I0824896

CHICAGO HOMES

CHICAGO HOMES

A Portrait of the City's Everyday Architecture

CARLA BRUNI
PHIL THOMPSON

ILLUSTRATIONS BY Wonder City Studio

A MIDWAY BOOK

AGATE

CHICAGO

First printed in October 2025

Printed in the United States of America

10 9 8 7 6 5 4 3 2 6 27 28 29 30

Art direction and cover design by Morgan Krehbiel
Cover illustration by Phil Thompson
Author photo (Carla) by Mariah Karson
Author photo (Phil) by Edison Vuong
All illustrations by Phil Thompson unless otherwise noted

Library of Congress Cataloging-in-Publication Data

Names: Thompson, Phil (Artist) author illustrator | Bruni, Carla (Preservationist) author
Title: Chicago homes : a portrait of the city's everyday architecture / Phil Thompson & Carla Bruni.
Description: Chicago : Agate Publishing, [2025] | Includes bibliographical references. |
Identifiers: LCCN 2025015185 (print) | LCCN 2025015186 (ebook) | ISBN 9781572843578 hardcover | ISBN 9781572849013 epub
Subjects: LCSH: Architecture, Domestic--Illinois--Chicago--History | Architecture and society--Illinois--Chicago--History | Chicago (Ill.)--Buildings, structures, etc.
Classification: LCC NA7238.C4 T46 2025 (print) | LCC NA7238.C4 (ebook) | DDC 728.09773/11--dc23/eng/20250519
LC record available at https://lccn.loc.gov/2025015185
LC ebook record available at https://lccn.loc.gov/2025015186

Midway Books is an imprint of Agate Publishing. Agate books are available in bulk at discount prices. For more information, visit agatepublishing.com.

For Katie, and for my parents.
None of this would be possible without you.
—Phil

For Terry Tatum, who forever tethered me to the small, local stuff with his scandal-woven storytelling and relentless love of home. We miss you.
—Carla

CONTENTS

"The Chicago accent is the night shift, the factory worker, the airport baggage handler. It is firefighters, garbage collectors, and bus drivers. It is bad coffee, the funniest guy in the breakroom, and the six days a week for one day off with your family. It is neighborhood know-it-alls and backseat loudmouths. It is complaining about the weather, the mayor, the city that you love. It is a BBQ with family and the first snap of a sausage when you bite into it. If the Chicago accent is ugly, then it is an acknowledgment that work in America is ugly, for nobody works like Chicago."

—**Gus Menary,** Chicago Producer and Theater Director

INTRODUCTION

"A building is not just a place to be but a way to be."
—Frank Lloyd Wright

Who Is This Book For?

This is a book for people who casually crane their necks to look into other people's living room windows, people who take pictures of unusual brickwork patterns and maybe get a little too far off the public way while doing so, people who know what a greystone is but maybe not a what a cornice is, architectural historians, bakers, baristas, runners, visual learners, architects, academics, accountants, locals, tourists, artists, and anyone who has ever been in or around a house.

This book is for people like us. It hopes to honor the everyday wood, masonry, and limestone buildings that do the real work of our lives with their sheltering porch roofs and sagging window air conditioners, oversized radiators and wonky wood windows, non-functional closets and creaky floorboards that disrupt the downstairs neighbor. It's a very long and well-informed love letter.

What Does This Book Do?

Chicagoans are a practical lot, and we wanted to make a book that looked good, but also worked hard. With this book, you should be able to:

- Identify the style of an old house or understand what makes it a transitional style if you can't pin it down
- Get a sense of what materials make up a house just by looking at it
- Have a good idea of the time period in which a house was built
- Reference moments in Chicago history that affected the design and use of homes, from the Great Chicago Fire to building codes and demographic changes
- Know why a Chicago home looks like a Chicago home (and not, say, a Savannah home or a Baltimore home)

How Does This Book Work?

While the book takes you through a chronological history of Chicago's built environment, don't feel like you need to read it through like a mystery novel. Use the Table of Contents to look up the architecture and planning-related histories that kick off each chapter/era, or look up a particular style that you're keen on and then follow it through each chapter to see how it evolved locally over time. Or read up on a particular historic event or topic because you want to geek out on the limestones used in Chicago or learn why we have wooden back porches as a fire escape when wood, well, burns. Don't be afraid to hunt and peck!

What This Book Finds Architecturally Shameful

Nothing. This is decidedly not a book that will slap the hand (or eye?) of the reader who has altered their old home in some way. It's a curious book that examines the built environment and tries to understand it. As the great Stewart Brand wrote, "Almost no buildings adapt well. They're destined not to adapt; also budgeted and financed not to, constructed not to, administered not to, maintained not to, regulated and taxed not to, even remodeled not to. But all buildings adapt anyway."

The story of Chicago is not about cataloging a bunch of buildings; it's the story of how we actually live, survive, and attempt to thrive as Chicagoans. It's about how back porches became our private sanitariums. It's about how the length of a surveyor's chain shaped where the sunlight enters a room. It's about how inequity informed the kinds of alterations that happen in disinvested neighborhoods. It's about how a Perma-Stone salesman made a killing on Keeler Avenue and the homeowners felt like they lived in castles for a little while. Maybe they still do. We frankly hope they do, because we should all feel like kings and queens, and because that stuff is really hard to get off once it's on there.

Our homes are a physical expression of our history and if you know how to have a conversation with them, you can learn a whole lot about Chicago and its residents. Be warned—some are big talkers.

A Few Caveats

There are, it turns out, a whole lot of homes in this city. More than a million, actually. There are also many transitional styles: quirky structures built by a guy who worked for a lumber company or brick manufacturer; houses that have been so completely reclad and reshaped that they no longer form an allegiance to any particular style (anarchist architecture!); garages turned into single-family homes; a company town and planned developments; pockets of neighborhoods where an architect had free rein to be clever in their designs . . . you get the idea. We cover what we believe to be the most common home styles and forms in this book, as well as sub-types and sub-styles.

Building Types Versus Styles

A building *type* is the form of a building, meaning the overall shape. A rowhouse is a row of attached houses, so in that case, when we say rowhouse, we mean the type. Classical Revival is an example of the *style* of a house, meaning it describes the more decorative elements of the house. Think of a style as being like the clothes a building wears. In the case of Classical Revival style, this includes triangular pediments, columns, cornices, decorative shields, etc. You can often smack a style onto any building type. For example, workers cottages (a type) can come in many different styles. Conversely, Italianate (a style) is like a one-size-fits-all dress that is imposed on numerous building types, regardless of their shape and size.

That said, the distinctions are not always cut and dried. A greystone is called a greystone because of the building material that is stuck to its primary facade, and it manifests as a variety of types and styles. The Queen Anne *style* can adorn a variety of house types, but there is certainly an unmistakable Queen Anne *type* of home as well. In general, we apologize for the disorder of the field—these builders tinkered like scientists. We will do our best to clarify throughout the text.

Covering Our Bases

We are aware that we are missing numerous delightful expressions, additions, quirky enclaves, architectural anomalies, micro-trends, and other wonderful variations that contribute to our local vernacular.

We also weave in countless building materials and social, political, and technological events, but surely missed some things that you think should be included.

We pored over countless books, newspaper articles, sources of useful data, sources of conflicting data, pamphlets, city reports, catalogs, websites, microfilm reels, and century old display ads to gather this information. We walked an endless number of city streets, burdened librarians, and spoke with dozens of people who work in architecture and planning-related fields. We asked people we deeply respect to read over the early, ambitious, perhaps slightly overboard drafts of our chapters. It's been a group effort and we are so grateful to all of you. So, have at it. Let us know how we did. And don't forget to look up.

CHAPTER

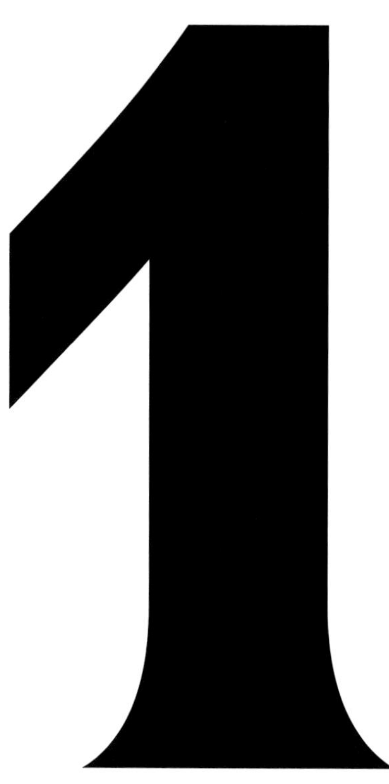

Early Inhabitants, Early Homes

1780–1837

“Nothing would be so agreeable to me as to talk to you by the hour of ancient Chicago, when the wild waters of the lake, on the one hand, were rarely vexed by the ships of commerce, and the wild flowers which covered the broad prairies on the other, were undisturbed by cultivation and uncropped by flocks and herds—save the wild deer that roamed at large over their broad bosoms; but I fear you will think I am becoming a little senile in my enthusiasm.”

—**Jonathan Young Scammon,** 1879, *Reminiscences of Early Chicago*

SOMETIME AROUND 1780, Jean Baptiste Point DuSable, a trader of African lineage, took a long ride up the Mississippi River. He paddled his canoe through the northern tributaries, then portaged his packed vessel over land to a lazy river that eased him out to the enormous freshwater lake then called Lac des Illinois. He found a spot perched on the river’s north bank, about five hundred feet from the lakeshore, to settle in and make a home. It was there he would live with his Potawatomi wife, Kitihawa, for the next twenty years. This is often considered Chicago’s first known settler home, and it was built from local timber (probably black oak or white pine). In the area were groves of sugar maple and basswood, in the shadows of which thrived *Allium tricoccum*, a wild ramp—similar to spring onions or leeks—with an Algonquin name that evolved over time into “Chicago.”

The DuSable home was located at a critical geological juncture: the waterways around the home offered up a tantalizing proximity between the massive Great Lakes system to its east and the Mississippi River to its west. Settlements and trading posts dotted the waters all the way down to the Gulf of Mexico. From the day French Jesuit explorers Marquette and Joliet first documented the area in 1763, states and commerce were seduced by the prospect of a canal. By this time, the French had lost all their land in the French and Indian War, but French holdovers, the *coureurs des bois* and the *voyageurs*, continued to hang around. The French legacy persisted—and does so to this day—in words like "Illinois," their pronunciation of the Native tribe along that river; and "prairie," their word for meadow or grasslands.

Jean Baptiste Point DuSable himself came from a French or once-French territory, though his birthplace is hazy. He may have been from the French Caribbean—some think Saint-Domingue, modern-day Haiti—or he could have made his way up from somewhere in the Louisiana territory, like St. Charles (in present-day Missouri). With possible ties to these places and Africa, he might be categorized as *creole*, a word with a similar origin and a broad latitude of use, though he defies easy labels. His life along the Mississippi, from his birth around 1745 to his death in St. Charles in 1818, variously put him among Native, Spanish, French, British, and colonial American influences and jurisdictions.

Allium tricoccum | commonly, wild ramp or onion | "Chicagoua"

The Early Chicago Homes

Prior to DuSable's arrival during the French colonial period from 1673 to 1763, there may have been temporary houses in Chicago as part of trading outposts or small missions. We know, for example, that Father Jacques Marquette, the French-Canadian Jesuit missionary who, with Louis Joliet, explored and charted the Mississippi River, built a log cabin somewhere around Chicago over the winter of 1674–75. We also know that they were nearly flooded out of house and home in the spring thaw. Unsurprisingly, time has destroyed any structures from these earliest settlements.

Some French colonial homes still exist in southern Illinois and Missouri that might give us clues as to what a French outpost around Chicago looked like—perhaps even the DuSable home. Their construction methods combined some practices from Normandy, where many of the French settlers originated. For example, the pitch of the roofs, the trusswork (the framing that holds up a roof), the raised foundations, and even the practice of using vertical timbers filled in with a mud and plant fiber mixture called *bousillage*—all of this can still be found in Norman homes in France today. The addition of distinctive covered porches likely evolved from the needs of the French colonials living in the hot and humid Caribbean. In lieu of being able to flip on the air conditioning, a full-length gallery (porch) was the next best way to cool down. That design tradition carried over to New France, and northward to the Upper Mississippi.

The DuSable (and Later, Kinzie) Home

Could the DuSable home have been a French colonial home? As there weren't architects wading through the ramps at this time, we don't have blueprints, or even any drawings of the DuSable house by contemporaries. We do, however, have a few breadcrumbs. According to the home's bill of sale to its next owner, uncovered by early Chicago historian Milo Quaife, the main house was 40 × 22 feet and accompanied by various outbuildings: a large barn spanning 40 × 28 feet; another barn at 30 × 24 feet; a horse mill; a bakehouse; a poultry house; a workshop; a dairy; and a smokehouse. In short—this complex was stocked! Jean and Kitihawa were well provisioned as the sole settled residents at the crux of a continent, no doubt with the help of Kitihawa's family and their long history and knowledge of the land.

The most precise description of the DuSable home comes from an 1891 book, *Industrial Chicago*. There are no sources, however, and the specificity of the description is eyebrow-raising (including the exact number of logs and

The DuSable cabin, per *Industrial Chicago* (1891). The roof was said to be thatched with grasses and covered by strips of bark.

the height of the doorway). That said, the illustration above shows what the DuSable cabin may have looked like based on that particular description.

We know from accounts at the time that the DuSables were in the business of farming and selling goods to travelers and soon-to-be residents of Chicago, and what we know of their home and surrounding buildings seems to confirm that. Eventually the home would come into the ownership of John Kinzie, a trader who provisioned Fort Dearborn. Kinzie's daughter-in-law, writing her memoirs, described the home from Kinzie's time, which would've been more than forty years after it was first built:

> It was a long, low building, with a piazza extending along its front, a range of four or five rooms. A broad green space was inclosed [sic] between it and the river, and shaded by a row of Lombardy poplars. Two immense cottonwood-trees stood in the rear of the building, one of which still remains as an ancient landmark. A fine, well-cultivated garden extended to the north of the dwelling, and surrounding it were various buildings appertaining to the establishment—dairy, bake-house, lodging-house for the Frenchmen, and stables. A vast range of sand-hills, covered with stunted cedars, pines, and dwarf-willow trees, intervened between the house and the lake, which was, at this time, not more than thirty rods distant.[1]

It's important to note that Juliette Kinzie was describing the house as it was then, several owners removed from the DuSables. But the way she describes the home as long and low, with the "piazza," makes it sound like one of the many French colonial homes that date to the same year DuSable built the home.

In 1800, DuSable sold the home to a man named Jean La Lime for 6,000 livres, the French currency at the time, which is about $20,000 in today's dollars. After leaving Chicago, DuSable lived out his final years in St. Charles. Four years later, John Kinzie bought the home. In 1812, Kinzie got into a quarrel with La Lime, then stabbed him to death in what he claimed was self-defense. It was the first official murder in Chicago, some say brought about by La Lime's threat to expose Kinzie's shady business practices. This may also have been the first official documentation of shady business practices in Chicago, now a tradition.

The Kinzie (and formerly DuSable) home, as described by his daughter-in-law in 1831.

Indigenous Homes: The Wigwam & the Summer House

DuSable was notably the first non-Native to settle in the area, but he wasn't the "first" resident of the Chicago area, of course—not by a long shot. The best available archaeological evidence reveals human habitation since the end of the Ice Age, about 12,000 years ago. Tribes of seminomadic hunter-gatherers moved through the land with the game and the seasons, using the extensive waterways and ridged paths left in the wake of the melting glaciers. Though the region was low-lying, swampy, and muddy, it also had the fanned-out rivers that made travel easier for Native tribes in dugout canoes. By 1673, when French explorers like Marquette and Joliet were voyaging through, the Potawatomi tribe was the largest tribe in the region. Potawatomi means "those who tend the sacred fire," in reference to their long-standing alliance with, and primacy among, the Ojibwe and Odawa. Together this trio was, and still is, referred to the Council of Three Fires.

Not only were the Potawatomi here long before DuSable had built Chicago's "first" home, but each Potawatomi family had *two* homes. One home—the wigwam—was for the winter season, late fall through spring; the summer home, somewhat similar to what other tribes call a longhouse, was for the warmer season. Like the homes of the earliest settlers, the homes were derived from the abundant trees and vegetation available. Both the wigwam and summer house used bark or woven mats of reeds to cover the outside.

The Wigwam

Typically, a married couple, their children, and even some extended family would live in a wigwam. When it was time to move on for the season, they would often remove the outer covering and leave the wooden support structure standing. Then they would bring materials to cover the support structure of their new home for the season. Here's a look at the structure of a wigwam. Anyone familiar with the lattice design of Frank Gehry's Pritzker Pavilion in downtown Chicago might notice the resemblance.

The wigwam used a dome structure made of branches or saplings, which was then covered.

A Potawatomi wigwam.

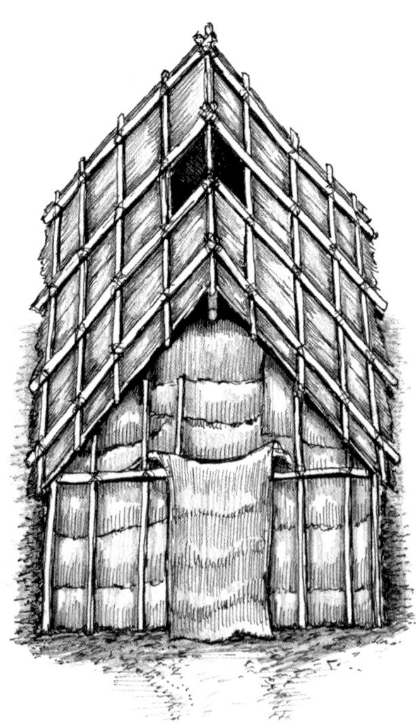

The summer house, a common habitat for Great Lakes tribes like the Potawatomi. Occupants slept in rows along each side of the house.

The Summer House

This structure was more communal than the wigwam, offering more space and designed to accommodate multiple families. A frame of tall, notched saplings was made into a rectangular or oblong form with a gabled or rounded top to let the water drain off, and covered with bark. Because there were entrances at either end, this summer house had far better ventilation than a wigwam and allowed for cool breezes to come in and for heat to escape.

The Log Cabin

In 1803, a few years after DuSable split for St. Charles, the government of the newly independent United States built a white pine log military fortress—a wall of vertical, spiked logs, an elevated and fortified "blockhouse," and dorms—right across the river from his old home. The construction of Fort Dearborn was a way of asserting control over the region and providing protection to settlers. Throughout the early decades of the 1800s, settlement in Chicago was limited to a handful of families who lived in clusters of modest homes around the fort and the fork of the Chicago River called Wolf Point.

We've come to know them as the stuff of dioramas in dusty museums, but based on existing evidence in the region, log cabins had a definite presence and utility for American settlers. They were simple structures, usually one or two rooms (called "pens"), consisting of roughly hewn lumber stacked horizontally and interlocked, then chinked (mortared) with a mix of material like mud, small stones, and corn husks to seal the gaps between the logs. These would have been built with the sturdiest timber available. In the Chicago region, that may have been oak, hickory, or white pine. They would almost certainly have had a chimney of stone or brick, when available.

For many settlers, these cabins were not just homes, but also doubled as "the office." Work-from-home life has been popular for a long time, it turns out. A "saddlebag" cabin would include a home and something like a trading post or small storehouse—the "saddlebag" being the workroom addition. A "dog-trot" cabin had two pens separated by a covered breezeway. Most settlers from this era were not employed in the modern sense—they were entrepreneurial, skilled tradespeople who made their own hours and avoided a commute.

Recollections of Chicago from the early 1800s usually describe some roughshod log cabins. Until the first sawmill came along in 1831, Chicago's settlers were dependent on their own axe to hew logs to size and fit them together, which could no doubt look a bit clumsy. The sawmill was a revelation. It could produce smooth, dimensional lumber for building components like siding, which settlers were quick to acquire and nail over their log walls to spruce up their digs. At around the same time, in 1833, Chicago also got its first brickyard, located near the bank of the Chicago River, between Dearborn and Clark, which certainly would have enhanced the cabins' chimneys.

This log cabin is now situated in Naperville's Naper Settlement, but it was originally located in southern Illinois. It dates to the 1840s.

The Making of the Chicago Grid

Anyone who's spent time in (or flying above) present-day Chicago knows it's a city built on a grid. Row after row of homes and buildings are neatly arrayed in lots along city streets. Alleys run behind the homes with parallel arrays of garages and garbage cans. So why does Chicago's urban landscape look the way it does? The origin of this layout goes back to the original survey in 1830, but the real story goes even deeper.

On achieving independence from Great Britain, the United States came into ownership of the land that would become modern-day Ohio, Indiana, Michigan, Wisconsin, Illinois, and part of Minnesota. But there was little official control. Native tribes, the British, and even some of the original American states fought over the land. The state of Virginia, for example, lay claim to the entire Northwest Territory after its state militia

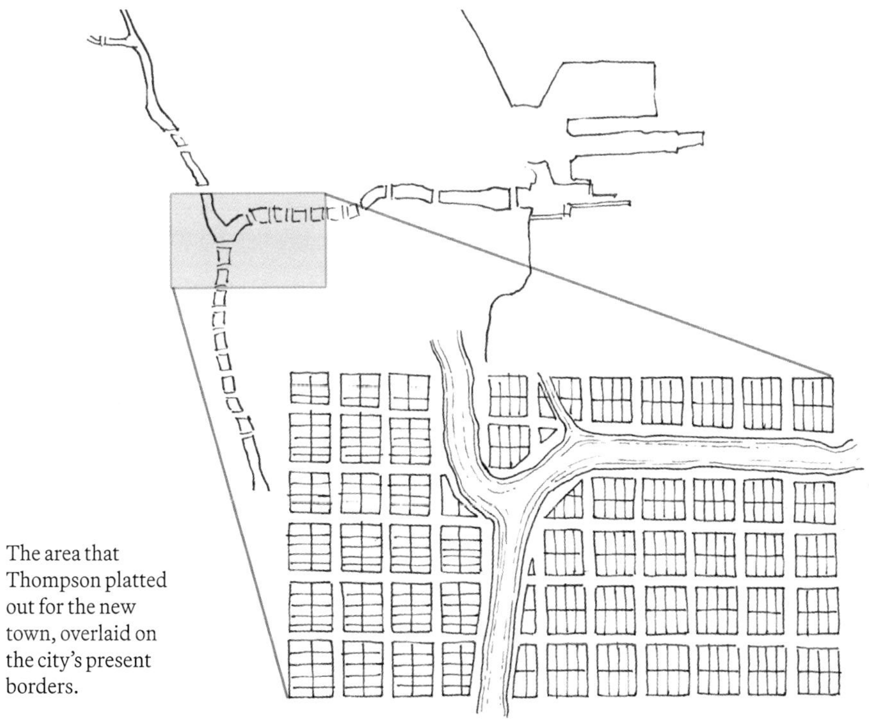

The area that Thompson platted out for the new town, overlaid on the city's present borders.

defeated the British there, calling it "Illinois County, Virginia."

In 1784, in light of the wrangling and fighting, Thomas Jefferson, who was then a delegate of the Continental Congress, proposed two ordinances to help resolve the land disputes. The first laid out a structure with which to carve out new states from the territory. The second outlined the methods by which new towns would be surveyed. The plan called for creating towns that would be six miles by six miles, or thirty-six square miles, with a certain allotment for public use—public education, for example—and future use by the federal government. It was highly influenced by New England town planning, with allotments for community and public spaces.

The U.S. officially established the land as the "Northwest Territory" in 1787. Jefferson's proposals became law and gave Chicago and other "western" towns in the territory their strict grid pattern. With permission from the federal government, but not funding, the new state of Illinois's Canal Commission in 1830 assigned a surveyor named James Thompson (no known relation to the co-author/illustrator) to plat out Chicago. The plan was to sell off the new plots to fund the canal, finally realizing the dream of connecting the Great Lakes and Mississippi River. The canal was critical. It was so important to the founders of the state of Illinois, in fact, that they insisted on drawing the state's northern border far enough north that it included the future canal. If not for that decision, Chicago might have ended up in Wisconsin. We shudder to think what that would mean for football today.

James Thompson, like many other surveyors of the day (Abraham Lincoln had been another Illinois surveyor), used the standard tools: a Gunter's chain, a compass, and a few other tools, some of which are on display at the Chicago History Museum. The measurements from the original survey tools are relevant today. His Gunter's chain was the standard sixty-six feet. Ten lengths of a Gunter's chain is 660 feet, or one-eighth of a mile, also called a furlong (in medieval England, a "furrow long" was the length of one furrow in a plowed field). The length of a modern-day Chicago block is 660 feet. Eight full Chicago blocks make up a mile. The

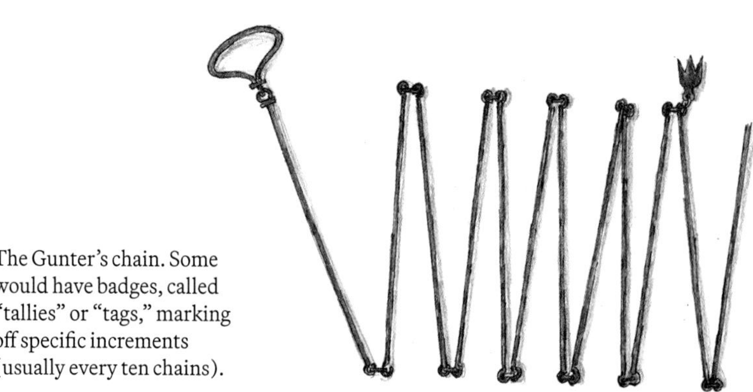

The Gunter's chain. Some would have badges, called "tallies" or "tags," marking off specific increments (usually every ten chains).

standard width of a Chicago road? Sixty-six feet. A quarter-chain? It's about sixteen feet, the standard width of a Chicago alley, and the width of streets with no parking on either side. A two-way local street is double that width, or thirty-two feet. All of these measurements are enshrined in Chicago's current "Street and Site Plan Design Standards."

However! It's important to note that for Thompson's *original* plat of Chicago, Thompson measured using a bit more generous dimensions: 80-foot by 180-foot lots, with 18-foot alleys and 80-foot street widths—measurements that continue to reverberate in today's modern, bustling Loop.

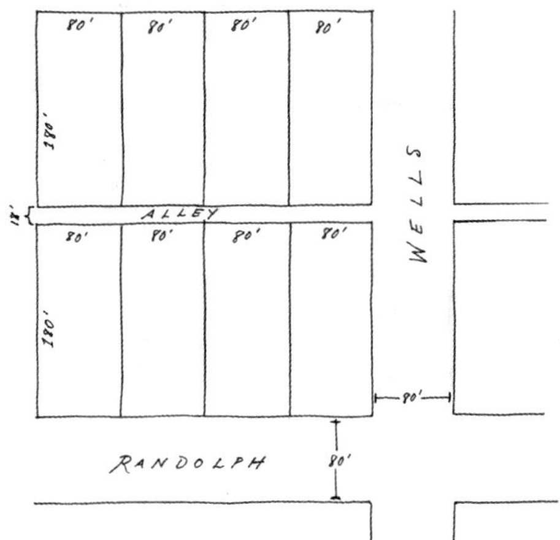

Thompson's original plat of Chicago—note the lot sizes are larger than the "typical" 125 by 25 feet Chicago lot.

Thompson divided the town into a grid of fifty-eight blocks (the "Block 37" shopping megaplex is located on what was numbered "block 37" on the grid) and subdivided in such a way that lots were long and narrow, with the narrow end facing the street, giving Chicago homes a distinct (and some would say, pleasingly cohesive) look. That said, while there's a kind of rhythm and order to the layout, don't let anyone fool you into believing that Chicago lots are all exactly 125 by 25 feet—they weren't originally and many lots are not that size today, although most bear some proximity to those dimensions. Whenever someone says Chicago lots are all that standard size, show them a random sampling of real estate listings.

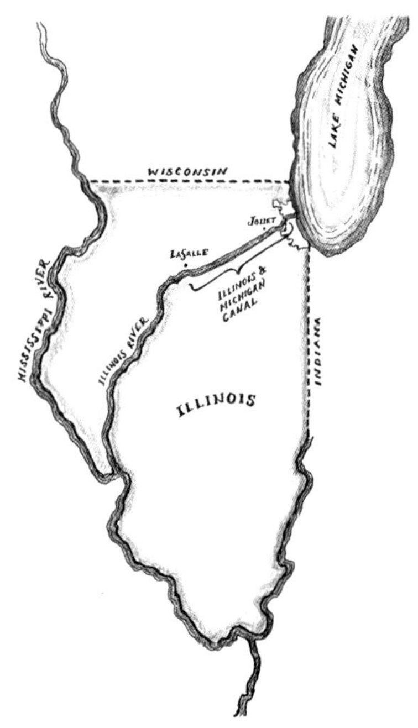

It was the vision of the canal as a vital connecting waterway that put Chicago on the map. The sale of land parcels helped fund its construction, but the canal wouldn't be completed until 1848.

Once James Thompson finished the massive job of dividing up this young city into a relatively tidy grid, he was offered a choice of either three hundred bucks or a few parcels of the muddy new town. He took the money. ■

Federal Style: East Meets "West"

By 1833, the few dozen residents who had settled in Chicago voted to officially form a town (the city founding was still a few years away). It was also the year that the settlers pushed out the Native tribes. The Blackhawk War of 1833 was the final spasm of violence between Indigenous groups and the new settlers, the outcome of which was the Treaty of Chicago. The treaty forced the Potawatomi and others to cede five million acres of lands in Illinois and Wisconsin for about six cents an acre. The other stipulation was that they had to move to lands west of the Mississippi. A wave of new settlers from the northeastern U.S. set off a wave of land grabs in towns throughout Illinois. By one estimate, one-third of all towns in central Illinois were founded between 1835–37. These new settlers brought to Chicago a type of home that was then popular in their towns, the Federal style home.

A Federal style side-gable building, based off of the Sauganash Hotel, which had a "side-saddle" log cabin.

This home type is most recognizable by its strict horizontal symmetry, modest ornamentation, prominent windows, and central doorway. One easy mnemonic device is "five over four and a door": five windows on the second floor, four windows on the first floor, and two on each side of the door. It derives from the Georgian style, which prevailed in Great Britain through the reign of the three King Georges from 1714 to 1820, and was based on classical ideals of symmetry and proportion. In the United States, historians often refer to Georgian homes built pre-independence as "Colonial" and those built post-independence as "Federal," with some marginal stylistic evolution.

Federal Style Side Gable

One of the variations was the side-gable home. The "side gable" simply means that the gables are positioned facing the home's neighbors, rather than the street. This was one of the home types brought from the East Coast to Chicago; original examples are rare in Chicago today, but there are many examples in cities along the East Coast in preserved Colonial and early American historic districts.

We know Chicago had a few Federal side-gable buildings and it likely had more that are lost in the historical record. Federal style buildings certainly coexisted with log cabins in the city's early days, but they were most likely the domain of the more well-to-do class—the merchants and tradespeople who could afford to build more expansively.

Some of the early examples were hotels. The Sauganash Hotel, originally the Eagle Exchange Tavern, was built at the fork of the Chicago River in 1831 but destroyed by a fire in 1851. If you're willing to wander an hour or so outside of Chicago, you can still see the "Pre-Emption House," built in 1834, at Naperville's Naper Settlement, a collection of historic buildings that were moved from their original location into a kind of outdoor museum. Another great local example is Stacy's Tavern in Glen Ellyn, Illinois, which was once a waystation for travelers between Galena and Chicago and has been restored to what a tavern may have looked like in the 1840s.

Federal Style Front Gable

All that grid work done by James Thompson in the 1830s was useful in making neat little building borders on wide, open swamp and prairie land, but it also forced some stylistic modifications. Take the Federal style side-gable home, for example: Its character-defining broad front couldn't be squeezed onto these narrow Chicago lots. To adapt these homes to the lot space, they were turned so the broad side of the home was not the side being shown to the public, but rather the narrow side and its triangular gable.

This gave the homes a distinctive "cottage" look that would come to define so many Chicago dwellings, perhaps most notably the workers cottage (spoiler alert). These Federal front-gable homes had everything in common materially and aesthetically with side-gable homes—just rotated 90 degrees.

This shift also meant that the front door was moved to the narrow, street-facing side, and the broad sides of the home, enclosed by neighbors, were now freed up for less glamorous materials. In later years, that's where the less expensive Chicago common brick would be used, while the facade would use something like fancy St. Louis pressed brick, with a rich, uniform red. This is just one example of the ways in which Chicago provided some regulatory or normative guardrails on architectural forms and styles. These parameters posed new and interesting problems for homeowners, builders, and architects to creatively solve.

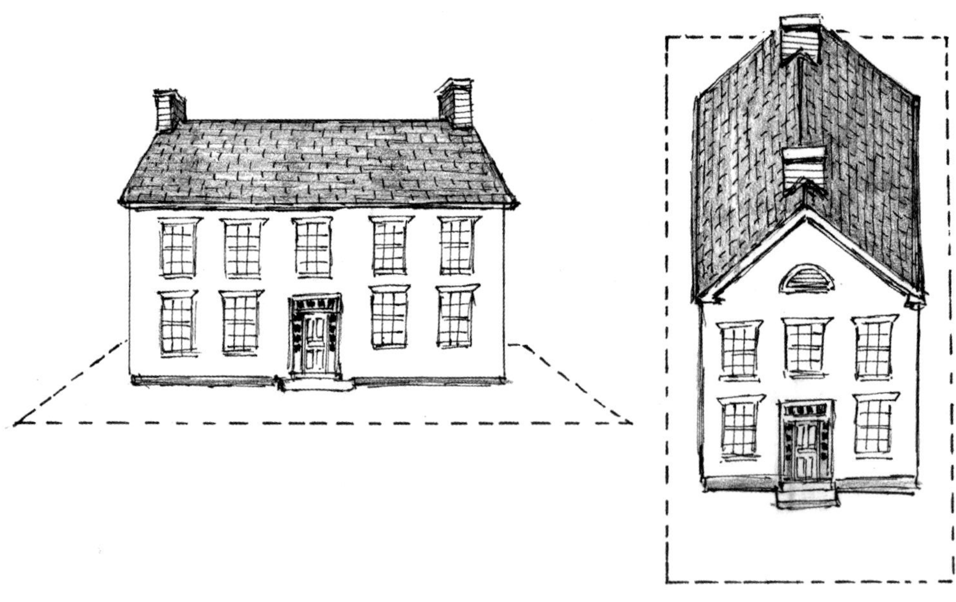

Different lot shapes make for different expressions of home styles, and sometimes a 90-degree spin, like this Chicago version of Federal style on the right.

A Federal front-gable facade.

Chicago's front doors are on the narrow end of a home due to the shape and orientation of our lots.

From Timber to Balloon Frame

One of the most significant architectural advancements in this period was the transition from timber-frame to balloon-frame construction. This is not just notable for Chicago (though many, especially locals, believe it occurred here first), but for home builders elsewhere and thereafter. Let's just say that at a minimum, Chicago was a very early adopter of this construction method, and it led directly to a building boom of tens of thousands of quick, inexpensive wooden homes.

Timber-frame construction involves the careful assembly of large, cut lumber via a system of interlocking parts. One way to connect the lumber is with a "mortise and tenon" joint. Simply put, a mortise is a hole in wood, and a tenon is the wooden piece that goes into that hole.

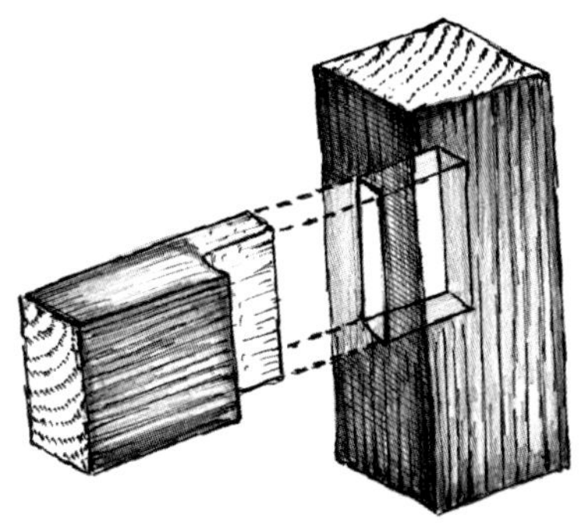

Mortise (right) and tenon (left).

Timber-frame construction existed in places like ancient China, Mesopotamia, Egypt, and medieval England before colonists brought it to North America.

Enter carpenter Augustine Taylor, who built St. Mary's Church on Lake and State Streets sometime around 1833 using a method that came to be known as a "balloon frame." Some sources claim he invented it; others say George Snow was the mastermind. Still others argue it was more an evolution of existing adaptations that had been taking place in construction regionally. Initially, the term "balloon frame" was derisive—a frame so light it would float away—but the structure became so common that folks just co-opted it as the accepted term. Taylor used thin, dimensional, mill-sawn lumber in order to create a lighter structure that was easier to assemble. In contrast to the bulky and expensive timber-frame method, the balloon frame could be erected and assembled with nails (rather than labor-intensive joints) by a carpenter and a helper in about a week.

In the decades to follow, the balloon-frame method came to dominate home building throughout Chicago. It was tailor-made for the population boom and the relentless demand for housing. As lumber mills abounded and nails became mass-produced rather than hand-forged, the cost of

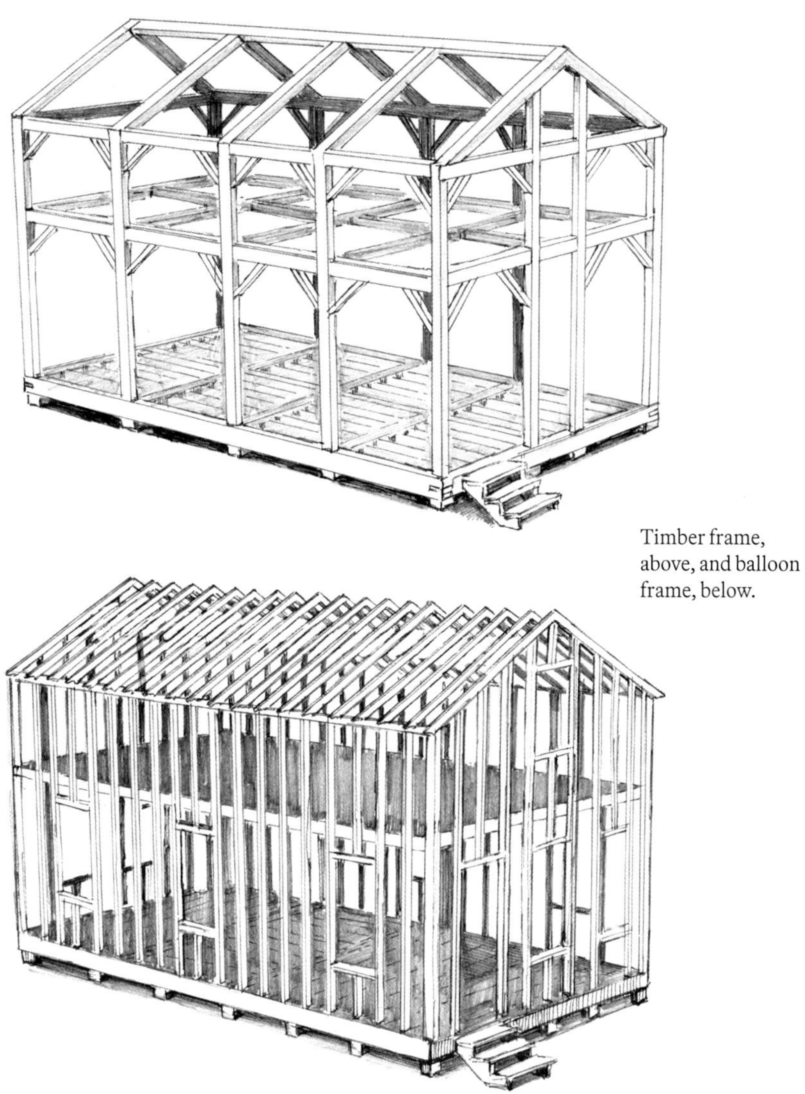

Timber frame, above, and balloon frame, below.

building declined. As for timber-frame homes, very few still exist in the city today, though demolitions are revealing timber-frame construction in homes that, from the outside, appear much newer. Even now, a variation of the balloon frame is used in most American home construction: the "platform frame," which also uses thin, dimensional lumber but provides more fire protection between floors. Instead of the studs going from floor to ceiling in the balloon frame—which allows fire to roar upwards—platform framing puts a barrier between floors. ■

The Parthenon, an exemplar of the original Greek architectural style revived in early 1800s American locales like Chicago.

Greek Revival: Breaking with the British

The Greek Revival style was not unique to Chicago; the whole nation got the bug. A few factors came together to make the style so popular. First, it was decidedly un-British. Folks were eager for a break from the Georgian, Colonial, and Federal homes that had dominated the nation. The newly independent Americans took a measure of pride in breaking from the British monarch to form a style of self-government that harkened back to ancient Greece. In 1821, the Greeks themselves began rebelling against the Ottoman Empire, and Americans naturally rooted for the sort of autonomy and self-determination they also had just won. The Greek Revival style called to mind a Greek temple, often with the same grandiosity.

Chicago at this time was still a small city and not yet flush with wealthy tycoons that might have telegraphed their wealth with elaborate ornamental details, so the style was rather pared down. Some of the known examples of Greek Revival style were the Clybourn House, built in 1836 by meatpacking magnate Archibald Clybourn; and the home of another prominent early

GREEK REVIVAL

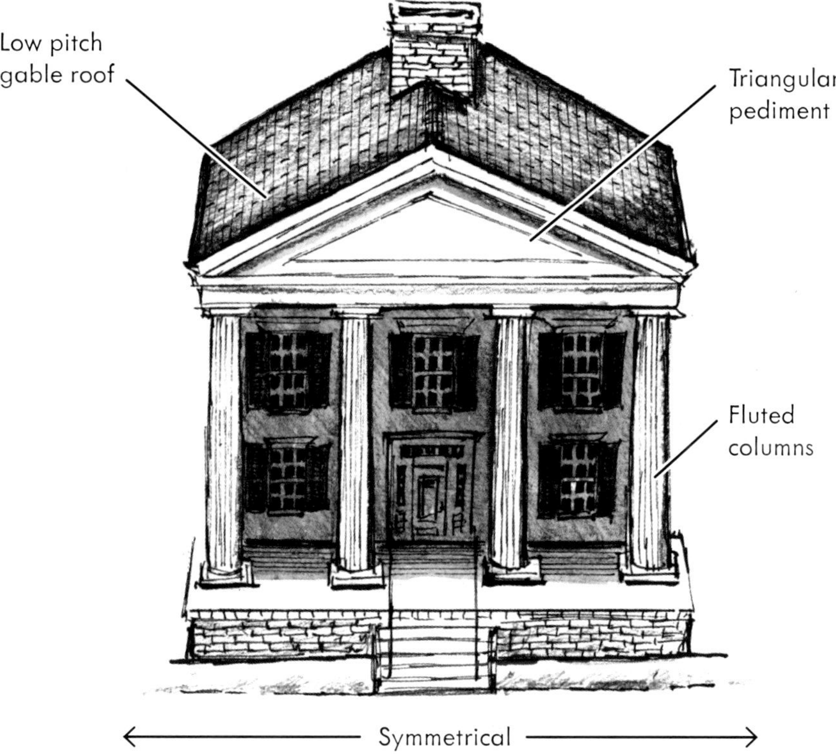

Example of an American Greek Revival home. These early homes gave strong Parthenon vibes.

COMMON FEATURES

- Horizontal symmetry
- Low-pitched gable roof forming a triangular pediment
- Prominent columns, fluted or unfluted
- Decorative details like egg and dart patterns, or other Greek-inspired motifs
- Windows with decorative crowns, the horizontal elements that adorn the tops of windows
- Prominent use of white to mimic marble; this could be wood painted white or covered with stucco. Trickery!

Chicagoan and mayor, William Ogden. Though the style faded in popularity for homes in the 1840s, it remained in vogue for many decades for banks and government offices. The most famous existing residential example in Chicago from this time period is the Clarke-Ford House.

A quick refresher on column types (left three are Greek; farthest right is Roman).

The Clarke-Ford House

Built circa 1836 for New Yorkers Henry and Carolina Clarke, the home was originally located on a twenty-acre property on Michigan Avenue between 16th and 17th Streets. It was moved twice in its history, the last time in 1977 to its present location on Indiana Avenue in the Prairie Avenue Historic District. Henry owned a successful hardware business, which grew as other northeasterners poured into Chicago and built homes of their own.

The Clarke House was built on a mortise and tenon timber frame, set atop a brick foundation. The house has white clapboard siding, Doric columns supporting a pediment over a grand entrance, and generous first-floor windows that let in lots of natural light to high-ceiling rooms. The *pièce de résistance* is the rooftop belvedere—a type of large cupola allowing for windowed views—which is an Italianate addition built in the 1850s. After Henry Clarke died in 1849, Caroline lived in the house until 1860, selling off most of the land to support herself and her children. In 1941, Bishop Louis Henry and Margaret Ford took a lead role in preserving the home for the next three decades, and it was renamed the Clarke-Ford House in their honor in 2022.

The Clarke-Ford House, now located at 1827 S. Indiana Avenue.

CHAPTER

From Founding to Fire

1837–1871

“New York society may have come over on the Mayflower, but Chicago society came over on the Rock Island line.”

—**Bob Greene,** Columnist, *Johnny Deadline, Reporter*

After 1833, Chicago went from a sleepy town to a bustling city of four thousand. The period saw rampant land speculation, as fortune-seekers poured in and prices for lots went up and up. Though there was real estate speculation throughout towns in Illinois, investors knew that the planned canal near Chicago would make the city a critical site for trade and shipping. In a haze of optimism, Chicagoans incorporated as a city on March 4, 1837. Credit flowed too easily, though, and a banking panic that originated in New York City in May of 1837 spread to the rest of the country, including Chicago. The credit needed to purchase land quickly evaporated and land values crashed, resulting in a few years of lost fortune and economic misery.

At this time, Chicago was a smattering of wood-frame homes hugging the fork, stem, and branches of the river, with muddy roads and a handful of brick buildings. Some dismayed speculators left for good, convinced Chicago’s best days were behind it. The federal government decommissioned Fort Dearborn. The future looked bleak.

But of course it’s foolish to bet against Chicago. In the years after the 1837 crash, optimism rose around the city’s original reason for existing: the Illinois and Michigan Canal. The ninety-six-mile-long, hand-dug canal was completed in 1848, creating an unbroken waterway from New York City to the Gulf of Mexico, a boon for traders, the shipping industry, Natives, farmers, French fur traders, and even migratory birds. The canal opening just happened to coincide, too, with Chicago’s definitive debut into the Age of Rail. That very year, the city’s first rail line started running service between Chicago and the Des Plaines River. Others followed in rapid succession—Chicago to the canal, Chicago to the Mississippi River, Chicago to the East Coast—all built in the mid-1850s. By 1871, the city had over twenty railroads connecting Chicagoans and their goods to and from all corners of the country. We were right in the center of the matrix.

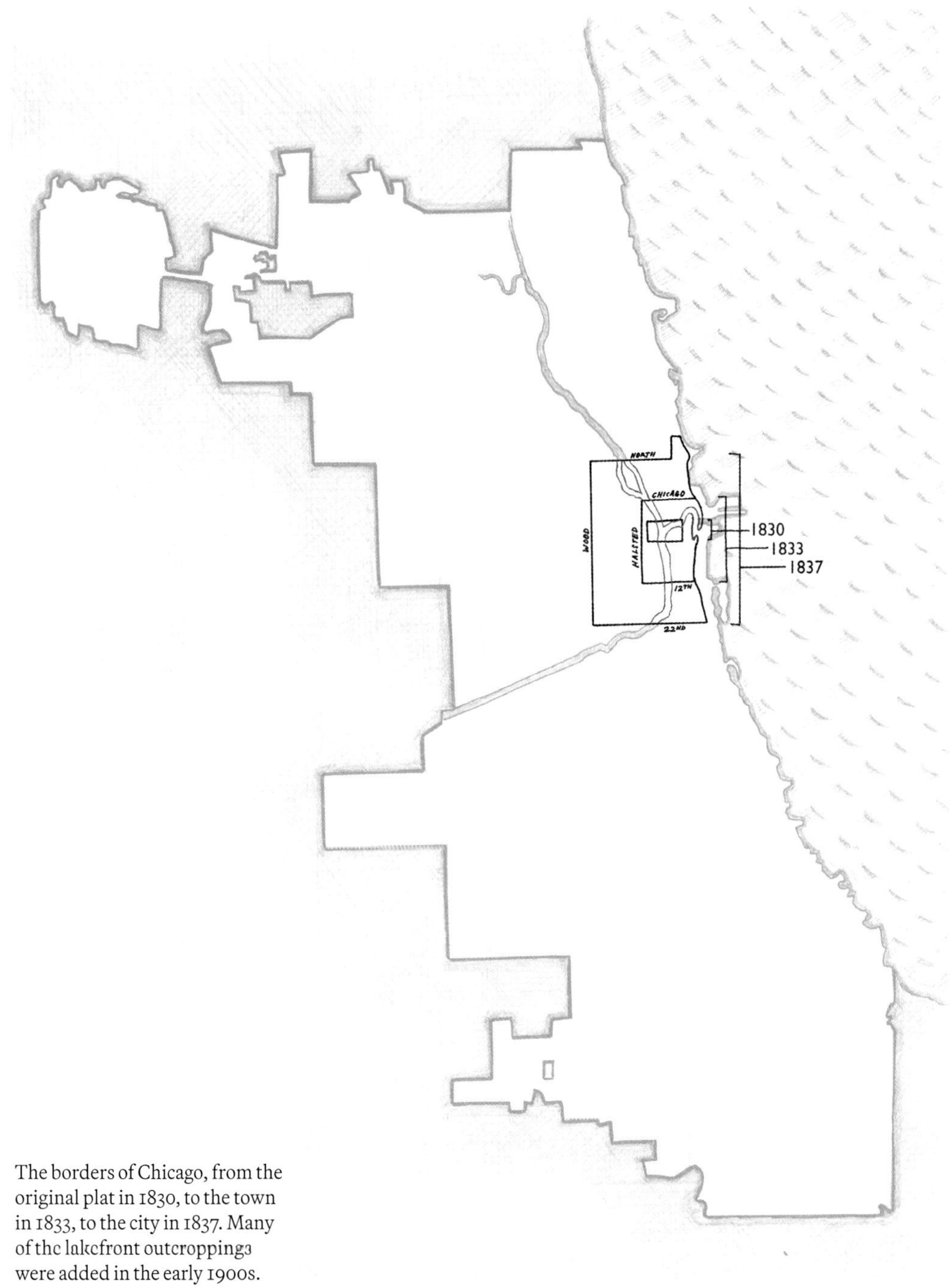

The borders of Chicago, from the original plat in 1830, to the town in 1833, to the city in 1837. Many of the lakefront outcroppings were added in the early 1900s.

These connections set up the city as the trader and transporter of the heartland's products. Farmers brought their produce by the tonnage to Chicago to be processed, resold, and traded. Timber outfits from the north country woods in Wisconsin and Michigan sent barges stacked with raw lumber to be sawn and sold at mills that lined the south branch of the Chicago River. In 1848, the same year Chicago got its first telegraph connection, the Chicago Board of Trade was founded as a brokerage operation to streamline buying and selling wheat, corn, oats, livestock, and a litany of other commodities. During the Civil War years, from 1861 to 1865, the city's profiteers benefitted as the Southern states could no longer access their usual suppliers in the Northeast. At the same time, Northern states' demand for wartime goods boomed, and they were often routed through Chicago.

It was hard and decidedly unglamorous work building Chicago in this period—digging a giant canal, slaughtering hogs, assembling McCormick reapers to harvest crops. It was manual and it was immense and it meant a huge demand for labor. The population of Chicago grew from about four thousand in 1837 to about three hundred thousand in 1871, with folks arriving in droves from crowded cities like New York and Philadelphia. In this period, wages in Midwestern states were about 20 to 30 percent higher than in places like New York and Pennsylvania, which attracted tens of thousands of job seekers.[1] Immigration also boomed during this period, adding mightily to the labor force. They all needed a place to sleep and keep the rain off. As the population rose, the number of homes rose with it, spreading outward from the once-sleepy original settlement at the river's fork.

The Irish and the Germans arrived in the greatest numbers. Blight had swept through Ireland from 1845 to 1852 and destroyed the country's staple potato crop. Many families suffered, starved, rioted—and over a million boarded ships bound for the United States.[2] Failing crops and rising food prices affected other parts of Europe, too. Millions of rural and urban folk clamored for relief and reform, including those in the German Confederation. They wanted more civil, labor, and political rights and freedoms. When monarchs rejected their demands, droves of disillusioned masses left for cities like Chicago.

As Chicago's population grew with the new arrivals, so too did the city borders and civic improvements. Aware of growing health and safety needs, city leaders installed gas street lighting in 1850 and created significant improvements to municipal freshwater delivery in 1854. In 1855, they also took up the massive task of installing a sewerage system, which required raising up the streets and sidewalks, piece by piece, in order to accommodate the

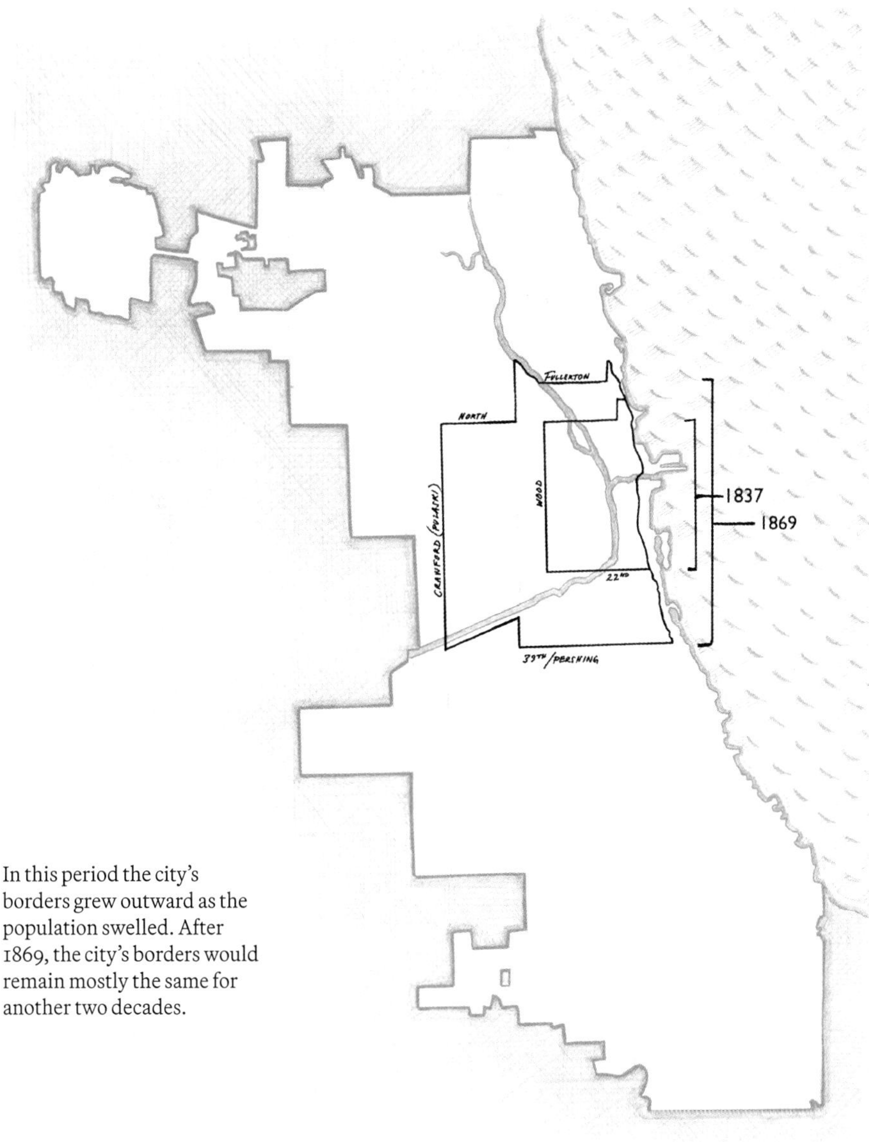

In this period the city's borders grew outward as the population swelled. After 1869, the city's borders would remain mostly the same for another two decades.

drainage. Whole buildings were lifted on jacks, and house lifting and house moving became cottage industries. Social infrastructure also grew during this period. By 1869, the state legislature created three distinct park districts to oversee the construction of large public parks and the tree-lined boulevards that connected them. They were Douglas Park and what would become Humboldt and Garfield Parks, as well as an extension of Lincoln Park.

Homes for the Working Class

Housing was in serious demand, and this "inland metropolis" had one thing going for it: Unlike the crowded cities of the East Coast, where families were stacked on top of one another in tenement buildings or side-by-side in tiny rowhouses, Chicago promised laborers their own homes. In many cases, workers also were given a plot of land from which they could derive other income: a rented rear cottage, a yard in which to raise livestock, or even a barn in back of the home. Homes were attainable, especially if one was willing to live in the polluted shadows of the stockyards and factories. A *Chicago Daily Tribune* classified ad from 1865 promised cottages on the West Side for between $1,000 and $1,600. A few years later, the advertised rent for a cottage with eight rooms was $25 a month.

It was the promise of being able to build and own a home of one's own, in fact, that drove many new residents to cities like Chicago. Most of the housing built at this time was for wage laborers, as they made up the majority of the population. Elaine Lewinnek, in *The Working Man's Reward*, credits Chicago as one of the early cities in which the American dream of wealth and prosperity were tied to the notion of homeownership. A smaller portion was for the merchants and managers of the middle class with the means to build bigger homes, and perhaps move out to the commuter suburbs along the new rail lines. Then there were the tycoons like Marshall Field and Philip Armour, who built massive homes along Prairie Avenue. Being south of the river meant not having to wait out the constant ship traffic.

The flip side to thousands of workers owning individual frame cottages that were crunched together was the systemic risk of a major fire. This was a known risk. The city's firefighters were frequently outmatched. The property insurance companies, which had the most to lose in a catastrophic fire, were pushing hardest for reforms, asking for better firefighting strategies, better waterworks, and stricter rules with regard to construction.

Building Materials

The abundance of wood from northern Michigan and Wisconsin meant that there was plenty of cheap lumber available in Chicago for all kinds of construction: homes, storefronts, streets. Huge stacks of raw lumber lay in yards lining the south branch of the Chicago River. Some of the early city streets were simply "plank roads" laid on mud. Some of the more pleasant streets were created with Nicolson paving—wood block pavers covered with tar. In the years leading up to the Fire, there were 57 miles of wood-paved streets, 88 miles of paved streets, 450 miles of unpaved, muddy messes, and 561 miles of wooden sidewalks.[3] That said, most people wouldn't wear a suit made of wood and tar to protect themselves from fire, and there's a good reason for that. These delightful wooden streets didn't fare well when the city was set ablaze.

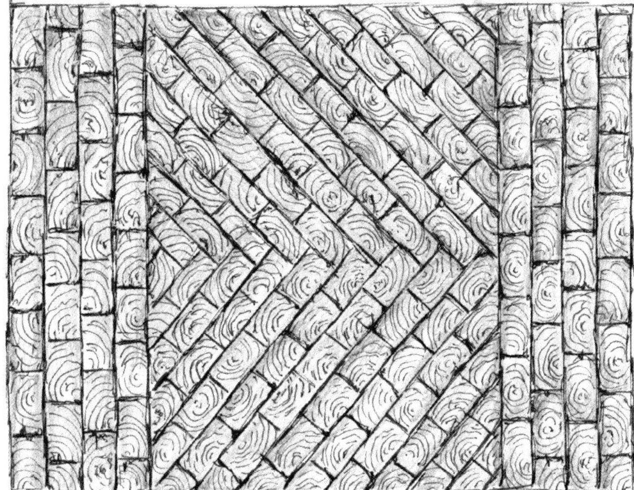

These wooden Nicolson pavers can still be found covering a few Chicago streets. The most well-known survivor is behind the "Cardinal's Mansion" between State and Astor Streets.

Chicago wasn't *entirely* a city of wood. Its "central business district" was filled with stately brick and stone buildings. As land values rose in the core of the city, buildings grew taller and more robust. As Chicago's city center—the modern-day Loop—became more valuable, wooden cottages were physically moved on big blocks to make way for more extravagant buildings. Here's a description of the city by a resident from that period:

> In the heart of the town the stranger beholds blocks of stores solid, lofty and in the most recent taste, hotels of great magnificence and public buildings that would be creditable to any city. . . . Now it is a gorgeous and enormous carpet house that arrests his attention, now a huge dry goods store or a vast depot of groceries. The next moment

> he finds himself peering into . . . a dining room window, where in addition to the delicacies of the season there is a spacious cake of ice covered with naked frogs, reposing picturesquely in parsley.[4]

As indicated by the naked frogs in repose, things were getting fancier in Chicago.

In addition to churches built of limestone, there were so-called fireproof hotels of cast iron and brick. In 1853, the city constructed a massive courthouse in the Greek Revival style. That courthouse—the city's second after the one built in 1835—took a prominent place at Clark and Randolph and its cupola could be seen from miles away. Photographer Alexander Hesler climbed into that cupola and took a series of photographs that, when stitched together, made a lovely panorama and commemoration of the city at that time. In 1859, the *Chicago Tribune* wrote that "a London Insurance Company, having instructed their Chicago agent to take no risks in our 'wooden city,'" was sent a copy of Hesler's panorama, to show them that the city *definitely*

A Greek Revival courthouse with an especially extroverted cupola at Clark and Randolph Streets in the 1850s.

was not at risk of going up in flames.[5] Chicago was no podunk city, and it wasn't taking any lip from across the pond.

Beyond Hesler's vantage point of stately masonry buildings in the central business district stood row upon row of wooden homes. According to an 1868 Chicago Board of Health survey, 38,000 out of the city's 40,000 buildings were of wood construction; out of those, 31,700 were used as residences.[6] Even the brick and stone buildings in the central business district had interiors composed of wooden braces and floorboards.

Here's an account from a resident in 1867 about the rest of the city beyond the view of the panorama:

> Along the lake, south of the river for two or three miles extend the beautiful avenues which change insensibly into those streets of cottages and gardens which have given Chicago the name of the Garden City. In all Chicago there is not one tenement house. Thrifty workmen own the houses they live in, and the rest can still hire a whole house. Consequently, seven-tenths of Chicago consists of small wooden houses in streets with wooden sidewalks and roads of prairie black.[7]

Anyone with a passing knowledge of Chicago history—or the story of Icarus—knows where this ends. We'll get into the Great Fire in the next chapter, but for now, let's take a look at the homes that were built in the period between 1837 and 1871.

The Pre-Fire Homes Still With Us

One of the minor tragedies to come from that epic tragedy is that present-day lovers of old Chicago architecture have so precious little of Chicago's built environment from the pre-fire era. What the fire did not destroy was largely taken care of by the indelicate nature of age and demolitions. Much of the pre-fire architecture that survived consists of a handful of larger brick and masonry buildings that somehow escaped the inferno: churches like Old St Pat's in the present-day West Loop and St. James Cathedral in River North, or functional structures like the Water Tower on Chicago Avenue.

There are homes that existed within the pre-fire boundaries of Chicago that did, in fact, survive both the fire and the years since—likely more than anyone has yet identified. Pre-fire records are sparse. The earliest fire insurance map we have for Chicago is from 1868–69, and it covers the modern-day Loop, where buildings have been turned to rubble more frequently than any other sections of the city since its inception. But there are pre-fire homes that continue to stand stubborn and proud, like the good Midwesterners they are, within the pre-fire city limits, bounded by Fullerton Avenue to the north, Crawford (now Pulaski) Avenue to the west, and Egan (now Pershing) Street to the south.

There are also homes that existed before the fire but were built *outside* the original city boundaries. Those can be found in small clusters, mostly in the communities that sprung up along the rail lines. Stately homes in places such as Norwood Park, Morgan Park, Hyde Park, and Austin became part of the present borders of the city as more land was annexed over time. The city of Chicago gobbled up these formerly "suburban" homes, most significantly in 1889, and gave them fancy new urban identities.

Old St Pat's, one of the rare surviving pre-fire buildings and a well-known beacon among Chicago's Irish.

Interior Spaces in the Mid-1800s

It's difficult (and maybe a little unpleasant) to imagine, but folks didn't always have the luxury of flicking on a light or flushing a toilet at home, and it's worth noting the limits of available technologies during this period. Houses were dark and cold in the winter, hot as Hades in the summer, and using the bathroom was no picnic either. (Hello, outhouses and chamber pots.) As with most modern conveniences today—say, soft-close kitchen drawers—the upper classes tended to adopt them first, followed by the middle and then struggling classes. In Chicago, which was very much a working-class city in this era, most homes lacked even the most essential modern conveniences of the day.

Heating & Cooling

Heat is one example. Fireplaces, which were never very efficient at spreading heat throughout a house (most of the heat escaped up the chimney), were replaced in the early 1800s by wood stoves. The primary challenge of using fire to heat a home was keeping the heat in and the smoke out. Improvements in expelling smoke—something Ben Franklin had worked on—meant that stoves could be situated in the center of a room and spread heat more effectively. By the 1850s, most homeowners had replaced wood with the much more energy-dense coal.

Still, the lack of particularly effective heating options meant that the rule of the day, particularly for common laborers, was compact living. During the colder months, home dwellers spent the majority of their time in a space heated with a stove in the middle of the main living area. Better-off cottage dwellers of this era had two stoves and two chimneys: one for the main living space in the front of the home, and one for the rear, for cooking. As for cooling off during the hotter months of the year, the choices were a bit more limited. There were built-in options such as windows for cross-ventilation, overhanging eaves, and covered porches that blocked sunlight. For more well-to-do Chicagoans, high ceilings allowed warm air to rise and collect above.

Lighting

For much of this era, Chicagoans would have been using candles or oil lamps to light their homes. In 1846, cleaner and brighter-burning kerosene was discovered as a better lighting source and was widely adopted, replacing oil lamps. Gas lighting, which was powered through a network of pipes carrying coal-fired gas, made its Chicago debut in 1850. At first, it was primarily used for street lighting, but soon connections were built to businesses downtown like hotels and theaters and mansions. Because interior residential lighting was so dim, homes were designed to bring in more natural light, and that meant large windows, particularly on the first floor and street-facing side where most of the living and entertaining occurred. Electric lighting wouldn't be available in Chicago until the 1880s.

Plumbing

Oh, plumbing, how we appreciate you! Until city-provided water and sewerage lines were laid in the 1850s, households were on their own in acquiring fresh water and disposing of their waste. The lines were first installed in a limited zone, but by 1857, the city's water and sewerage district enabled any household within the district boundaries to access those amenities, and by 1858, more than seventy-two miles of water pipes and four thousand water taps—both for public fountains and private home connections—made life a little easier and more sanitary for certain lucky Chicagoans. By 1904, nearly two thousand miles of pipe and three hundred thousand taps had been installed.[8] In the following years, many more households would hook up to the public water and sewer lines. It was a far better option than dumping raw sewage into the river and letting it flow right into the lake. The expansion of these services had additional effects. Lured by all these sexy service lines, surrounding towns began champing at the bit for the same amenities, with many ultimately agreeing to annexation by the city. ■

The Preeminent Workers Cottage

This era saw the rise of the workers cottage—specifically, the one-and-a-half story, front-gable home that was constructed with the balloon-frame method of building pioneered in Chicago's early years. This building type would not only come to dominate this period of Chicago's history, but it would also endure for many decades, going through various iterations of material construction and style. For a rapidly growing city, the workers cottage checked several boxes: It was in vogue; it was cheap and easy to build; it could house a worker's family; and it was compact enough that additional space on Chicago's generous lots could be used for a rented coach house or raising livestock.

The cottage became so prevalent and important to the state of Illinois's identity that a key feature of its contribution to the Paris Exposition of 1867 was the American Cottage. Not a workers cottage, exactly, but a cottage that was gussied up and dressed nicely for a Parisian audience. According to one analysis of the Western influence on the Exposition, these homes were "concrete embodiments of the doctrine of self-reliance and its special connections

Example of a typical workers cottage from this period,
with a stovepipe on one of two centered chimneys.

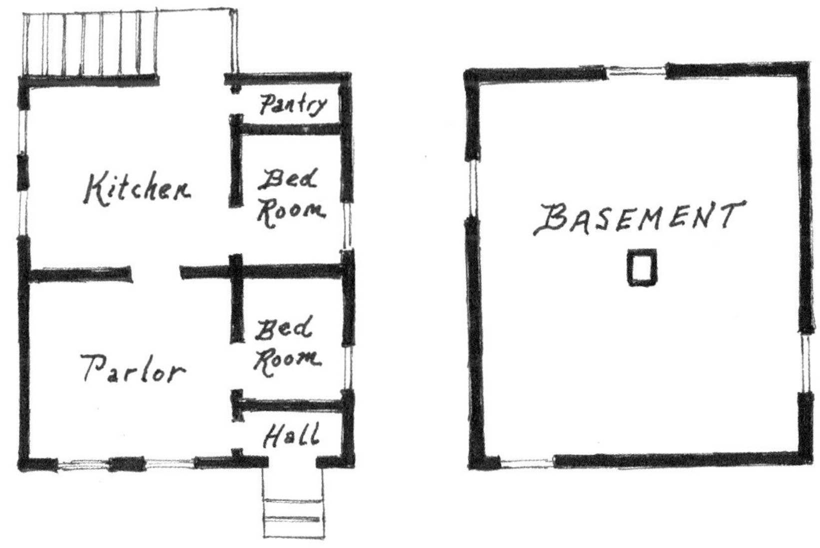

Example of the floorplan of a typical workers cottage from this period.

to farming and education—and, more specifically, symbols of the hope of Western prosperity and opportunity. . . . Showing that luxury in the new world was to be found in simplicity and space, they were exemplars of the simple, robust construction adapted to the necessities of new lands."[9]

In the first chapter, we discussed the ways in which the once-common side-gable homes were rotated 90 degrees to fit on Chicago's narrow city lots, orienting the gable to the street. The specific look of these homes was supported with influential, illustrated texts. One writer of such texts was Andrew Jackson Downing, who, through his illustrated publications, popularized a variety of cottage designs, including the simple, unadorned cottage for the urban laborer. But perhaps the more practical and direct influence were books such as *Carpentry Made Easy*, which popularized the quick, balloon-frame building method and spread the availability of workers cottages built in this era. Easy to construct, cheap, and well-fit to the narrow lots, these cottages proliferated in Chicago in the mid-1800s.

Illinois's "American Cottage" at the 1867 Paris Exposition.

The early Chicago workers cottage, at its most prevalent, was one-and-a-half stories, with a front-facing gable. Builders constructed the home with the gable facing the street and the long sides extending to the rear, with one or two chimneys. The interiors were quite simple.

The construction plans for the wood framing that held up these early workers cottages were available and disseminated in carpentry handbooks with diagrams like the one shown below. Generally, the earlier workers cottages—up to those in the early 1870s—exhibited a gable with a shallower pitch than the later workers cottages from the 1880s to early 1900s, which had a steeper pitch. Note that the shallow pitch is reminiscent of the angles of a classical pediment, the Greek proportions "revived" by Greek Revival homes. This stylistic influence in the early Chicago cottages may have been imported from upstate New York and the Erie Canal. The more equilateral triangle of the gable to the right, on the other hand, appears strongly as a recurring form in the later Queen Anne period.

The type of wood frames from carpentry books that helped guide and spread common workers cottage forms. A gable with shallower pitch (left) was common for early workers cottages; a gable with steeper pitch (right) was common later on.

House Moving & House Raising

Compared to the heavy timber-framed cottages they replaced, the lightness of balloon-frame homes—coupled with the lack of modern utility hookups that would come later—meant that homes were easy to move. Early owners took full advantage of this feature, as homes were frequently rolled from lot to lot, and sometimes even stolen and resold to naive buyers.[10] House moving was so prevalent that visitors to Chicago in the mid-1800s often reported major traffic jams involving a cluster of cottages on rollers. In 1846, Chicagoans even asked the city council to put limits on the number of buildings that could sit in the middle of traffic at any given time. The other advantage of the lightness and mobility of these early cottages was that they could be easily lifted upward, which was handy for a city that would soon need to create a whole layer of infrastructure beneath itself.

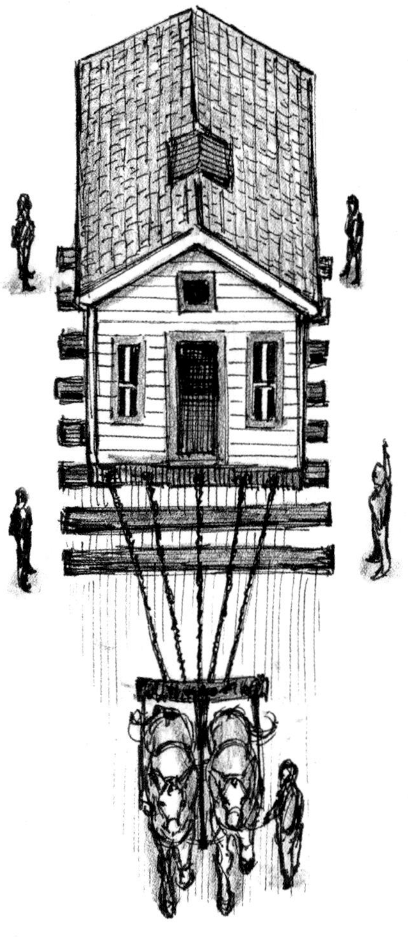

Chicago's origins as an ancient glacial lakebed meant that its residents were long dealing with muddy roads and standing water that did not absorb easily into clay soil. It was hard enough for residents to avoid sinking in the mud, but as masses of people arrived and congregated, the standing water and waterborne pathogens created far worse problems than dirty boots. Typhoid, dysentery, and cholera also decided to get to work in this growing city. In 1854, one outbreak of cholera killed about 2,000 people in a population of only 80,000.[11] An equivalent proportion of Chicago's present-day population would be about 67,000 people.

The city finally accepted that it needed a sewerage system. The plan was to install drains and raise the street levels between four and five feet, which the city adopted in two stages during 1855–56 and 1857–58. The city would lift the streets and sidewalks, but home and building owners were responsible for raising their own properties. For those who didn't have the in-house expertise and a crew of gullible friends, there was a small industry of house- and building-raising companies available for hire, including one owned by George Pullman, later and better

Moving day! A cottage on rollers was not an uncommon sight.

A raised cottage with a frame second floor and a masonry first floor.

known for founding the Pullman Palace Car Company and the company town of Pullman. Entire hotels, like the elegant Tremont Hotel, were hoisted up by crews of hundreds, using jacks, while hotel patrons went about sipping their tea, hardly aware that they were levitating. But besides these large raising projects, individual house raising was done on the order of thousands, as the street grade was raised in various parts of the city.

Houses weren't just raised to meet a higher street grade. In some instances, they were raised simply because the owners had the means to add a new floor under the existing house, which added the opportunity for extra residents or tenants. Today, there are numerous examples of homes that were lifted up to a higher level, with a brick first floor constructed as the new first floor, and a front door added for ground-level access.

In instances where homeowners refused to meet the new levels of street and sidewalks, some would build a bridged walkway from the higher sidewalk to what was previously their upper floor, leaving their first floor below the new ground level. Examples of these "sunken homes" can still be found around the city. Some of them remain sunken below the street grade; some of them are raised to meet it, with a little staircase down to the previous first floor doorway.

The typical evolution of a cottage on a street that has been raised.

The Homes of Chicago in Its Pre-1871 Borders

Recall that Chicago's borders pre-1871 made for a much smaller footprint than that of the city today. Within those boundaries, very few pre-fire homes still stand. Those that do exhibit the architectural trends of the day: Gothic Revival, Second Empire, and Italianate. There are vanishingly few examples of the former two. Italianate came to dominate the stylistic preferences in the middle of this era and well beyond it. But let's start with the first two.

Gothic Revival: Inspiration from the Middle Ages

Like the Greek Revival style of the early 1800s, Gothic Revival's lifetime as a residential style was fairly short-lived. But, also like Greek Revival style, Gothic Revival hung around for quite a while outside of residential architecture and was incorporated into churches, schools, and colleges (see, for example, the romantic, black lipstick-inspiring Gothic buildings of the University of Chicago, founded in 1890). As expressed in Chicago homes, the style borrowed motifs from France and England's late medieval period.

Here's a home in Wicker Park, dating to the mid-1800s, in a pared-down Gothic Revival style. The giveaway in this case is the steep pitch of the cross-gable roof (when a front and side gable "cross" one another).

GOTHIC REVIVAL

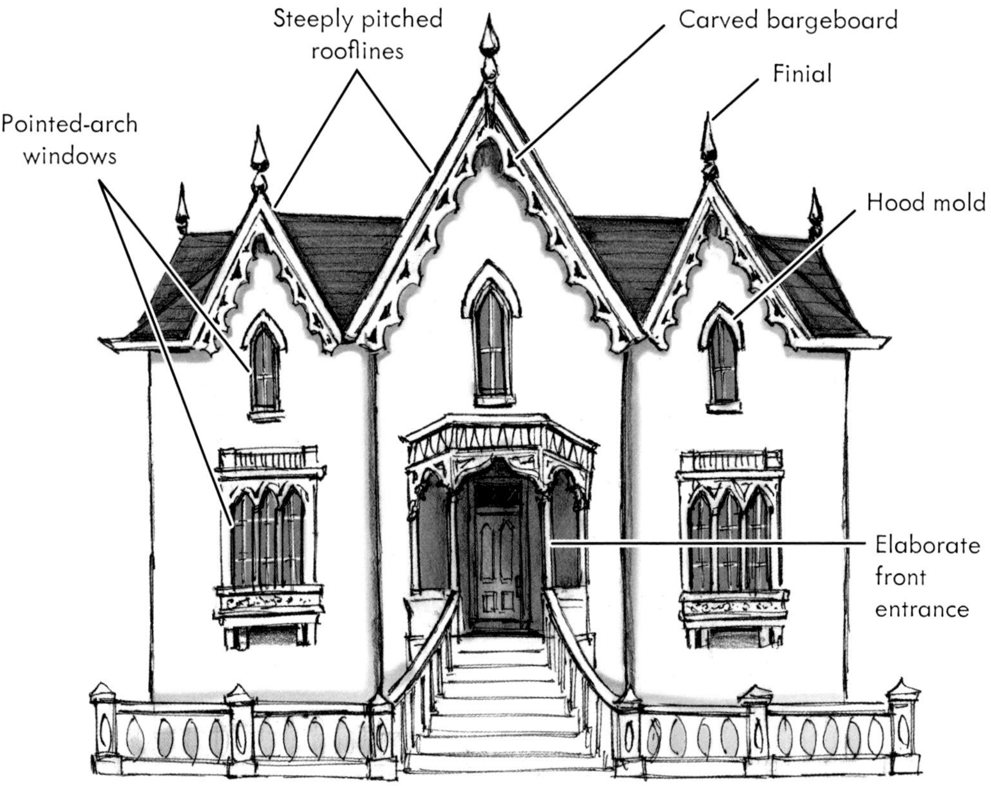

A Gothic Revival home near present-day Wabash and Grand Avenue based on a lithograph from 1866.

COMMON FEATURES

- Distinctive pointed-arch windows, often with a drip mold as a crown
- Steeply pitched rooflines, typically a front gable or multiple gables, with a cross gable
- Carved bargeboard—the decoratively carved wood that adorns overhanging rooflines—topped with a carved finial
- Front entrance with a porch adorned with Gothic detailing

One other prominent example in the Chicago area is the Francis Willard house in Evanston. Built in 1865, the home's steep front gables with decorative bargeboard, cross-gable roof, and vertical board and batten siding put it in the wood-forward sub-style often called Carpenter Gothic. Through the late 1800s and early 1900s, this style would live on, particularly popular for farmhouses in the heartland (think of the house behind the stoic couple in Grant Wood's painting, *American Gothic*, which is hanging at the Art Institute of Chicago).

Second Empire: Inspirations from Paris

The Second Empire style, often represented in pop culture as a "spooky" architectural style, is also ushered into Chicago in this era. Think the Addams Family mansion. During the reign of Napoleon III from 1852 to 1870, the supposed "second empire" of France after its first under Napoleon Bonaparte, Paris underwent a major architectural transition that, in many ways, made it the Paris we now fantasize about while we sit through long staff meetings. These fashionable Parisian buildings emphasized the roofline with the steeply pitched mansard roof, usually with one or multiple dormers. The bonus living space afforded by this building topper was often, in Paris anyway, the dwelling for servants and staff. After all—who'd want the apartment with the lowest ceilings on the highest floor in an era before elevators were common?

The most conspicuous feature of the Second Empire home, the mansard roof.

The Paris Expo, or *Exposition Universelle*, of 1867, where Illinois showed off its American Cottage, helped spread the popularity of the Second Empire style in developing American cities. In Chicago, the love affair was short-lived.

Many of the mansard roofs that were built in the 1860s—perhaps most notable on the Crosby Opera House—fell victim to the Great Chicago Fire. As Gerald Larson, Professor Emeritus of Architecture at University of Cincinnati, has pointed out, when Chicagoans rebuilt after the fire, they hesitated to reintroduce the mansard roof. It was seen as a major fire liability, being both made of wood and hard to reach for firefighters. In his *History of Chicago,* A.T. Andreas wrote that the Board of Police reported a variety of issues to the city council, including consistent warnings about mansard and tar roofs.

Some of the mansarded Second Empire homes in the posh part of town did manage to escape the fire. Here's Prairie Avenue on Chicago's Near South Side in 1874.

Of the pre-fire Second Empire homes in the Prairie Avenue district, only the Keith House and the Wheeler-Kohn House, both from 1870, survive to this day.

SECOND EMPIRE

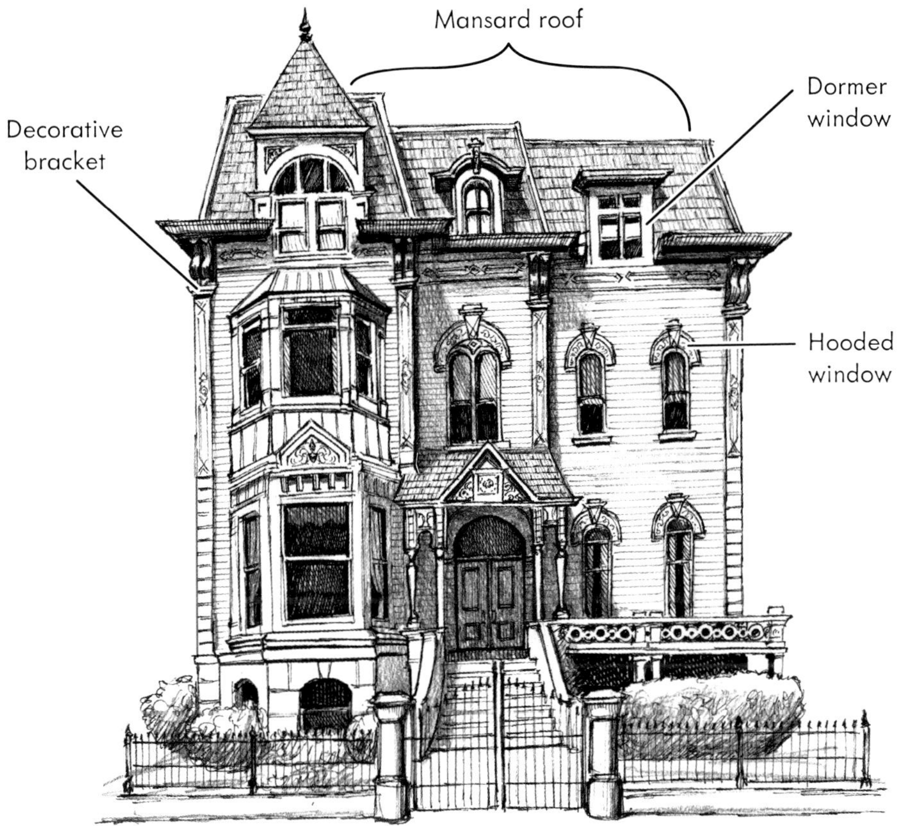

The Wheeler-Kohn house, which is not far from the present location of the Clarke-Ford House.

COMMON FEATURES

- Mansard roof, in some cases adorned with ornate iron cresting
- Dormer windows
- Decorative brackets beneath the eaves
- Hooded windows in a consistent repeated pattern
- Occasionally a prominent, centered tower or offset wing

Italianate: The Tuscan Villa Comes to the City

The Italianate style originated from examples that gained popularity in England and the eastern United States. One of the earliest examples is Blandwood in Greensboro, North Carolina, designed by Alexander Jackson Davis and built in 1844. He partnered with Andrew Jackson Downing, illustrating books that spread and popularized various picturesque styles in the 1850s, including those based on the "Tuscan villa," or what became known as the Italianate style. The style was also popular outside of Chicago, but really got a grip on towns west of the Appalachian Mountains that were booming in the mid-1800s, like Chicago. In cities such as Cincinnati and St. Louis, the enthusiasm for the Italianate style coincided with a relatively blank canvas and massive amount of housing construction.

The Italianate style was a reaction to the cramped urban living conditions present in industrializing East Coast cities. It was meant to elevate a country style by expressing an integration with nature and a return to the elevated ideals of the Italian Renaissance—such as harmony and proportion. Just as the Greek Revival style called back to ancient Greek ideals and meshed its aesthetic with American material conditions and needs, so did the Italianate style. Chicago saw a steady incorporation of Italianate features in the 1850s, leading well into the 1880s, when it would be eclipsed by the Queen Anne style.

One of the great examples of an existing early Italianate home in pre-fire Chicago is the Hull House.

Notice the marks of the Italianate style: the distinctive cornice with spaced brackets, rounded windows, and a belvedere. This home was built in 1856 by real estate developer Charles Hull and was made famous by Jane Addams and Ellen Gates Starr, who bought it in 1889 and made it the namesake part of an extensive campus for vast social support services. The Hull House Museum is now stewarded by the University of Illinois Chicago, spared while eleven other associated buildings were demolished to make way for the construction of the university campus.[12]

Another Italianate home that survived the fire was the late-1860s Bellinger Home in Lincoln Park. This home was miraculously spared while many of its neighbors were engulfed. Notice the aesthetic throughline from the Hull House: the symmetry, the distinctive gable with decorative cornice and brackets, and the rounded windows and door.

ITALIANATE

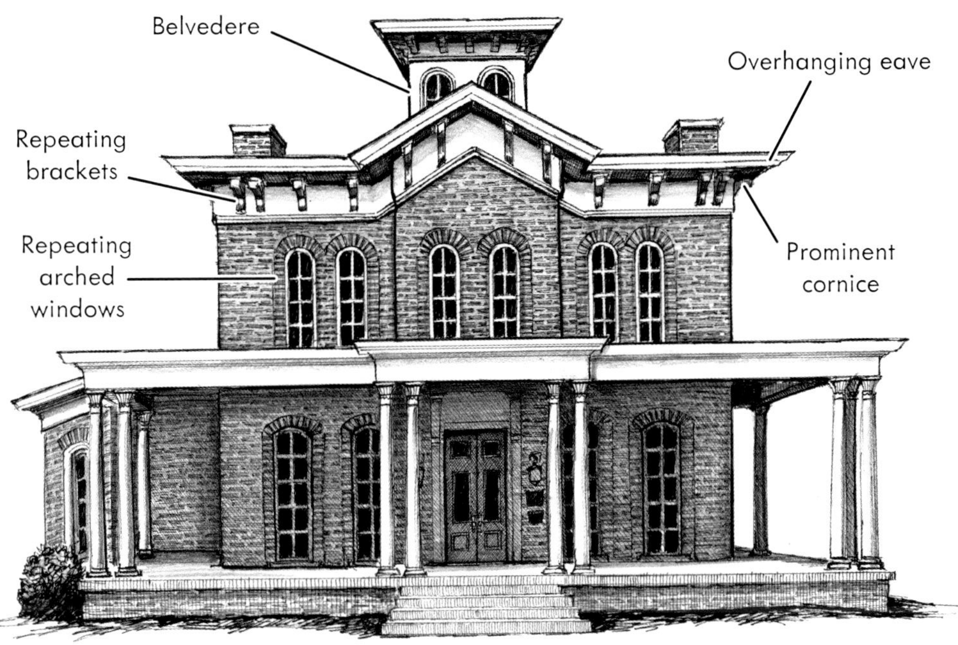

Hull House, situated just southwest of the Loop near the University of Illinois Chicago, made famous by Jane Addams.

COMMON FEATURES

- Attention-grabbing and deep cornices, often highlighted with one or several colors and decorative molding and ornament
- Large, repeating brackets supporting the overhanging eave
- Prominent windows and doors, typically with the same repeated arched or rounded curve
- Distinctive hoods or lintels with incised ornament (carved patterns) and/or a prominent keystone over the tops of windows and doors
- Strong horizontal symmetry (Chicago's Italianates more often had the front entrance offset, but otherwise were symmetrical)
- In some earlier cases, a tower or a belvedere

Former home of police officer Richard Bellinger, who reportedly saved it from burning by dousing it with water and, when that ran out, cider. The home was designed by W.W. Boyington, who also designed the famous Chicago Water Tower.

Pre-Fire Homes in the Former "Suburbs"

The surviving pre-fire homes also include those that are situated within modern-day Chicago borders, but in 1871 existed outside the city limits. These fall within a few clusters: along a northwestern axis, in Old Irving and Norwood Park; and along a southern axis extending to Hyde Park and Englewood, through to Morgan Park. There are a few outliers. These homes mostly sprung up along a few of the commuter rail lines: the Chicago and North Western to the northwest, and the Illinois Central Railroad to the south. These homes, in contrast to those that were within the original city limits, were built on generously-sized lots and weren't restricted to the narrow facade of the typical Chicago home. The majority of these are Italianate, but there is a little Gothic Revival and Second Empire representation as well.

The Northwestern Suburbs: Old Irving & Norwood Park

The Old Irving cluster includes a handful of pre-fire homes sporting the beloved Italianate belvedere. Here are some examples of those homes, among them the Phebe and John Gray House, which some historians think may have been a stop along the underground railroad, and a home on Keeler Avenue. Note the other Italianate features that adorn these homes.

The Phebe and John Gray House.

Another Irving Park Italianate.

The Norwood Park cluster may have the largest number of known pre-fire homes in the city. The original portion of the Noble–Seymour–Crippen House dates to 1833, technically bumping the Clarke-Ford House off its pedestal as the oldest home in modern-day Chicago, though the Noble–Seymour–Crippen House was not built within the original Chicago borders.

The Southern Suburbs: Hyde Park, Kenwood, Englewood, and Morgan Park

Let's take the nearer-south first. Hyde Park Township existed from 1861 until its annexation by the city of Chicago in 1889. Its footprint was enormous, extending from 39th Street (Pershing) on the north, to State Street on the west, all the way to 138th Street—the southernmost border of present-day Chicago. It included Kenwood as well. To the west of Hyde Park Township was the town of Lake, which included present-day Englewood.

There are some beautiful examples in Hyde Park of large, Italianate homes that were built in the mid-1860s, including this cottage with the telltale gable, cornice and brackets, and semicircular window hoods.

While a lot of Chicago's Italianate homes have strong front symmetry and prominent cornices with brackets, we also see some with hipped roofs and facades with paired windows. A hipped roof, unlike the two-sided gable roof, has four sides that slope toward all the sides of a home, typically with a gentle pitch. We'll see hipped roofs used in full force in bungalows and Foursquares in later chapters.

Italianate front-gable cottage of Hyde Park.

Two-story Italianate in Hyde Park with a hipped roof.

It's also worth taking a ride farther south to Morgan Park, where there are two other great examples of Italianate homes—the Hopkinson (or Platt) House from 1871[13] and the Iglehart House, the original portion of which dates to 1857. Out to the west of downtown, in the former suburb of Austinville (now the neighborhood of Austin), there is the still-standing Seth Warner House.

Many pre-fire homes that managed to stand for more than a century were eventually lost to the wrecking ball. The remaining few are therefore worth

Home of Austin's Seth Warner, who was a blacksmith, abolitionist, and lover of the arts.

protecting with pitchforks and battle cries. They're a critical window into the styles, tastes, and living arrangements of the generation of Chicagoans who arrived as the city was riding a huge upswing of growth and industrialization. In 1871, the Great Fire took out about 17,500 homes. Its aftermath and wrangling between various groups—immigrants, social classes, insurance companies, and city leaders—would set the stage for a rebuilding of the city's homes in brick and stone.

CHAPTER

Rising and Rebuilding

1871–1882

1890 1900 1910 1920 1930 1940

"The wiping out of the whole of the material wealth of a great metropolis was indeed an event for which we as a community were unprepared; and if the enormity of the calamity was not brought home to us at once, it was principally because we lost our homes simultaneously with our city."

—Editorial (unsigned), 1873, *Chicago Daily Tribune*

What is Chicago's central, defining story? Ask an outsider, and they might say that at Chicago's core is Al Capone or the '90s Bulls' dynasty. But step inside Chicago for longer than a layover at O'Hare and a local might bring you in close and tell you the city's founding mythology. First, we built this city by a big lake, only for it to burn to the ground in 1871. Then, we rebuilt it bigger and better to host the best event the world had yet seen: the 1893 World's Fair, where we introduced the Ferris Wheel, Pabst Blue Ribbon beer, *and* Cracker Jacks.

Like all good origin stories, Chicago's has a great structure and gives its tellers a deep sense of spirit. There are nuances often lost in the retelling, however—particularly with respect to the architectural changes that emerged in the aftermath of the Great Chicago Fire. The typical story has it that the fire created a "blank canvas," the city banned wood construction, and architects rushed in to create and innovate in brick and then steel. As we'll see, there were other forces at work, including political opposition, economic booms and busts, and the flowering of a showy upper class. But the outlines of the story are true: fire left an enduring mark on the city's architecture.

During Chicago's massive, sprawling, wood-supported growth of the mid-1800s, some residents had deep anxiety about the risk of a catastrophic fire. There was a sense of impending doom from astute observers, like the Chicago Board of Fire Underwriters in June 1871: "Unless the suggestions here made, and repeatedly made by our predecessors, are adopted, Chicago may have a conflagration sweeping over miles of territory and destroying millions of dollars' worth of property." Just four months later, dry, hot, steady winds had laid out the worst possible conditions for this prophecy to come to pass.

Sometime after 9:00 p.m. on October 8, 1871, citizens were alerted by the sound of alarm bells or neighbors pounding on their doors. From the height of rooftops or second floors, they were aghast to see the approach of a massive wall of fire moving from the southwest edge of the central business district. With an unnerving speed, the line of fire moved northward while fanning outward in an upside-down teardrop shape. It was "fenced in" by the north branch of the Chicago river to the west and the lakefront to the east. The flames burned through the wooden shanties as well as the brick and stone buildings of the central business district, so hot that it buckled and melted cast iron. Grand establishments, like the Crosby Opera House, the Court House, and the Palmer Hotel, which had just opened two weeks earlier, burned to the ground.

The gray shape shows the area consumed by the 1871 fire, which roared south-to-north and jumped the river twice.

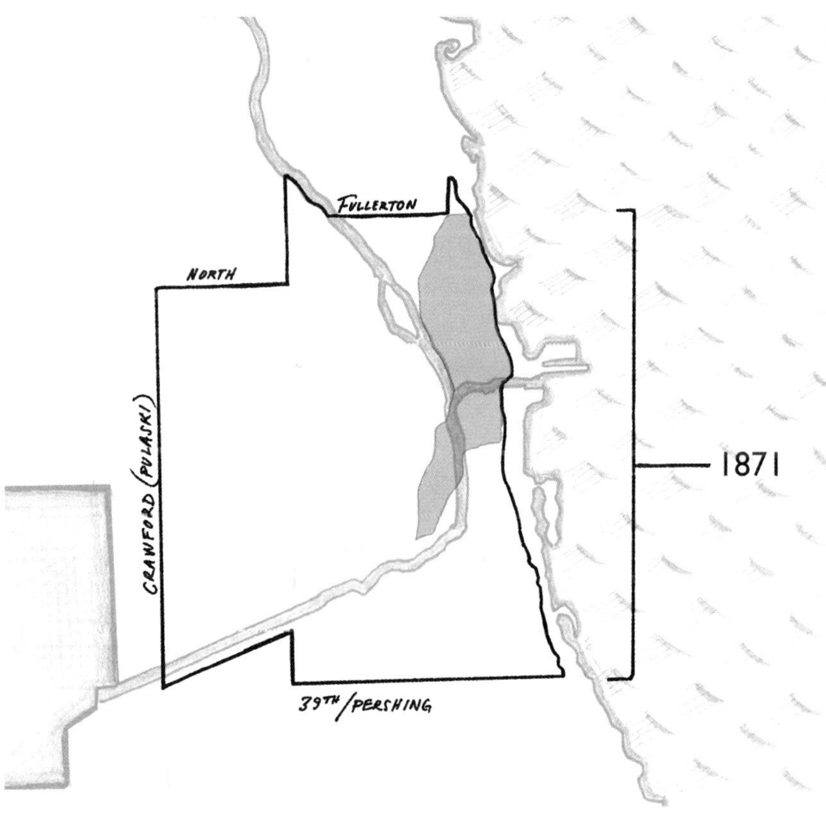

Some residents on the far north of the city saw a large fire to the south and figured that the firefighting crews would handle it before it got near their homes. But the water pumps were failing while the fire gathered in strength. The fire roared north and burned up everything in its path. People fled, many running eastward to stand in the lake for the remainder of the night, watching the fire burn before finally petering out at Fullerton Avenue, which was then the city's northernmost border.

The next day, most of what had been the city, including tens of thousands of wooden cottages, was a smoldering pile of rubble and ruins. It wasn't long before investigators pinpointed the origin of the fire as a wooden barn behind the O'Leary family cottage. The fire was not, as later rumored, ignited by a cow kicking over a lantern. But no one knows the exact source, because no one was there or copped to witnessing it. From Mrs. O'Leary's testimony:

> I was in bed myself and my husband and five children when this fire commenced. . . . I could not tell anything of the fire, only that two men came by the door . . . and said "Kate the barn is afire." I ran out and the whole barn was on fire. Well I went out to the barn and upon my word I could not tell anyone about the fire.[1]

The O'Leary homestead: a rented front cottage, with the O'Learys residing in the back one. The barn had been at the furthest rear of the lot.

There had been, of course, other "Great Conflagrations" throughout history: London in 1666, Moscow in 1812, New York City in 1835. The Peshtigo Fire in northwestern Wisconsin ranks the worst in American history in terms of loss of life, with between 1,500 and 2,500 dead. It occurred on the very same night as the Chicago Fire. The Chicago Fire, by contrast, killed an estimated 300 people. What made it especially dramatic was that it was such a calamitous humbling for a city that had been on an unprecedented, two-decade tear of population and construction growth.

The inescapable reality of the situation was that the city residents would need to rebuild. Tens of thousands of structures had burned down, leaving about a third of the city's population homeless, and most city services in shambles. According to one witness, "For three days after the fire we walked through the streets, covered everywhere with heaps of debris and parts of walls, and could not help comparing ourselves to ghosts wandering through a vast grave-yard. 'Am I really awake, or am I having a horrible dream?'" For many of the affected citizens, they were not just homeless, but without savings or a place to work.

An extant shelter cottage in Old Town, which was likely much more pared down at the time it was built.

Many started rebuilding the next day. As news of the fire traveled the world, donations poured in for relief. The Chicago Relief and Aid Society stepped up to disburse donations to beleaguered residents. They also provided lumber and plans for "shelter cottages." Chicagoans built more than 5,200 of these. At least one of them still exists and is inhabited in the Old Town area.[2]

Of course, the city would rise again—the phoenix from the ashes. But the fire was never far from the collective memory of the people, and it would shape the built environment in enduring ways.

Although not a well-known part of the Chicago Fire mythology, the rebuilding decade also was beset by an economic depression. In September 1873, while a group of city boosters was set to open the grand Inter-State Industrial Exposition along the lakefront on the present-day site of the Art Institute—a bank panic was brewing, thanks to a huge bubble of over-extended credit in the railroad industry. In the same month the exposition was to open, the implosion of a major bank in Philadelphia set off a national panic, resulting in a long economic depression that would last until 1879.

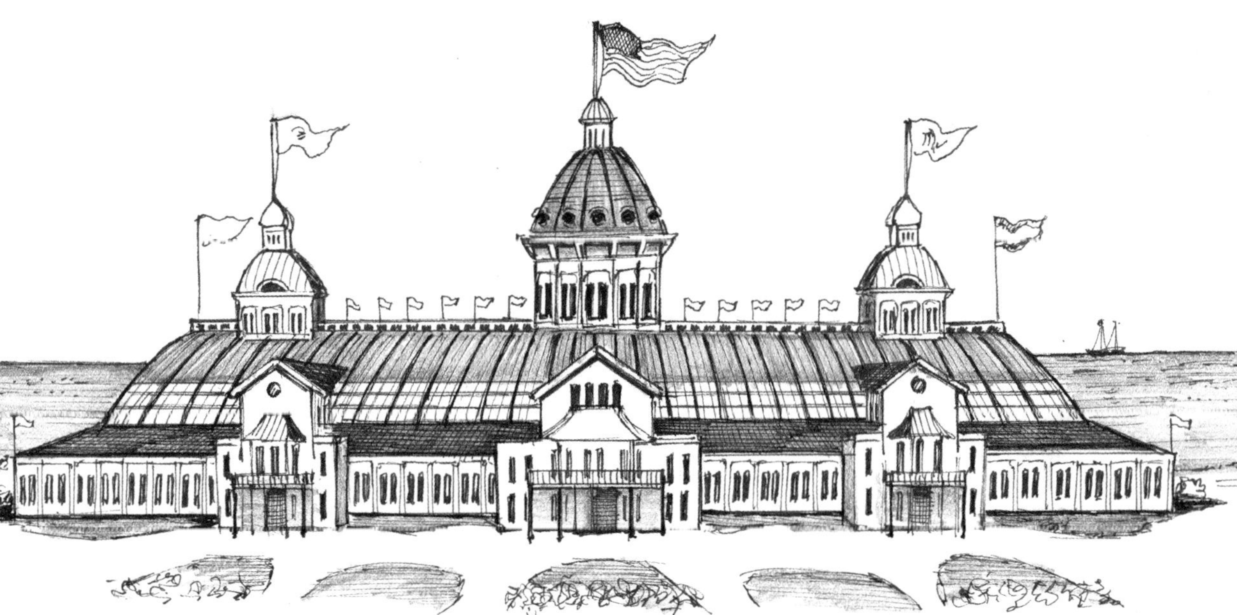

Site of the Inter-State Industrial Exposition.

In fact, this economic period was so uniquely immiserating that it was called the "Great Depression" until the depression of 1929 took that moniker; thereafter, it was referred to as the "Long Depression." There was 8.25 percent unemployment, and even in the busily rebuilding Chicago, many laborers went unemployed.[3] A major mass Socialist rally of angry workers took place in December 1873 and other labor turmoil followed. In 1877, railroad workers and allied laborers nationally went on strike, and in Chicago, it culminated in the "Battle of the Viaduct" at Halsted between 12th and 16th Streets. Mobs and police faced off, exchanging rocks and gunfire, and at least eighteen workers were killed in the violence.[4]

In spite of all of this strife, people continued to pour into Chicago. Optimism still reigned. The city's population in 1870 was about three hundred thousand and by 1880 had grown to about five hundred thousand. Immigrants were still coming from Germany and Ireland, but also increasingly from other countries: Canada, Sweden, Bohemia (now Czech Republic). The 1870s would not only see the depression brought to a merciful conclusion by the end of the decade, but also three major inventions: Alexander Graham Bell's telephone (1876); Thomas Edison's phonograph (1877); and the electric incandescent light bulb (1879), though widespread adoption was years away. The city's mass transit was still horse-drawn street cars, but the cable car was soon to come.

It would not be an overstatement to say that the 1870s were one of the most formative years in Chicago's history, in terms of its built environment but also its psyche. For years thereafter, few architects or civic leaders cutting a red ribbon in front of a new building or civic landmark could fail to mention the founding lore around the fire and resurrection. The notion of resilience is baked into the local ethos. Barack Obama incorporated it into his personality during his presidential term: "I'm from Chicago; I don't break."[5] The post-fire homes of Chicago also seem to reflect this ethos: They have a certain muscularity to them, a fortress-like quality, and we'll look at the ways that this came to be.

Fireproofing the City

The common narrative about Chicago's architecture before and after the fire often emphasizes that the city was predominantly built with wood, and after the fire, wood was prohibited in favor of brick and stone. The reality was more complex.

As early as 1845, the city council recognized the danger of fire in crowded, combustible buildings, and instituted the first fire limit, which covered the central business district. This meant, in practice, that buildings within the fire limit had to be made of approved, fire-safe materials like masonry and iron. However, enforcement was weak and exceptions were issued all the time. We can see in pre-fire photos of the business district that there were wooden cottages in between brick commercial buildings. But even the recommended fireproofing measures were too meager for what they promised; the then-popular cast iron facades melted, and the brick and masonry buildings were filled with wood interiors. The Great Fire of 1871 exposed all of these vulnerabilities.

The first mayoral election following the fire saw the victory of "Fireproof" Joseph Medill, who made a promise to take a hard line on fire risks. Those with means to build fireproof buildings—the well-to-do residents, the businesses, and the fire insurers—generally wanted to extend the fire limit to the entirety of the city. But on the other side of the argument, there was a large contingent of working-class residents worried about being bricked out of their city. At a city council meeting on the issue, a huge group of angry Germans from "North Town" (today's Old Town/Gold Coast), rioted and threw a brick through the window of city hall.[6]

So in 1872, the city voted to extend the fire limits in such a way that provided a "carve out" for the working-class who wanted to build affordable homes. There were a number of other safety provisions laid out, but all in all they were considered quite weak. The revised code "amounted to nothing more than a whitewash, as the only improvements in construction over the existing 1865 code was the *de facto* elimination of cast iron fronts and stone veneers."[7]

The fire insurance companies continued to press for more fireproofing, and they were on the verge of canceling all policies within the city before a business association stepped in and satisfied most of their demands. They remained unsuccessful, however, in pressing for the fire limit to extend to the city border until July 1874, when another huge fire made their case for them. Cause unknown, it started on the southern edge of the central business district and ripped through forty-seven acres, affecting predominantly Black and Jewish neighborhoods.

Though not nearly as destructive as the 1871 Great Fire, the fire of 1874 was reminiscent of the previous conflagration and re-traumatizing to its recent survivors. Finally, the city council had the political capital to overcome opposition and extend the fire limit to the edge of the city. Anyone building within the fire limits needed permits from the Board of Public Works; wooden buildings could not be enlarged or moved within the fire limits, only moved *out* of the fire limits. They also created the country's first standalone Department of Buildings in 1875 in order to enforce the rules.

In practice, this meant that there was still a plethora of wood-frame homes, many of them cottages that had been built between 1871 and 1874 within the city limits. Some of these are still standing and we'll look at them later. The homes and buildings built post-1874 were mostly brick and stone, as permitted by the city. This would become an enduring reality of the

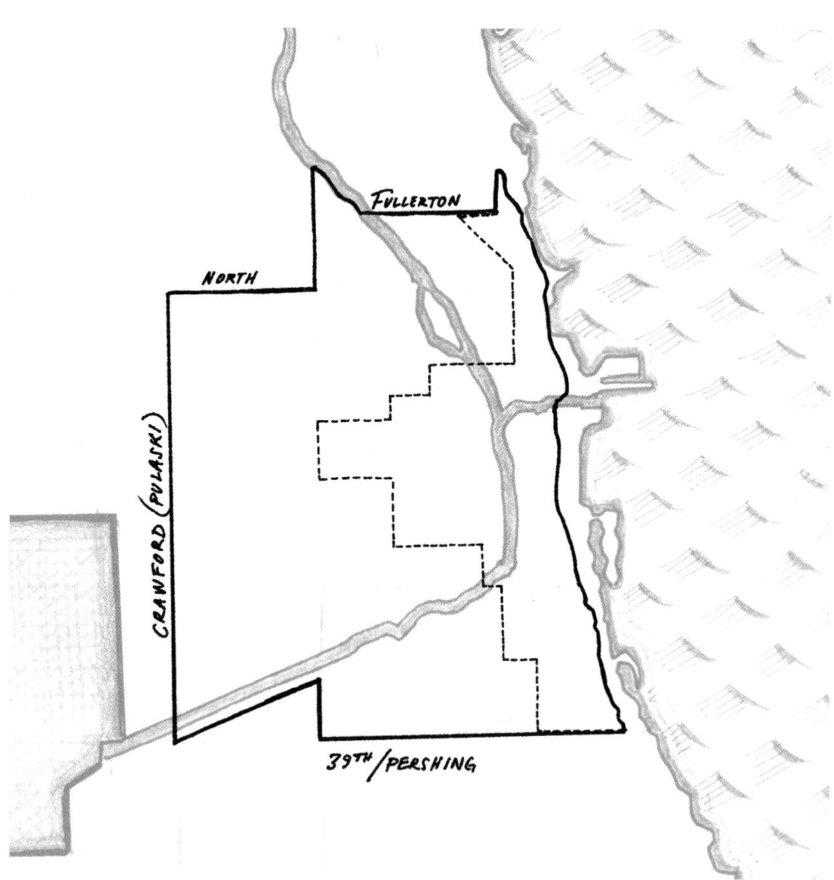

The dotted line shows the fire limit of 1872, which allowed a substantial portion of the city to ignore most of the fire code requirements.

post-fire city architecture. Meanwhile, many Chicagoans, native and new, looked to the suburbs beyond the fire limits. The increasing access from the suburbs to the city with horse-drawn streetcars and commuter rails made life there more feasible for more people. Some simply were traumatized by the events and turmoil of the fire engulfing their crowded city, and the siren song of wider lots, more space, more greenery, and bigger homes was powerful.

Decline of Pine, Uptick of Brick (and Stone)

It wasn't just the fire limits and building codes that were pushing the population toward masonry buildings. It was economics. The old-growth white pine forests from Wisconsin and Michigan, which had been so readily razed for Chicago's wooden homes, had been plundered for other growing cities in that period. The declining supply was showing up in the prices for white pine, doubling in 1870 from their pre–Civil War levels and moving upward from there.[8] If the city was having a difficult time convincing home builders to use masonry, the fact that white pine was making homes so expensive to build was argument enough.

Enter brick. Chicago to this point had been importing a massive amount of brick from other parts of the country, such as St. Louis and Philadelphia. Local brick manufacturing, sourced from the clay of the Chicago River, was relatively small by comparison. The fire limits became a boon to the industry, a gift of supply and demand that ramped up production in a major way for existing manufacturers and brought new manufacturers to market. These increases in supply supported a robust domestic market and eventually such economies of scale that the brick manufacturers started producing for other markets as well.

This brick wasn't the best looking or most impermeable, however. The local clay had more lime and iron, giving it a discolored, uneven reddish-tan appearance. It was typically reserved for a building's non-street-facing walls, while the street-facing facade would be composed of the "nicer" brick, called face brick, from other producers: St. Louis or Philadelphia were still the preferred choices for face brick facades.

Joliet Limestone, a.k.a. "Athens Marble"

One building material that clads both the remaining pre-fire structures in Chicago as well as those built in the immediate post-fire years is the yellow buttercream limestone from Joliet. Its name speaks to its provenance: The limestone was extracted initially from quarries around Joliet and used for a variety of lock and bridge operator houses—locally known as tender-houses—for the Illinois and Michigan Canal. In 1853, the Illinois Stone and Lime Company was formed to begin provisioning Chicago with what would later, in the spirit of real estate rebranding, be referred to as "Athens Marble." Writing in 1876, former Lieutenant Governor William Bross said, "Cheaply quarried and easily accessible by water, Chicago owes much of her prestige and prosperity to these Athens marble quarries."

Joliet limestone was used for a wide variety of buildings in the 1850s into the 1870s, often with a Gothic Revival "castellated" look. Several of the most prominent examples of wholly clad Joliet limestone structures include the Joliet prison (1858, famous for having housed Leopold and Loeb and the fictional "Joliet" Jake Blues of the Blues Brothers); the Union Stock Yard gate (1875, designed by Daniel Burnham and John Root); the Rosehill Cemetery gate and Chicago Water Tower (1864 and 1867, respectively, both by William Boyington).

Joliet limestone was extensively used until the 1890s, when another limestone swaggered onto the scene: Bedford limestone. Bedford limestone came from its namesake town in south-central Indiana, and while it didn't have a fancy-sounding nickname like Athens marble, it offered a number of benefits that put Joliet limestone on its heels. According to an article written for an Illinois History symposium:

> [Bedford] limestone is a true limestone. It is cut from solid beds and, hence, is not layered like the dolomite limestone from the Joliet area. It had many advantages over the [Joliet] stone. It could be cut and laid as a veneer over brick masonry; it did not have to be laid as the weight-bearing element. It was also easier to carve, being not quite so hard as the Joliet stone. It was easier to saw, and it gave a uniform gray look on a building, unlike the various subtle hues of the dolomite limestone (although to my eyes this stone has the dullness of concrete). However, the Bedford Limestone appealed to early 20th century taste, which exhibited a bent for classical buildings with uniform walls, uniformly laid with uniform color.[9]

Because we kicked Joliet limestone to the curb at a certain point in our building history, we use that switching point to roughly date Chicago masonry-built homes and buildings. For the homes and buildings built in the post-fire period from 1870–80, Joliet limestone is used liberally. In some cases, it made up the facade or even the whole building—but in many cases, it was used to create some lovely accent marks on homes. One of its primary uses throughout much of this era was as window and doorway hoods. It was the perfect match for the Italianate style, a key feature of which, as you may recall from our last chapter, was adorning and ornamenting windows and doorways.

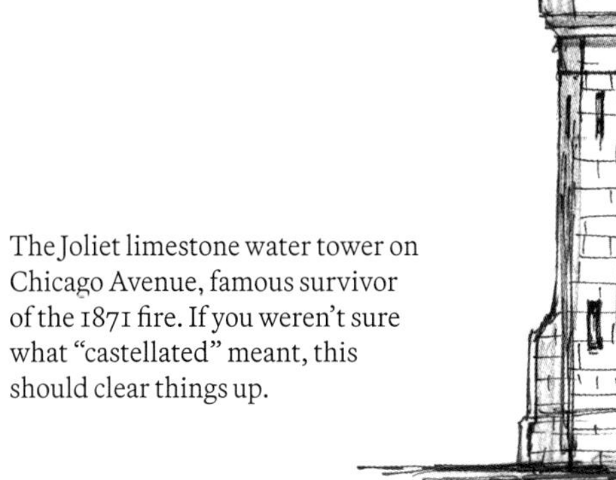

The Joliet limestone water tower on Chicago Avenue, famous survivor of the 1871 fire. If you weren't sure what "castellated" meant, this should clear things up.

Post-Fire Patterns of Population Growth

There are three broad categories of homes from this era:

- Wood-frame homes built within the original city limits between 1871–74
- Masonry homes built within the original city limits
- Wood-frame homes built outside the city limits

In the decade following the Great Fire of 1871, the population pushed further outward from the central business district. For three years, until the fire limits were extended to the city limits, Chicagoans were able to build wooden homes within the city limits. Some of those homes from that three-year period exist—notably in what was then "North Town," or today the area of Old Town. Many of these are workers cottages built by German immigrants, like the one on Eugenie Street that's pictured here.

Frame workers cottage in Old Town, also home to a number of other early 1870s frame cottages.

After the fire of 1874, these neighborhoods came to be dominated by masonry homes. Little by little, the frame homes, more prone to deterioration and easier to tear down, were replaced by brick. The home on the right below is an example of an 1874 stunner that was recently demolished to make a decidedly less charming vacant lot.

The Post-Fire Limits, Pre-Annexation Homes of the "Suburbs" (1874-1889)

For almost two decades after the Great Fire, the city borders were quite stable, with only a minor annexation of a parcel of land in the area we now call Avondale. This was unusual given the city's pattern of gobbling up surrounding land to this point. But the fire had quieted the expansionist voices—and perhaps it was the case, too, that the towns around Chicago were waiting to see what new amenities the city might offer them. Of course, in 1889, the city made its most substantial annexation in its history, but we'll get to the specifics of that in the next chapter. The main consideration for our purposes is that, for fifteen years between the establishment of the stricter, expanded fire limits in Chicago and the city's big annexation, many residents were enticed to leave the city in order to build cheaper, wood-frame homes. As a result, the neighborhoods that had not yet been annexed during this fifteen-year post-fire period have a good variety of interesting, wood-frame homes still available for today's viewing pleasure.

A home in Lincoln Park on Fullerton, where the fire had come to a stop, likely built in the early 1870s.

Another Lincoln Park Italianate built just after the fire. This one was torn down in 2023.

Architecture as a Profession

One of the enduring stories in Chicago's fire mythology is that architects came running to the city for jobs, making Chicago an architecture epicenter. You may be noticing a theme, but the truth is more nuanced. Some came to the city; some were already there and thrived. William Le Baron Jenney had been in Chicago since 1867. John Wellborn Root moved to Chicago in 1871 and would ultimately join forces with Daniel Burnham, who had been in the city since 1855. Louis Sullivan moved to Chicago in 1873; Frank Lloyd Wright didn't get there until 1887.

We take for granted the existence of architects trained at accredited universities, but they were actually a rarer commodity for much of the early years of Chicago—or really anywhere. Those that worked in Chicago were primarily employed for larger jobs and were not necessarily formally trained. Before schools of architecture were established in the United States—MIT was the first, in 1865—a person became an architect by apprenticing as a craftsman, usually a carpenter, and then by studying the work of an established architect's books and journals. Then you'd learn by drafting and doing. Of course, you could also study in Europe, but given that you couldn't just book a cheap flight using your credit card miles, that wasn't an option for most.

In this era, architects had less influence on residential design than local builders, using local traditions. The term *vernacular* is liberally applied among architectural historians to describe homes that arise from a local language of sorts: local materials, building traditions, climate realities, local preferences. But the immediate post-fire period in Chicago starts to show glimmers of the ever greater importance of trained architects. The second architecture school to be established in the United States after MIT was the University of Illinois, which graduated its first architect in 1873.[10] By the 1880s, architects would start to form associations, clubs, and magazines to share designs, and would begin to assert themselves over residential buildings. But until that change, the vast majority of the homes in this era reflected much of a continuation of the styles and practices of the pre-fire years. ■

Italianate: The Style That Outlasted the Rest

You might recall from the previous chapter that the Italianate style dominated architecture, while Second Empire style had a moment in the mid-1860s. In this post-fire period, the Second Empire style continued, but was far less popular. The signature mansard roof—high up and constructed of wood—was considered a major fire liability and was quickly phased out. Italianate became the undisputed style champion and marked the vast majority of homes and buildings of the era.

The defining features of the Italianate style from this era include the distinctive window and doorway shapes and hoods, which often feature adornments that highlight the home's facade. These details might be crafted from Joliet limestone, showcasing incised ornamentation or keystones, or from milled wood painted in striking colors. Additionally, the style is characterized by a prominent cornice with brackets—especially double brackets—and sometimes dentils, which emphasize the verticality and height of the home.

We'll look at the way that this style manifested in some actual homes from this period.

The Brick Workers Cottage

The workers cottage doesn't just survive the post-fire era—it's living its best life! It shares the same basic form as the earlier workers cottage, but where once it was built using wooden balloon-frame construction, it is now made of sturdy brick and limestone. The brick workers cottage accounts for a large majority of the housing stock of this era within the original city borders.

Rowhouses

This era saw the appearance of rowhouses much like those of New York City. In Chicago, rowhouses of this period tend to have prominent bracketed cornices in keeping with the Italianate style. Some stellar examples are clad in Joliet limestone.

BRICK WORKERS COTTAGE

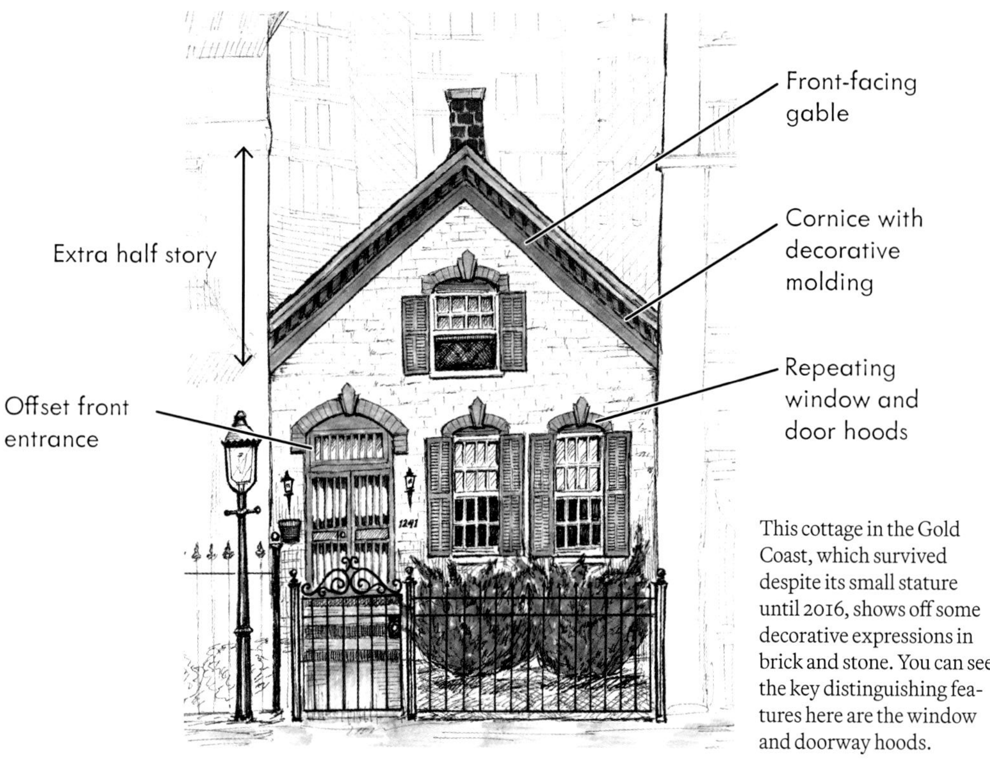

This cottage in the Gold Coast, which survived despite its small stature until 2016, shows off some decorative expressions in brick and stone. You can see the key distinguishing features here are the window and doorway hoods.

COMMON FEATURES

- Front-facing gable with a cornice that might have brackets or decorative molding, like dentils
- Long and narrow, shotgun-style floor plan
- Strong horizontal symmetry, typically with the front entrance offset with two separate windows
- One-and-a-half stories, often with a habitable (or at the very least, usable) half story with its own window
- Most built with an elevated first floor; typically, the later the cottage, the more likely it was to have been built elevated or raised from its original level
- Repeated ornamental window and door crowns, usually with modest decoration

ROWHOUSES

An Italianate rowhouse.

COMMON FEATURES

- Exteriors that form a uniform, uninterrupted facade along the street
- Roofs that are joined or have a consistent parapet, creating visual unity along the row
- Connected by shared "party walls," the structural walls that separate units
- Narrow frontage but extends deep into the lot
- Often have stoops or small steps leading directly to the sidewalk

Unlike some of the denser northeastern cities, Chicago doesn't stay as in thrall with rowhouses and will see them, in a manner of speaking, torn from their siblings and turned into single-family homes and flats buildings. You can see, for example, the lineage between the 1870s Italianate rowhouse above and the later (probably late 1880s) Italianate two-flat below.

Two-flats are essentially sections of rowhouses living like independent women.

The Rise of "Flats" Buildings

One of the most significant and lasting building types to come from this era was the "French flat." Recall from the last chapter that the Paris Expo of 1867 brought new attention to the country in its Second Empire, during Napoleon II's reign. One of the architectural imports we got from that city was the mansard roof and iron cresting—hallmarks of the Second Empire style. The other architectural import would stick to the Second City in a big way: the flats building.

In 1857 the Hotel Pelham in Boston was the first American apartment building, inspired by examples from the re-blossoming Paris, created in response to a shortage of middle-class housing. Its builder, Dr. John H. Dix, had spent some of his medical education in Paris and in those years, he fell in love with the French apartment flat. He commissioned a young architect, Alfred Stone, to build a five-story building in that manner and named it after his wife, Helen Pelham Curtis. Unfortunately, it didn't exactly take off at the time—Americans associated apartment living with poor tenement housing and anyone with the means could simply move outward to cheaper land. It was also limited by the lack of private kitchens and washrooms—and elevators. This was true, too, of the Parisian apartments, where the upper floors were reserved for the staff servants; now those same units are luxury housing.[11]

Nonetheless, as land values in American cities rose, builders turned back to the style as a product for middle-class families that wanted to be centrally located but couldn't afford a single-family home. A new flats building, the St. Cloud Hotel, opened in Boston in 1870. Another influential example emerged in New York City in 1869–70, when Rutherfurd Stuyvesant built a French flat designed by Richard Morris Hunt in the Victorian High Gothic style. Hunt also designed the Marshall Field mansion on Prairie Avenue, as well as the Administration Building of the World's Fair, both demolished. (He's perhaps most well-known today for the Biltmore Estate, the Vanderbilt home in Asheville, North Carolina.)

Pictured on page 82 is an early Chicago "French flat" building, once situated near Dearborn and Erie. Harold Mayer, in *Chicago: Growth of a Metropolis*, calls it the first of its kind in Chicago when it was built in 1878, though certainly some buildings were laying claim to the name in their marketing earlier than that. One of them was Potter Palmer, developer and hotelier behind the Palmer House Hotel. According to one published complaint in 1875, "There are a great many buildings in the city designated as French flats which do not possess the least right to the title, and are in fact nothing more or less than tenement-houses."[12]

A Chicagoan in 1880 sent a missive back from New York City, published in the *Tribune:*

> One of the curious results of the new apartment-house system is to greatly enhance the value of property in their vicinity. It is argued that a French-flat house of five floors, with a family on each floor, populates an ordinary city lot with forty or fifty opulent people, while a single dwelling on the same space, would only give seven or eight persons a location. The consequence is that . . . retail-store property has greatly appreciated through the multiplication of wealthy customers in the neighborhood.[13]

Another early flats building, the imposing Hotel St. Benedict Flats, was designed by James Egan in 1882 in a Victorian Gothic style. It still stands at the corner of Chicago and Wabash Avenues and is listed in the National Register of Historic Places. It's definitely worth a look.[14] Though the building believed to be the first "proper" French flats building at Dearborn and Erie no longer exists, it can be argued that Chicago wrapped its sinewy arms around the flats form more aggressively than many other American cities. It would go on to become one of the city's most common housing types, as we'll discuss in detail in later chapters. The proliferation of a variety of flats buildings presented city residents with a solid base of the "middle housing" that is missing from many other American cities that have either single-family homes or high-rise apartments with very little in between.

An early "French flat" building in Chicago, once situated near Dearborn and Erie (now gone).

Chicagoans Push the Boundaries

As Chicagoans built brick and stone single-family homes and flats within the city limits, others left the city, lured by the opportunity to build more economical wood homes on cheaper land. Public transportation was still somewhat limited in this period, and while certain suburbs like Hyde Park and Ravenswood had commuter rail, for many, commutes into the city were constrained by the speed of horse-drawn cars. In short, one couldn't be too far afield of the city limits. These ex-Chicagoans were building many of the forms and styles that Chicagoans were building: lots of Italianate homes and some scattered Second Empire. But these suburban homes were often a bit taller, a bit roomier, with wood siding and wood ornamentation.

Chicago's boundaries held firm through the 1870s, and the remaining homes from this period of Chicago history can be seen in neighborhoods like Bridgeport and Pilsen, or Bucktown and Wicker Park. These older neighborhoods, while not immune to teardowns, are still rife with brick homes from this era that have managed to escape the bulldozer. Many homes in neighborhoods that hewed too close to the business district were demolished. In the next decade, as new transit options made vast, undeveloped spaces available, Chicagoans raced to fill in these newly accessible pockets with housing. They were the settlers of suburbia. Eventually they would come back into the city limits—or rather, the city limits would find them. If the 1870s saw a tempering of the city's appetite for the annexation of surrounding land, the next decade would gobble up suburbs like hot dogs at a Sox game. ■

A home built sometime in the mid-1870s, just outside the city borders in what was then Lake View township.

CHAPTER

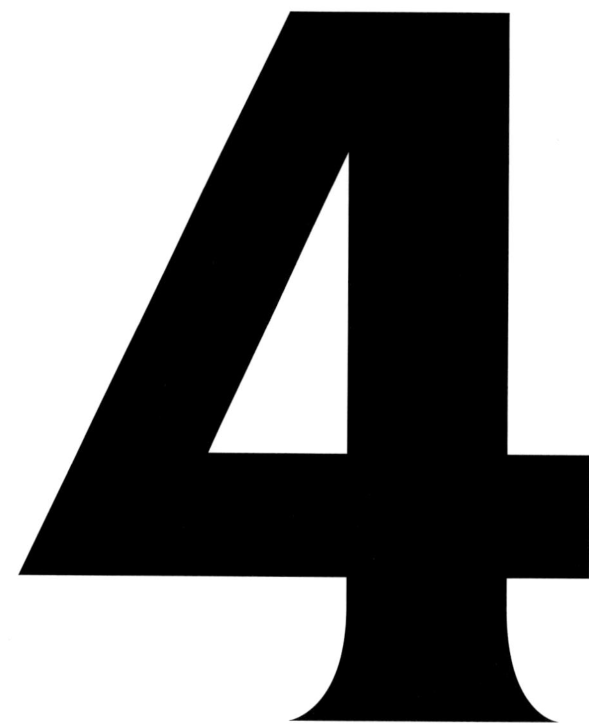

Annexation and Elevation

1882–1892

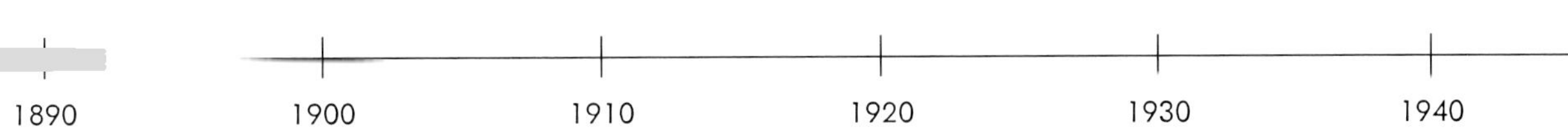

"In order to gain and to hold the esteem of men, it is not sufficient merely to possess wealth or power. The wealth or power must be put in evidence, for esteem is awarded only on evidence."

—Thorstein Veblen, *The Theory of the Leisure Class*

IN 1879, SAMUEL NICKERSON approached architect Edward Burling to design a family mansion to sit at the corner of Erie and Wabash. He wanted a showpiece, something to display the Nickerson family's enormous wealth from banking, rail, and distilled adult beverages. Burling delivered, completing the home in 1883 with all the cutting-edge technology: electric lights powered by a basement generator, a central coal furnace, and layers of fireproofed masonry walls. While the home's exterior took on a more sedate Italianate style than what was in fashion, the home's interior exploded in an eclectic celebration of styles, muddling up Moorish, Greek, Italian Renaissance, and other revivals. It's always the quiet ones. The Nickerson home was in many ways a bold projection of Chicago homes in general during this period, with a focus on technological changes to interiors and an aesthetic playfulness, but always with a practical, trauma-informed eye toward fireproofing.

Chicago's built environment underwent a transformative makeover in the decade between 1882 and 1892. Through annexation, the city quadrupled its land to 169 square miles (today it's 227). The population doubled to about 1.2 million as immigrants began arriving in droves from Sweden, Poland, and Bohemia. Black Americans began migrating in greater numbers from the former Confederate states, which had been moving toward the new Jim Crow regimes. Coal-powered manufacturing and railroads boomed and whistled, and the newly rich showed off their wealth (though it be "gilded," or "thinly luxurious," as Mark Twain famously said). Laborers organized into new trade unions, and tycoons and monopolies pushed back. The world's first skyscrapers erupted from the flat landscape of Chicago. Just outside the city, developers bought large swaths of land to be transformed into neighborhoods like Edgewater and Austin (originally "Austinville"). In short—Chicago's industrializing economy pushed the city up and out. Cities were expanding across the United States, but Chicago was on fire. So to speak.

The Nickerson mansion, now the Richard H. Driehaus Museum, is open for tours.

Technology spurred the city on. Chicago was literally electrified in this era, most visibly by the incandescent electric lights adopted by hoteliers, business owners, and wealthier residents. When Frank Lloyd Wright arrived in Chicago in 1887, he got his first glimpse of electric arc lights, which he described as "dazzling and ugly."[1] The telephone saw a massive adoption in this decade, from its first appearance in 1878 to connections in over 7,700 homes by 1890. Public transit was also transformed. No longer were pokey, horse-drawn streetcars the only means of public surface transit; Chicagoans could ride cable cars (1882), then electric streetcars (1890), and then a train on lines elevated above the city streets (1892). As the city expanded, so did its public transit—starting mainly on the South Side but eventually spreading citywide—making even the farthest parts of the city more accessible.

In this era of heady economic growth and technological change, notions of social improvement, if not utopia, abounded. In the midst of pollution, child labor, and fourteen-hour workdays, the Chicagoans powering this relentless progress began a steady pushback: This can't be it. The push for labor rights and women's suffrage was hitting a new stride. This was the threshold of the "Progressive Era," the name that characterized American history from 1890 to 1920, in which activists and reformers targeted many of the ills of the prior decades. Jane Addams and Ellen Gates Starr founded Hull House on the present-day Near West Side of Chicago (the current site of the University of Illinois Chicago campus) in 1889, which became a vast organization dedicated to improving the life of working-class immigrants in terms of housing, health, and jobs training.

In 1890, the U.S. Congress awarded the city of Chicago the hosting privilege for the World's Columbian Exposition over Chicago's rivals St. Louis, New York City, and Washington, D.C. The momentous announcement set off a flurry of speculative activity and building in Chicago for the following three years, particularly near the planned site for the fair in Jackson Park and the Midway Plaisance on the South Side. It also led to the creation of a handful of large apartment hotels and the first "courtyard building," the Mecca Flats, in 1892. In its totality, the World's Fair would cap off Chicago's frenetic decade of urban improvement by inviting the world to experience a wonderland of architectural and technological marvels.

Bold New Architecture in Chicago

The 1880s was one of the most dynamic periods for architecture in Chicago. In fact, a case could be made for it being one of the most dynamic periods in American architecture up to that point in history. First, the economic boom and rapid growth of new industries meant that more residents were wealthy, and some extremely so. At the same time, the Aesthetic movement, a movement that originated in England in the mid-1880s, was capturing the imaginations of the middle and upper classes. This movement was a call for beauty and refinement—art for the sake of art—a luxury that would have seemed impossible amid the smoldering rubble of the city a decade earlier.

This romantic ideal gave Chicago's newly wealthy—and those striving to join their ranks—a way to stand out, using bold ornamentation and eclectic styles in their homes. It also gave license to the architects who were increasingly asserting their independence from European and East Coast influences. In 1883, an editorialist identified only as "F.B.W." said it well:

> A few years ago residents did not build for anything more than temporary purposes; they wanted merely shelter until they could make money. . . . Now men are making fortunes, and the first use to which they are putting their wealth is the erection of permanent dwellings . . . not only for themselves and their descendants, but they are rearing to themselves monuments.

> We have now Boston architects who give us Boston architecture, New York architects who give us New York architecture, English architects who supply us with Queen Anne and mildly Gothic models; what is imperatively needed is architects who will become imbued with the peculiarities of Chicago and supply us with Chicago architecture.[2]

Keep in mind that there were still relatively few trained architects in this period. In 1883, only 126 were listed in the census, but among them were some of the names we now know well, like Daniel Burnham and John Root. They designed houses both for wealthy clients and the moderately well-to-do, though they would be most well-known for their expansive civic and commercial contributions. Nonetheless, some architects operating in Chicago would make their name in residential architecture, like Joseph Lyman Silsbee and Henry Ives Cobb. Others exerted a gravitational pull through the influence of their commercial designs. In general, there was always some tension and ongoing dialogue between the high style of the "real" architects and the bottom-up vernacular style from the builders and homeowners.

This decade saw the rise in assertiveness of "western" architects in Chicago, who set themselves apart from the East Coast and European establishment. What did that look like? It took shape in a number of ways: the first architecture journal for the region, *Inland Architect* (1883); prominent Chicago architects splintering off of the American Institute of Architects to form the Western Association of Architects (1884); and the Chicago Architectural Sketch Club (later the Chicago Architectural Club) forming and becoming a critical medium of exchanging new ideas (1885).

Chicagoans with money built stately homes along prestigious boulevards with green space and access to new, faster transit. Within the city limits (which at that time ran from Fullerton on the North to 39th—or Egan, now Pershing—on the South, and from the lakefront on the East to Crawford—now Pulaski—on the West), arose tall homes with exuberant facades in brick and stone. Think: Grand Boulevard (now King Drive) and neighborhoods like Gold Coast, Wicker Park, and Lincoln Park.

Meanwhile, the working class built their homes in places like Pilsen, Bridgeport, and Bucktown. While these were relatively modest digs, they were showy in their own way, as dressed-up workers cottages and multi-flat buildings with brickwork and flowery incised ornament. The city started to take a different shape, with upscale neighborhoods emerging at the outskirts and linked by a modernized transit system that carried commuters and shoppers through older neighborhoods filled with new immigrant arrivals.

The areas beyond the city borders saw the greatest population growth and relative change in home building activity, along with a rise in land values. From 1880 to 1890, the city's surrounding suburbs witnessed a major population surge. While the population within the city limits increased 57 percent, from 503,145 to 792,377, the population of the outlying areas grew 650 percent.[3] The South Side townships exploded: Lake and Hyde Park went from fewer than 20,000 residents each, to over 100,000 and 130,000 residents, respectively. Meanwhile, Lake View grew from about 6,500 to 50,000 in that same period. Some of the most luxurious housing went up in Hyde Park on Drexel and Grand Boulevards, from just south of the city (39th Street) to 51st Street.[4] In Humboldt Park, a six-room cottage ran you $1,400, but a showy home on the boulevard would set you back $6,000.

The irony was that, while residential architecture became more lavish, a group of Chicago architects was exploring a variety of commercial projects in the 1880s and early 1890s that took a different approach altogether. As the value of land in the central business district rose, developers could extract ever greater rental income by building upward. That provided architects and engineers the opportunity to design buildings to previously unheard-of heights of ten-plus stories. To some architectural historians, their commercial style came together as the "Chicago School." In the words of Gerald Larson, Professor Emeritus of Architecture at the University of Cincinnati, it was a "new architectural language . . . that expressed (. . . not the same as "exposed") the structure of the building and enriched it with a modern, ahistoric style of ornament."[5] The roster of architects working on this new architectural vocabulary included William Le Baron Jenney, the team of Dankmar Adler and Louis Sullivan, and the team of Daniel Burnham and John Root, among others.

Some of the stylistic developments from these commercial buildings would go on to influence the approach to residential architecture. Though firms like Adler and Sullivan found commercial work far more lucrative, many of their residential commissions translated to bigger projects further down the road. These commissions were not coming from aristocrats on the level of a Field or Palmer, but rather mostly upper-middle-class families located in the prestigious South Side communities, particularly among German-Jewish families to whom Adler had connections.[6] Through 1886, about 47 percent of their commissions were residential, though that changed following their massive Auditorium Building project, as their dockets were increasingly consumed with large commercial projects.

Sullivan's approach to architecture was embodied in his famous tenet, "form ever follows function," and his focus on harmonious and organic forms influenced many young architects, but one most notably: Frank Lloyd Wright, his former draftsman and chief assistant. By early 1890, Wright was lending a hand on projects like the Sullivan-designed Charnley-Persky House in Chicago's Gold Coast, which was completed in 1892. By the time of the World's Fair in 1893—the design of which mostly took on a conservative Beaux Arts line from Europe—residential architecture was already off on a whole new trajectory.

New Heights

Rising from the soaring land values of Chicago's present-day Loop came the skyscraper, defined originally as a building with ten or more stories.[7] The first skyscrapers emerged in the 1880s, and their descendants would define city skylines for years to come, eventually turning into T-shirt logos as symbols of city pride and identity. But these towering marvels weren't without their critics. One writer at the time called them "huge money-making schemes in brick and terra cotta" built "solely with an eye to rent-rolls"—although he made a begrudging exception for the Auditorium Building.[8]

People also complained that the buildings blocked the sunlight. It's difficult to fully grasp the impact of these early, massive shadows as they first loomed over the streets, darkening rooms in shorter buildings that depended on natural light. These shadows might have been the inspiration behind the ominous darkness that gradually spreads across a city in movies depicting alien invasions. No doubt these giants seemed oppressive and futuristic, but their innovations in foundation engineering, elevators, and the skeleton-frame structure would move beyond the commercial and help set the stage for high-rise residential buildings in the future.

The drive for more profits led to a drive for more height. This pushed engineering minds to solve more riddles and create more miracles. One of the early challenges was Chicago's soft clay soil, which could only withstand so much weight before it started to give way. Architect and author Thomas Leslie put it well: "Geographically, Chicago is one of the best places in the world to build tall buildings. . . . Geologically, it's one of the worst places. Sitting at the junction of a slow-moving river and a very large lake, the soil underneath the city of Chicago is largely fluid, compressible, squishy, and tends not to stay in one place when you put a heavy object on it."[9]

Taller and heavier buildings put higher demands on the foundations, and the architects and engineers of the day experimented with a variety of methods to meet them. At the time, digging all the way through to the bedrock, eighty or more feet below the surface, wasn't the most technically or economically feasible option. So attempts were made to "float" a foundation on the squishy clay soil. For their vaunted Auditorium Building, Adler and Sullivan used a foundation of large, isolated, pyramidal piers that acted like feet to support the building's weight. Unfortunately, it wasn't enough and the building sank eighteen inches in its first year. (To this day, entering the building means walking down to the ground floor.) Burnham and Root employed a new method for the Montauk Block (demolished in 1902), using a bed made of interlaced steel rails and concrete, which worked effectively enough to use in other projects, including the Rookery (1888) and Monadnock (the northern part of the building from 1891). Not to be outdone, Adler and Sullivan used caissons—wells dug all the way to the bedrock and then filled with concrete—for the Chicago Stock Exchange Building in 1893.

Transporting tenants to the top floors safely and effectively presented another challenge. The hydraulic elevator had been introduced to Chicago in the 1870s,[10] but it had its limitations, including the need for a deep basement. The availability of electricity and the Otis Company's improvement of the electric elevator in the early 1880s made transporting passengers to new heights possible.

Fireproofing was another essential feature. The Great Fire exposed the vulnerabilities of even materials that had previously been thought to be fireproof. Cast iron buildings, which were believed to be "totally fireproof," were "destroyed as easily as those that had made no such pretensions."[11]

Just as insurance companies had enforced fireproofing measures in Chicago before and immediately after the fire, they also highlighted the additional risks associated with skyscrapers:

> It is an indisputable fact that all buildings reaching an altitude of six or seven stories and not thoroughly fireproof are a menace to surrounding property in case of fire. . . . [The] Board of Underwriters of this city, after a failure to get the city authorities to act . . . declares if property owners will put up buildings of excessive height they must construct them as nearly fire-proof as possible, elsewise the underwriters of this city will decline to write any insurance upon them except at excessive rates.[12]

The innovation that would allow buildings to achieve the stratospheric heights they'd eventually reach was the creation of a skeleton-frame exterior and interior. But to make this kind of framing strong enough would require a new kind of material, one that outperformed iron in a number of key dimensions, including strength, flexibility, and weight. You guessed it: steel. Steel is created by mixing iron with carbon and additional elements, enhancing its strength, flexibility, durability, and resistance to fire and corrosion. With a steel frame bearing the building's weight, the exterior wall no longer had to support the structure and could instead function as a "curtain."

The structural steel skeleton that elevated Chicagoans to new heights.

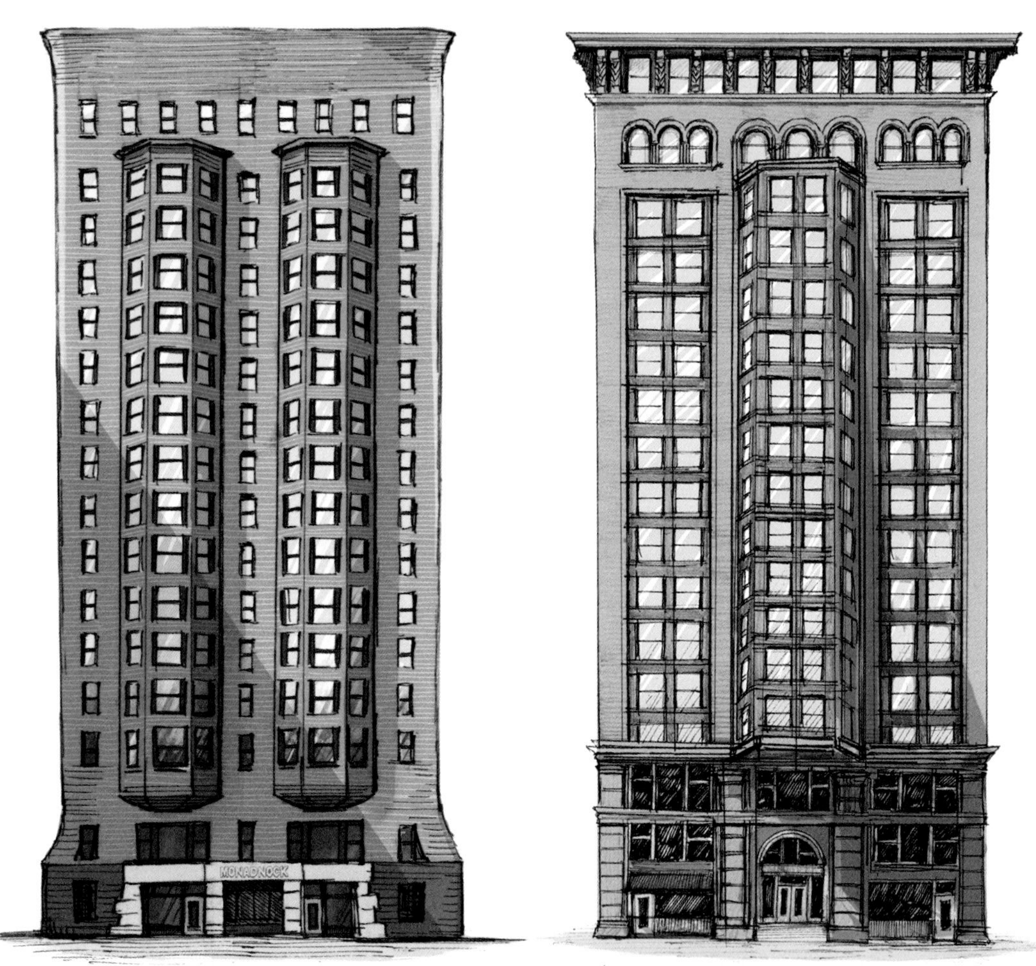

Monadnock north, built with structural masonry (left), and Monadnock south, built with a steel structure (right).

The Monadnock building in the Loop straddles both worlds. The northern portion, the Burnham and Root–designed structural masonry side begun in 1881, has six-foot-wide walls at its base to support the building weight. The southern portion, a Holabird and Roche–designed steel and terra cotta structure begun in 1891, is a fraction of the weight and had no such need for a thick base. According to Robert Bruegmann, professor and architecture historian at the University of Illinois Chicago, it "cost 15 percent less, weighed 15 percent less, and had 15 percent more rentable space than the north half."[13] Just think of how much more window space you can have for retail when the walls aren't as thick as a fortified castle wall.

The Home Insurance Building, designed by William Le Baron Jenney and completed in 1885, is often cited as the world's first skyscraper. It represents one of Chicago's chief architectural claims to fame and was the first skyscraper to incorporate structural steel for support. Of course, New Yorkers dispute the title. Of course, we have a healthy self-esteem and brush this silliness off. Regardless of any disputes about Jenney's masterpiece, Chicago did play host to the world's first all-steel framed skyscraper, the Rand McNally Building, completed in 1889 and designed by Burnham and Root. This city was certainly on the frontier of innovation in this space.

Apartment Hotels & the First Courtyard Building

Commercial buildings weren't the only structures climbing to new heights in this decade. Several high-rise residential hotels in Chicago were constructed to accommodate the influx of visitors for the World's Columbian Exposition, most located with convenient access to the fairgrounds in Jackson Park. They provided the luxurious amenities and status associated with high-end hotels, offering both short-term accommodations for fairgoers and longer-term residences for wealthier individuals seeking comfort and convenience close to the exhibition.

Significant examples included the Lexington Hotel (1892), the Chicago Beach Hotel (1892), the Metropole Hotel (1891), and the Virginia Hotel (1891). While these and several of their contemporaries were ultimately demolished, you can still lease an apartment at the Hotel Windermere (1893) in Hyde Park or stay at the Auditorium Annex (1893), now called the Congress Plaza Hotel.

APARTMENT HOTELS

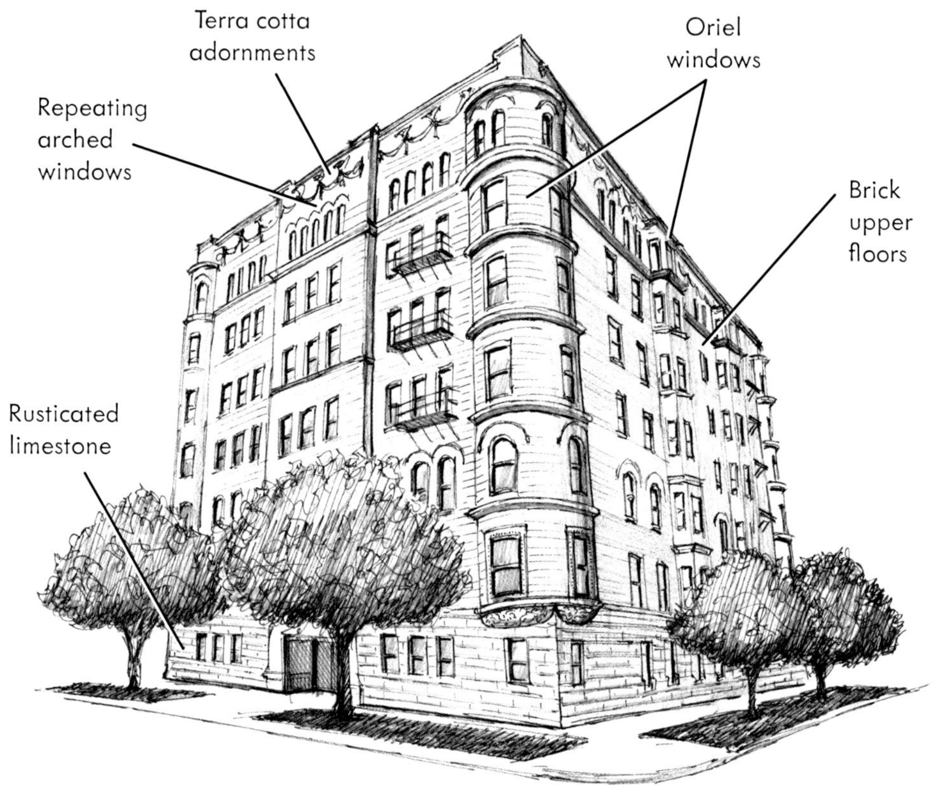

The World's Fair-era Yale Building in Englewood.

COMMON FEATURES

- Typically six to ten stories
- Extensive use of bay windows, like oriels, which are bay windows found on upper stories
- Use of repeated, arched windows in the Romanesque Revival style
- Terra cotta adornments
- Bold masonry; sometimes rusticated limestone for the first floor, with upper stories in brick
- Modern building amenities of the time like fireproofing, elevators, electric lighting, and modern sanitation

Preservation efforts saved this building and its handsome entrance.

Another high-rise that is still with us is the Yale Building in the Englewood neighborhood, which opened in 1892 and was saved through preservation efforts in 2003. Now used for subsidized senior living, the Yale Building, like several of the other apartment hotels, features corner curved bays, an interior atrium, and Romanesque Revival styling with rusticated stone and a prominent arched doorway and windows. Inside, the building is a real stunner, with a seven-story skylit atrium featuring a cage elevator and walkways that rival the balconies of New Orleans's French Quarter.

Another apartment hotel built for World's Fair housing was the Mecca Flats, considered the first courtyard apartment building to appear in Chicago. It is a significant building, both in terms of its architectural and racial history. Designed by Willoughby Edbrooke and Franklin Pierce Burnham (no relation to Daniel) and completed in 1891, the building featured what would become the distinctive mark of the type: a large U-shaped footprint surrounding a large, landscaped central exterior courtyard. It was only five stories tall but offered up ninety-six units. Every unit had access to light and ventilation, allowing for integration with nature and community interaction. This massive structure also offered semi-private front entrances, in contrast to high-rise buildings, where every unit shares the same entrance. Unlike later courtyard buildings, the Mecca Flats also had two large atria to provide even more light via an interior courtyard.

The Mecca Flats inspired musicians, poets, and architects as an early model for the Chicago courtyard apartment building until it was demolished in 1952.

The issue with the World's Fair-era apartment hotels, of course, was that the demand from the fair-going public only lasted for the duration of the event. As a result, many of the owners struggled to find longer-term tenants. Many structures were demolished. The Mecca Flats lasted another fifty-plus years, becoming a cultural and social hub in the Black Belt, a corridor along State Street that stretched southward from 22nd Street (Cermak). The Mecca Flats even inspired a jazz tune by Jimmy Blythe in 1924, "Mecca Flat Blues," and a poem called "In the Mecca" by the great Gwendolyn Brooks. It was demolished in 1952 after an intense battle, a sacrifice to the expanding Illinois Institute of Technology campus. Nonetheless, the Mecca's courtyard form would roar back into Chicago neighborhoods in the booming 1910s and 1920s and, with some modification, become a common and beloved residential building type.

The Real Estate Developers

The expansion of Chicago's residential areas during this time was driven in part by the emergence of "suburban" developers. Many of Chicago's current neighborhood names date back to their original names as suburban developments in the surrounding townships. Some of them can trace their own distinctive character to the efforts of the founding developer, whether that was arguing for a transit stop or favoring winding streets instead of the grid. The developers also influenced the type of homes bought, impacted how they

THE MECCA

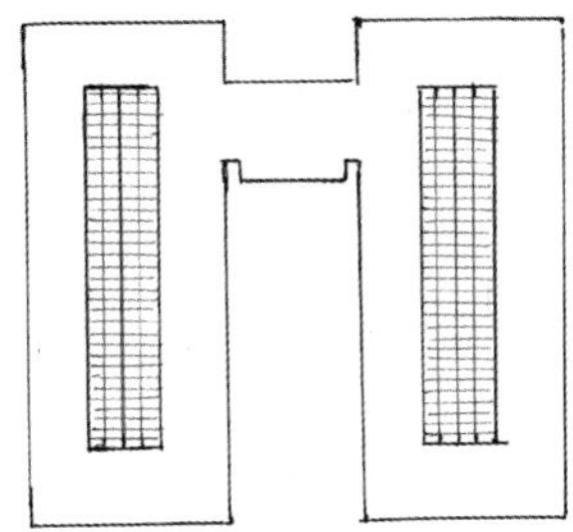

were financed, and sold Chicagoans on the dream of homeownership as a means of building wealth.

There had been developers operating in the Chicago and surrounding region in prior decades, but on a more limited basis and often constrained by a lack of commuter rail access. Pre-fire examples include Henry Austin's modestly named "Austin" settlement on the West Side, and the Ravenswood Land Co. and Irving Park Land & Building Co. on the North Side, among others. These communities would remain somewhat limited in population, however. According to Craig Turnbull in *Chicago in the Progressive Era,* "Until the late nineteenth century, speculation dominated all sectors of the Chicago real estate market . . . Capitalists, business entrepreneurs, and small investors typically held individual lots and parcels of land in anticipation of values rising with urban growth."

The 1880s and 1890s were another matter. Spurred by the availability, or prospective availability, of faster and more frequent transit—cable cars, electric streetcars, and elevated lines—developers gobbled up massive swathes of open land. They put fancy names on these new subdivisions and developed the local amenities, built some model homes, and then promoted and sold them like they were going out of style. Developers were, according to Turnbull, "actively directing urban growth and settlement patterns using a strategy that relied on installing a range of amenities prior to the sale of residential land."[15] That meant "preinstalled paved roads, trees, landscaping, sidewalks, curbing, and sewers." Their efforts, importantly for our purposes, also influenced the types of homes that were built and sold.

The developers' influence on Chicago's built environment was substantial. Samuel E. Gross was one of the most prominent of the day. His company was responsible for a whopping twenty-one subdivisions and ten thousand homes.[16] It would have been hard to miss his company's ads if you were scrolling through *Chicago Tribune* classified sections—or if you were out in public, as his sales-folk fanned out through city streets. Other developers followed. John Lewis Cochran purchased the land that he would name "Edgewater" in 1886. One of his guarantees was that his oasis north of Chicago would be wired for incandescent light, even while the neighborhood still lacked transit access. He delivered. Cochran actually created the Edgewater Light Company to provide inexpensive street and residential lighting, not only for the convenience of homeowners, but also to draw attention to the development. In later years, there was also Ravenswood Manor, where anyone purchasing before a certain date was given "free carfare for one year." The slogan for the development was "Cultured people of moderate means."[17]

These developers made choices that affected the type and quality of homes purchased. Samuel Gross, who famously supported the workers' aspirations for homeownership (a phenomenon referred to as "The Workingman's Reward," according to one locally famous advertisement), sold modest, wood-frame workers cottages that could be legally built outside the city limits. Rows and rows of these went up in places like his "New City," a community area that contains the Back of the Yards and Canaryville neighborhoods.

To be fair, they weren't all modest cottages. Gross's Alta Vista Terrace was inspired by the rowhouses of London, and its own rowhouses took on an eclectic variety of classical and revival details. John Cochran in Edgewater included "Louis Tiffany glass windows to 'brand' his residential landscapes."[18] In the same way that one might recognize a certain developer's suburb by its homes today, so it went for the late nineteenth-century suburbs, although the city of Chicago has grown around these developments and a bit of their distinctiveness has been lost over time. You just have to know where to look.

Often developments had distinctive branding, like this particular title script for Edgewater.

Terra Cotta, Fully Baked

The steel frame was revolutionizing high-rise construction, but other materials were coming into their own as major contributors to the built environment of this era. Terra cotta ("baked earth" in Italian) was one such material. It's a material composed of clay that is fired in a kiln to an extremely high temperature. It may then be either glazed and fired again, or left unglazed. Though incorporated as structural elements, roof tiles, or ornamentation in ancient civilizations, terra cotta had not been widely used in building construction in the U.S. until it found its moment after the Chicago Fire, when it became particularly useful in Chicago's high-rise buildings of the 1880s and 1890s. It had a variety of great qualities—it was malleable and versatile in its shapes and color options; lightweight (because it was porous) while being highly durable; and, most importantly for Chicago's purposes, it was fireproof.

The English ceramicist, James Taylor, had arrived in New York City in 1870 and found lukewarm interest in the notion of architectural terra cotta. He then moved to a superior city, where he brought his experience to the Chicago Terra Cotta Company. The company had been founded a few years earlier but lacked expertise in the use of terra cotta in buildings. Taylor was happy to take up the challenge. In the ensuing years, architects found that terra cotta was well-suited as a fireproofing material for tall buildings, using it to clad iron frames and even entire facades, as in the case of the Reliance Building at Washington and State Streets.[14]

A home on "Terra Cotta Row," a street in Lake View that was home to Northwestern Terra Cotta executives. They built homes that extensively showed off their product, like this one, as a mighty fine form of advertising.

From this point onward, Chicago became a major terra cotta production hub for the country with the Northwestern Terra Cotta Company forming in 1877 and the American Terra Cotta & Ceramic Company beginning production in 1881. The salespeople at these firms must have been charmers, because they continued to work their product into a variety of Chicago's notable buildings. Louis Sullivan's floral ornamental details in the medium became iconic masterpieces. Through the next decades, Chicago terra cotta would be incorporated into commercial and residential buildings, culminating in the explosion of ornamented buildings in the 1920s. ■

Company Towns, Company Housing

Another driving force that affected home building was industrialization. Chicago in this era saw major growth in manufacturing, which required labor, which required housing. Some neighborhoods in Chicago still show the natural patterns that emerged. The Union Stock Yards, a major employer, gave rise to rows and rows of workers cottages in the area behind the factory buildings. This neighborhood was fittingly, if not cleverly, named Back of the Yards. Bucktown, Pilsen, and parts of Roscoe Village sprung up along the Ravenswood industrial corridor created by the old Chicago and North Western (C&NW) Railway. Many of those factory buildings have since been converted into residences or subdivided into commercial spaces, surrounded by what is left of the former workers' homes. Today, these include what are now million-dollar brick workers cottages.

Some creative solutions emerged out of the need to house workers, though not all pleasant. According to an article called "Work Culture" in the *Encyclopedia of Chicago*, "Industrial workers, especially if they were white, often lived near their jobs at the mills, stockyards, or factories." As a result, multiple strategies emerged to supply housing for workers at the time, though some were exploitative. In a few outlying industrial areas, there were large commercial boarding houses. Some of them didn't have enough dedicated beds, so workers would sleep in shifts in a "hot bed." Tenants occasionally "preferred to lodge without common meals or to live in larger, more anonymous rooming houses, where a 'light housekeeping room' included a gas fixture for cooking on a single burner. In a rooming house residents could keep their own hours, enjoy greater privacy, and perhaps entertain guests more easily."[19]

One of the most famous examples of company housing—and so much more—is the town of Pullman. George Pullman made his name in Chicago as a major building raiser when the city's buildings had to be lifted up so they could be fitted for municipal sewer lines. In 1864, perhaps seeing fewer buildings to lift, he pivoted careers and designed a sleeper car to ride the rails. The luxurious Pullman car would eventually become the signature product for a company that would dominate its market. Pullman thought that he might increase employee loyalty and productivity by creating a planned town fully tricked out for the Victorian worker and his family.

In 1880, Pullman secretly bought 3,500 acres of land south of Chicago in what was then part of the Village of Hyde Park. Over the next three years, he built a fully functional "all brick" company town called Pullman, which

An array of rowhouse styles that can be seen in Pullman.

provisioned the workers and their families with all the accoutrements and moral restrictions of the Victorian lifestyle: churches, public square, stables, and even a reflecting pool called "Lake Vista" that collected the industrial by-product condensation. The town had its own gas and water infrastructure and sewage disposal plant.

Pullman also provided all of the housing, electing a type that was more in keeping with the East Coast. Designed by architect Solon Spencer Beman, there were neat rows of two-story brick rowhouses with indoor plumbing and access to alleys in back for daily trash collection. Built mostly between 1880 and 1883, the rowhouses and the grand Hotel Florence, named for Pullman's daughter, predominantly feature the Queen Anne style, and certain larger factory buildings, like the Administration Building, reflect an early Romanesque Revival style.

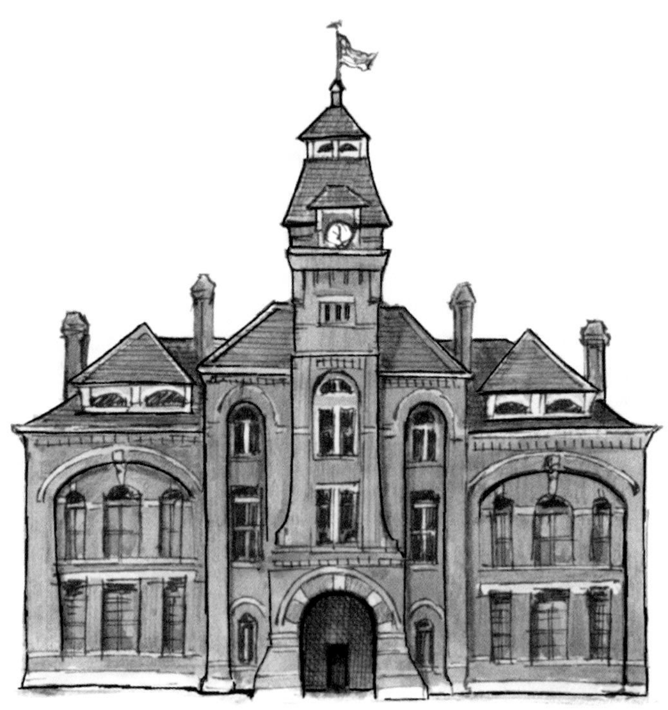

The Pullman Administration Building.

Though living conditions were initially considered well beyond the standards of the day, the promised utopia of a corporate-planned town contained the seeds of its own destruction, as workers were not willing to accept rent increases while they saw wage cuts. By 1894, Pullman had devolved into a now-infamous labor cataclysm that got the president and National Guard involved; the company would never be the same. Suffice to say, George Pullman was so reviled by the time of his death that his coffin was wrapped in steel and concrete, ostensibly to prevent desecration by disgruntled employees. There's an 1897 *Chicago Tribune* article that goes into excruciating detail about the process of how it was done, from tar paper to multiple pours.[20]

Annexation & the Changing Fire Limits

In 1889, Chicago annexed five surrounding townships, representing an area four times its size at the time. It remains the largest annexation in the city's history, and perhaps that's a good thing; if we had continued expanding at that rate, Chicago might be bordering Dallas by now. The decision was motivated by two main factors. First, Chicago's boosters wanted to stick it to their rivals by expanding the city's land area, surpassing a population of one million—making it the second-largest city after New York—and securing the tax revenue that came with it. Second, there was a genuine demand from surrounding communities for improved municipal services, particularly sewage and clean water, which the city could provide more efficiently and affordably. Though there was plenty of opposition in the annexed areas, a majority of the electorate did vote for it in a referendum.

The question of fire limits came up often in debates leading up to the annexation. After all, one of the major drivers of population growth in Chicago's surrounding townships, but especially in Lake and Hyde Park, was the opportunity to build less expensive wooden homes by avoiding Chicago's more stringent fire codes. The residents of townships lying beyond the city borders were concerned that annexation would also extend the fire limits to their areas. In the same way, the teetotalers were concerned that their dry laws would be made null and void once they joined the sin-filled city.

As noted in earlier chapters, the fire limit gradually expanded from a small, loosely enforced zone around the central business district to a politically negotiated carve-out due to protesting constituencies in 1872, before finally being extended to the city's borders in 1874. Now that talk was getting serious about greatly expanding the city's borders, the boosters needed

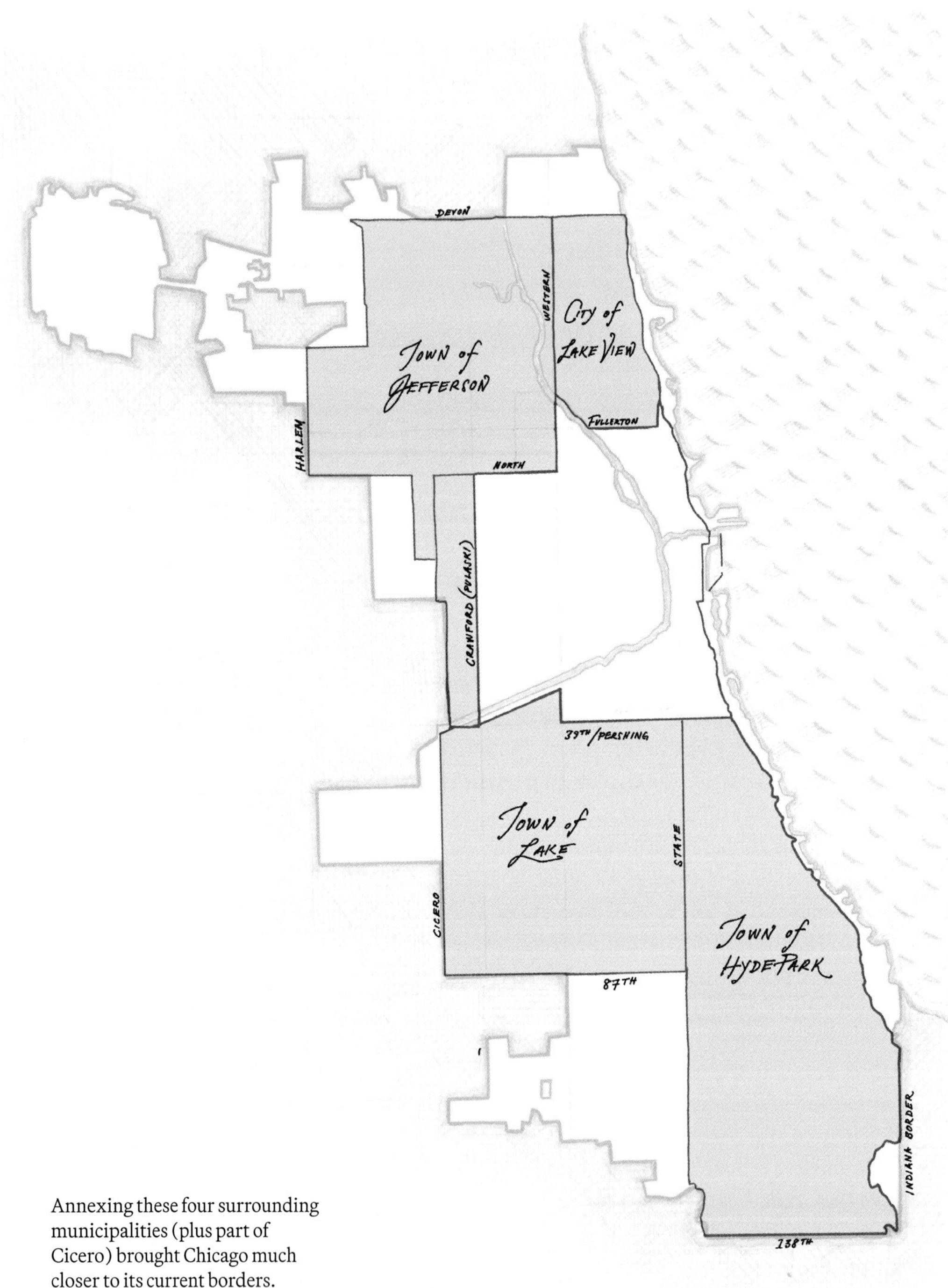

Annexing these four surrounding municipalities (plus part of Cicero) brought Chicago much closer to its current borders.

to set the question to rest. In 1889, the city finally mandated that any newly annexed territory would not be subject to the fire limits.[21] So the wood-loving opponents of annexation could rest easier.

Or could they? One of the lesser-known facts about this topic is that some of the surrounding townships had their own fire limits. In 1886, Hyde Park created fire limits from the city border south to 41st Street, then again to 47th Street. Then, ahead of annexation, the township created fire limits to cover the prestigious boulevards: Hyde Park Boulevard, Drexel, and Grand (King). The fire limits were sometimes used as "a form of zoning to keep out cheap wooden buildings and the kind of people who lived in them," according to Patricia Morse of the Hyde Park Historical Society. Lake View, for its part, voted in 1887 to create its own fire limit in a swath of its borders from Fullerton to Belmont and Halsted to Lake Michigan. Perhaps anticipating that its fire limits would supersede, or at least preempt, any eventual city fire limit extension, its ordinance applied only to residential buildings taller than two stories, as well as to public buildings and businesses.

The thing is, Chicago has a way of making promises . . . flexible. In 1890, when the city was awarded the World's Fair to take place in the non-fire-zoned Jackson Park and the Midway, civic leaders started to fret about the possibility of wooden shantytowns popping up all over the area ahead of the opening. Consequently, they extended fire limits all the way to 67th Street, the southern end of the park, and State Street to the west, covering the transit. Exceptions were made, not least of which were for some of the fair buildings themselves. Wooden concession stands along 57th Street stood there until they were demolished amid the neighborhood's urban renewal of the 1960s. There were other extensions, too, including an additional twenty square miles in 1915, and the entirety of the far-south 9th Ward in 1950.

The legacy of the fire limits, of course, affect the built character of the residences in the neighborhoods we see today. The neighborhoods inside the pre-1889 city limits have a whole lot more brick and stone to them than those outside. Hence one can find kindred-spirit homes in different parts of the city that are alike in form and style, but that are composed of wood versus masonry. This rule is not hard and fast; it's not as if crossing north, say, over Fullerton Avenue, is moving from a world of brick into a world of frame homes. The economics did not always favor frame construction because by the 1880s, the supply of white pine was dwindling and prices were rising.[22] By comparison, brick homes became more economical than they had ever been. However, there is a distinctive character shift between the old neighborhoods of Chicago and the neighborhoods annexed in 1889.

Workers cottages with similar forms but different materials; brick in the older Ukrainian Village neighborhood (left) and a wood-frame cottage in Lake View (right).

City Light, City Heat

In the 1880s, Chicagoans saw massive improvements in lighting and heat technologies. Early residents used firewood and then coal for stoves, and kerosene for lamps. By the mid-1800s, gas created from coal (coal gas) was first utilized to illuminate streetlamps, then gradually became more common in buildings used by the wealthy, particularly Chicago's downtown hotels, theaters, commercial storefronts, and private mansions. Gas had its downsides, however: it was explosive, smelly, polluting, sooty, and did not make for terribly bright lighting.

By the 1870s, the harnessing of electricity for lighting became a major quest. In 1878, an arc light inventor wowed Chicago crowds with a demonstration of the technology. Unfortunately, arc lights proved to be too bright, short-lived, loud (they buzz), and quite capable of burning down your house. It was Thomas Edison's incandescent electric light in 1880 (he was then known as the wizard behind the talking telegraph, or phonograph) that proved the most enduring and commercially practical. The incandescent light also seemed to offer the most direct and meaningful use for electrifying a house, building, and city.

Initially, electric companies sold hardware such as individual generators. But in 1888, the Chicago Edison Company centralized power generation with an electric station in the financial district at 139 Adams Street. This single station was capable of powering ten thousand lights.[23] Things only grew from there. Harold Platt, writing in *The Electric City,* explains, "The spread of the new technology in the central business district was steady and cumulative as Chicagoans increasingly linked things electrical with notions of amenity, class, and modernity."[24] In the 1890s, Samuel Insull acquired and ultimately centralized a power company that would become Com-Ed (Commonwealth Edison Company), the regulated monopoly that is still the city's primary electricity provider.

The two entrenched gas players, Chicago Gas Light and Coke Co. and the People's Gas Light and Coke Co. (each overseeing a separate portion of the city), meanwhile, did not take the competition "lightly" and, with sharp elbows, fought to continue providing the city with gas for lighting. Ultimately, the people preferred the clearly superior electric incandescent lights, and so the gas companies began pushing for the use of gas and coal for other applications such as heating, and for appliances such as stoves. And they did succeed in dominating in those arenas. To this day, the People's Gas Light and Coke Co. (People's Gas, today) is still the one and only gas company that Chicagoans use.

At this point in time, the availability of centralized systems that would move heat from a basement through the rest of the home was becoming more widespread. Such heating systems had been around for decades but were unreliable. James Walworth & Company, for example, built a steam heating system in 1859 for the Illinois governor and Chicago railroad baron, William Ogden. The fear of exploding boilers kept many would-be customers and insurers at bay. By the 1880s, classified ads were promising boilers that "would not explode" and steam heating became much more widespread.[25]

One particular advantage of steam heat was that it flowed through pipes under its own pressure, with no need for pumps or electric motors. It was thus a good fit for heating Chicago's increasingly tall flats buildings, apartment hotels, and commercial buildings. Boilers were fed with coal, which could be delivered through chutes accessible via the ever-useful Chicago alleys. For decades, until natural gas took over, Chicago buildings expelled nasty plumes of black smoke. This was regulated by the city, which encouraged snitching on offenders. Apparently there were a lot of snitches. In 1940, 85 percent of Chicago households were using coal for heating; by 1975, it was 1.5 percent.[26] Cleaner and more efficient natural gas took the reins from coal, but one can still see the coal chutes here and there on the sides of buildings. ■

Late Italianate: *Ancora Vivo*

In previous chapters, we covered the Italianate style, variations of which dominated Chicago's residential architecture from the mid-1800s. This style dies hard. In the 1880s, it persisted among various common housing types: workers cottages, two-flats, three-flats, and more.

Notable marks of the 1870s and early 1880s Italianate style are limestone lintels with incised ornament, prominent and typically painted cornices with brackets, and a dark red face brick contrasting with the Chicago common brick composing the sides and rear walls of the home.

The Rise of the Queen Anne

The Queen Anne became one of the more impactful styles throughout the country in the 1880s and into the 1890s, but particularly in Chicago. Many architectural historians trace the origin of the style's popularity to the influence of British architect Richard Norman Shaw, who was active from the 1860s to the early 1900s, and to the Philadelphia Centennial Exposition of 1876. But in Chicago, the style likely arrived via locals returning home from trips to the East Coast and reporting on the latest styles in well-to-do vacation spots. Like this *Chicago Tribune* observer of the "Queen Anne Cottages" in Saratoga in 1877:

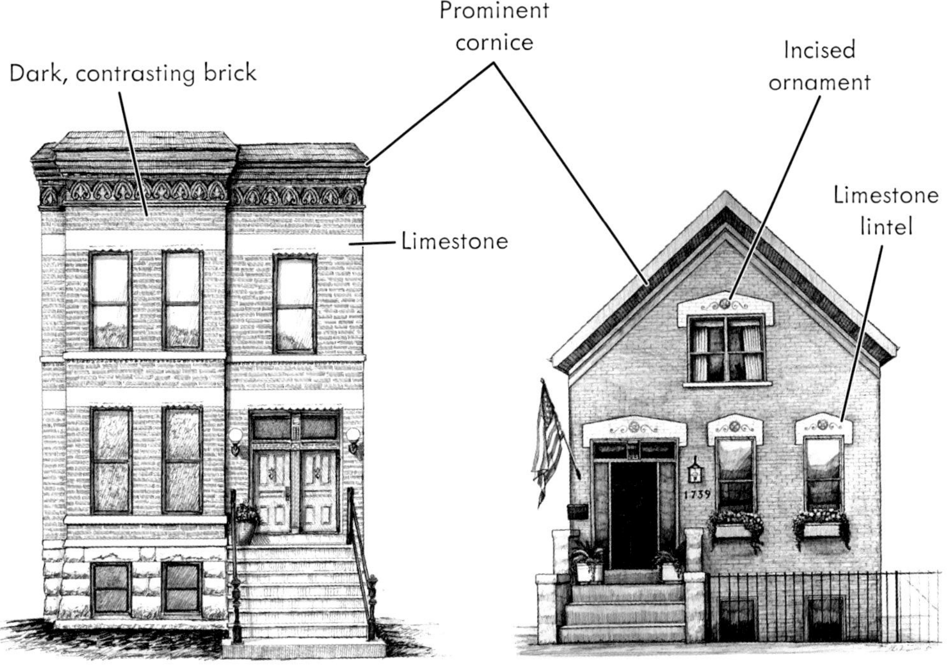

Late Italianate homes in Ukrainian Village (left) and Bucktown (right).

> These cottages are perfect of their kind, and were built without regard to cost. . . . The fancy for the Queen Anne cottage has taken root in many quarters, of which fact the Jersey coast is a good illustration. There is every reason why it should extend wherever summer or suburban villas are to be built, for no cottage is more homelike and simple, and cozily to be arranged.[27]

One factor that set ablaze the popularity of the Queen Anne style was the rising popularity of pattern books and home magazines that propagandized design ideas via print to builders and homebuyers. Another was industrialized machinery. Spindlework, the delicate wood detailing that you see around some porches and under roof overhangs, or as a transition element between stories, was not, in fact, made by some old guy with a carving knife and knobby knuckles. Spindlework was only possible in these quantities because of the availability of equipment like machine lathes and scroll saws, which had actually been around for a few decades at this point. As the country's major nexus for manufacturing and transit, Chicago was the source for a substantial amount of building material. According to Gwendolyn Wright in *Moralism and the Model Home,* two thousand men worked in local mills "turning out doors, sash, dressed lumber, and ornamental detailing for houses around the country," which sometimes included entire ready-made houses that were shipped all over the world.[28]

The Queen Anne style is a devious misnomer. It appears during the Victorian era, so named for Queen *Victoria*'s reign from 1837 to 1901, which is confusing enough. Even more confusing is the fact that the forms it popularized were pulled from an era *before* Queen Anne, who ruled from 1702 to 1714. Richard Shaw and others drew inspiration from the late Tudor era, which included Queen Elizabeth's reign in 1558–1603, and the Jacobean, which refers to the reign of King James I from 1603–1625. It was the era of Shakespeare.

But in general, this style likes to break rules, so maybe the name is apropos. Queen Annes like to be different. They're known for their asymmetrical facades with partial or full-length porches that sometimes wrap around the side of the house, and for their varied rooflines that allow for funky features like turrets. Their main visual objective is to avoid symmetry and a uniform appearance. As a result, there's a playfulness to them even while they maintain a certain sophisticated appearance. In Chicago, the style was used in both commercial and residential buildings, and it presented as a standalone form (you could see a shadow of a Queen Anne and know exactly what style it is projecting, with its tell-tale asymmetrical massing and lumpy forms) or ingratiated itself as a style onto other forms like rowhouses, flat buildings, and greystones.

A hallmark of the Queen Anne style is their patterned and textured exterior walls. Wood-frame Queen Annes were often clad with shingles, while masonry versions achieved textural effects by mixing up different brick courses or colors, terra cotta panels, or other kinds of masonry. Different materials might be used on different levels, such as a brick first floor and a stucco or frame second floor. Think of them as theater students raiding the costume room before a show—you can tell the cast is all from the same general period in history, but to call them cohesive is a stretch.

The Queen Anne style is perhaps most closely associated with our idea of a "Victorian home." Not only was it popular throughout the country, but it was flashy and adopted for use in a variety of residential types. One of the qualities that differentiates Chicago Queen Anne homes from those in

QUEEN ANNE

A wood-frame North Side Queen Anne in Logan Square.

COMMON FEATURES

- Bright colors and color variation
- Fanciful woodwork like decorative spindles and trim around the gables
- Prominent stained glass with colorful, symmetrical patterns
- Generous use of asymmetry with turrets, towers, and squared or angled bays
- Wide and deep front porches, often wrapping around one side of the home
- Prominent, attention-grabbing equilateral gables (a gable that forms an equilateral triangle), sometimes cross gables
- Pattern shingles, sometimes like fish scales

many other parts of the country is that the style has to adapt all of its sprawling traits into our long and narrow lots. A Queen Anne in rural or suburban America has breathing room to broadly spill out its asymmetry. Unless it sits on a double or corner lot, a Chicago Queen Anne typically has to express itself in taller and narrower proportions, almost like it's sucking in its stomach.

The Queen Anne showed up at a time when the city was developing in brick and masonry within its city limits and wood-frame beyond the city limits. The brick Queen Anne can be found in abundance, therefore, in neighborhoods that developed in the 1880s within the city and fire limits—Bronzeville, Pilsen, Gold Coast, Lincoln Park—while the wood-frame Queen Anne can be found in abundance in neighborhoods that developed in the 1880s outside the city and fire limits of the time—Austin, Hyde Park, Lake View.

Wood-frame North Side Queen Annes in Lincoln Park (left) and Andersonville (right).

Note that the Logan Square example on page 113 has a multi-sided turret, as do the Chicago masonry Queen Annes that follow. The use of the octagonal or polygonal shape in architecture had its roots in classical and Renaissance precepts, then popularized anew in the mid-1800s by Orson Squire Fowler, who argued for octagonal design to the extent that it formed the entire house. Though that idea didn't last, the polygonal bay window—forming just the three sides of the octagon, commonly called a "canted bay"—became a vital shape in Chicago exteriors for many decades:

A Queen Anne greystone in Ravenswood.

Here's a festooned Queen Anne with a corner turret on North Southport Avenue. The large plate glass and corner entrance indicates the first floor was meant for a business.

There are also a variety of larger buildings that take on the Queen Anne style, including flats buildings and corner storefront buildings with residences above. On the preceding page you can see a common feature of the day: an attention-grabbing sheet metal bay over wooden frames or turret that offsets a brick facade, and a decorative cornice. Festoons and garlands abound. It's designed to catch your eye.

The Queen Anne style adorned the humble workers cottage in various ways. The "Claremont Cottages," a collection of cottages built as a speculative development, are an exceptional example of how playful yet reserved the style could be on narrow lots.

The "Claremont Cottages," along the 1000 block of South Claremont Avenue.

Related Styles: Stick & Eastlake

Nestled within Queen Anne are arguably several sub-styles. These are worth a mention, although in Chicago they are much less common. They are Stick style, a related style called Eastlake, and Shingle style. These forms were also imports to Chicago. Stick and Shingle style arrived from the East Coast, and in particular the resort towns like Newport, Rhode Island, and Long Branch, New Jersey. Wealthy northeasterners were inclined to give a bit more free rein to their architects to experiment. The Eastlake style came our way from California, with origins in England.

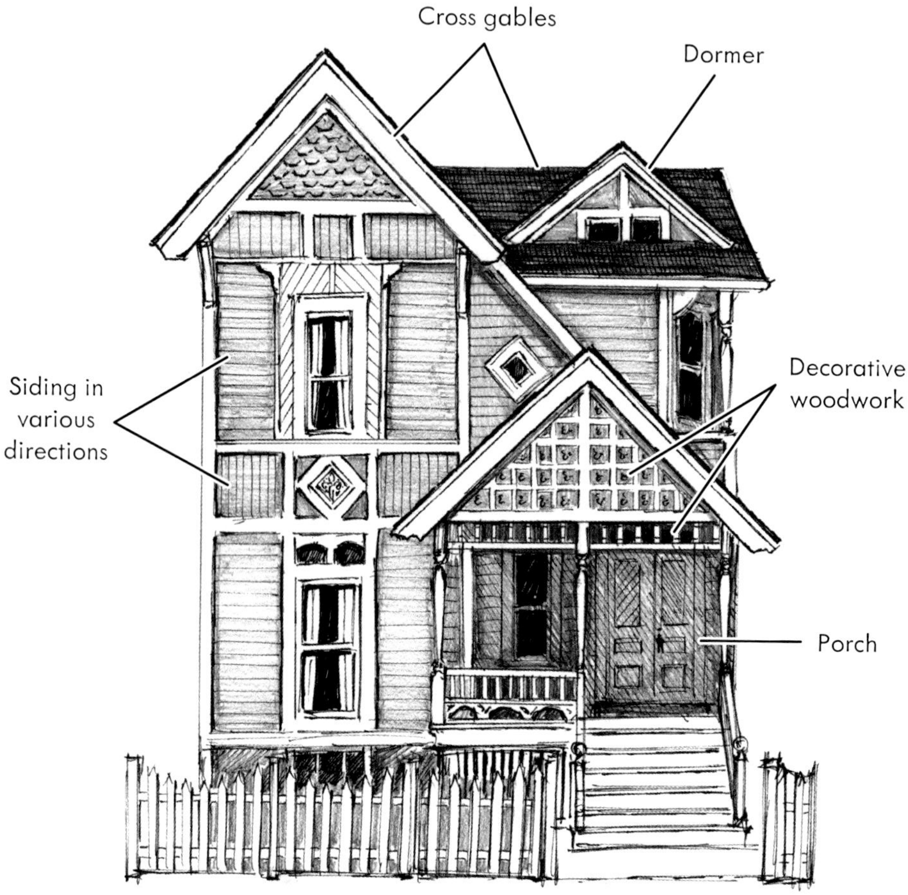

A Stick style home in Uptown.

Stick style shares some of the characteristics of Queen Anne, with its highly ornamented exterior (and typically a fanciful interior as well), decorative woodwork, and often asymmetric appearance with prominent gables and cross gables. One of the distinctive features of the Stick style home or building is the matchstick-like look of the facade, as if the builder's aims were to show every piece of lumber installed in the home in a showy, patterned way, but with a light touch.

Eastlake style, the name deriving from British architect and furniture designer Charles Eastlake (who ironically didn't have a direct hand in his

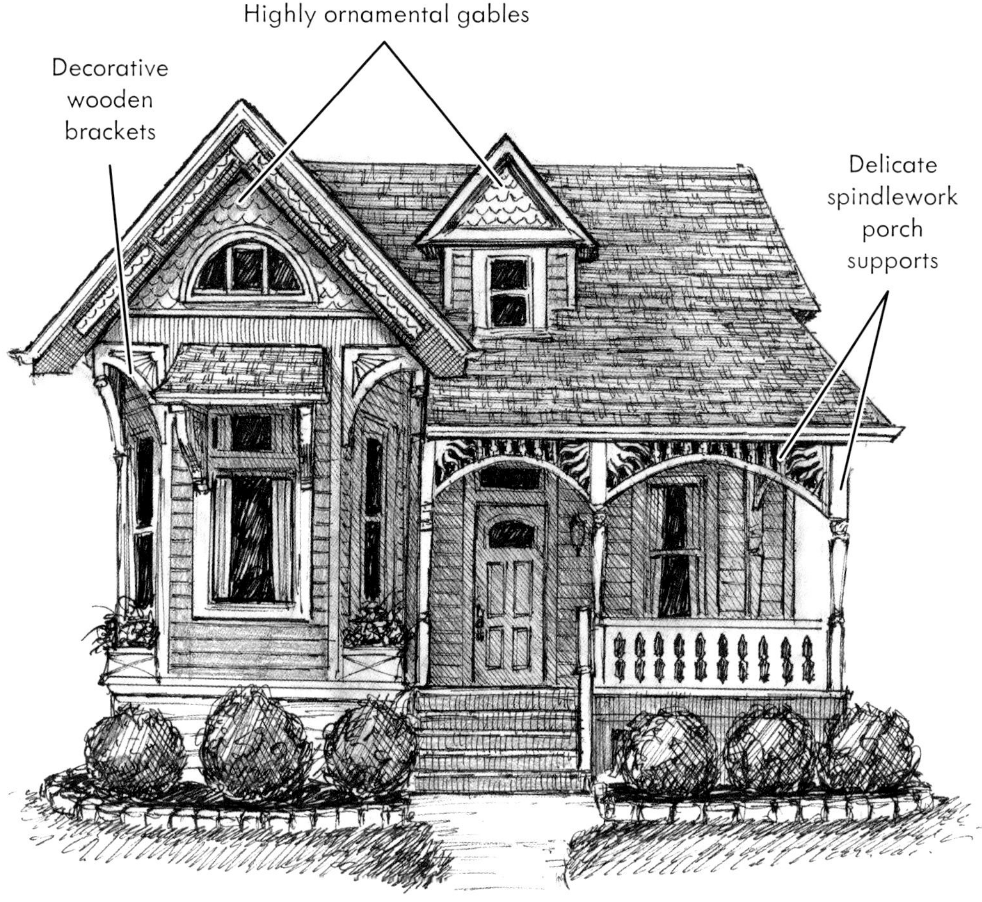

An Eastlake style home in Beverly.

namesake style and was a bit aghast at it), is perhaps even more difficult to find in Chicago. Like Stick style, this style also found its maximum expression in wood. The most distinctive feature of the Eastlake house is the highly decorative woodwork that adorns the gable, windows, and doorways, with lots of spindles. Cities like New Orleans and San Francisco that boomed in the 1880s and 1890s have these in abundance. There are also some famous examples in the Los Angeles area in Echo Park and Angelino Heights that you may recognize, like the abandoned home in Michael Jackson's "Thriller" music video, or so-called Halliwell Manor from the television show *Charmed*.

Shingle Style

Another sub-style of Queen Anne is the Shingle style home. Its most notable feature is an attention-grabbing front gable covered in rough-cut irregular and unfinished wood shingles. Typically, other parts of the facade are covered in shingles as well. As a variation of the Queen Anne style that was, virtually by definition, constructed in wood, these homes were confined to outside the city borders when they were built.

One of the great practitioners of the style was Joseph Lyman Silsbee, who moved from Syracuse to Chicago around 1882, and thereafter spread his particular take on the Shingle style to Chicago. One of his residential clients was John Cochran, founder of the Edgewater development mentioned earlier. Unfortunately, Silsbee's Edgewater homes did not survive Chicago's industrious ways, possibly because the expense of maintaining a home covered largely in wooden shingles likely made upkeep increasingly cumbersome. Survivors in the city are often found in the former "commuter suburbs" on the South Side, like Kenwood and Hyde Park, and Austin on the West Side. A Shingle style home that survived just outside Chicago is one of the more famous and widely visited: the Frank Lloyd Wright Home and Studio in Oak Park. Wright had worked for Silsbee and must have fallen under the spell, building the home in 1889 and adding a studio later.

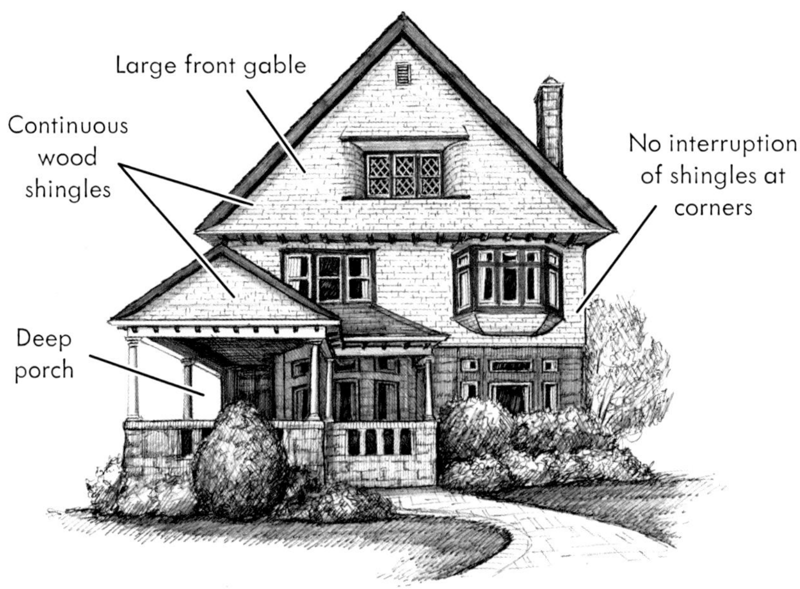

A Shingle style home in Kenwood.

Richardsonian & Romanesque Revival: Expressions in Stone

While Queen Anne homes, typically built from wood, were populating Chicago's outer, annexed townships, Romanesque Revival became a dominant masonry style within the city's historic core. The style first gained traction on the East Coast in the mid-1800s, with late-Roman architectural features being applied to a number of public buildings. Church of the Pilgrims in Brooklyn, built by Richard Upjohn in 1846, was considered the first. Romanesque Revival is often characterized by repeating patterns of arches, colonnades, and strong vertical massing via features like towers and steeply gabled roofs. This style is hulky, but it also makes you want to look up.

In the late 1870s, architect H.H. Richardson took a look at Romanesque architecture and thought, "Needs more drama." So, he put his own bold, heavy-handed spin on it—now famously known as Richardsonian Romanesque. This new expression of Romanesque was rooted in the earlier revival style, but gave an even heavier appearance with bulked up rough-cut stone. You're going to need an enormous door knocker to be heard at the entrance. The style also played around with asymmetry and structural polychromy—using natural, contrasting masonry colors to add different tones to the facade. He originally applied the style to public buildings, famously and firstly the Trinity Church in Boston, before taking other commissions like the Allegheny County Courthouse in Pittsburgh. It was the Richardsonian Romanesque style that would captivate other architects, especially in Chicago. Richardson had been known previously in Chicago for his seven-story American Merchants' Union Express building, constructed just a few years after the Chicago Fire, and which suffered a number of structural foundation issues.

In 1885, Richardson came back and more than redeemed himself. He designed three projects in Chicago that would influence a generation of architects and cement his reputation here. But he did not live to see the completion of any of his projects, due to his untimely death in 1886. These projects were:

- The Marshall Field warehouse (1887), which was in the present-day Loop, now demolished.
- The Glessner House (1887), which is located in the Prairie Avenue district on the Near South Side, now a museum.
- Franklin MacVeagh House (1893), in the Gold Coast along the lake, now demolished.

RICHARDSONIAN ROMANESQUE

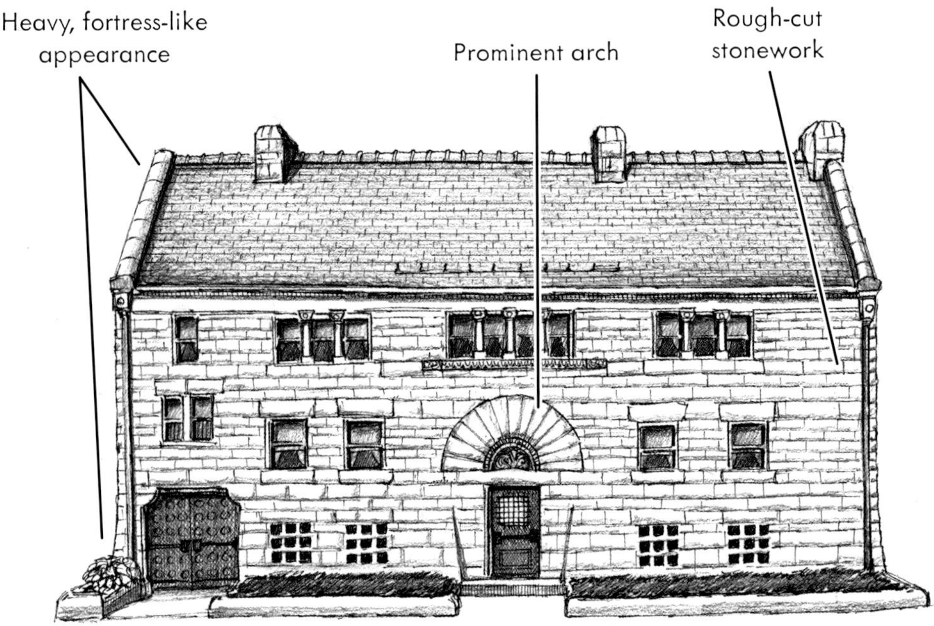

The Glessner House.

COMMON FEATURES

- Extensive rough-cut (rusticated) stonework on the exterior
- Asymmetrical facade
- Built with Bedford limestone (in Chicago; stone will vary elsewhere)
- Prominent use of arches, supported by squat columns; typically larger arches on the lower floors, and smaller on the upper, typically emphasizing entrances and windows
- Decorative stonework, typically organic floral or botanical patterns, to accentuate certain elements, particularly the front entrance and facade windows
- Many have towers topped with conical roofs
- A heavy massing: these homes looked strong, solid, well-built, almost impregnable

The work of Richardson, albeit limited in Chicago, was critical at a time when architects were struggling to find a uniquely "American" architecture. Even though his style had "Romanesque" in its name, it still served to influence other architects who were eager for a homegrown style that departed from European precedents. If Europe wasn't doing it contemporaneously, then it could be American. It was also perfect for a city that had a few specific features: a regulatory need to build masonry homes; access to abundant quantities of brick and durable limestone in the Bedford quarries, as well as brick; and booming demand from customers with sufficient income. Richardsonian Romanesque found Chicago to be the right place at the right time.

From the mid-1880s, thousands of Chicago homes were built with some lineage to Richardsonian Romanesque, many in the rusticated Bedford limestone that defined Richardson's signature Chicago buildings. Examples include the rowhouses along Grand Boulevard (now King Drive in Bronzeville) and the Gold Coast, but more modest examples abound, too.

A Richardsonian Romanesque rowhouse in the Gold Coast. Note the exuberant use of arches and columns.

The Wathier home from 1891 by architect Oliver Marble, on the Near West Side. It's all about the rusticated stone and the heavy arches.

CHAPTER

1830 1840 1850 1860 1870 1880

White City, Blight City

1893–1900

1890 1900 1910 1920 1930 1940

"Well Susan, it paid, even if it did take all the burial money."

—World's Fair Visitor, 1893[1]

CHICAGO IN THE 1890S was big, bawdy, wealthy, impoverished, and powered by immigrants. As was mentioned in the previous chapter, it had doubled in size between 1880 and 1890, growing to over a million residents. This was thanks to the massive arc of land annexed in the late 1880s—conveniently just in time for the 1890 census. This population increase would bump the city into the rank of second most populated city after New York, much to the ire of the now third-place Philadelphians who considered our rapid boundary expansion a dirty way to grow population numbers. Chicago just shrugged its big shoulders.

By the late 1890s, Chicago's population had grown to 1.7 million, with half of the population crammed into a three-mile radius around the city center. Given that you couldn't jump in your Toyota Camry and head to work, and public transportation was limited to certain areas, much of the land around the outskirts of the old city boundaries had yet to be developed in earnest. Still, we kept pulling in new residents. By 1899, three out of four Chicagoans were born abroad—mostly from Europe—or were children of immigrants.[2] African Americans were also entering the city in significant numbers for the first time. Arriving from Southern states and looking for work, a majority worked as day laborers or domestic workers after being barred from higher paying factory work.

Hope & Panic

If you ask a Chicagoan today what happened here in the 1890s, they'll likely bring up the World's Columbian Exposition of 1893. Maybe they'll mention a serial killer as well, thanks to that other very famous book about Chicago. Whether you called it the World's Columbian Exposition or the Chicago World's Fair, it sounded a lot better than "the Panic of 1893," which is how newspapers described the economic depression that settled in right as the Expo was being built.[3]

It was, in fact, the eighth such "panic" in Chicago's history, but it turned out to be a doozy. While speculators had been gobbling up land to build on before the Fair, there was a significant drop in the sale of lots and vacant property after the gleaming Beaux Arts wonderland closed its gates. In 1894, real estate prices plummeted, and by 1896, the demand for vacant property had reached the lowest point in the city's history. The volume of building activity dropped from over $63 million in 1892 to $28 million in 1894, which, in addition to the exhaustion of forests in the Upper Great Lakes region, did damage to a lumber industry that would never recover.[4] By 1897, it was said that real estate was "a liability instead of an asset," and finally, five years after the panic began, foreclosures hit their peak in 1898.[5]

Part of the problem, of course, was that the pre-Expo housing and hotel boom had led to overbuilding. As soon as the Fair ended, neighborhoods like Hyde Park and Woodlawn were smattered with "Vacancy" and "For Sale" signs. The University of Chicago helped to put bodies into some of the buildings, but it would take about thirty years before there was a need to build more housing.[6]

Some still found a silver lining. Unlike hotel owners and landlords, saloon owners were crowd surfing on the miseries of their patrons. While the local saloons had a way of making many an unfortunate situation worse, they could also be surprisingly benevolent. Saloons at the time filled a social service gap in the city—they offered free lunches to patrons. In some cases, the lunch was truly free, ignoring the old adage about there being no such thing. Some saloons did expect the purchase of a five-cent beer, but in return the patron received both the beer and a better lunch than they could get at a regular restaurant for a nickel. It's possible these saloons filled more bellies at the time than all other charitable organizations combined. They may have also caused more marital problems than any other institutions combined.

Where the Working Class Lived

Most of Chicago's working-class families were renting a unit in a two- or three-flat or living in tenements or boarding houses at the time. They'd hunt for deals, buying used furniture from the street vendors like those at Maxwell Street Market, an open-air market on the Near West Side. The market was located in an area mostly inhabited by Eastern European Jews until the 1920s, and conveniently near Hull House. Middle- and working-class families having a bit more success may have been able to snag a home in one of Samuel Eberly Gross's new developments for as little as one hundred dollars down and ten dollars a month. They may also have filled it with the latest fashions from local shops or department stores; many provided financing options so furnishings could be paid for over time.

The massive immigration that occurred during this period resulted in ethnic cohesion in certain neighborhoods of the city, some of which remains to this day. Poles moved to the northwest part of the city, Czechs and Italians settled southwest, Germans collected in the near north, and so on. Black migrants also populated certain South Side neighborhoods but had far less choice in the matter. As more African Americans migrated to Chicago, racism intensified and racial covenants, uncooperative landlords, and outright violence found Black residents confined to the city's most run-down housing with the most overcrowded and hazardous conditions.[7]

Transportation

While the timing of the Fair was lousy from an economic standpoint, the infrastructure created before it and afterwards changed how the city moved. While real estate tanked in the mid-1890s, transportation plans managed to barrel forward. The elevated lines, or "L" tracks, were first constructed in 1892 and 1893 to the South Side and West Side. They used small steam locomotives until 1897, and heavy tentacles of track were rapidly unfurling into various parts of the city that would eventually connect at the turn of the century. These lines reached densely populated neighborhoods as well as wide-open speculative areas that would soon give birth to new subdivisions, thanks to a stretch of steel and enterprising developers.

The cable car, which had been so important in the eighties and early nineties, was surpassed by the more efficient electric street cars in 1890, though they existed concurrently for years. Despite their bumpy and unpredictable operation, it wasn't until 1906 that the last cable car skidded and jerked down a Chicago street. Electric street cars had their own challenges. Operators struggled with higher speeds, frayed wires, and the newness of the electric beasts. In short, they had a habit of treating pedestrians as speed bumps.[8]

Having electric street railways, horses, carriages, pushcarts, bicycles, cable cars, and elevated trains operating simultaneously allowed for a plethora of transportation options in Chicago. It also meant that all of these intersecting paths created a dangerous tangle of movement downtown, now with more workers and shoppers than ever entering the gauntlet.

With all of these zippy transportation options, why were horses still clomping down busy streets? This was partly due to their role in several critical industries. One by-product of Chicago's prolific slaughterhouses was an abundance of leather, which helped Chicago become one of the leading manufacturers of saddles and riding gear. By 1895, there were 245 blacksmiths, 398 horseshoers, and 325 livery stables that rented carriages.[9]

If you were looking for a way to get in a cardio workout on your commute, you could join in on the bicycle mania. By 1899, there were nearly 2,000 miles of road in Chicago—1,266 of those miles paved with asphalt or cedar blocks[10]—as well as numerous parks and tree-lined streets.[11] Chicago became an epicenter for the sport. This craze was also a game changer for women, who suddenly had increased mobility outside of the home, and led to the "rational clothing" movement, which called for emancipation from the constraints of Victorian fashion. A daring woman might even wear bloomers while riding about town.

To protect pedestrians from the relentless onslaught of clomping hoofs and spinning wheels, this era also brought a huge investment in sidewalks. While sidewalks had existed in some sections of the city for decades, they were often barely passable thanks to merchants and signage, or were in a compromised state. The city created a Department of Sidewalk Construction, and in 1899 alone, a total of 244 miles of sidewalk were laid and almost 70 miles underwent repairs. Sidewalk inspectors were a serious lot. Property owners were responsible for the upkeep of sidewalks at the time, and inspectors notified them of complaints—over 20,000 notices were sent in a single year.[12]

Work

Outside of leather-making industries and slaughterhouses, work could be found in pig-iron, coal, and steel industries. Less dirty work could be found making telephones, a newer technology primarily used for businesses, though these communication devices were finding their way into middle-class homes in the 1890s. Chicago was a principal manufacturer of telephone equipment, and by 1905, 100,000 Chicagoans had their very own telephones. Unsurprisingly, Chicago was also the bicycle manufacturing capital of America in the 1890s, with eighty-eight local companies producing nearly two-thirds of the nation's bicycles.[13]

It was relatively common for everyone in the house to work. A man's salary in the 1890s may not have paid all of the bills, especially amid a depression. "Work-from-home" jobs were critical at this time and everyone who was able participated. To add income, women tended to boarders, did laundry, made and mended clothing, made and sold other goods, and did pretty much anything they could from the kitchen table or any corner of the home that was available. Children also worked off the books, peddling items on the street or hawking newspapers. Of course, there were also sweatshops, and children often quit school at a very young age to contribute to the family wages.

And Still, the City Grew

Slowly, the economy began moving in a positive direction and things began to turn around for Chicago and its residents. In 1899, there was a general improvement in workers' conditions, with wages up 5 to 10 percent. Flats that were vacant in 1898 were filling up again in 1899. Office rents went down and residential rents began to stabilize. All of the new transportation infrastructure continued to connect people to new opportunities, and the literal connection of the South Side, West Side, and finally North Side elevated tracks created a loop in the central business district in 1900, thereafter known as the "Loop." The North Side would grow rapidly in the early twentieth century while the existing housing infrastructure on the South Side continued to struggle in the aftermath of the World's Fair—though it held on to its massive industrial plants and a large portion of its population. Despite this lopsided improvement and a lingering glut of vacant housing from the Columbian Exposition, there was a pattern of growth that affected all of Chicago. Elevated lines kept pushing into previously undeveloped tracts of land, and along these newly constructed lines sprang up rows and rows of apartment buildings.

Electric streetlamps illuminated the World's Fair. There are a handful of these in front of the Museum of Science and Industry.

The World's Columbian Exposition

"The damage wrought by the World's Fair will last for half a century from its date, if not longer. It has penetrated deep into the constitution of the American mind, effecting there lesions significant of dementia."

—Louis Sullivan, from *The Autobiography of an Idea, 1924*

On February 25th, 1890, Chicagoans and New Yorkers held their breath during a series of vote counts that would determine the location of the next world's fair. The winner would have a chance not only to show their city to the world, but to also save face for the entire country. The United States had made a lackluster showing at the 1889 Exposition Universelle in Paris and it was time to change minds about this young and enterprising country. The U.S. also had a personal beef with the French after they effectively emasculated our capitol city at the Exposition by doubling the height of the Washington Monument—then the tallest structure in the world—with their 984 foot Eiffel Tower.

Spoiler alert: Chicago won the bid. This was thanks to a collection of its leading capitalists, significant financial support from the city and state, and over $5 million in stock subscriptions from everyday Chicagoans who just really wanted something to look forward to. Less than sixty years after becoming a city and twenty years after enduring a fire that burned down 18,000 of its buildings, a resurrected city was bustling and cocky and gearing up to welcome millions of visitors. Speculators snapped up land and buildings, and land values near Jackson Park exploded, sometimes increasing 1,000 percent in a year. Sections of the South Side were rapidly transformed and new development corridors emerged along the lake and the newly built "L" train line, today known as the Green Line. Housing blocks were constructed for the Fair's workers, while entertainment venues and hotels multiplied in nearby Hyde Park and Woodlawn.

So what, exactly, is a world's fair? These massive global exhibitions expose visitors to arts and crafts, industrial and agricultural products, technology, scientific achievements, and any and all unique expressions of other cultures, in an attempt to inspire and entertain. It's a lot to put together. In fact, the fair was supposed to open in 1892 to celebrate the 400th anniversary of Christopher Columbus's arrival in the New World in 1492, but there were numerous come-to-Jesus moments that moved the schedule into the next year. One might say that Columbus missed his original mark, and so did Chicago.

Daniel Burnham, a Chicago architect and the fair's chief designer, worked with Central Park's famed landscape architect Frederick Law Olmsted to turn the swampy six hundred acres of Jackson Park into a gleaming Neoclassical and naturalistic urban mecca—a challenge that was not for the faint of heart.

Barriers like ailing architects, labor strikes, challenging landscapes, deluges of rain, an economic depression, and far too little time left Burnham scrambling at every turn. At the height of construction, a mind-boggling 40,000 workers labored day and night to make up lost time while some of the best-laid plans continued to be foiled.

An exposition of this magnitude becomes a tiny city unto itself, with infrastructure such as running water and sanitation, electricity, places to eat and recreate, and transportation to and within the grounds. But it also has to educate and entertain. While pulling in exhibitors from all over the

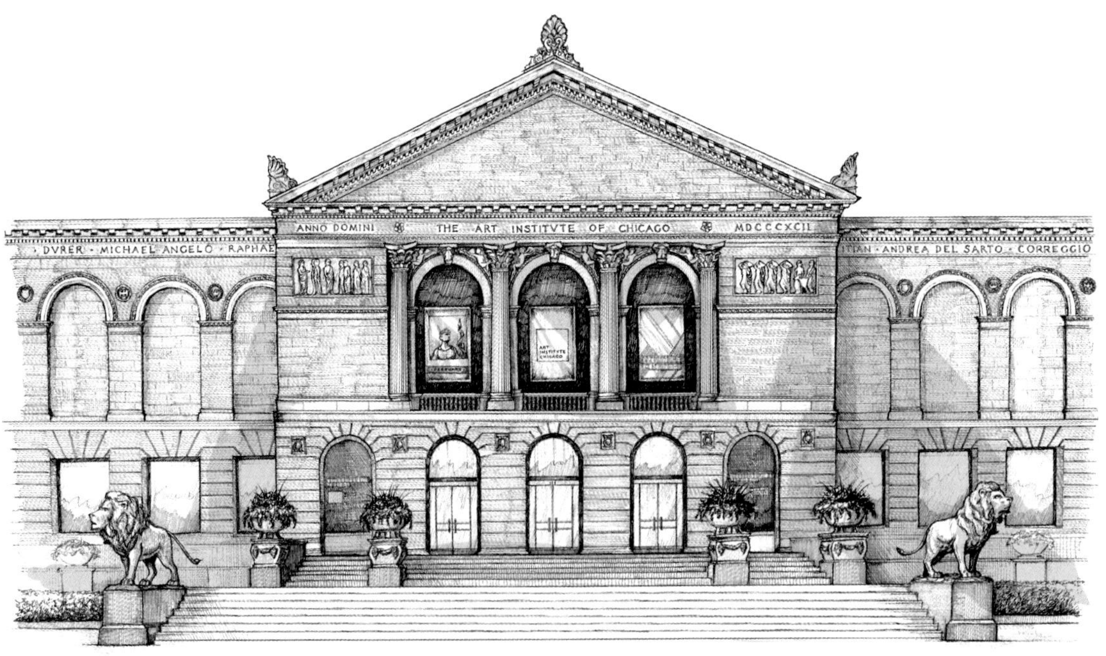

The Beaux Arts style Art Institute of Chicago, one of the original Expo buildings.

world to show off their unique cultural practices—forty-six countries to be exact—the fair must also have order and cohesion. And, you know, be stunningly beautiful.

Burnham decided to look to the past, opting for powerful and romantic Beaux Arts buildings. This style of architecture is influenced by classic Roman and Greek architectural forms that stress symmetry, with details like columns and pediments, statues and figures embedded into facades, and stone or stone-like materials. Think cultural institutions and train stations. This was an unpopular choice among architects who saw the fair as an extraordinary opportunity to define what *American* architecture could look like, and they were right to believe that this would influence architectural styles for decades to come.

Chicago was a young city, and Chicagoans were known to much of the world as a bunch of scrappy hog butchers. New Yorkers, who felt especially snubbed from losing the bid to Chicago, would certainly underscore this view. And so, to defy this reputation, Chicago put on a crispy white shirt, wrapped some pristine garlands around its shoulders, and cleaned itself up to become the White City. From a practical standpoint, painting every building the same color was also a simple and cost-effective way to create cohesion. The contrast of white against the backdrop of bloodied meat packing plants, smog, and bubbling rivers of industrial waste also served to create a sort of magical halo around the fair.

This contrast also underscored the disparity felt by many during this decade of economic peril. The fair wasn't for all Chicagoans, and the fifty-cent ticket price excluded many of the city's working class and those struggling to get by. To show that organizers were interested in being inclusive, there were numerous "nationality days" aimed at groups looking for recognition and a way to celebrate their various ethnic identities and neighborhoods, which Chicago is known for even today. Black Chicagoans were also largely disappointed in the fair's representation of their achievements and felt like they were reduced to tropes.

With construction *mostly* complete, the gates of the fair swung open on May 1, 1893. Despite innumerable challenges and inequities, "the fair that changed America" drew 27.5 million visitors, which was almost 40 percent of the U.S. population at the time. On top of creating an entire city amid tremendous pressures and an economic depression, Burnham also managed to pull off the goal to "out-Eiffel, Eiffel." After reviewing countless proposals that lacked the complexity and awe required to one-up the Parisians, a structural engineer from Pittsburgh (by way of Galesburg, Illinois) sent in a plan to build a terrifying contraption with incalculable amounts of iron and the ability to hold over two thousand squirming humans. It was also a gigantic spinning circle that would soar over the fair and offer views from heights few had experienced before. And so, the proposal was ultimately accepted and George Washington Gale Ferris Jr. built his jaw-dropping wheel, which thankfully did not crush thousands of fairgoers while rolling down the center of the Midway Plaisance.

New Technologies

On a less imposing scale, but ultimately a far more impactful one, the fair introduced some modern technologies that would transform our everyday lives. A new technology of electricity—alternating current—would revolutionize transportation and lighting in both the home and workplace. It also completely transformed recreation by introducing visitors to new, electrically powered inventions. The kinetoscope was a contraption with a viewer that featured a sequence of photographs seen in quick succession—the precursor to moving pictures. The phonograph brought sound into homes and allowed people to listen to music in a private space on their own schedules for the first time in history. It also allowed people to record and replay music.

Practical inventions like elevators, dishwashers, and spray paint—a solution born of the need to manage the extensive painting and upkeep of buildings at the fair—would also become the stuff of our day-to-day existence. An automobile exhibit featured the Daimler Benz Victoria, an early gasoline-powered car that offered an alternative energy option for the rare automobile owner in the 1890s.[14] Soon-to-be mass-produced food staples were introduced into our kitchen, like Cracker Jacks, Aunt Jemima pancake mix, Cream of Wheat, Juicy Fruit gum, and, much to the eternal gratitude of future college students, Pabst Blue Ribbon.

Lasting Effect on Chicago's Landscape

Rental properties created for throngs of fairgoers and the transportation improvements needed to move bodies to and from the Expo led to the rapid urbanization of the South Side. While many newly built apartment buildings would struggle to remain occupied after the fair, the transformation of the landscape was permanent. As for the fairgrounds . . . well, most of it went up in smoke after the Expo closed. A headline from January 9, 1894, read, "The White City in Flames; Fire Destroys the Fairest of the Beautiful Buildings." Still, two notable buildings that would become critical cultural institutions—the Art Institute and the Museum of Science and Industry—remained intact, and defining land features like Olmsted's Wooded Island and the Midway Plaisance are still enjoyed today.

Chicago's rich history of artist colonies can also be tied to the World's Fair. In 1894, Anna and Lambert Tree erected Tree Studios at 4 East Ohio as a way to keep artists in Chicago after the Expo. Tree Studios offered cheap rent and studio space so artists could live, work, and be part of an arts community. You can read more on artist colonies in Chapter 8.

Projecting beyond Chicago, the Exposition kicked off the City Beautiful movement, an architectural and urban planning campaign that flourished in the late nineteenth and early twentieth centuries. The goal was to improve cities aesthetically, functionally, and socially, through beautification and the construction of classically inspired buildings. The movement hoped to uplift urban environments for all city

The U-shape plan of still-extant Tree Studios surrounds a courtyard. The west facade is composed of a full-length cast iron arcade at ground level for retail. The second story is covered in a buff-colored Roman brick with large windows for the artists' studios.

dwellers. In a sense, it was a "fake it till you make it" mentality, but it also emerged as part of the broader progressive social reform efforts of the 1890s and 1900s, driven by the upper-middle class. Daniel Burnham and Edward H. Bennett's 1909 Plan of Chicago, considered one of the principal guides of the City Beautiful movement, was the result of many lessons learned in planning the fair. This guide became a kind of urban planning bible for cities all over the U.S. and the globe. If you see a civic plaza with white columns, It's probably a hangover from the Expo. ■

Classical Revival & Beaux Arts: A New, European Chicago

Also called Neoclassical, though one could quibble about the formality implied by that word, Classical Revival is a more "everyday" version of Beaux Arts—the slightly less ambitious sister in a respected family. The style is a generic term for architecture that has some classical features, like pediments, columns, decorative shields, finials, and balustraded flat roofs. It was one of the most widespread styles in the United States during the late 1800s and early 1900s, which is evident when you notice how many buildings have early Greek and Roman details thrown onto their facades. Often, these buildings have a mix of various classical elements that never would have been grouped together in their original iterations. They aren't precious, but they're still classy.

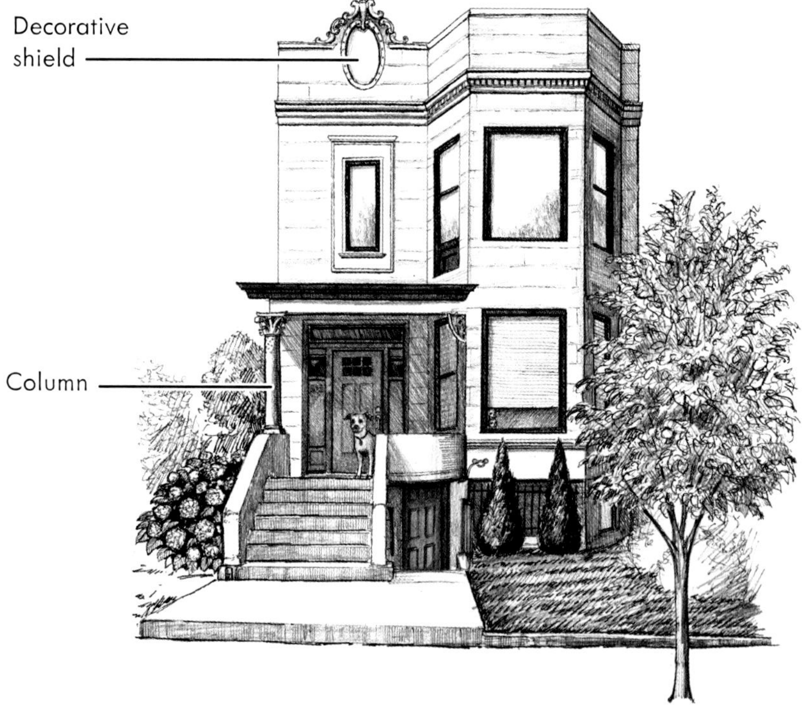

An example of a greystone with pared-down Classical Revival details—a simple, decorative shield adorning the parapet wall and a column near the entryway. Done and done.

CLASSICAL REVIVAL

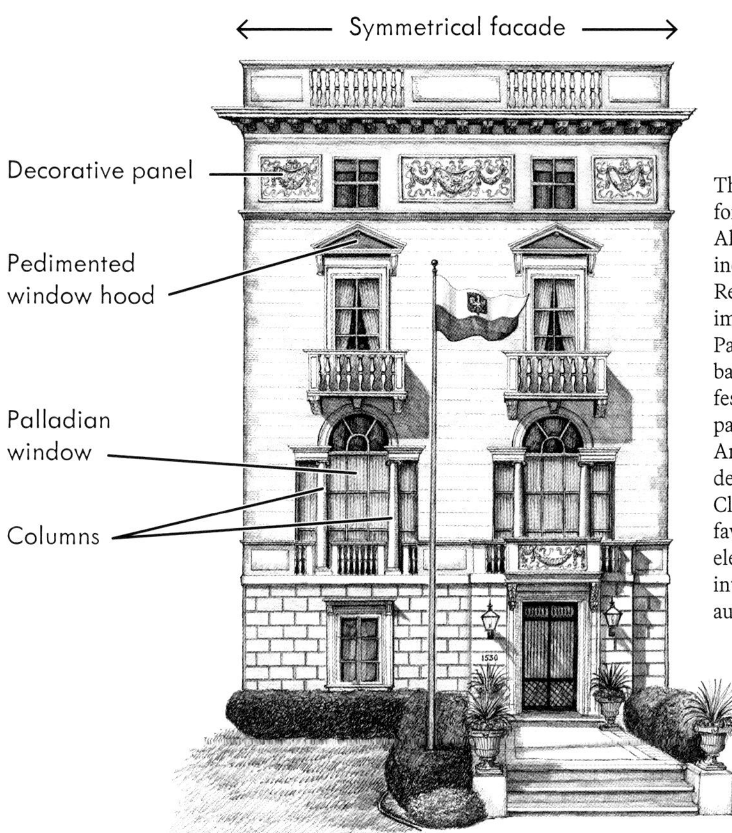

The Polish Consulate, formerly the Bernard Albert Eckhart mansion, incorporates Classical Revival details like pedimented window hoods, Palladian windows, and a balustraded flat roof. The festoons and decorative panels push it into Beaux Arts territory, the more decorative version of Classical Revival that favored adding sculptural elements and decoration into traditionally more austere designs.

COMMON FEATURES

- Symmetrical facades
- Minimal use of bays, towers, or other projecting building elements
- Cornices, triangular pediments, and flat roofs with balustrades or parapets
- Details like columns, finials, and decorative shields
- Front door often flanked by pilasters or sidelights and topped with a pediment or rounded fanlight
- Use of a variety of materials, including brick, stone, terra cotta, and wood

BEAUX ARTS

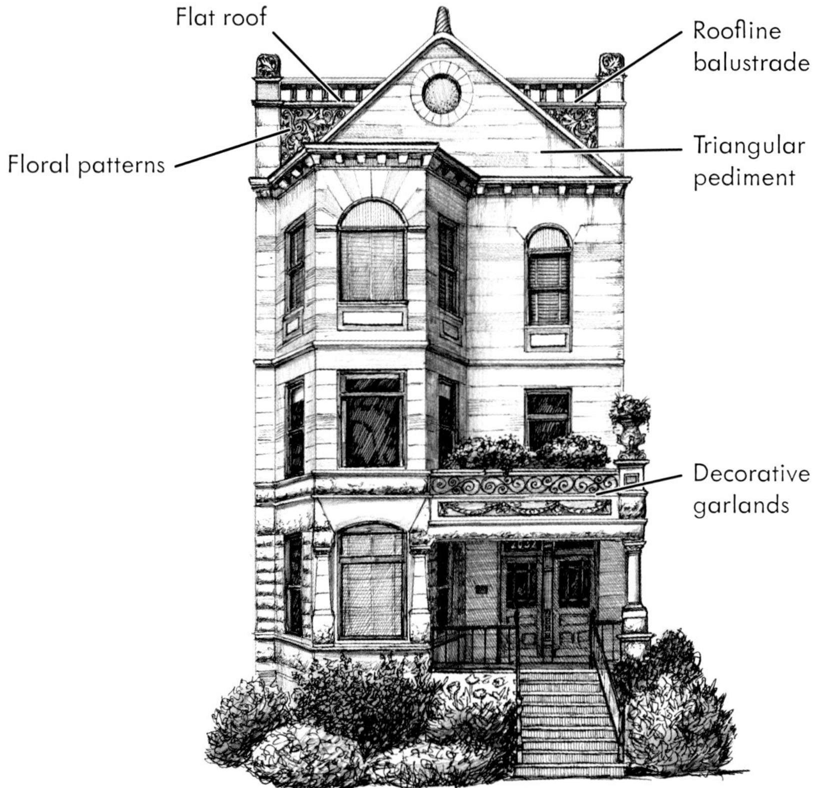

Section of a Beaux Arts rowhouse at 1521 N. State Pkwy.

COMMON FEATURES

- Flat or low pitched roof (occasionally, a mansard roof)
- Classical ornament, including columns, cornices, and triangular pediments
- Wall surfaces with decorative garlands, floral patterns, or shields
- Symmetrical facade
- Roofline balustrade
- Minimal use of bays, towers, or other projecting building elements
- Wide variety of exterior materials, including brick, stone, terra cotta, and wood

The Beaux Arts and Classical Revival styles are inextricably tied. Beaux Arts is essentially a version of Classical Revival with its own philosophies and a lot of festoons. The Beaux Arts style was named for the premier French school of architecture, the École des Beaux-Arts, and American architects like Richard Morris Hunt studied at the school and brought the style back from Paris in the early 1890s. With a fancy name like Beaux (rhymes with "hose") Arts, it may not surprise you to learn that the style was most often seen in places where wealth was concentrated, like big cities and resort communities. This style could be laid over a variety of building types, including greystones, rowhouses, and flats.

When they weren't at their drafting tables, students of the relentless, perfectionistic École were no doubt dreaming about columns, cornices, and triangular pediments from classical Greek and Roman buildings. They were taught to emphasize grand arrival halls, and to convey a sense of stubborn, eternal heaviness—these were not buildings meant to be picked up and flung around like workers cottages. They seemed built to last forever. Or at least, until urban renewal.

The popularity of Beaux Arts was advanced by the World's Columbian Exposition in 1893. Given that one of Chicago's goals was to one-up the 1889 Paris Exposition, it was an interesting choice to go with a style that came directly out of the prestigious Parisian school—a point not lost on a gaggle of enraged Chicago architects. With its grandiose treatment of classical architectural forms, the Beaux Arts style was seen as an expression of both wealth and civic pride. Buildings of this style are formal and monumental with loads of decorative details.

A Beaux Arts festoon.

If you want to look at buildings that exemplify the influence of the École des Beaux-Arts and its design traditions on American architecture, take a gander at the Art Institute of Chicago, the Museum of Science and Industry, and the Chicago Cultural Center. The first two were also part of the larger Beaux Arts plan of the Columbian Exposition—meaning the collective layout of the buildings followed École des Beaux-Arts planning philosophies, in addition to each individual building exterior expressing the style. The Chicago Cultural Center was built in 1897 and survived the indiscriminate demolition of buildings in the 1960s and '70s by the skin of its dentil molding.

When you read about this style, the most commonly used word will be "grandiose," so it's no surprise that the style is best suited for museums, courthouses, train stations, and other large public buildings. That said, elements of the style were woven into countless mansions, rowhouses, and greystones. One trick that usually works to distinguish Beaux Arts from any old Classical Revival residential building is looking for the style's signature decorative garlands and festoons.

Romanesque Revival (and Interment)

This style came back for another round in the 1890s, which is no great surprise since Chicagoans in the 1890s were bonkers about stone buildings. And this style was one of the stoniest. While H.H. Richardson died in the 1880s, just as he was creating an exciting "new" style in America, architects continued to run with the massive arches and hulking, rough-cut stonework popularized by Richardson. In addition to institutional and commercial buildings, the already stone-clad greystone flats and rowhouses basked in the bulky embrace of this style until it faded out in the late 1890s. In general, that boulder look was out of style after the turn of the century.

Chateauesque: Bonjour et Au Revoir!

The Chateauesque style became fashionable in Chicago in the 1880s and punctuated rooflines for a couple of decades. The style, which was based on the sixteenth-century French chateaux, was initially used for the mansions of the city's social elite on South Side streets like Prairie Avenue, but quickly spread to middle-class residences. The homes of the wealthy are marked by dramatic verticality and Gothic flavor, and often conical towers or turrets (or

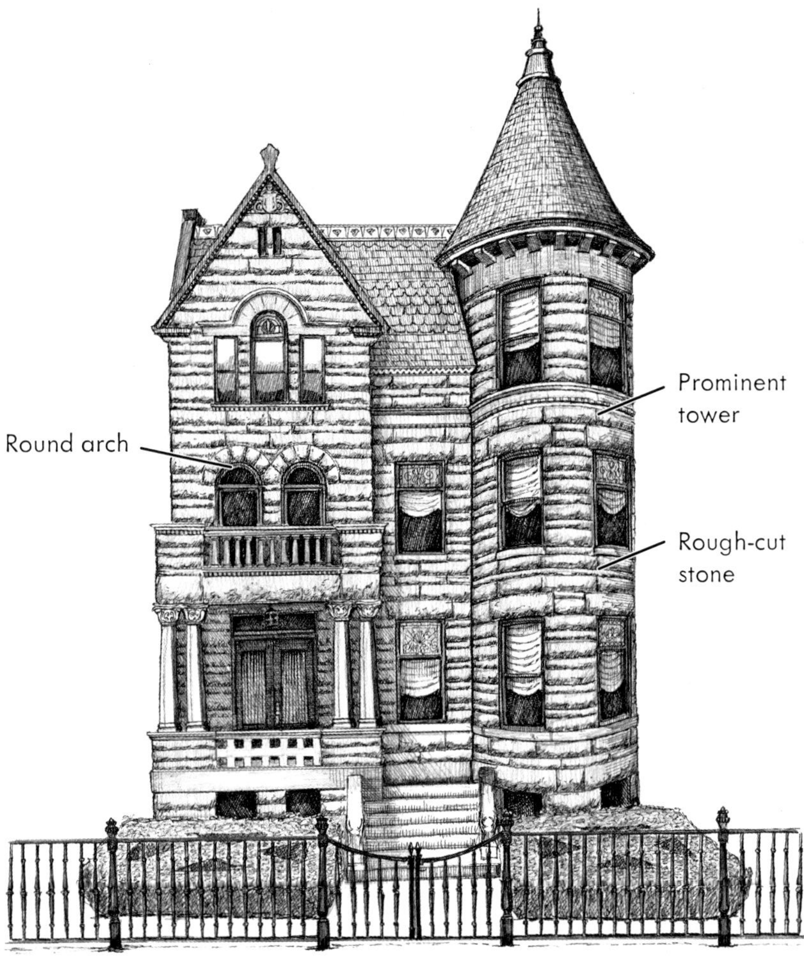

Romanesque Revival continued to be defined by its heavy, rough-cut stone walls, round arches and squat columns, deeply recessed windows, and pressed metal bays and turrets, like this fine specimen in Lincoln Park, built c. 1893.

both) that frame a steeply pitched hipped roof. The everyday Chateauesque is decidedly tamer.

There are several high-style examples in Chicago from this era. Richard Morris Hunt was a famous practitioner of the style, his Biltmore Estate in Asheville, North Carolina, being one prime example. He also designed the now-gone William Borden mansion in the Gold Coast along the lakeshore.

CHATEAUESQUE

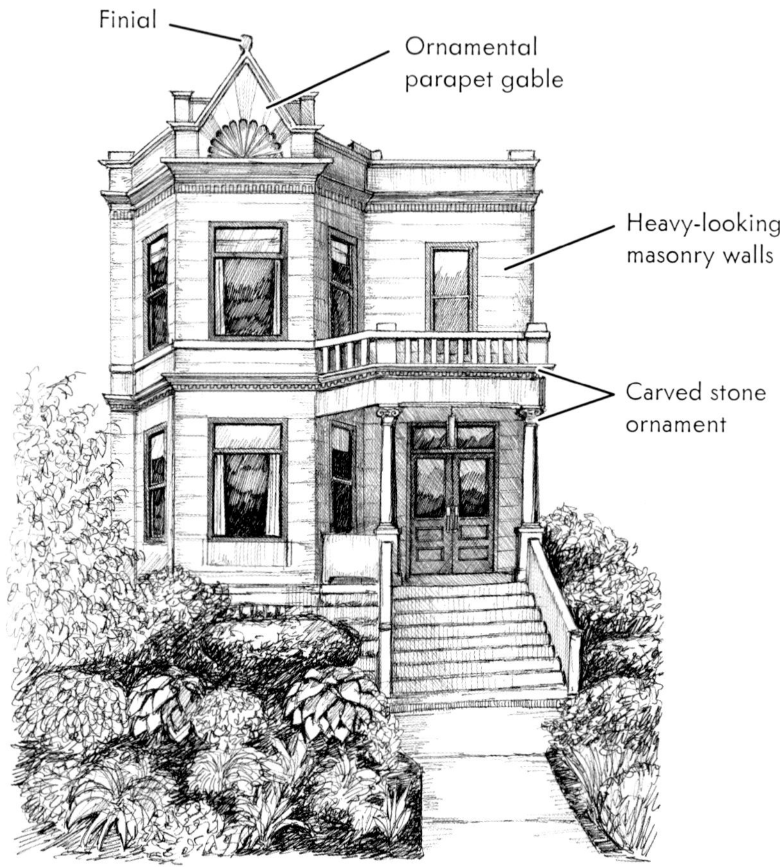

A Chateauesque greystone in Logan Square.

COMMON FEATURES

- Vertical proportions
- Massive-looking masonry walls
- Ornate carved stone ornament
- Ornamental parapet gable(s)
- High-peaked hipped or gabled roofs, sometimes with cresting
- Finials
- Elaborate dormers
- Tall chimneys

The steepled, street-facing parapets on these stone-faced mansions, flats, and rowhouses were a Chateauesque signal, making sure you knew this was not your typical Chicago home, but instead something a little . . . *je ne sais quoi*. Of course on the inside, many of these flats and rowhouses actually were pretty typical Chicago homes at the time—but as they say, dress for the job you want. The style dwindled after the early 1900s, but you'll still see them around the city, especially fancying up greystone facades. Often, the style is so pared down that the only clear signal is an ornamental parapet gable topped by a finial, but it's distinct enough to get the job done.

The 1890s William Kimball house on Prairie Avenue is not holding back with its finial game.

Chateauesque rowhouses on South Dr. Martin Luther King Jr. Drive in Bronzeville that are also showing off a mix of Gothic and Renaissance ornament, tall chimneys, and some sweet peaks.

Clarifying Windows

It's easy to take windows for granted, but it wasn't until the technological improvements and competitive mail-order catalogues of the late nineteenth century that there was nationwide standardization of window sizes and hardware. This was a feat that robbed future architecture nerds of quirky vernacular window variations, but also led to more affordable, quality-controlled construction. To understand how long it took to get to this level of mass production, let's start with a little history of the window.

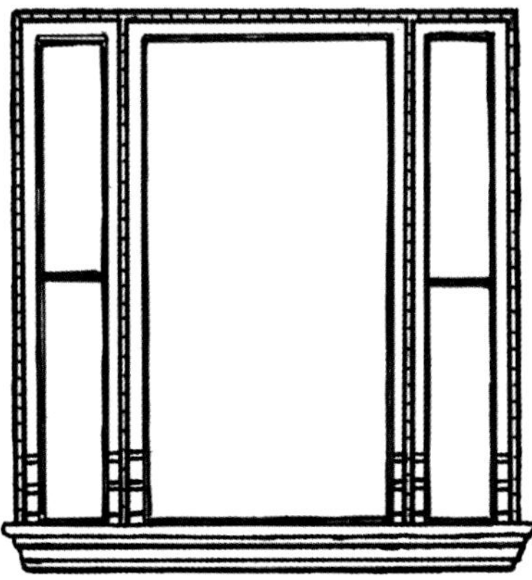

A Chicago window.

Victorian-Era Windows

While there is mention of glass being created by the first ever blacksmith in the Book of Genesis, we're going to skip ahead a little to the early colonizers of America. Americans have been obsessed with glass since we first barreled into Jamestown, Virginia, in the early 1600s. Settlers were keen to have a booming glassmaking operation and a substantial amount of time and money was dedicated to this new industry. But those early experiments within colonies were not known for their success. Glass production attempts were a spectacular failure thanks to a variety of technical issues and other distractions, like starvation. Things were uphill from there, however.

By the middle of the nineteenth century, mail-order companies were supplying a wide variety of building materials and components via catalogs. In the early days, these companies, based in Boston, Philadelphia, New York, Chicago, Detroit, and a few smaller cities, offered a variety of window sizes and tailored their windows to the styles cities favored. In 1887, an organization called the Wholesale Sash, Door and Blind Manufacturers Association was formed, creating a system that further standardized and quality-checked windows, distilling trends and improving durability. By the 1890s, catalogs were far more extensive, catering to all areas of the country, which created more standardization in window sizes and hardware.

Despite this standardization, there was still room for some new, niche configurations. The Chicago School, a school of architects active in the city in the late nineteenth and early twentieth centuries, focused on improved

An example of oriel windows on a six-flat. It wouldn't be wrong to call these bay windows, just less descriptive because oriels are found only on upper stories. The first-floor windows beneath the oriels are typical double-hung sashes.

An 1880s stained-glass window with organic forms, originally installed in a two-flat.

The Manhattan Building, built by William Le Baron Jenney in 1890, has some mighty fine oriel windows. Looking up from the street level, pedestrians can see grotesques with faces (or *mascarons*) on the bottoms of the oriels.

technologies, steel frame construction, and bringing more natural lighting into interior spaces. The "Chicago School" window is a style found primarily in skyscrapers, and consists of a large, fixed, central pane window with two narrower, double hung sash windows on either side. A sash is a full pane of glass, and a double-hung sash features two vertically sliding sashes—one on the top and one on the bottom. This allows for a fair amount of unobstructed light to enter a space as well as ventilation via the side sashes, which slide open for air. Bay and oriel windows were also popular with the Chicago School because they extend outward from the main walls, allowing more natural light and airflow to enter from multiple directions.

The most typical windows in the 1890s were double-hung wood sashes with multiple lights (panes of glass), though the number of lights decreased as we closed in on the twentieth century. Glass for these sashes typically came in two sizes: single glass that was one-twelfth of an inch thick, or glass that was a heartier one-ninth of an inch thick. The thinner glass could be used in windows that had a lot of smaller lights, and the thicker could be used for larger expanses of glass. Most commonly, the glass would be blown into a cylinder, cut lengthwise, and then flattened.

Plate glass was a different animal. For the production of plate glass, molten glass was poured flat, left to harden, and then ground and polished for clarity. It was also thicker, and extremely expensive to manufacture. By 1890, Chicago had become one of the country's primary plate glass suppliers.

Queen Anne sashes from an 1890s catalog put out by Paine Lumber Company, based in Oshkosh, Wisconsin.

Because so many styles were marching through town in the 1880s and 1890s, there were quite a few varieties of windows available, even as they were standardized. The "Queen Anne" window was likely the most popular. These had a multi-light sash over a single sash. Some incorporated stained glass or cut, etched, or embossed glass. The most common of these windows could be easily recognized by their small blocks of brightly colored (or sometimes clear) glass that surrounded a larger central pane of clear glass. In addition to catalogs, lumber yards also sometimes stocked varieties of Queen Anne windows in the 1880s. While the more conservative Colonial Revival style became more popular in the 1890s, Queen Annes took a hint and became less colorful to fit in.

"Cottage" or "cottage front" windows were also common at this time. These consisted of a single pane on top that had either clear or stained glass, paired with a large clear glass sash below. These windows could be a double-hung sash, a single sash, or a single-hung sash with a transom top sash.

Homes that still have their original wavy glass windows—a kind of subtle, rippled look—are the result of old-fashioned glassmaking methods. There is an urban legend claiming that glass is actually a liquid substance that is slowly moving downward from the pull of gravity. According to the MIT School of Engineering, which is made up of people you likely don't want to argue with, glass is actually a highly resilient elastic solid that is completely stable. So, if it is wavy, it was wavy from the day it was born. Pro-tip: If you happen to have a cracked window, it can be pretty expensive to try and replace the original wavy glass. If you need a piece of glass, look for a gut rehab in the surrounding area and then run around to the back alley to nab some original sashes before they're hauled away to the dump. You can have this glass cut to size by a local glass cutter. ■

Example of a cottage front sash, which featured a decorative transom over clear glass.

Farewell to the Queen (Anne)

While there were plenty of Queen Annes built in Chicago in the 1890s, especially on streets like Goethe, Scott, and Huron on the Near North Side, the truth is that the stately cohesiveness of the Columbian Exposition made the Queen Anne's twisting turrets, lopsided proportions, and mix-and-match coloring look a little unkempt. The White City and its neatly aligned Neoclassical and Beaux Arts buildings were projecting strength through uniformity. These buildings were serious—the stuff of banks and civic order and grand residences. They couldn't be bothered with fairytale towers or finicky spindlework or basically anything you could knock off a facade with a baseball bat. Suddenly, Queen Annes looked a bit rumpled, and as a result, these creative, cheery art teachers of architecture fell out of favor. Louis Sullivan foresaw this effect and called it out in his autobiography, claiming that the fair's emphasis on European classicism sucked the fun out of American experimentation and set back American architectural thought for the next forty years.[15]

An early 1890s Queen Anne rowhouse with brick walls, rusticated stone base, and a pressed metal turret in the Gold Coast.

Queen Annes continued to take some hits beyond this 1890s revival of classicism, however. If you look at the Chicago Historic Resources Survey, a twelve-year research effort by the City of Chicago to note the historic and architectural importance of all pre-1940 buildings in the city, you'll notice that quite a few of the documented Queen Annes have disappeared. The survey was completed in 1995, so a large number of these were obliterated in the past few decades. The fashion police can be ruthless.

Colonial Revival: Reimagined Roots

While examples of Colonial Revival homes exist from the 1880s, Chicago's 1893 Columbian Exposition definitely had a hand in the revival of this style both here and across the U.S. The Exposition's New Jersey Pavilion held a two-story, forty-by-sixty-foot reproduction of George Washington's Colonial style headquarters at Morristown, New Jersey.[16] Complete with its revolutionary relics, the reproduction got architects worked up about the demigods of American history—our tough, powdered, founding fathers—and their stately lives. In addition, architects like Shepley, Rutan & Coolidge, Bostonian architects who opened an office in the 1890s and designed the Art Institute of Chicago, the Chicago Cultural Center, and other local gems, also designed some iconic Colonial Revival homes. While the style hadn't fully taken off in Chicago yet, you can find concentrations of these earlier examples in Kenwood and Hyde Park.

A lot of imagination was inserted into this architectural retelling of history, as is generally the case with historical recreations. It would take a couple of decades for the style to smooth out and become more unified and less ostentatious, with some earlier examples suffering from what one critic referred to as "columnitus giganticus."[17]

The Horace E. Horton Mansion in Beverly.

COLONIAL REVIVAL

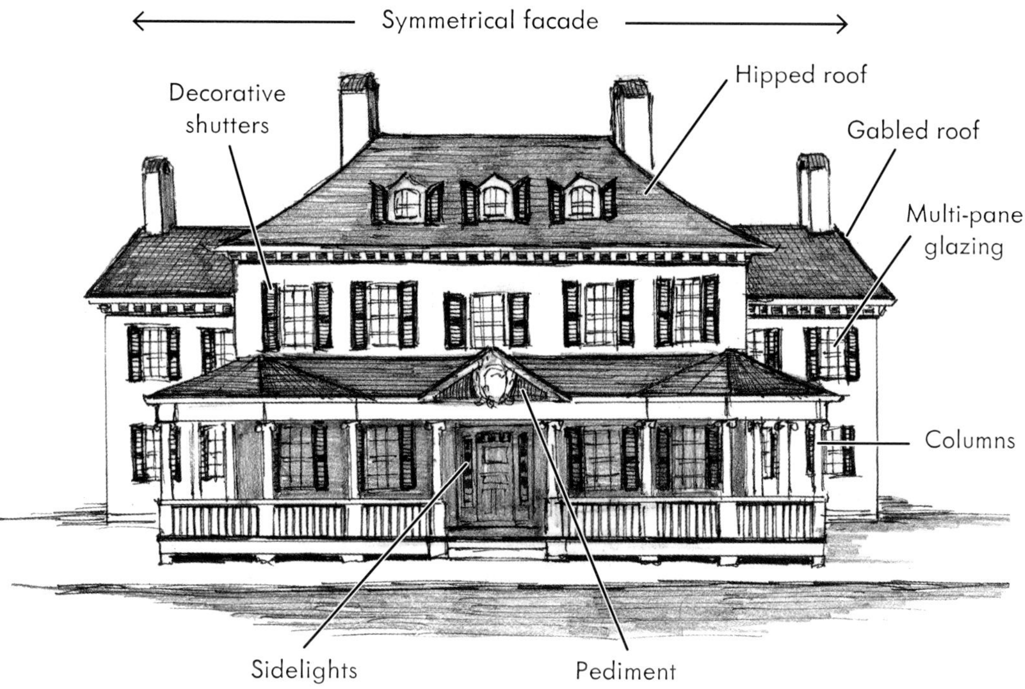

The New Jersey Building from the 1893 World's Fair helped inspire the revival of the Colonial style.

COMMON FEATURES

- Symmetrical facades, often with side porches
- Red brick or wood clapboard walls
- Accentuated entrances decorated with sidelights, transoms, columns, and pediments
- Either hipped or gabled roofs (usually side gables), often with dormers
- Windows usually have double-hung sashes and multi-pane glazing
- Decorative shutters

The Burly Greystone (and Brick Flats)

Greystones were constructed by the thousands from around the mid-1880s until about 1915, and they continued to be built in lesser quantities until around 1930. In fact, there are around thirty thousand greystones in the city—not as numerous as Chicago bungalows, but still an iconic Chicago building type that dominated before the bungalow was born. The greystone building boom began around the time of the Columbian Exposition, possibly because light-colored stone became popular with all the White City hoopla. Romanesque Revival greystones built before 1893 started morphing into Neoclassical and Beaux Arts expressions from the mid-1890s into the 1910s.

These meaty neighborhood staples are often found clustered along Chicago's boulevards and parks because many were built when these landscapes were first laid out in the late nineteenth century. You can find them all over the city, but there are large groups of them in Jackson and Washington Parks to the south, in Logan Square and Lincoln Park to the north, and Garfield Park and North Lawndale to the west. North Lawndale may have the largest concentration of greystones in the city, and it's especially worth checking out its K-Town Historic District.

Sub-Types

- Mansions
- Multi-flats and one-flats (sometimes called "shoebox" greystones)
- Rowhouses

Cladding Variations

- Sandstone, redstone, and brownstone-clad buildings
- Even more rare: Joliet limestone and early forms of cast concrete

Sub-Styles

While most were eclectic in style, borrowing elements based on the whim of the architect or builder became common in the later years of building. That said, there were some prominent details from Romanesque Revival, Queen Anne, Chateauesque, and Classical Revival styles in this era.

GREYSTONES

A delightful, pared-down greystone in Wicker Park.

COMMON FEATURES

- Front of building clad with grey limestone (or, rarely, sandstone)
- Flat roof
- Continuous limestone parapet with occasional pressed metal or faux mansard
- Occasional turrets topped with conical roofs
- Cornice made of limestone or pressed metal
- Raised basement
- Prominent front porch
- Off-center front door
- Generous front steps
- Brick along sides and rear
- For mansions—massive, hipped or pitched roofs covered in slate shingles

ROMANESQUE REVIVAL GREYSTONE

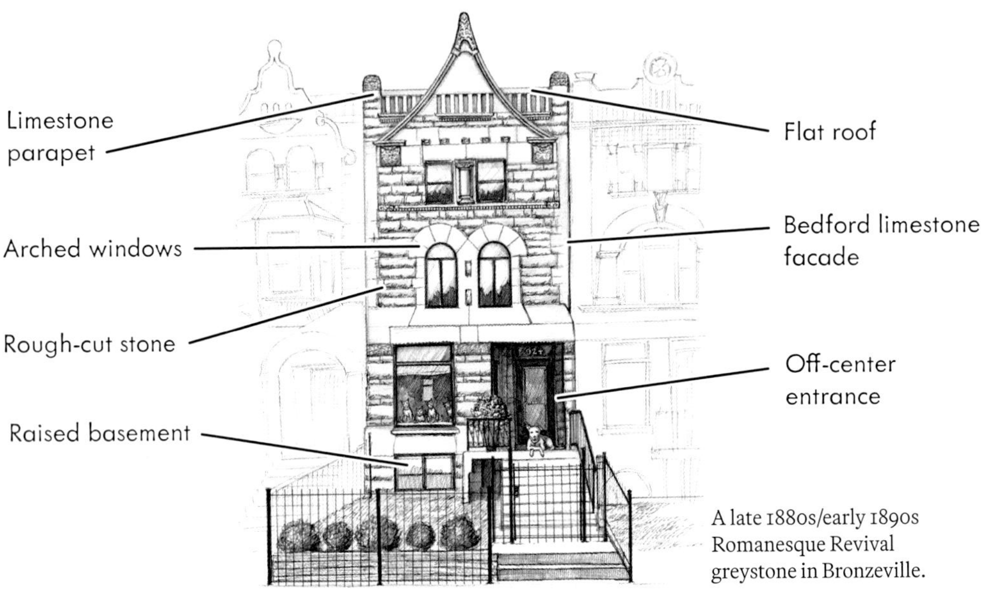

A late 1880s/early 1890s Romanesque Revival greystone in Bronzeville.

QUEEN ANNE GREYSTONE

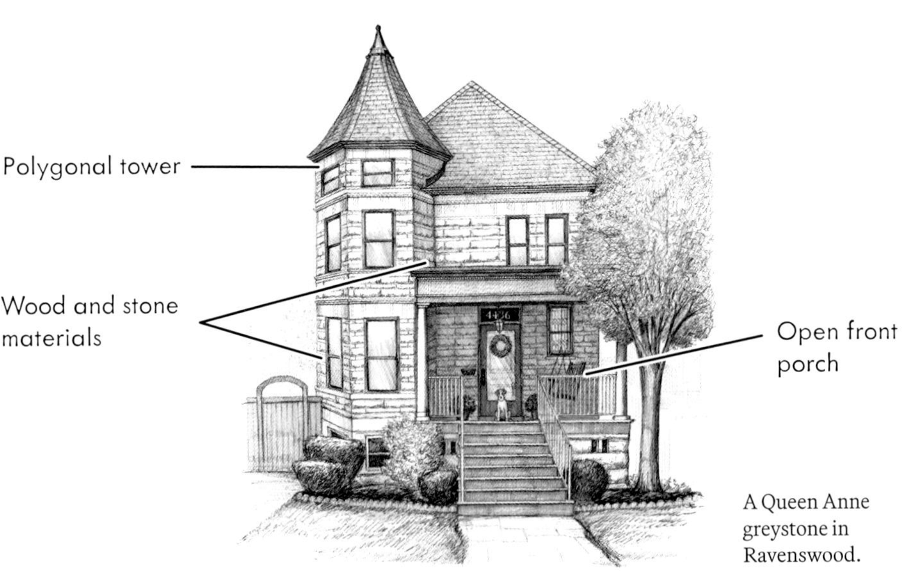

A Queen Anne greystone in Ravenswood.

CHATEAUESQUE GREYSTONE

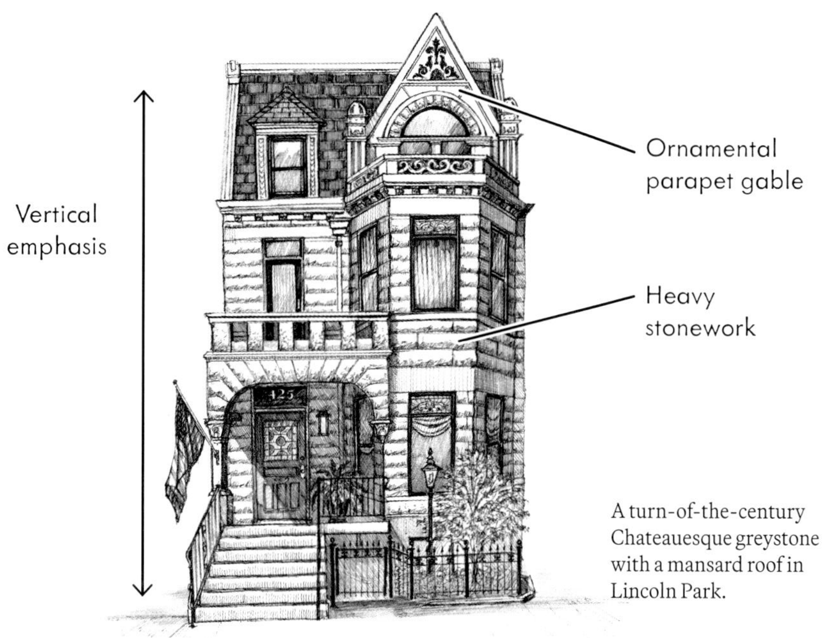

A turn-of-the-century Chateauesque greystone with a mansard roof in Lincoln Park.

CLASSICAL REVIVAL GREYSTONE

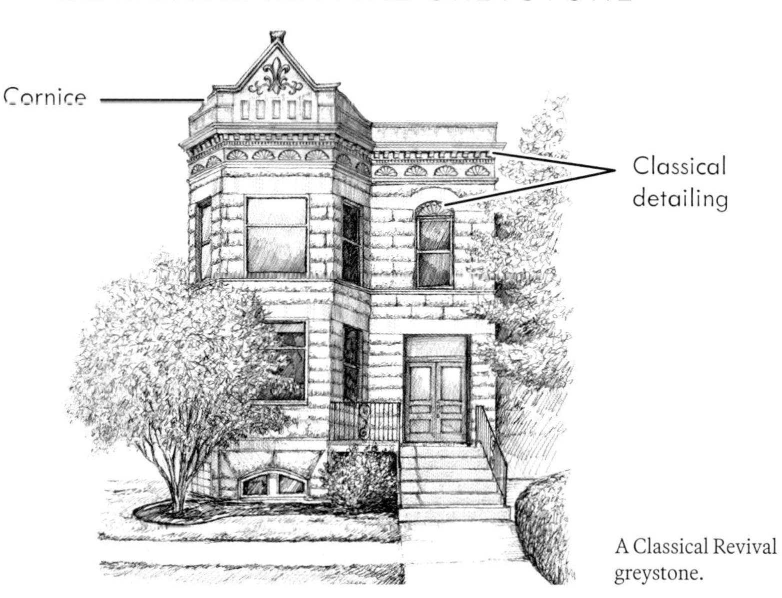

A Classical Revival greystone.

Greystones were a stepping stone for many working-class families as they inched their way up the economic ladder. Because so many greystones were stone-fronted two-flats, the idea was that a single owner would purchase the building, live in one unit and rent out the other to help pay down the mortgage. While they offered a path to stability for the working class—and even upward mobility—greystones could also be large single-family homes and vary from modest to imposing and elaborate. To read more on the two-flat form as a path to upward mobility and many other wonderful things about Chicago's flats buildings, see the "Brick Two-Flats and Variations on a Theme" section in Chapter 6.

What Makes a Greystone a Greystone?

The defining feature of the greystone is, unsurprisingly, its gray stone facade, which consists of either rock-faced or smooth-faced Bedford limestone. What this means is that the term "greystone" refers to a style of construction—it's a masonry building with a front facade made of Bedford limestone quarried from south central Indiana—rather than a singular architectural style. It can wear any style of clothes it likes as long as they're made of stone.

That said, for whatever reasons, Chicagoans also refer to less-common buildings with red, brown, and buff sandstone facades, along with a few rare granite and marble-clad facades, as greystones. These non-grey sandstone greystones (that clear?) were more common in the 1890s, usually expressing styles like Chateauesque, rather than the slightly later Neoclassical or Beaux Arts expressions of greystones. While these buildings are less common than the Bedford limestone greystones in Chicago, they share many of the same characteristics, as well as the same care and maintenance needs. These other-stoned "greystones" are typically found on the same blocks as their limestone-clad counterparts, like teenagers hanging out together and wearing the same outfits but in different colors, for subtle individuality.

Greystones are generally only clad with stone on the street-facing facade and have common brick on the other three sides—the exception being mansions that may have more than one street-facing facade because they're on an extra-large lot and more exposed, or situated on a corner lot. The stone is only a covering, not a structural element, and leaving the common brick exposed on the side and rear exterior walls saved builders a bundle of cash. And homeowners, too. This is why greystones were eclipsed by brick flats in the next century—a simple matter of cost.

The structure itself is designed with a raised basement with a stone or stone and brick foundation (later concrete), and stairs leading up to a prominent porch on the first floor. The main entrance is usually an off-center door and once you're inside, you'll find a vestibule with two doors on the interior—one opens up to a stairway leading to the second floor, and the other leads directly into the first-floor apartment. Inside these long, stacked apartments, you'll find living rooms in the front, bedrooms and sometimes a dining room in the center, and a kitchen in back. Having a replicable layout meant builders could quickly and efficiently build out spaces, which saved time and money. This general layout is standard for most flats buildings and is even replicated with Chicago bungalows, which are essentially just one floor of a two-flat in terms of their interior plan.

Greystones have flat roofs, usually with a continuous limestone parapet. Because this "style" is only based on what material is stuck to its facade, it can take any form. While the two-flat form is most common, you'll also find mansions, rowhouses, three-flats, six-flats, and one-flats (sometimes referred to as "shoebox greystones"). Like so many styles of architecture at the time, these look . . . heavy. One of the most common styles expressed on greystones in the 1890s was Romanesque Revival, with hunks of rusticated limestone, arches, and robust cornices that gave tiny fortress vibes.

While it's easy to zoom down a street packed with greystones and assume they all look the same, they are actually subtly differentiated so that every building owner can still describe their home in a way to set it apart from their neighbors: "Mine's the one with the fancy triangle at the top" or "Just look for the lion heads." Even with the differentiation, a street lined with greystones will give an imposing sense of cohesion and grandeur in a way that a block full of workers cottages or lower-density housing just won't be able to pull off.

Many greystones were demolished in the decades after World War II as factories closed and residents fled to the suburbs.[18] Urban renewal and blockbusting in the decades after likely encouraged more vacancies. Many South and West Side neighborhoods, which were the birthplaces of these iconic buildings, fell on hard times in the decades after, thanks to local disinvestment and racist housing practices. In 2006, North Lawndale residents launched the Historic Chicago Greystone Initiative to support greystone owners with resources like grants, financing, and workshops, eventually expanding to include all vintage homeowners as the Chicago Greystone & Vintage Home Program. The program ended in 2018 but the guides are easy to find online and continue to be a popular resource.

Bedford Limestone

A bit about the famous gray stone that covers tens of thousands of our buildings seems warranted. By the early 1870s, Chicago had at least six stone companies, some of which had been around as early as the 1850s. In the last two decades of the twentieth century, these companies merged into larger organizations like the Western Stone Company and the American Stone Company. Despite the large industry and employee roster, our local limestone wasn't ideal for building, and boy did we like to build with limestone. In the 1890s, these stone companies shifted their focus and began to crush the stone into aggregate for road paving as well as for lime production, which could be used as a binder for mortars and plasters. Chicago builders decided to switch to the more durable Bedford limestone, quarried about 250 miles south of Chicago in Bedford, Indiana.

According to a Bedford limestone walking tour brochure, this oolitic limestone—sedimentary rock made of tiny spherical grains cemented together by lime mud—was found near Bedford in the 1830s. The railroads of the 1850s turned these quarries into gold mines. Your greystone facades or windowsills keep some mighty fine company—they are made of the same stuff that was used in the Biltmore Estate, the Empire State Building, the Pentagon, and thirty-five of the fifty state capitol buildings.[19]

Bedford limestone is also what was used as detailing on countless other building types in Chicago. You'll see it in the form of windowsills, embedded decorative details, and stone slabs that top brick cheek walls—the walls that sit at either side of the front steps on many Chicago bungalows and brick flat buildings. If you want to know if that windowsill is made of Bedford limestone or concrete, get up close and personal with it and look for tiny pebbles embedded in the sill. If you see tiny pebbles (aggregate), you'll know it's concrete. If the surface appears pebble-free, it's limestone. ■

Workers Cottages: Just Keep On Working

Workers cottages continued to pop up like weeds (desirable weeds) around Chicago in the late nineteenth century. Housing booms were happening in other parts of the country as well, and our cottages were the equivalent of the small, affordable shotgun houses of the South, or the armies of rowhouses being built to create opportunities for new homeowners in Baltimore. Towards the end of the 1800s, workers cottages continued to feature a long, narrow rectangular footprint and a simple gable (peaked) roof. Most were one-and-a-half stories tall, with an attic or smaller upper floor. While there might have been decorative details added to the front facades and cornices to fit with the more elaborate styles of the 1880s and 1890s, they remained relatively simple in appearance, and often had raised basements and wooden stairs leading to an offset front door, balanced by two or three windows next to the door, and a centered attic window in the above half story.

Workers cottage two-flats in North Center and Lincoln Square.

Workers Cottage Two-Flats

A two-flat version of these was also popular at the end of the nineteenth century and into the twentieth century. One might just refer to them as a "gable-front two-flat," but many of them sure do look like two-story workers cottages, so they're worth mentioning here. These have the same roofline and details as a typical workers cottage, but are two-and-a-half stories tall and contain two separate units, likely with identical floorplans. Basically, they were just two cottages stacked on top of each other.

Typically, as with a single-family cottage, an offset front door would have grouped windows next to it. But with a two-flat, there are two doors next to each other (sometimes only one), and a set of grouped windows on the second floor, directly above the first. Above the front entrance is a single window. Sometimes the grouped windows are in a projecting bay on both floors, sometimes not, but the first and second floor match. In some cases a front staircase was added so there is a front door on both levels.

Brick cottages constructed at the end of the century often used pressed, patterned brick, limestone details, painted wood elements, and wrought- and cast-iron railings, as well as materials newly available in the late nineteenth century like architectural terra cotta and galvanized metal, which was used for cornices. Chicagoans still had an appreciation for highly decorative, well-built houses, even at a modest scale, and that can be seen even in workers cottages. Queen Anne details on cottages were typical in the 1890s, and these homes were only pared down to more straightforward Craftsman style details after 1900.

Machines for manufacturing brick had been used for decades at this point, and one could order a variety of brick types ranging from common brick to a more defined, finely textured, and uniformly colored pressed brick for the street-facing facade. In the late nineteenth century, pressed brick was manufactured around the country, but St. Louis, Chicago, Philadelphia, and Kansas City were the big suppliers. Brick type was sometimes specified using the name of the place of manufacture with a number following it; the number indicated how dark the brick color was, and the larger the number, the darker the brick. For example, the Schnitzius Cottage at 1925 North Fremont Street used a deep red "St. Louis 7" pressed brick, and you should probably take a stroll past that particularly charming early 1890s cottage to get a sense of the color scale, as well as a sense of just how adorable these cottages could get.

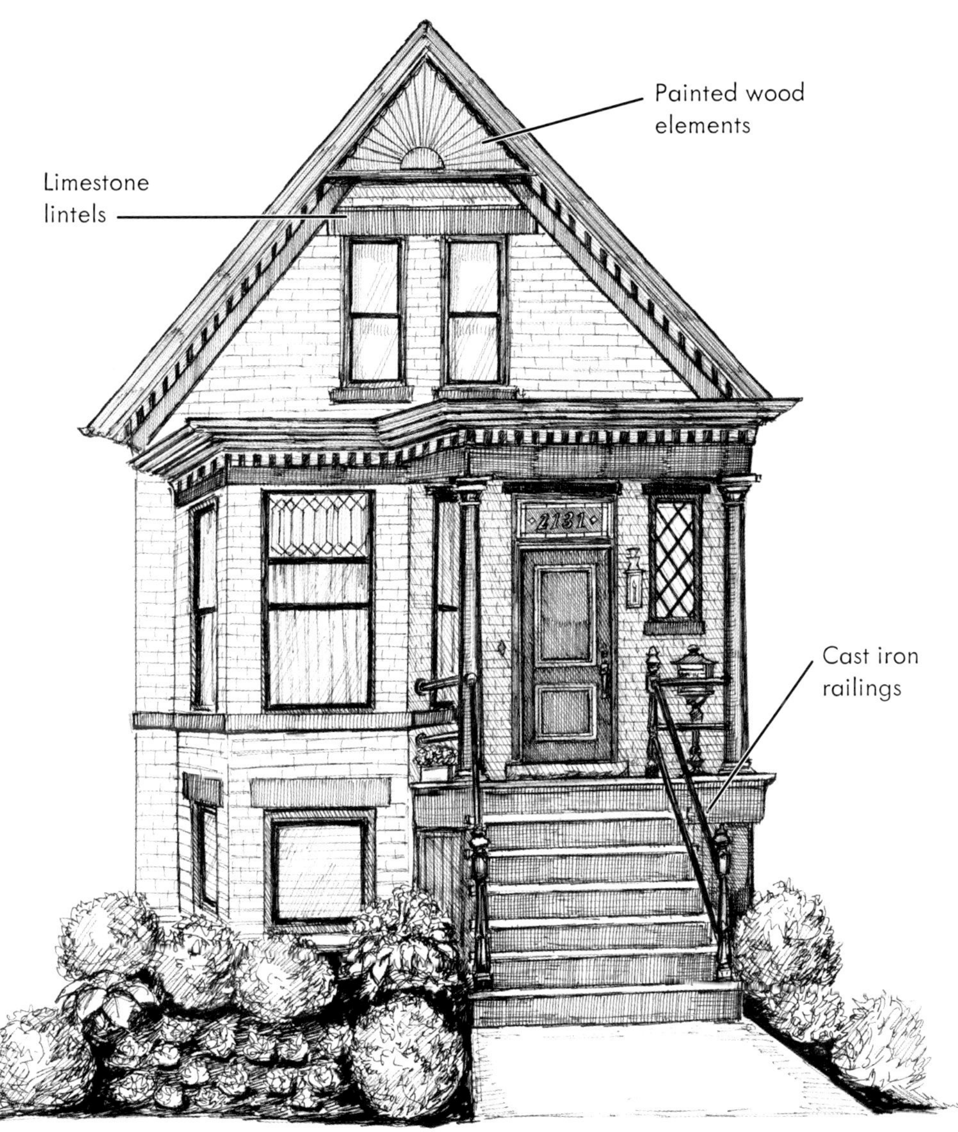

An 1890s brick cottage in Ukrainian Village showing off some decorative detailing.

Working-Class Domestic Life

Today, we sometimes use "working class" and "middle class" interchangeably. This may be because nowadays, trade work tends to pay well overall and can't be outsourced, so the economic realities are sometimes similar or even inverted between "blue-collar" and "white-collar" jobs. See, for example, the young adult with a master's degree who can't afford rent versus a plumber of the same age who owns a single-family home and has more work than they can shake a pipe at. Regardless, the line between "working" and "middle" was considerably clearer in the late nineteenth century.

Some historians divide the late nineteenth century and early twentieth century into a before-and-after story for the working class. The Gilded Age of the late nineteenth century was the pits, full of countless social and economic issues caused by urbanization, immigration, and industrialization. The Progressive Era of the early twentieth century came along and tackled these issues through reforms and legislation, getting rid of horrific living and working conditions and creating paths towards homeownership (for white native and European-born Chicagoans) and improved labor laws and age reforms to broaden opportunities for younger generations. The division between eras is an oversimplification, of course, as many of these problems dragged into the twentieth century, but at least there was hope on the horizon in the new century and increased awareness. People were mobilizing around inequities that had long been ignored.

Amenities & Layouts

So, what did the conditions of a working-class home look like before 1900? Well, let's say there was definitely an economy of rooms. Whether you lived in the city or the country, your house usually contained two major rooms: a kitchen and a room for work and sleep. Sometimes there were one or two additional, smaller rooms for added storage or sleeping.

The Vernacular Architecture Forum published an article called "Examining the American Dream: Housing Standards and the Emergence of a National Housing Culture, 1900–1930" that described in great detail the home lives of workers at the end of the twentieth century. Housing amenities typically consisted of a stove to heat both your home and your food, a cold-water sink, oil lamps or candles, and an outhouse. Rooms had multiple functions and were also used to "work remotely" for added income. You might find a woman hemming pants for pay in a kitchen that also has a bed in it. Beds might also be

According to U.S. census data, it was not unheard of for a 1,200–1,400 square foot home in the first decades of the twentieth century to house over a dozen people, along with a boarder to help pay the mortgage.

used by different people at different times of day, when day shifts and night shifts came into play.

Families took in boarders for extra income, because why not find a fourth use for that room? While many of these spatial realities would change for the better in coming decades, census data from the first couple of decades of the twentieth century also shows that on occasion, recent immigrant families (especially large Irish-Catholic families) were living with fourteen family members and a boarder crammed into a 1,200-square-foot bungalow. This would have been a nightmarish time for a working-class introvert.

The changes in working class homes in following decades were significant and can be seen in the following rooms and amenities:

Bathrooms with three fixtures. Bathrooms with a bathtub, toilet, and sink solved countless issues related to disease and privacy. For most of the working class, bathroom fixtures were rare until after 1900. Outhouses, public toilets, and public bathhouses were the norm and had remained largely unchanged since the medieval period.

The dining room. Working-class families would have seen dining rooms as luxurious, given that they were used to eating and sometimes even sleeping and bathing in their kitchens. A whole room just for eating? Of course, economic realities and thrifty mindsets meant that the additional room could also be used for non-dining functions like added workspace or beds. In wealthier homes of the era, the separation of activities reflected Victorian ideas about privacy and property. Pocket doors, for example, were an elegant way to close off rooms to hide domestic activities without large, clunky doors swinging between interior spaces.[20] Interestingly, in some ways today we live more like the working classes, regardless of income, often eating in our kitchens or opting for open kitchen/dining floor plans where food preparation can be easily witnessed by guests.

Public amenities. Most of the writing about technological improvements centers on the middle class. Electric refrigerators and vacuums came much later to the working classes, sometimes decades later, but there were some victories. Before 1900, the only public utility that may have been typical in working class houses was cold running water. The addition of a sink with plumbed or pumped water would have made life incalculably more bearable, especially for women. Other public amenities like sewage, electricity, gas hook-ups, and garbage collection were front of mind for Progressive Era reformers who made huge headway in the early 1900s. In the near future, thousands of working-class families moved into electrified, single-family homes during the boom of 1910s bungalow neighborhoods.

The private bedroom. It goes without saying that a private bedroom would have been a game changer. An amorous couple with children might slip away into a small room, if that was an option, for a brief expression of affection, but a separate room for parents or other family members was a rarity in immigrant and working-class homes before 1900. Best not to think too hard on that.

Closets. For many Chicagoans, it's easy to gripe about how small or impractical the closets are in many of our apartments. Granted, building owners sometimes converted shallow Murphy bed alcoves into "closets" that are good for little more than an ironing board and a frozen pizza turned on its side, but that's another matter. The reality is that closets didn't even exist in workers' homes until after the turn of the last century. While people in the 1890s had a fraction of the clothing and items we have nowadays, a built-in, enclosed storage space would have been a huge luxury, hiding personal items and keeping out the smells of food and the airborne coal soot that swirled around, landing on fabrics (and in lungs).

The front porch. An open porch was another amenity gained only after the 1890s for the working class. While single-family Queen Anne homes had luxurious porches stretching across the entire primary facade, sometimes wrapping around the side of the home, flats and workers cottages might have had some front steps at best. The porch was seen as a place of leisure and an outdoor extension of living space that must have been a godsend for someone cramped into two-to-four rooms with family, day and night. Interestingly, outdoor front porches fell out of favor in the 1920s when new construction opted to enclose such rooms into bays for added interior living space. This may also have been due to housing reforms that required improved indoor living conditions and better wages for workers. Less precarious livelihoods made an escape room (porch) less attractive than added interior space. Additionally, fire codes that required back porches as a second means of egress in the early 1900s meant that one could still avoid Uncle Giulio's fiery monologues after he'd come home late from another union meeting. ■

An open front porch on an early 1900s workers cottage in Avondale.

Prairie Style: Low-Slung but Lofty

Unlike most of the styles in this book that gallivant from building form to building form, Prairie style architecture is primarily concerned with single-family homes. The style is defined by its horizontal form, and Prairie houses tend to be long and low-slung. Frank Lloyd Wright, who is most associated with the style, described it as "married to the ground," and its crawling orientation can make even tight lots look deceptively spacious. Unlike most buildings, where the layout is determined by the structure's footprint (the exterior border of the house), Prairie style houses are designed from the inside out, and spread across the lot like a cowboy lying back and chewing on a piece of hay at lunchtime. Significant examples can be found in Edgewater, Hyde Park, Beverly, and, most notably, Oak Park.

Prairie homes are uniquely American because they literally respond to America. Instead of looking to display classical ideals of beauty or giant columns of power, these homes are directly inspired by the low landscapes of the Midwest. Given the inspiration, it also stands to reason that they're built with materials rooted in the natural world. Pine, oak, limestone, stucco, and brick were the primary culprits, and to stretch the house even a little longer, visually at least, sometimes even the brick units were elongated. The interior woodwork was often stained and waxed to reveal the grain of the wood, and exterior wood elements were often un-planed and stained, instead of painted, as a nod to the natural surroundings.

While Prairie style is most associated with Wright, the style was directly inspired by the philosophies of Louis Sullivan, who put the crazy idea into architects' heads that nature should inspire the built environment. In addition to Wright, Sullivan's apprentices included George Grant Elmslie, William Purcell, Parker Berry, William E. Drummond, and William L. Steele. Others, like Barry Burne, apprenticed under these architects. Architect George W. Maher, who worked with Joseph Lyman Silsbee, Elmslie, and Wright, opened up his own practice in 1893 and designed Oak Park's Pleasant Home mansion four years later, one of the most well-known Prairie homes of this decade.

There was still an intense desire to find a unique American architectural style at this time, not only because the challenge was irresistible, but because these were the years directly after the Chicago World's Fair when Daniel Burnham had, in some minds, squandered his opportunity to do something contextual and innovative. If you can't look to other buildings for inspiration, perhaps look to the unbuilt environment? The Prairie School by definition centered on open, asymmetrical floor plans and connected indoor

PRAIRIE STYLE

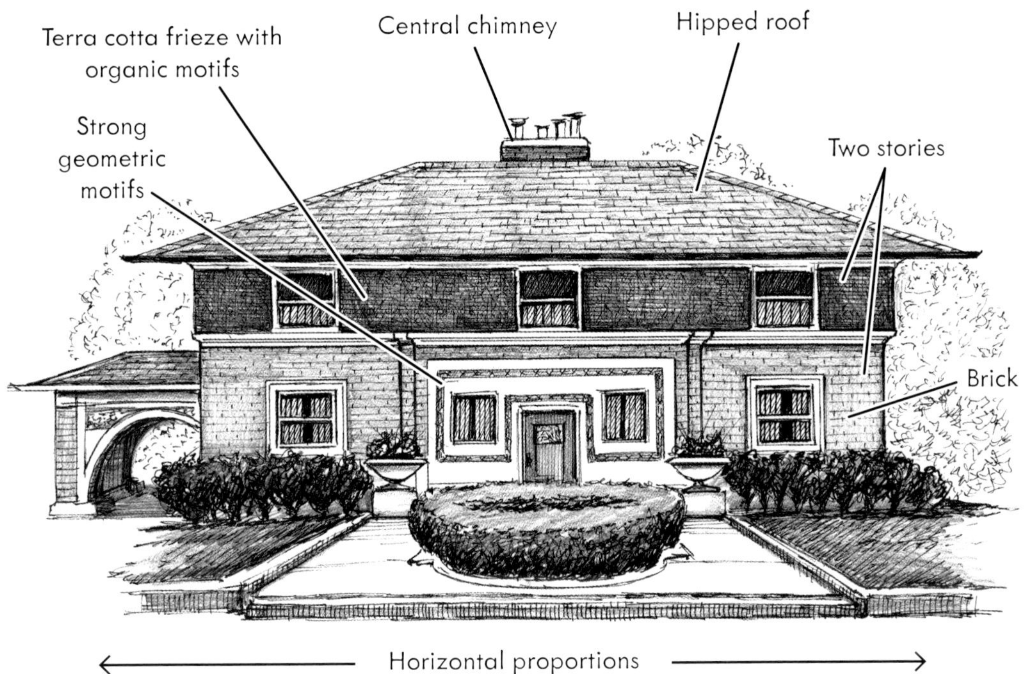

Winslow House (1894–95), 515 Auvergne Place, River Forest, IL. This was Frank Lloyd Wright's first major commission as a solo architect. He later described it as "the first prairie house."[21]

COMMON FEATURES

- Brick or stucco exteriors
- Horizontal proportions
- Strong geometry and massing
- Hipped or gable roofs with wide, overhanging eaves
- Two stories
- Brick or stucco exteriors
- Stained-glass windows with abstract, geometric ornament
- Large square porch supports
- Large central chimneys
- Restrained use of applied ornamentation (not fussy)

and outdoor spaces where nature and the built environment blurred. Wright opened up his architectural practice in the sleepy Western suburb of Oak Park in 1893, the same year as Burnham's Beaux Arts bonanza.

While intensely inspired by the landscape, Prairie architecture wasn't *only* about nature. It was perhaps a bit loftier. In addition to looking to the environment for inspiration, Wright and other architects developed the style as "a modern architecture for a democratic American society." Prairie architecture spoke to Chicagoans at a time when anti-industrialist sentiments were high. In fact, another important contributor to the movement was Jane Addams. Addams's Hull House, a settlement house that offered social services to the community, was the site where the Chicago Arts and Crafts Society was founded in 1897. Many architects, including Wright and other early Prairie Schoolers, were charter members. It was also at Hull House that Wright read his manifesto titled "The Art and Craft of the Machine," his justification for turning away from Morris's more purist version of Arts and Crafts, which insisted on a literal hands-on approach to everything.

Although they were pro-machine, these architects valued quality craftsmanship and paid attention to details—right down to something like the length of brick. Roman brick, used on buildings like the Robie House (built 1909) in Chicago's South Side neighborhood of Hyde Park, was much thinner and longer than the standard brick we are used to seeing. The brick was called "Pennsylvania Iron Spot Roman brick,"[22] and Wright traveled to another great Midwestern city—St. Louis—to retrieve it. The homes weren't ornate like the Victorian homes of the era, but the devil was in the details. Architects like George W. Maher would often take a motif or plant form and bring it through everything from the plaster to the art glass to the furniture.

Prairie style was relatively short-lived, but it made its mark. The style managed to spread across the Midwest and ultimately around the world, especially in north-central Europe and Australia. Still, we're the luckiest. Because it was largely developed in the Chicago area, we have some of the most extraordinary examples of Prairie style homes in Chicago and our surrounding suburbs. Go to Chapter 6 for more on the style during its heyday in the early 1900s.

"Had I been taller, all my buildings probably would have been proportionally higher."

—5'8" architect Frank Lloyd Wright

5132 S. Woodlawn Ave., Isidore H. Heller House (built 1896). Architect: Frank Lloyd Wright.

American Foursquares: Roomy & Accessible

In the 1890s, we were introduced to the first American Foursquares, though they still dressed up in styles that had peaked a decade before. In a handful of years, they'd be wrestled from their petticoats, thanks to the Prairie School and the popularization of the Columbian Exposition's stoic Classicism.

These homes are cube-shaped with roughly equal rooms, typically four on each floor, though occasionally two of the rooms would be combined. A dormer window usually poked through the center of the front roof face, and there was often a large front porch that spanned the entire front of the house. This is a house for porch swings and checkers games on wicker tables.

These 1890s Foursquare homes are really hamming up the Victorian-era details. The one above has an unusual second-story window layout with a central bay flanked by two oculus windows. The Foursquare on the facing page is showing off some spindlework, classical columns, a central dormer on the roof, and even some Beaux Arts detailing.

AMERICAN FOURSQUARES

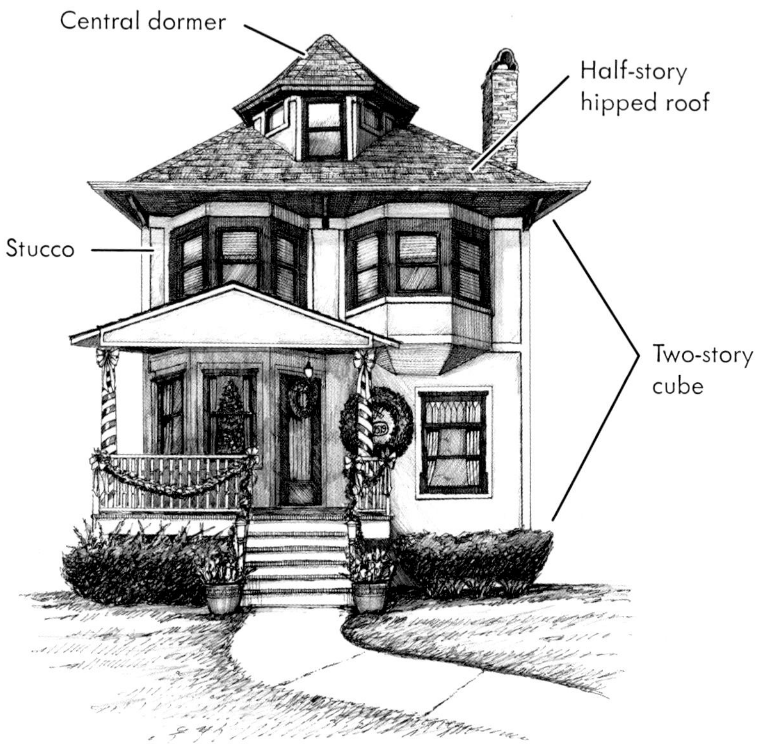

This 1897 Foursquare in Rogers Park shows a mix of Classical Revival and Queen Anne characteristics. Later Foursquares will simplify and have a "flatter" appearance all around, like their Prairie style relatives.

COMMON FEATURES

- A simple two-story cube shape
- Hipped roof with a central front dormer
- Wide one-story front porch
- Built with a wide variety of materials, including wood, brick, and stucco, but most often brick locally
- Symmetrical facade
- Two-and-a-half stories
- Simple square or rectangular plan
- Low-pitched hipped roof
- Usually a central front dormer
- Broad front porch, sometimes enclosed
- Little use of ornament

Sub-Styles

- Queen Anne
- Classical Revival
- Colonial Revival

Because Foursquares weren't common in Chicago until after 1900, there is more information on the style in the next two chapters. It's important to note, however, that these were some of the first single-family homes that were roomy and relatively affordable to the middle class while featuring both electricity and a standard bathroom with sink, toilet, and bath. These luxuries and new technologies hadn't been around long, and this was a turning point where they were accessible to everyday folks.

The Foursquare made it to Chicago through the magic of pattern books, architectural journals, and department store catalogs, according to Chicago historian and former Chicago Park District planning guru, Julia Bachrach, who also happens to live in a Foursquare. Catalogs, like *Lambert's Suburban Architecture,* published in New York in 1894 to show off new suburban homes, introduced the style around the country, and certainly to Chicago. There wasn't a name for the style yet, so it would just be referred to as something like "a design of the popular square type." Lambert himself described this new kind of house as a "straightforward" variation of the Colonial style, with "good square spacious rooms and a large attic."[23]

Tudor Revival: Mixed-Up Medieval

These rustic-yet-whimsical homes with their decorative wood accents, gigantic chimneys, and steeply gabled rooflines have folks longing for the Renaissance Faire year-round. And, like the Renaissance Faire, these homes are not attempting to be historically accurate—they are more like, "Hey, you can wear 'peasant' sandals, a leather vest, elf ears, and carry a bird of prey on your shoulder and be right at home here!" While wildly charming, the details take numerous liberties and are a hodgepodge of medieval English styles that once existed, as well as some stylings that only existed in the villages of fairy tales.

While the style doesn't really take off until the 1910s and '20s, there are some examples in Douglas, Beverly, Kenwood, and Uptown from this period. Tudor Revival homes in the U.S. spanned the 1890s through 1930s and are named after the Tudor Dynasty (1485–1603)—a period of time in England when the country was shifting from church-inspired Gothic architecture to medieval and Renaissance-inspired architecture. This shift took the heaven-stretched spires and flying buttresses off of buildings and grounded them into more modest, human-scale structures. Materials like exposed timbers and plaster and thatch roofing were accessible, down-to-earth, and charming yet casual.

The Tudor Revival style was generally more popular as a suburban housing type throughout the country, but its ornamentation can be stuck onto any building type. If there is half-timbering on a skyscraper, it would be identified as Tudor Revival style.

The American version of the style was often eclectic, though some pared-down versions began to appear in the 1890s, like these rowhouses. While lacking all the Victorian doodads and whimsy, the basic characteristics of steeply pitched rooflines and decorative stone quoins are unmistakably Tudor Revival.

Late nineteenth-century Tudor Revival rowhouses in Bronzeville.

TUDOR REVIVAL

This 1893 Tudor Revival has rich textures, curves, long flat planes, a mix of earthy colors (reds, whites, browns), a broad porch, and ample stonework that blends the Queen Anne form with Tudor stylings to create an almost psychedelic effect.

COMMON FEATURES

- Steeply pitched roof
- Various gable configurations
- Tall, narrow windows ranging from double-hung, casement with decorative glazing, dormer, oriel, and bay windows
- Multiple panes of glass in each window (multi-pane glazing)
- Multiple types of exterior wall cladding on the same house
- Large chimney
- Stucco wall cladding, with and without decorative half-timbering
- Brick and stone cladding, with and without half-timbering
- Brick or stone first story with stucco upper story and/or gable with half-timbering
- Stone first story with brick upper story and (false) gable

Coach Houses

Oh, coach house, you are the location of so many disastrous Hollywood movie affairs. These obsolete buildings definitely do not belong in urban environments as we understand them today, and so we city dwellers can't help but be enamored by these out-of-place structures.

As you might guess, the coach house was where the horses and carriages were kept, as well as any additional equipment. These buildings, which often look like smaller, reconfigured versions of the house they belong to, were the precursor to the garage, though not nearly as numerous for a couple of reasons. First, there simply weren't as many houses during this era as there were in the 1910s when automobile garages began popping up and lining alleys across the city. Second, they were often used for horses and not everyone had their own horses—most people actually used public transportation to commute in the late nineteenth and early twentieth centuries. Even if a homeowner did have a horse, they may not have had the means to build a coach house and would have instead put the horse up at a nearby stable.

Larger, more ornate coach houses might have also had a milk cow or living spaces for a groom or coachman. Fancy ones like the one behind the Charles Gates Dawes house in Evanston (built 1894–95, with the coach house built a year earlier) had their own architect. The mansions of Prairie Avenue, built in the 1870s and 1880s, certainly had coach houses for the elite of Chicago. You can certainly find less elaborate versions in many communities, perhaps most commonly in areas like Lincoln Park, Lake View, Hyde Park, Kenwood, and Wicker Park.

Once the automobile entered the scene, some coach houses were converted into garages. Wealthier homeowners may have converted an upstairs coachman dwelling into a room for the chauffeur. Others were converted into offices or additional living spaces we now call accessory dwelling units (ADUs). We would guess there's a coach house dojo or two out there as well.

Some coach houses were never meant for horses but were instead built at the outset as an additional living space, either for extra income or, in some cases, as the original house until more money was cobbled together to build the main house in the front of the lot. A particularly delightful version of this is the "garalow," a 1920s phenomenon that consisted of building a tiny version of a Chicago bungalow, the size of a two-car garage, on the rear of the lot.[24] The garalow was designed to easily convert into a garage once the main bungalow was built on the front portion of the lot. In still other cases, early cottages, which averaged five hundred square feet in size, were constructed without permanent foundations so they could be moved to the rear of the lot once the homeowner could afford to build a larger house.

A late 1880s "coach house" in Lincoln Park. Originally, this was the main house on the lot, but it was then moved to the back of the lot when funds were available to build a greystone three-flat.

Often, additional family members remained in the rear cottage and used it like an in-law suite.

But there is one coach house conversion that rises to the top of the list in this city: the coach house turned convent. The "Cardinal's Mansion," owned by the Catholic Archdiocese and built in 1885 at State Parkway and North Avenue, converted its 5,800-square-foot coach house to lodge nuns.[25] If you go check out this mansion—and you certainly should—definitely stop and look at the alleyway directly behind it between State and Astor Streets. You'll find one of the three remaining wood-paved alleys in Chicago. ■

CHAPTER

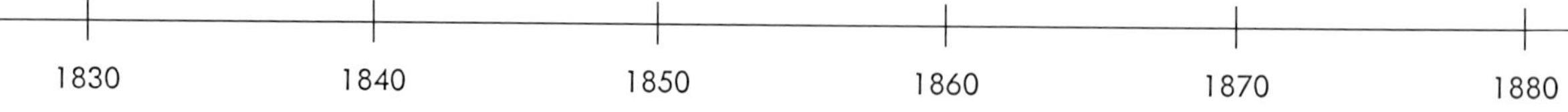

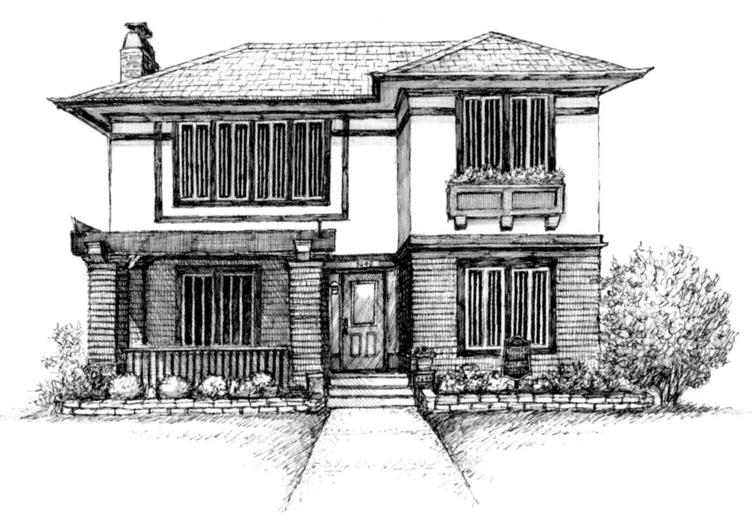

New Century, New Chicago

1900–1917

"I give you Chicago. It is not London and Harvard. It is not Paris and buttermilk. It is American in every chitling and sparerib. It is alive from snout to tail."

—H. L. Mencken

On January 1, 1900, the century opened in Chicago with a literal bang. Workers blasted the last of the earth separating the Chicago River from the canal, reversing the flow of the Chicago River and sending the sewage created by more than 1.5 million people, in addition to the filth of the stockyards, violently downstream. It was somebody else's problem now. As had often been the case in this city, the work of destruction in the name of progress was done in the dead of night before a lawsuit could be filed to prevent it.

While there was plenty of opposition to what was, admittedly, an engineering marvel, the truth was that the city had a major sewage problem and a population that was both proliferating like buckthorn and dying in droves. The Chicago River, once teeming with life, had become the city's gutter. Even worse, that gutter flowed into Lake Michigan, where Chicagoans got their drinking water. Lacking a better plan, Chicagoans sent their waterborne illnesses merrily downstream in an effort to save their own hides.

Chicago at the turn of the century was rapidly transforming its technologies, industries, and demographics. It was a city of dichotomies. There were wide expanses of countryside beside dark, crowded tenements. Shiny new skyscrapers went up near hastily constructed shacks. Great mansions of the Gilded Age peacocked just a few blocks from a massive, open red-light district containing hundreds of brothels. A strong temperance movement with dry districts bumped up against areas like the Stock Yards and its 500 saloons. In all, there were close to 6,400 saloons along 31 miles of street frontage in Chicago. This is what happens in the absence of liquor licenses.

It was the twilight of the Victorian era. Queen Victoria herself died in 1901 and although the zeitgeist of her era lingered, it quickly succumbed to competing influences. This was reflected in shifting cultural preferences and dramatic changes to the built environment. In the first decades of this era we see the paring down of buildings with simple, well-crafted homes and detailing. The frilly ornamentation, historicism, and eclectic nature of the Victorian-era buildings were tone deaf and out of fashion. Architects like Frank Lloyd Wright pushed for an "organic architecture" that naturally erupted from its surroundings. The flattened and geometric patterns, both in terms of a building's form and style, streamlined production and emphasized an economy of construction.

Companies like Montgomery Ward, Sears Roebuck, Aladdin, and Lewis Homes offered complete housing kits with pre-cut materials packed onto trains and dropped at the site of one's choosing. The catalogs advertising these homes were last century's equivalent to online shopping. They promoted new architectural styles, like Chicago bungalows, far and wide, sometimes building up entire neighborhoods. At the same time, Chicagoans renumbered their homes and renamed their streets between 1909 and 1911, erasing the confused and inconsistent mapping of the previous century. Amid the relentless change and chaos that successfully expanded this city, there were at least some attempts to create order.

The first decade of the twentieth century brought unprecedented immigration, and ramped up its public transportation to shuttle workers across an ever-expanding city. Traffic on the elevated lines increased by 258 percent between 1898 and 1918, and the areas being developed were generally located along new train lines. New buildings were sprouting up at the end of the Northwestern elevated line near Wilson Avenue, southeast of 63rd and Cottage Grove Avenue, along the Metropolitan elevated line between Cicero and Crawford Avenues, and from Madison to Harrison Streets. Neighborhoods such as Kenwood, Englewood, the stretch of Milwaukee Avenue between Chicago and North Avenue, and the areas east of Humboldt Park also continued to grow.

By 1910, about a third of Chicago's population was foreign-born. Italian, Polish, and Russian Jewish immigrants were moving into the old residential areas while the older Irish and German immigrants were movin' on up, selling their properties to more recent newcomers and relocating to the areas along new elevated train lines. Industries were also pushing into old residential areas. Black residents were confined to the narrow belt of land bounded by 26th and 39th Streets, State and LaSalle Streets, and were forced to pay high rents for rundown housing. Also lacking alternatives, Chinese and Jewish populations were ghettoized and charged bloated rents for substandard dwellings along South Clark Street and portions of the West Side, respectively.

During this same period, Robert S. Abbott founded the *Chicago Defender*, which became the country's most influential Black weekly newspaper, with two-thirds of its readership located outside of Chicago. Pullman porters—African American men hired by the Pullman Company to maintain sleeping cars and tend to the needs of rail passengers—helped spread the paper along their routes in the Southern states, and it became a major contributor to the next wave of migration to Chicago. A long-term movement of African Americans from the South to the urban North—known as the Great Migration—transformed Chicago between 1916 and 1970. While reforms were beginning to reshape working and housing conditions for many European immigrants, African Americans endured even worse conditions than the Europeans had faced.

In the 1890s, Chicago's borders had continued to expand into a crescent shape around the old city, gobbling up existing settlements of wood-frame workers cottages that were intentionally built outside the city to avoid its fire codes. Beyond the ring of new growth were detached settlements that varied in size from tiny villages to city-like developments of fifty thousand people. South Chicago was the largest of these areas, with its iron and steel industry along the Calumet River. In a 1902 report on small parks created by the South Park Commission, South Chicago was described as "hemmed in by stretches of railroad tracks and ugly buildings" and "where scores of towering smoke stacks and furnaces put out smoke and dust day and night."

High-class residences for the most part ceased to be built during the first decade of the twentieth century due to plummeting housing values. Mansions that were purchased for $100,000 and $300,000 were sold for $33,500 and $65,500 in 1908. Fancy homes were being left for apartments and a person could rent an entire mansion for $200 a month.[1]

Meanwhile, others were putting down roots north and west of city limits in areas like Oak Park, LaGrange, Evanston, Wilmette, Winnetka, and Lake Forest. Wide stretches of vacant land within the city limits separated these newly settled areas from the smog and grime of industry and poor living conditions. The nature of rapid, unplanned growth had made movement through the city a dirty and chaotic hassle. Chicago was in dire need of a better circulation plan and lacked parks, playgrounds, schools, and adequate sanitation. In 1906 the Merchants Club commissioned architect Daniel Burnham to draw up a comprehensive plan for the city that would address these issues and more. Make no small plans, indeed.

City officials had lax attitudes about housing, thanks to the relentless influx of new labor coming in and the city's preoccupation with matters of larger infrastructure. Unsurprisingly, this led to catastrophes like the Iroquois Theater fire, which trapped thousands of attendees in a blazing inferno in 1903. This single fire led to the death of six hundred people and, thankfully, also led to desperately needed updates to building and fire codes.

These new codes and methods of enforcement were the kinds of improvements that social reformers like Jane Addams were pushing for to improve the overcrowded and unsanitary conditions of tenement housing. The city was finally being forced to pay attention to the floods of struggling European immigrants, if not the Black migrants, who turned the gears and stoked the engines of its progress.

Adapting the Workers Cottage

Since the 1830s, workers cottages had been put up as cheap, easy-to-construct homes for hardworking immigrants and subsequent generations, and they'd followed all the stylistic fads. This period ushered in the Craftsman style—a philosophy and style that emphasized handcrafted materials and simple, functional design—and it brought new elements to cottages like front porches with columns and railings, arched window openings, and decorative limestone or brickwork panels above or below the windows. Some workers cottages were also stretched a little wider, in contrast to the sometimes intensely vertical orientation of earlier cottages.

A simple, wood-frame workers cottage from the early 1900s.

In theory, workers cottages from the first two decades of this century would have been built with brick, limestone, and terra cotta. However, when you pull the original building permits or look at the old fire insurance maps, you discover that frame homes were definitely still being built in Chicago well after fire codes supposedly forbade this practice. There are myriad reasons for this, and certainly some were political. So, while brick construction was booming, you'd still find plenty of frame cottages (and other frame buildings) built during this time.

In addition to any stylistic shifts at the time, these homes were also raised up, pushed out, built on top of, clad in asbestos, cemented with artificial stone, plumbed, electrified, moved, and, finally, eclipsed by bungalows in the 1910s as the go-to home for the working class. Even now, more than a century after the last cottages were constructed, they continue to be monkeyed with and lived in by working-class Chicagoans.

Housing Realities for the Working Class

From the beginning, these cottages were constructed to be affordable, often to first-time homeowners. But the path to upward mobility was not smooth, and developers often took advantage of recent immigrants and those working hard to avoid tenement housing. In Upton Sinclair's 1906 novel *The Jungle*, the Rudkus family struggled to keep up with the monthly payments on their "new" cottage. They are informed by an indelicate neighbor that their home is indeed *not* new but part of a typical scam to trick poor first-time homeowners into impossible terms that will eventually leave them on the street, without equity and without recourse. These high-interest, unprotected lending practices were similar to the housing practices that, during the 1950s and 1960s, deprived Black families in Chicago from acquiring billions of dollars in generational wealth.

If, like the Rudkuses' neighbor, you were able to pull off homeownership in the early years of the twentieth century through red-hot spite and an unwed son's wages, it meant a hard-won bit of stability at a time when working-class jobs provided little economic security. It was common to take in boarders to help with mortgage payments by cramming another struggling soul into the small footprint. Or, if things were looking up, by investing in a rear addition. Some two- and three-flat buildings actually began as small workers cottages that were raised up and turned into a multi-unit property by adding an apartment underneath the original structure.

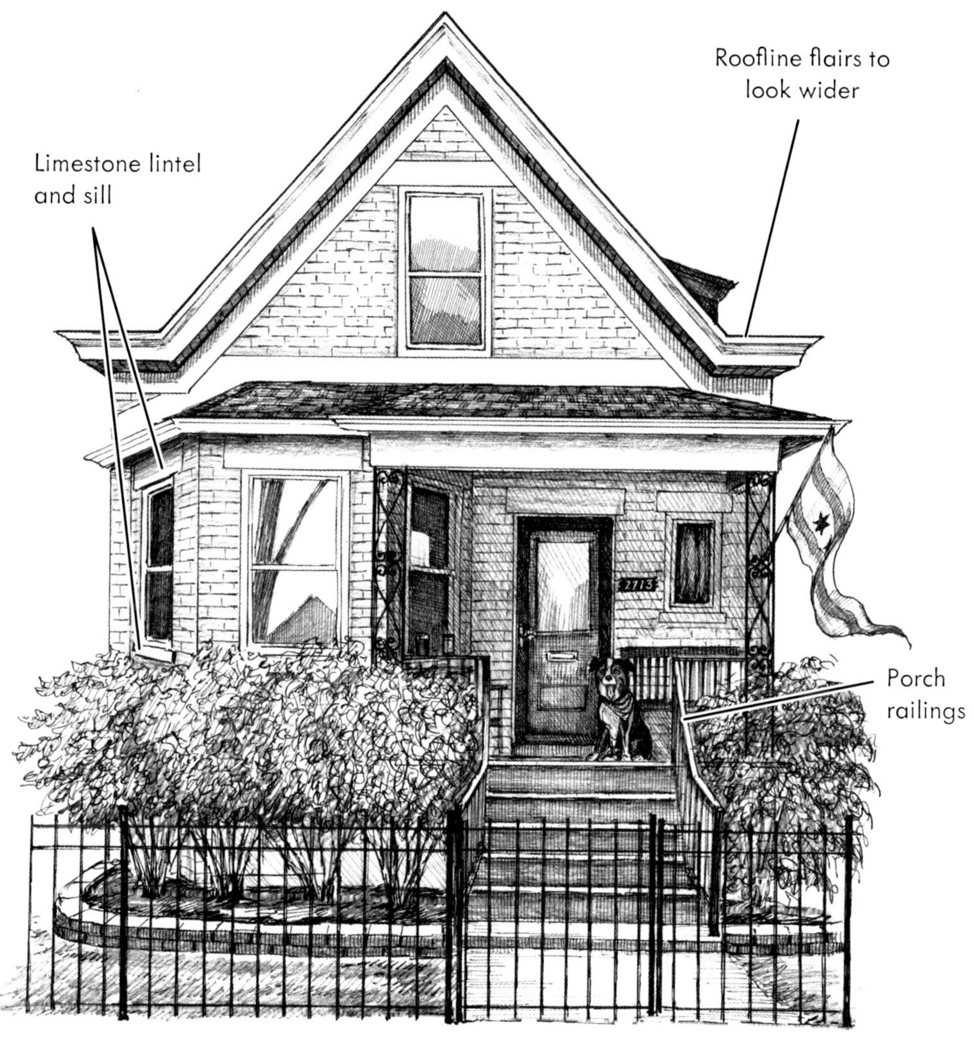

A brick workers cottage in Avondale built c. 1909.

The 1909 Plan of Chicago (a.k.a. the Burnham Plan)

Chicago was a transportation hellscape in the early 1900s. While some credit the years following the 1871 fire as the time when Chicago transformed and made order of a newly flattened landscape, that's just not how things played out. Thirty years of architectural anarchy reigned after the fire, creating intolerable conditions everywhere, including in the central business district. Even worse—those conditions were causing businessmen to lose money. Perhaps not surprisingly, the young executives of Chicago's Merchants Club took the initiative and selected Daniel Burnham, who was famous for his leadership role in the 1893 World's Columbian Exposition, to turn things around. Fortunately, in addition to helping the merchants of the city, Burnham was also insistent on making the city a more beautiful place to work and live.

For inspiration, Burnham and Edward H. Bennett, an architect and city planner Burnham hired to design and handle the technical aspects of this ambitious task, looked to Paris and other European cities. This research helped them to break down the Plan of Chicago into six categories: improving the lakefront; creating highway systems outside the city; improving rail systems for freight and passengers; acquiring an outer park system and circuits; systematically arranging the streets within the city; and developing centers of intellectual life and civic administration.

Much of the proposal focused on the business district. At the time, freight yards, train terminals, shipping warehouses, and countless establishments were smashed into a chaotic square mile. These had to be moved out of the district to ease traffic and free valuable downtown land for commercial development. Port facilities needed to move, and streets needed to be redesigned. Chicago also needed to extend Michigan Avenue north to Chicago Avenue to create a "Miracle Mile."

The Plan wasn't all about downtown changes, and perhaps its greatest legacy is the transformation of Chicago's lakefront. At the time Burnham and Bennett were laying their ideas out, only a quarter of the shoreline was publicly accessible. The Plan boldly declared that "the Lake front by right belongs to the people. It affords their one great unobstructed view, stretching away to the horizon, where water and clouds seem to meet. . . . Not a foot of its shores should be appropriated by individuals to the exclusion of the people." Burnham proposed that the city could create a lot more shoreline using the city's construction detritus (which had been used to expand Lincoln and Grant Parks). Park authorities used that idea to create Northerly Island, Burnham Park, and Promontory Point in the 1920s and '30s.

What did the Plan do for housing? It created order and it created amenities. The Plan envisioned a comprehensive network of boulevards, small parks, and the acquisition of reasonably priced forest land. Given the dark, cramped living conditions of the working class, planners envisioned the parks as a means of social betterment (and control), echoing the sentiments of playground advocates who believed Chicago needed more park areas to keep the working class happy and disease-free via all that fresh air. The residents simply viewed these beaches and green spaces as an extension of their homes. Beyond using them for recreational purposes, there are countless stories of families and, notoriously, businessmen sleeping along the boulevards, parks, and beaches in their suit pants and shirts, then dusting off their jackets in the morning and heading to work. These spaces would have been much cooler than the insides of apartments and homes on July and August evenings. In numerous ways, Burnham's seemingly romantic vision really did translate to an improved quality of life for many Chicagoans. ■

Frame & Stucco Bungalows: West Meets Midwest

From the late nineteenth century into the first decades of the twentieth century, "bungalow" was a generic term used to mean a small American home. It gradually replaced the ubiquitous "cottage" descriptor. The word "bungalow" is actually derived from the Bengali word *bangla*, though there is some variation in terms of what that word describes.

The Bengali *bangla* were huts with mud walls, thatched roofs, and a courtyard layout that looked a wee bit different from what we think of as an American bungalow. The huts remained largely unchanged until the British Raj came along and brought different ideas of how a house should look and function. For the British, the idea of a single, private, outward-facing dwelling was preferable. The layout was fairly standardized, with a large central room leading off to several others that could be used as bedrooms, studies, or dens. Most had a verandah—an opened gallery or porch—that surrounded the building on three or four sides.

These Raj-evolved bungalows also had more elaborate landscaping and required staff to help maintain the home and gardens. Perhaps most notably, unlike their Bengali predecessor, this version of bungalow had a general

A stucco bungalow in Oak Park.

A simple *bangla* hut.

association with leisure. As the world became increasingly urbanized and industrialized, the idea of a simple, single-family home in tune with the nature around it became popular and continued to evolve until we saw an expression of them pop up on the Western coast of the United States. The early bungalows of Chicago took their cues directly from their parents, the wood and stucco bungalows of Southern California, which were originally built as seasonal second houses or primary residences in mild climates.

U.S. Style Ancestors

California architecture firm Greene & Greene, established by brothers Charles Sumner Greene and Henry Mather Greene, took the lead in California bungalow design, and the brothers were masters of American Arts and Crafts architecture. But bungalows always had a Chicago connection. In 1893, the brothers embarked on a cross-country trip where they stopped at the World's Columbian Exposition and for the first time saw examples of Japanese architecture. This influence is evident in much of their later designs.

While Chicago's iterations are greatly pared-down versions of the "ultimate bungalows" that Greene & Greene designed in the first decade of the twentieth century, early frame and stucco bungalows are clear descendants of the West Coast bungalow and are easy to imagine outside of urban areas, surrounded by numerous trees and maybe some wildlife larger than the local, pizza-thieving squirrel population.

Of course, it was controversial to bring the pastoral vibes of Arts and Crafts architecture into an urban environment. Even Gustav Stickley, who proselytized the virtues of Arts and Crafts homes and published the Craftsman journal and other popular books on bungalow and furniture design, gave a big thumbs down to the urbanization of the bungalow form. But we showed him!

Chicago's frame and stucco bungalows are one-and-a-half story wood frame structures with the signature Craftsman (technically a later version of Arts and Crafts) styling, which stressed horizontal lines, overhanging eaves, and open or enclosed front porches. These were Chicago's bungalows before we fully localized the bungalow form—bungalows before they had a nasal accent and understood it was a crime to put ketchup on hot dogs.

FRAME & STUCCO BUNGALOWS

4517 N. Lawndale, a stucco bungalow built 1916.

COMMON FEATURES

- Frame (wood) construction, sometimes covered in wood shingles or fully or partially covered with stucco
- Low-pitched, gabled roof (occasionally hipped) with wide overhangs
- Sometimes very broad gables
- Simplified Craftsman details
- Roof rafters that are usually exposed
- Sometimes decorative (false) beams or braces added under gables
- Full or partial front porches with a roof supported by tapered, square columns

Amenities & Construction

Bungalows sprang up quickly in the first two decades of the twentieth century in new developments that boasted poured concrete curbs, sidewalks, and electric streetlights. Developers at the time were responsible for tying the homes they built into the street grid of the city and extending the utilities. Such conveniences had previously been unthinkable amenities for working-class Chicagoans.

Bungalows were quality homes built for people with moderate incomes. Developers would often buy up several lots at once—sometimes entire street faces—and build homes simultaneously to keep construction costs low. Materials were ordered in large quantities and purchased at a discount, and continuously employed workers were skilled and efficient due to the repetition that comes with building the same basic structure day in and day out. Having skilled workers also meant that a foreman may not need to be hired to oversee construction, saving the developer, and potentially the future homeowner, even more money.

Materials

While these early bungalows were primarily wood structures, developers experimented with materials and tried to adjust to new building codes. Some builders used structural clay tile for the walls, which they would then coat with stucco. On Arthur Street in Rogers Park, for example, stucco was laid directly over scored, stacked, hollow clay tiles, supposedly making the homes "nearly fireproof." More commonly, these were frame structures with stucco covering wood lath and board sheathing. Stucco itself was generally known to be a fire-resistant material, which was a big selling point even when the home was wood underneath. Yes, Chicagoans continued to tire of their homes burning down.

Cost

Homes could be purchased on an installment plan that would be around the same cost as a rental payment. Books of plans were also available for purchase, or even for free, if you wrote in to order them from places like the National Architectural Association. The Association was conveniently located in the Medinah Building at Jackson and Wells before its demolition in 1934.

According to an advertisement placed by Raymond G. Hancock & Co in 1917, you could purchase a frame, stucco, or brick bungalow for around

$4,000–$6,000 by choosing a lot, a housing style, and paying either $10 or $20 down until you paid a full $100. Once that initial chunk was paid, the house would be ready for occupancy and subsequent payments would be between $30–$50 per month, including interest that was determined by the total cost of the home. An article for a new development of North Side bungalows said they were selling some homes for as little as $3,000.

Upscale Versions

While bungalows were primarily geared towards working-class families, built into the roughly 25-foot-wide lots, others had massively broad gables that spread out voluminously and anchored street corners. There were ranges in lot and house size and even restrictions in developments like The Villa, located on the Northwest side of the city. This neighborhood was mostly constructed between 1907 and 1922 and is a stunning collection of California- and Chicago-style bungalows, American Foursquares, and other styles, including elements of Colonial or Tudor design. The homes were built by developers Haentze & Wheeler, who declared themselves to be "The Original Bungalow Builders."

A circa-1907 frame bungalow with wooden shingles in The Villa historic district.

The Villa bungalows were built along tree-lined streets and parkways and set themselves apart from other bungalow developments in numerous ways, including cost. The houses ranged from $4,000 to as much as $20,000 for mansion-sized homes. The development was, in many ways, a reaction to the stigmas and stifling conditions of crowded housing in the city. This tiny neighborhood had a distinctly suburban feel since apartments and businesses were not permitted, and each home had at least fifty feet of frontage, guaranteeing ample light and air. Promotional pamphlets included a section titled "Restrictions" that insisted that no house or bungalow could be constructed at a cost of less than $2,500.

Eventually, climate, durability, fire codes, and the booming brick industry evolved this style into the brick Chicago-style bungalow in the 1910s. Frame and stucco bungalows continued to be built concurrently with their brick offspring until brick finally won out. Still, family is family and it is believed their relationship remained amicable.

The Mighty Chicago Bungalow

Chicago bungalows are like Chicagoans—down to earth, hearty, adaptable, and practical. Locals might also add good-looking. Chicagoans don't need flashy things, but they do appreciate things that last and look nice. These brick homes are relatively roomy, inside and out, but also offer the option to grow into something a bit more expansive, as money allows, by popping out a couple of attic dormers to make the top half story into a livable space. The owners might eventually also build out an in-law suite containing a giant TV, sofa, bedroom, and bathroom in the massive rectangle of a basement, if, by the grace of some deity, they aren't situated in a flood zone like 30 percent of Chicago homeowners. Think before you carpet that basement.

In terms of appearance and their relationship to each other, bungalows are stocky, well dressed, and comfortably clustered. They line up along a street like friends and family holding their hands out for high-fives at a race. They are neighborly. If a bungalow owner pops their head out the front door or sits on the limestone ledge of their porch wall, the uniform setbacks of the homes allow them to see all the way down the block and holler to their kid or neighbor. These homes suit Chicagoans. Which is a good thing, because they account for about a third of the single-family housing stock.

The city lots in bungalow neighborhoods are typically tight and often only a narrow gangway separates homes. A fourth-generation plasterer once shared a rumor that during construction, plasterers would lay planks between the dining room windows of neighboring houses and just walk across them into the next home with their buckets to save time: "Bam, bam, bam down the block." Still, these subdivisions were planned in a way that allowed for lawns both in front of and behind the house, and gardens, along with window boxes, heavy stone planters and maturing trees anchoring the yards, have always been a part of bungalow neighborhoods. The expansive front windows and porches brought the outside world inside, and the low positioning of the bungalow kept it in touch with the nature around it. Today, gardening competitions in bungalow neighborhoods are fierce and citywide.

Despite their spacious feel and all the natural elements incorporated into the design, bungalows are extra sturdy, built with double-wythe brick walls, which means they have an inner brick wall and then an outer brick wall wrapped around it. Roofs were typically covered with asphalt shingles, except for those with clay tiles—although clay tile roofs were mainly seen on 1920s bungalows, and even then, they were relatively rare. Foundations were made of poured concrete, and wood floors and trim would have been made of oak, pine, and maple.

Chicago bungalows are sometimes criticized for being monotonous in their design and execution. To be clear, this is nonsense. The brick choices change from house to house, the entrances switch sides, dormers vary in size and shape, rooflines shift from front-gabled to side-gabled to hipped to the occasional gambrel. The variation in brick colors and patterning gives each building its unique stamp, and the limestone detailing also allows for differentiation—who wants to share a motif with their neighbor? This way of differentiating homes is an old trick. The 350-year-old rowhouses lining Nyhavn in Copenhagen distinguish themselves in the same way. In Nyhavn, despite each unit sharing walls and many of the same characteristics, one could easily point to a rowhouse from the vantage point of a far-off boat and know which uniquely roofed, brightly colored shop was which. Every homeowner, just like every shopkeeper, wants to feel special.

There was a period of time in which these beloved homes were not considered the sexy beasts of the local residential landscape and were being torn down or converted into unrecognizable forms at an alarming rate. In 2000, the Historic Chicago Bungalow Association was created under Mayor Richard M. Daley as a City of Chicago delegate agency and nonprofit dedicated to saving bungalows across the city. The Association dropped the "Historic" from its

CHICAGO BUNGALOWS

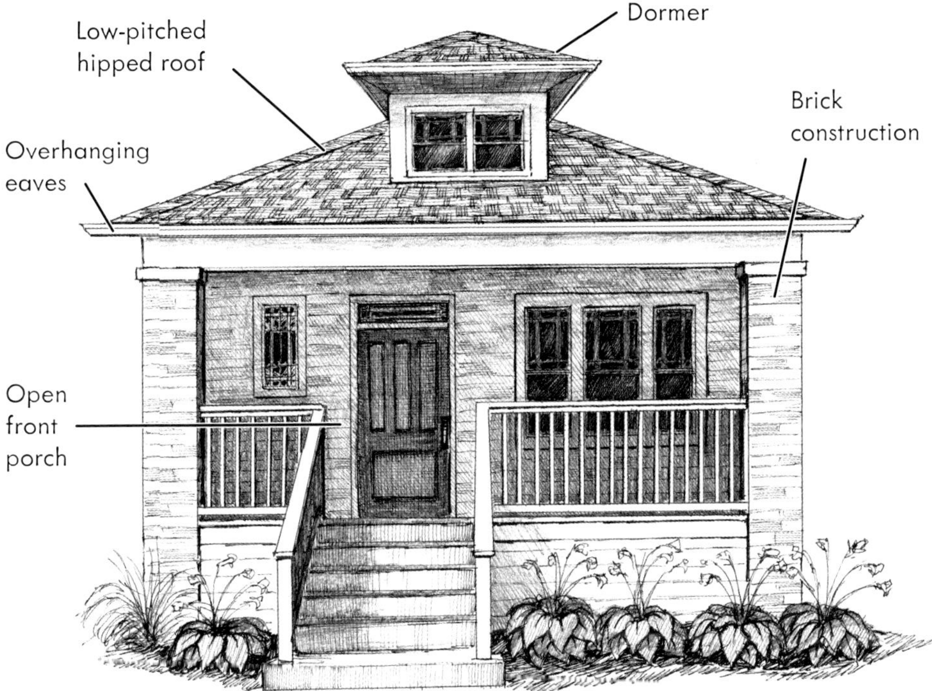

An open front porch was typical of Chicago bungalows in the 1910s.

COMMON FEATURES

- Brick construction—red, brown, orange, or a patterned mix. The brick could be quite textural.
- One-and-a-half stories
- Rectangular shape
- Limestone detailing
- Concrete foundation
- Open front porch or enclosed bay (mostly open front porch in this era)
- Generous windows
- Low-pitched roof with overhanging eaves; most commonly a hipped roof, but sometimes gabled
- Influenced by the Arts and Crafts movement

name in recent years and has grown to serve over 50,000 members since its inception—vintage homeowners who love their homes fiercely and are bent on maintaining and improving them.

Where Are They Located & Why Were They Built?

The Bungalow Belt contains many of the densest bungalow neighborhoods and stretches across the city in a massive arc, but there are plenty of these homes interspersed in neighborhoods outside the arc as well. The belt starts on the South Side, heads out to the West, and then curves up to the North. Some neighborhoods known for being part of the belt are Marquette Park, Chatham, South Shore, Gage Park, Hermosa, Portage Park, Belmont Cragin, North Mayfair, and Irving Park.

A 1910s Chicago bungalow in Belmont Cragin.

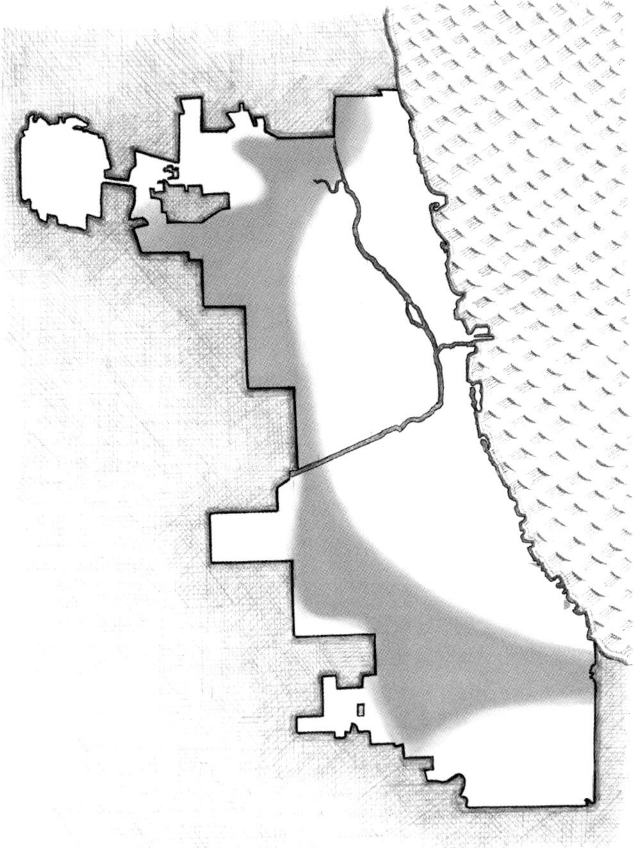

The Bungalow Belt.

From around 1880 to 1920, the City of Chicago was busy annexing surrounding farmland and suburbs and adding new infrastructure. Some areas of the city that were literal swampland got a major facelift, which was certainly the case for many bungalow neighborhoods. For example, where local amenities might have once included a contagious disease hospital, a garbage dump, and wooden stumps hovering over saturated ground to boost up foundations, you could now expect gas lines, water mains, paved streets, sidewalks, and public transportation lines. New residents and developers started changing the names of neighborhoods like Pennytown, named after a general store owner named Penny who sold homemade popcorn balls, to Avalon Park, named after the English Isle of Avalon where King Arthur was born.

So much of the early twentieth century was a reaction to the end of the previous century. Bungalows, for example, had a layout that was almost identical to a greystone or two-flat, which is to say that everything was on a single floor. To have bedrooms on the same floor as a kitchen or dining room must have felt almost scandalous for a homeowner. Single-family homes were usually two-stories, with the bedrooms and bathrooms—the private rooms—on the second floor.

But this all-on-one-floor model kept prices lower and allowed for the possibility to build out the upper half story as money allowed (or never, as it turned out in most cases). In 1917, you could buy a new brick bungalow with newly available domestic comforts thanks to recent innovations with heating, plumbing, and electricity for just $4,000–$6,000. Somewhere between 80,000–100,000 of these dream makers were built from around 1910 until the early 1930s, creating an ordered, urban grid over what was previously cheap, undeveloped land.

The builders and architects who built bungalows were, in fact, rather like bungalows themselves: practical, relatively modest, and successful in their mission. Bungalow builders were not part of the city's architectural elite; they were usually part of a broad, locally focused practice that didn't get a lot of recognition, but got a lot done. They often had their preferred contractors and architects, and sometimes they bypassed architects and formulated their own designs. The architects who worked with bungalow builders often maintained offices in neighborhoods rather than downtown, and while some were more prolific than others—sometimes building large swaths of them in every corner of the city, like architect Ernest Braucher—none were "starchitects" and no single builder or designer came to dominate Chicago bungalow production. Chicago bungalows were adapted and refined by literally thousands of small builders and architects, and some even worked on customizing bungalows purchased through mail-order catalogs. They were as down-to-earth as the homes themselves.

Sears Homes Catalogs

In 1888, Richard Sears, the son of a blacksmith and wagon maker, put out a thin catalog full of watches and jewelry claiming, "The Lowest Prices On Earth." The twenty-three-year-old telegraph operator started the R.W. Sears Watch Company after success selling watches for a wholesaler, and moved the business to Chicago a year later. He soon began selling anything and everything a person could want—mail-order bicycles, firearms, baby carriages, and, in 1908, houses.

Mail-order homes could be purchased through catalogs from as early as 1906 to as late as 1982. Purchasers received the architectural plans and all of the materials needed to build the home. What did that look like? You mailed in your order and then all of the pieces were collected and shipped via train car. Sometimes that meant that a load of bulk lumber would be dropped on a lot, ready for the future homeowner to cut it all to size for construction. But more often pre-cut lumber was dropped off ready to assemble. These pre-cut lumber shipments were called "kit" homes.

These kit home shipments would also include doors, windows, flooring, roofing materials, hardware, and even enough paint to cover everything with two coats. Everything fit together like Ikea furniture on a grand scale. Sometimes folks wanted to build their homes themselves, but often people hired contractors for the labor. There were copious design options, and the styles of the homes had alluring names like Starlight, which sounds more like a tiki drink or a showgirl alias than a five-room, frame bungalow with a large front dormer. Many of these models spanned years and even decades, including the Starlight, which was featured in catalogs from 1913 to 1933.

Cover of a 1908 Sears, Roebuck & Co. Homes catalog, the first year Sears began selling homes by mail.

Electric, plumbing, and heating fixtures were the only construction amenities that didn't come with the kits—but fret not, those were also available as add-ons. About 20 percent of the country subscribed to what became a massive catalog of around 1,400 pages. More than 100,000 items with a quality guarantee could be delivered right to your door, so when you ordered your house, you could also tack on everything from a kitchen sink to bath towels. The home styles ranged from American Foursquares to bungalows to Cape Cods—around four hundred different home styles were available. Even more remarkable was that buyers could submit their own blueprints to Sears and the company staff would then customize the materials.

Outside of convenience, the kits were hugely popular because they were affordable. Those on a tight budget who had some basic carpentry skills and a bit of patience could build their own homes, cutting out the construction labor. Sears also used simple balloon-frame construction and standardized cheaper materials like asphalt shingles and drywall.

Sears was not the only company selling homes through catalogs. There were eight major companies in addition to small, locally run companies that sold homes in both the U.S. and Canada—perhaps most notably the Aladdin Company and Montgomery Ward—but Sears was a giant. By the time the catalog was discontinued in 1940, Sears had sold a staggering 75,000 houses. In 1939, business was still booming, but in this regard and many others, World War II changed everything. Demand for lumber exploded and the Supply Priorities and Allocations Board issued an order that any nonessential construction must be halted. Only employees in defense industries could build homes.

Today, there are plenty of mail-order home enthusiasts documenting and writing about Sears homes and places like Pleasantville, New York, which had so many of these mail-order homes that a hill in town was named Sears & Roebuck. Sears kit homes have been listed in the National Register of Historic Places and can sometimes sell for huge sums of money. Some estimate that somewhere around 70 percent of Sears houses are still standing today. ■

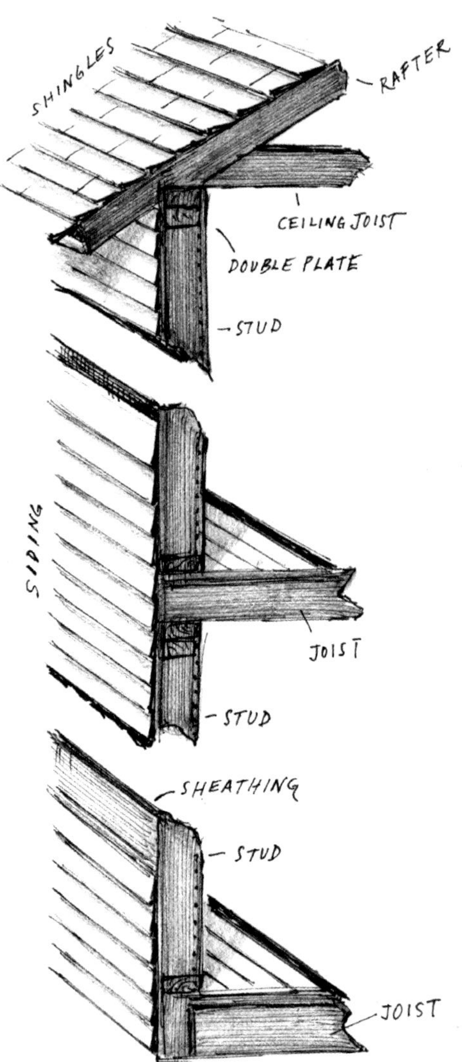

Roof and wall assembly detail as part of the "General Specifications" from a 1917 Aladdin Homes catalog.

A Simplified Tudor Revival

There aren't significant changes in terms of how Tudor Revival homes express themselves during this period except that these homes are no longer shaking hands with the nineteenth century styles. During this era, Tudors begin to look more like the "typical" Tudors you see around Chicago, though they were still on the large side—you won't find as many for the working-class budget. In the following decades, the more compact, single-family home and multi-unit versions came in droves. You can read more on the history and nuance of the style in the previous chapter and about its evolutions in Chapters 7 and 8.

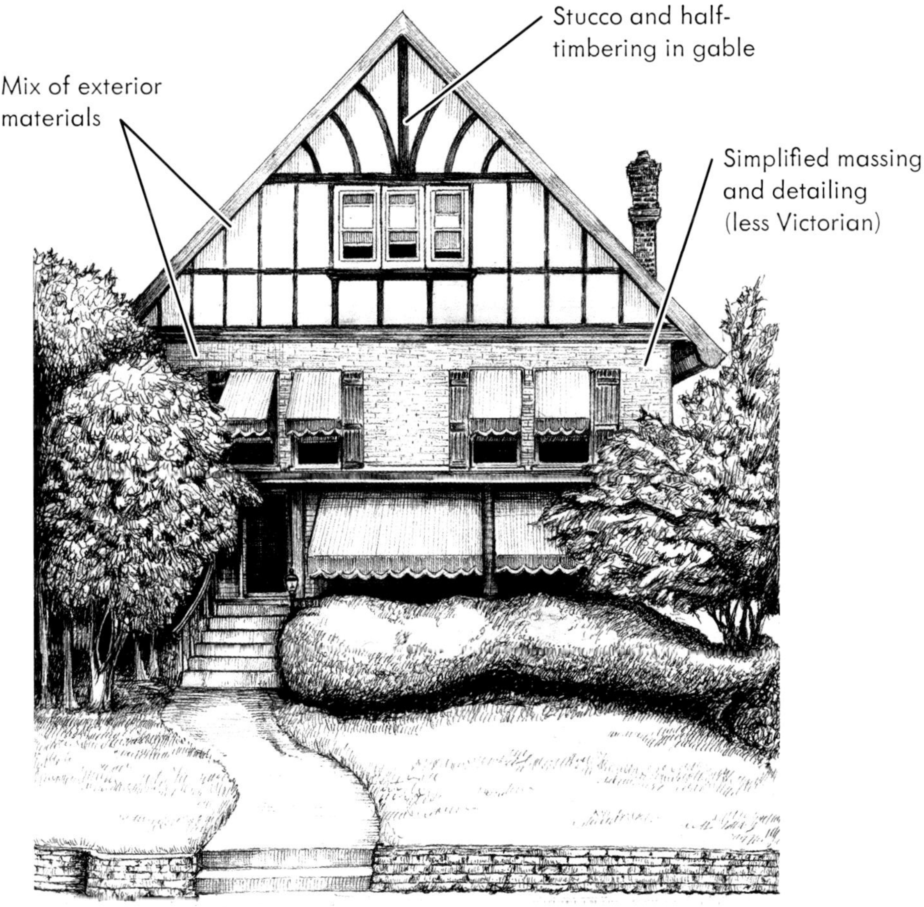

A 1912 Tudor Revival home with a broad front gable in South Shore.

Colonial Revival: The Return of the Traditional

Like the American Foursquare, the popularity of this style from the early decades of the 1900s was, in part, a reaction to the more ornate styles of the 1890s and an attempt to achieve order through a "pure" non-eclectic style. After getting through a bumpy transitional period in the late nineteenth and very early twentieth centuries, architects put a cool rag on their heads and snapped back to something resembling a more "true" form of Colonial Revival architecture. Essentially, the style grew up and became more like its parents after an experimental phase in high school. To underscore the return to a more conservative look, movies—both "classics" and recent films—often feature Colonial Revival homes when the intent is to convey wealth or the ideal American family, regardless of location. *Home Alone*, *Father of the Bride*, and Don Draper's home in *Mad Men* are just a few examples of how this style was used as shorthand for character development.

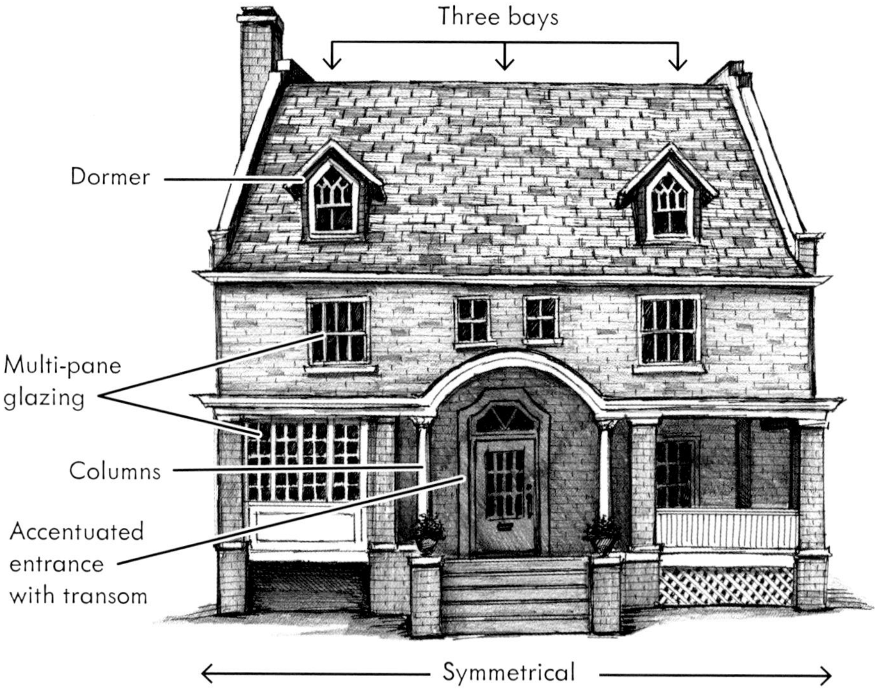

A Colonial Revival in Rogers Park, built 1912.

These Colonial Revival style homes are not interested in sporting a cutesy cottage look. They are substantial homes declaring that the owners have traditional values, pay their taxes on time, and dispose of their lawn clippings properly. These homes, which can be found in areas such as South Shore, Norwood Park, and Morgan Park, have a timeless look and timeless ethics, if you will. Chicago's narrow lots force this form into a three-bay width versus the elaborate five-or-more bay forms you'll find in the suburbs, yet they retain their dignity.

A sub-type of Colonial Revival is Dutch Colonial. These share the same characteristics but entrances are often to the side, and they're topped with a large, distinctive Dutch gambrel gable, which can be front- or side-facing, sometimes with a little flare at the eaves. If you were asked to draw a barn, you'd draw this roof. They may have either brick or wood clapboard walls.

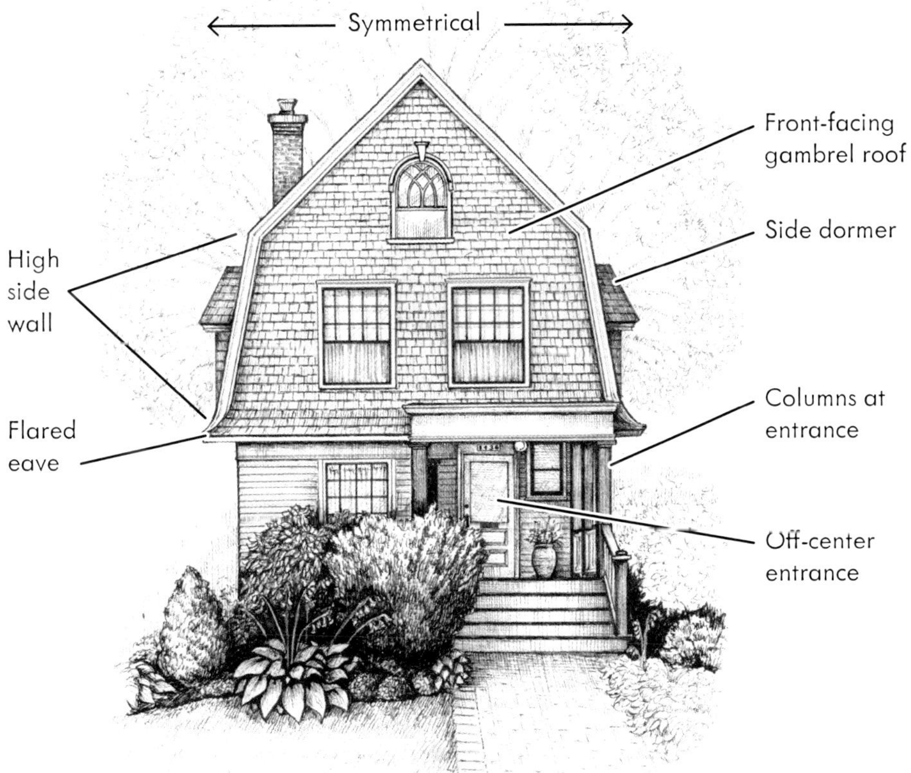

A 1903 Dutch Colonial in Evanston.

Prairie Style Peaks & Perishes

The early 1900s was peak Prairie. The public had embraced—indeed were a bit zealous about—the Arts and Crafts movement, which focused on hand-crafted materials and artisan guilds as a response to the social ills created by mass production. The new century also brought with it the modest, working-class bungalow, and this generation gobbled up the delightful propaganda of *The Craftsman* magazine and other publications that revered chisels, elbow grease, and honesty of expression. Of course, at this point, machines were going to be a part of construction no matter what the ideals. According to H. Allen Brooks's introduction in his book *Frank Lloyd Wright and the Prairie School*:

> The mechanical saw, press, or mold were able to produce boards, bricks, or terra-cotta and concrete blocks of distinctive character; steel beams and reinforced concrete made possible the far-reaching, cantilevered roofs and balconies. Unlike the Englishman William Morris, who had rejected the machine as an enemy of art, or the International Style designers, who would make a virtual fetish of

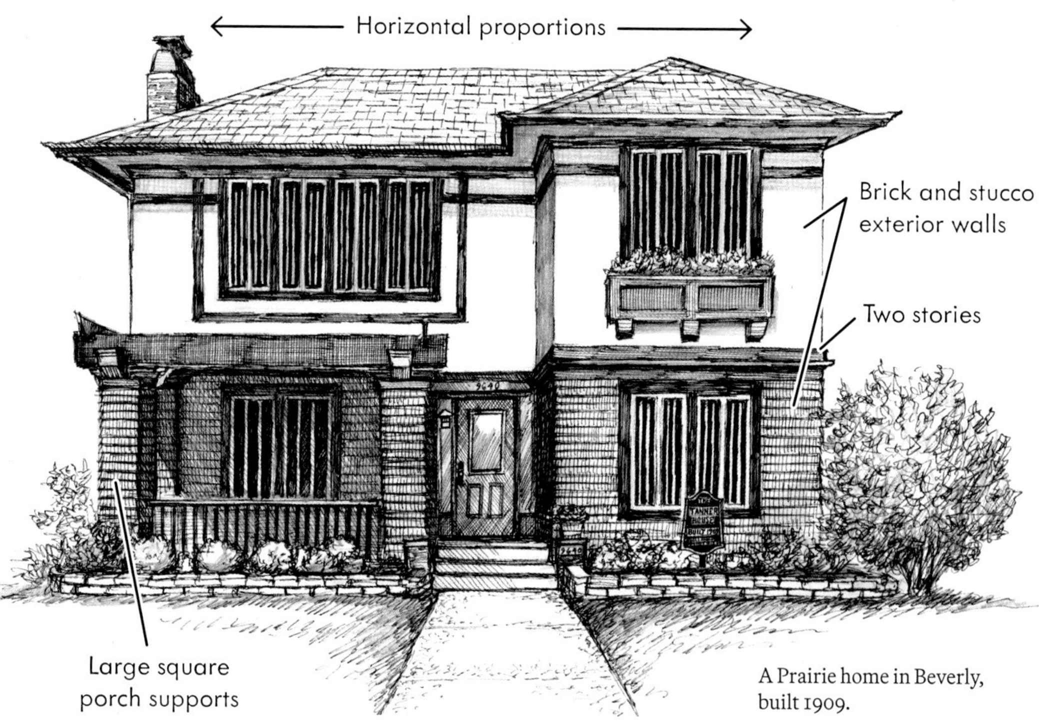

A Prairie home in Beverly, built 1909.

standardized, industrial parts and place a symbolic value on the relationship between the machine and art, the Prairie School architects, led by Wright, accepted the machine as part of their natural heritage and used it to shape, but not to dominate, their aesthetic.

The style reached its fullest expression in residences, like Wright's Robie House and George W. Maher's Pleasant Home, but schools, warehouses, and park buildings were also built in the style. Chicago is especially rich in examples: the suburb of Oak Park has the highest concentration of Prairie style buildings in the nation.

But, alas, almost as quickly as Prairie style came into favor, it was shown the Sullivanesque-ornamented door. Attitudes about what mattered changed during the First World War, and "practicality" trumped Prairie style's ideas about experiential architecture and anti-industrialization—these are not wartime ideas. The conservative attitudes at the end of this period killed even the beloved *Craftsman* magazine in 1916, when readership hit an all-time low. Today, you can find echoes of Prairie style in American Foursquares, bungalows, and even the low-slung midcentury ranches that eventually filled in many of the lots left vacant during the Great Depression. The style also influenced the craftsmanship, art, and clean lines of Bauhaus design and International Style. Romance is not dead!

American Foursquares: Back to the Basics

The American Foursquare, as we typically think of it, is the Foursquare of the early 1900s. When these first came around in the 1890s, they had simple and open plans inside but wore more elaborate details on their exteriors. In the twentieth century, they were distinctly post-Victorian on the outside as well. A 1917 Aladdin Co. mail-order catalog described a Foursquare as "inviting you into its big, strong protective walls to find comfort, pleasure and satisfaction."[2] It is a sort of well-dressed football player the parents would love to meet, provided it didn't drink all the beer.

If you ask a kid to draw a house, they'll draw a Foursquare. At least, they will if they aren't being raised by academics or architects. Bedrooms are upstairs for privacy, common areas and kitchen are downstairs. Tiny, compartmentalized rooms like those of Queen Annes, with dark wallpaper and fretwork, would make them grouchy and claustrophobic. If they had a tagline, it would likely read something like, "keep it simple," or "we make sense."

A 1909 stucco Foursquare in Albany Park with an upper-story bay window. Bays were less common with Foursquares, but they'd show up on occasion, especially in the earlier iterations of the style.

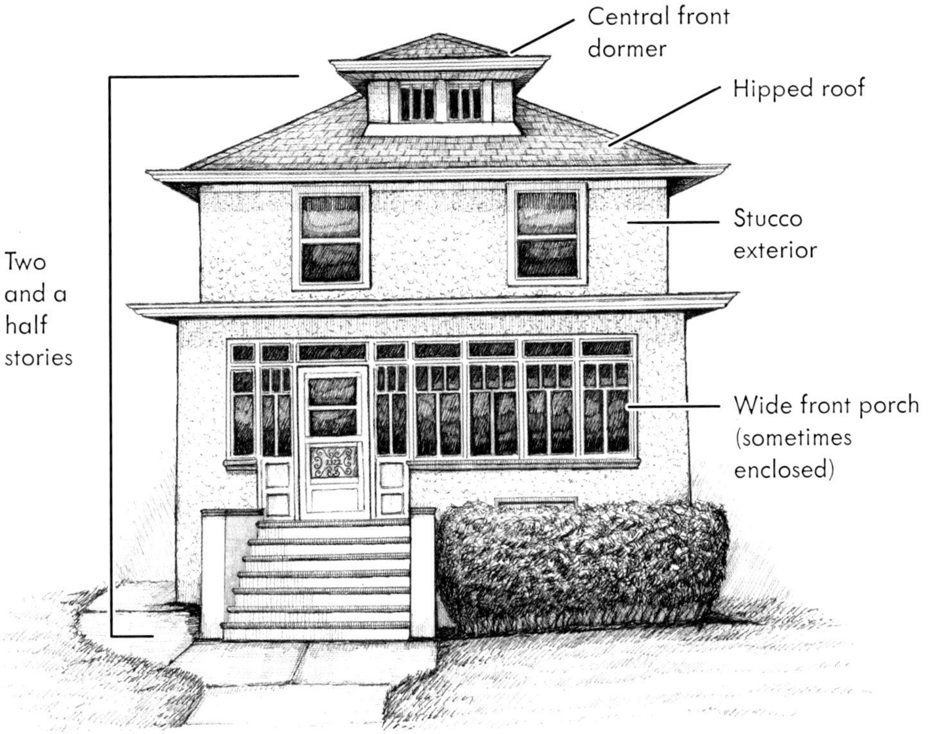

A stucco Foursquare in Ravenswood Manor, built 1913.

Affordability

Roomy and straightforward, the American Foursquare was relatively simple to construct and remained attainable for a range of income levels. As they proliferated through mail-order catalogs, Foursquares became increasingly affordable, in part because they didn't have any towers and complicated plans with lumpy exteriors. Squares are just cheaper to build. That same Aladdin catalog counted this housing style among its best-selling plans in 1917.

While this style is sometimes called the American Foursquare or Prairie Box, we tend to just call them "Foursquares" in Chicago. "Foursquare" refers more to the building's form than its style, describing the shape and layout of the home. The applied details were often from a collection of contemporaneous styles, such as Craftsman, Colonial Revival, and Neoclassical. Like other housing types at the time, Foursquares were simple but versatile, built in a wide variety of materials including wood, brick, and stucco.

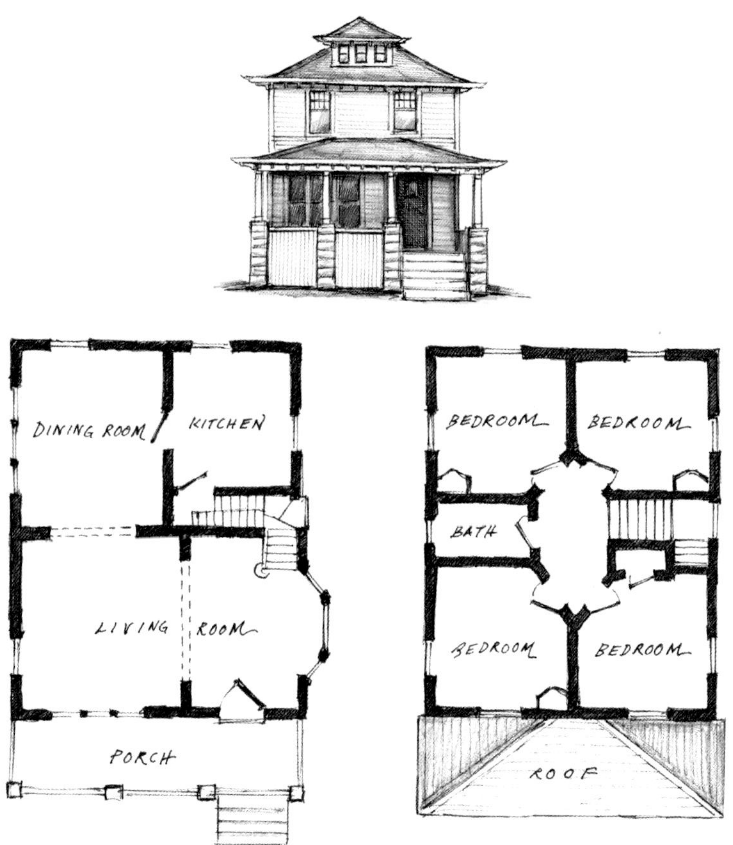

"The Virginia" with floor plan, from a 1910s Aladdin Homes catalog.

Ties to Prairie Architecture

The American Foursquare is often tied to the Prairie School, but there are some substantial differences between the two. The Foursquare has never been as philosophical or political as the Prairie School or Craftsman movements, although these homes and architectural philosophies all began manifesting at around the same time in Chicago. While some historians think of Foursquares as the simplest expression of Prairie style, these commodious boxes are not concerned with beefs against Daniel Burnham, democratic values, inspiration from nature, or job security in a changing world. They like being roomy and functional, and if they had stomachs, they'd probably appreciate a good, balanced meal involving steak and broccoli.

Bleak Housing Conditions and Tenement Reform

In terms of housing, it was a rough start to the century. The abysmal housing conditions of the working class were largely ignored by the city's health commissioner, who was preoccupied by the lack of an adequate water supply and sewer system. In 1906, Upton Sinclair's book, *The Jungle*, rocked the country by exposing the housing conditions of recent immigrants working in the meat-packing plants of Chicago. Early in the book, we see recent Lithuanian immigrants Juris and Ona arrive in Packingtown—more broadly known as the Union Stock Yards or Back of the Yards neighborhood—in hopes of earning good wages and working toward the American dream. What they find instead is endless corruption and filthy working conditions, equaled only by the filth that permeates the rooms they can afford to rent for themselves and Ona's family:

> Mrs. Jukniene was a wizened-up little woman, with a wrinkled face. Her home was unthinkably filthy; you could not enter by the front door at all, owing to the mattresses, and when you tried to go up the backstairs you found that she had walled up most of the porch with old boards to make a place to keep her chickens. It was a standing jest of the boarded that Aniele cleaned house by letting the chickens loose in the rooms. Undoubtedly this did keep down the vermin, but it seemed probable, in view of all the circumstances, that the old lady regarded it rather as feeding chickens than as cleaning the rooms.

Even for chickens, these were not ideal housing conditions. In response to the lack of action taken by the city to tackle this issue, the City Homes

Old houses on Liberty Street in a Jewish district of the city, near the old Maxwell Street market. Many of Chicago's tenements were not massive, multi-unit buildings, but crammed single-family homes.

Association was created in 1901 by middle- and upper-middle-class reformers, including Jane Addams. The purpose of the association was to improve the living conditions of the working class, address overcrowding and sanitation issues, and establish small parks and playgrounds in Chicago. The committee had only six months to make their case, and they needed to record housing conditions that spanned 187 miles of land under city management. Unlike New York, where there was concentrated poverty, Chicago's centers of manufacturing sprawled across the city, scattering working-class districts. As a result, the committee focused on three primary areas: a portion of the Near West Side occupied by Italian immigrants and Russian Jews; a Polish district near Division and Ashland; and a Bohemian district in what is now the Lower West Side. The culmination of this research was a publication titled *Tenement Conditions in Chicago*.

The report found that 43 percent of the homes that were visited housed 1.5 people per room, and that almost a quarter had more than two people per room. Addams noted in a separate article titled "The Housing Problem in Chicago," "If the average tenement house density of the three districts investigated were spread throughout the city, we could house within our borders 23,000,000 people." Almost half of the rooms were rated as "gloomy, dark, or very dark"—often completely lacking windows—and many districts had almost no bathrooms. The majority of these dwellings were only two to three rooms, with relatives or boarders crammed in as another source of income.

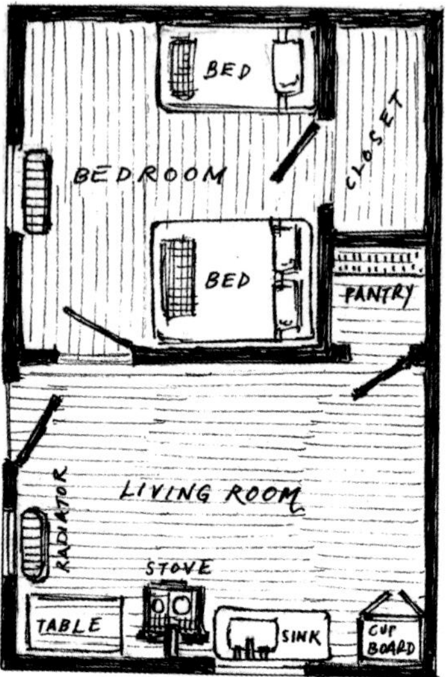

Plan of a two-room model tenement from 1900, "designed to meet the means of a working man earning $2 a day."

The City Homes Association reports, along with other reports that uncovered these conditions, led to a new building code. In fact, Chicago's 1902 Tenement House Ordinance in many ways reshaped, and was the template for, Chicago's unique multi-family housing types. The Ordinance effectively eliminated the use of the wood-frame tenement buildings that were popular with residential apartment developers and limited the majority of courtyard buildings to three-and-a-half stories. The low height of the courtyard building also meant that elevators were not necessary, further reducing the cost. Changes in the code around issues like height, materials, window, sanitation, green space and safety necessarily changed the way our buildings were designed and built going forward. ■

Courtyard Apartment Buildings: Dense but Good-Looking

You know these courtyard buildings. They're the U-shaped brick buildings that feel like oases with their landscaped courtyards and fountains; the ones you curse for taking up all the parking on the block even if you're one of the people living in them and taking up parking on the block. There are thousands of them stretched across the city, often dominating the corners of neighborhood blocks.

The typical U-shaped courtyard building is a three-story brick building with five entrances. In the middle of these entrances is a central courtyard that every tenant gets to look onto from their windows. Some building owners have modified these views by adding a small metal balcony that people throw grills onto but hardly spend time on because it's weird being so close to your neighbor's balcony. Each entrance usually has six apartments. As with flats in Chicago, the basement level is where you'll find the boiler and utility rooms, laundry rooms and tenant storage units. Basement-level apartment units are rare but when they do occur, they're generally limited to the front of the court and are commonly referred to as garden apartments. They are also the cheapest to rent.

Variations

- Half courtyard / side court (shaped like an "L")
- One-and-a-half courtyard / s-court (shaped like an "S" and usually on block corners)
- Double courtyard / multi-court (shaped like a "W")

The most common shapes of courtyard buildings. For more information on these typologies, it's worth visiting Larry Shure's *Ultra Local Geography* blog, where he calls these shapes the side court, u-court, s-court, and multi-court, respectively.

COURTYARD APARTMENTS

Section of a 1906 light brown L-shaped courtyard apartment building in Ravenswood.

COMMON FEATURES

- U-shaped footprint or a variation on that theme
- Brick exterior with limestone detailing and sills
- Flat roof with parapet walls
- Large, landscaped interior courtyard
- Multiple exterior entrances

These buildings are brick construction with face brick on all of the street- and courtyard-facing exterior walls and common brick at the rear. Foundations are poured concrete, and Bedford limestone was used for the sills, to cap parapet walls, and to create various geometric motifs. Brick colors were mostly browns and reds during this era with various textures, bonds, and patterning. If this sounds similar to the Chicago bungalow and brick two-flat material makeup, that's because it is exactly the same. Economy was god and a degree of uniformity—or perhaps it's better to call it cohesiveness—was smiled upon at the time.

Origins of the Courtyard Building

The population boom during the last decades of the nineteenth century meant that housing density was increasingly a priority, so architects sought out new multi-unit building forms to offer options beyond single-family homes, luxury high-rises, and tenements. This experimentation would continue for another couple of decades, driven increasingly by social reforms in the early twentieth century. The question of keeping density while still allowing for acceptable amounts of light and air was a central one for architects.

Experimentation with courtyard apartment buildings in the 1890s laid the groundwork for the iconic courtyard buildings we see anchoring so many Chicago streets. One particularly important example was pioneered by Anthony Schmitt, a wealthy candle manufacturer and developer. Schmitt's vision for the Arizona Apartments at 42nd and Greenwood Avenue was made manifest by the architectural firm of Treat & Foltz. The fifty-five-unit building was located near mansions (rather than being ghettoized), allowed for ample sunlight, and had an impressive landscape incorporated onto the lot. The seventy-by-seventy-foot courtyard was essentially a private park for its residents. There were seven distinct entries into the building, and these separate, exterior entrances were a departure from the long hallways of tenements, affording more privacy and getting closer to the American ideal of single-family homeownership.

Following the lead of experiments like the Arizona Apartments became the plan for creating more desirable and affordable housing. These new courtyard buildings would incorporate green space that made up a whopping quarter of the lot. Trees and flowers and fountains were now visible from every unit, which was a huge departure from the former crowded buildings that were built out to the lot lines and contained dark, windowless rooms. While two-flats were sometimes disguised as single-family homes to project the illusion of wealth, the courtyard apartment also attempted to meet some single-family home standards by having the next closest thing to a front yard, increased privacy, and ample light and air circulation. This added a level of respectability to the idea of multi-unit living. Instead of long interior hallways with anonymous doors and cramped common areas, these apartments had multiple exterior entrances with staircases and landings that led to only two apartments per floor. This design allowed tenants to experience something much closer to the feel of a single-family home.

Brick Two-Flats & Variations on a Theme

What Is a Flat?

First, a note about local terminology: In Chicago, "flat" refers to a specific type of apartment. Every floor of a flat apartment building is essentially the same as the floor below and the number preceding the word "flat" represents the number of units in the building. While "two-flat" and its variations sound more like the form of the building than the style, we tend to call them by that descriptive name rather than any style that is expressed on their facades. For example, if a single-family home has Tudor Revival details, we call it a Tudor. If a brick two-flat has Tudor Revival details, we still just call it a two-flat. The same goes for a three-flat and six-flat. The one-flat is called many things, but one-flat seems to make the most sense locally, given how we describe their taller siblings.

What we never call these buildings are duplexes and triplexes. Duplexes are newer construction and mostly live in the suburbs. Triplexes have nothing to do with the Chicagoland area—you'll have to travel if you want to use that word and not get a weird look. And while technically, all two-, three-, and six-flats are multi-unit buildings, we tend to just call those out by their names and reserve "multi-unit building" for buildings that have more than six units.

Greystones, which are most typically two or three stories and also a kind of flats building, are technically flats, but we just call them greystones because of their stone cladding. Don't question it.

Flats buildings in all their variations can be found in virtually all bungalow neighborhoods and beyond, stretching from the furthest southern neighborhoods to the furthest northern neighborhoods. Some particularly dense pockets of two-flats and their brethren are West Garfield Park, South Lawndale, Lower West Side, Brighton Park, New City, Fuller Park, West Ridge, and surrounding neighborhoods.

A 1910 two-flat with three-sided polygonal bay windows.

Why Are There So Many in Chicago?

According to one account in 1909, these "stacked apartments" were built for families grappling with the social and economic shifts of the times: "Forced partly by the high price of land in the desirable sections within reach of the city centers, partly by the increasing cost of all the necessities and luxuries of life, as well as the annoyance and difficulty of securing competent help, our

American families have been compelled in many of our cities and suburban towns, to abandon their natural preference for private and individual homes and enter upon what is probably an early phase of co-operative living." Surely that is true for some, but the two-flat was, and continues to be, notoriously successful as a way for people to achieve stability, and potentially, upward mobility.

Brick Flats

Chicago filled up at a faster rate than any other American city between 1910 and 1930, and the city struggled to keep up with places to stick all these people. Brick flats existed in the 1890s, especially in areas like Garfield Park, Lawndale, and Bronzeville, often sharing streets with greystones. But they exploded in the 1910s, when we could not build and fill these buildings fast enough. In fact, while flats by definition have only a single unit on each floor, there are caveats here as well. Some two-flats may have split off into front and back units to make them even more affordable, and basement units—legally or otherwise—could make a two-flat a kind of under-the-radar three-flat.

Two- and three-flats make up more than a quarter of Chicago's housing. In some neighborhoods, like South Lawndale and Brighton Park, they make up more than two-thirds of the building stock. In the earliest decades of their existence, immigrant families would pack the flats with family or others who had recently come over from their home countries. While this model of coexisting while maintaining a degree of privacy may have changed in some regards, it has stayed the same in others. Consider a common scenario today. For years, you and your closest friends or family talked about living together (but apart), and finally, you found a good deal and the timing was right. You leave the doors to your units open so your cats can go in and out of each other's homes. It's easier to borrow a cup of sugar this way, especially when it's raining. You have impromptu dinners. You also share the outdoor space, summer BBQs, a winter fire pit. You meet in the basement and coordinate laundry schedules. When you go out of town, your mail is collected and the aforementioned cats are fed.

These flats buildings were always bridge housing, building a path for generational stability. They allowed, and still allow, people to move up financially, possibly to that Chicago bungalow down the street.

BRICK FLATS

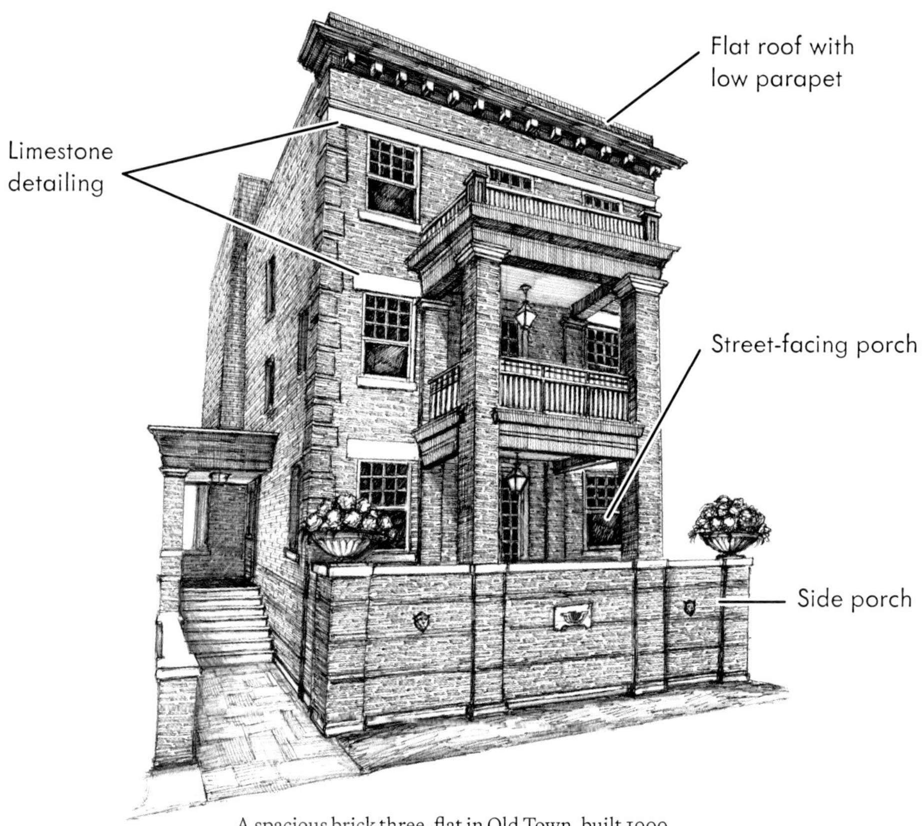

A spacious brick three-flat in Old Town, built 1909.

COMMON FEATURES

- Brick construction with face brick on the street-facing facade and Chicago common brick along the sides and back
- Flat roof with a low parapet wall
- Limestone detailing
- Generous windows
- Arts and Crafts detailing
- Street-facing open porches, enclosed porches with a small side porch, or open front porch on first level and enclosed porches above
- A basement level with a boiler and utility rooms, laundry rooms, and tenant storage units

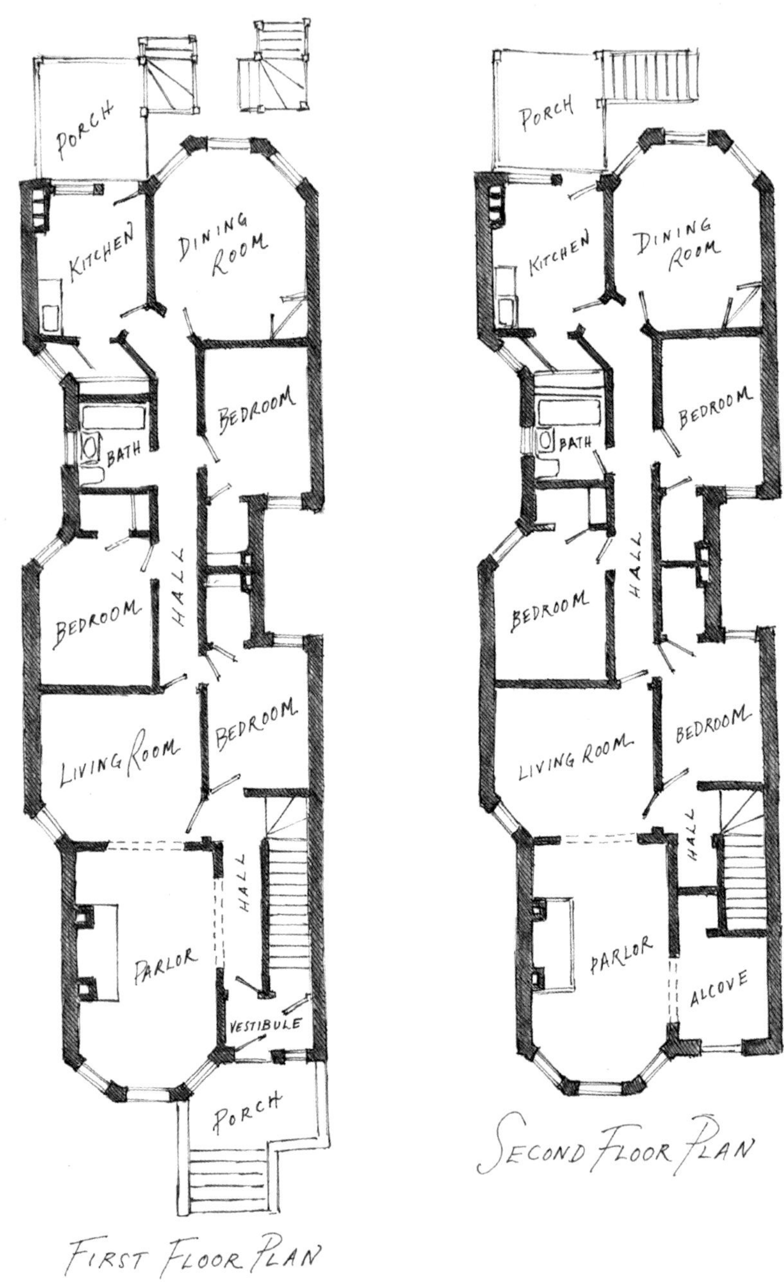

A greystone two-flat from a 1909 Radford's Stores and Flats catalog.
Note the identical first and second floor plans.

Two- and Three-Flats, Pushing Out Their Predecessors

While some two- and three-flats were clad as greystones, their brick-clad brethren were largely nudging them out. While their interiors were virtually identical—long, stacked apartments with living rooms in the front, bedrooms and sometimes a dining room in the center, and a kitchen in back—the economical brick facades were replacing the limestone-fronted greystones and their nineteenth-century flourishes. That said, the greystone did try and adapt, and many constructed in the 1900s–1910s featured Arts and Crafts details. Still, the brick flats used only limestone *accents* as part of their pared-down Craftsman detailing, and that cost builders less to construct.

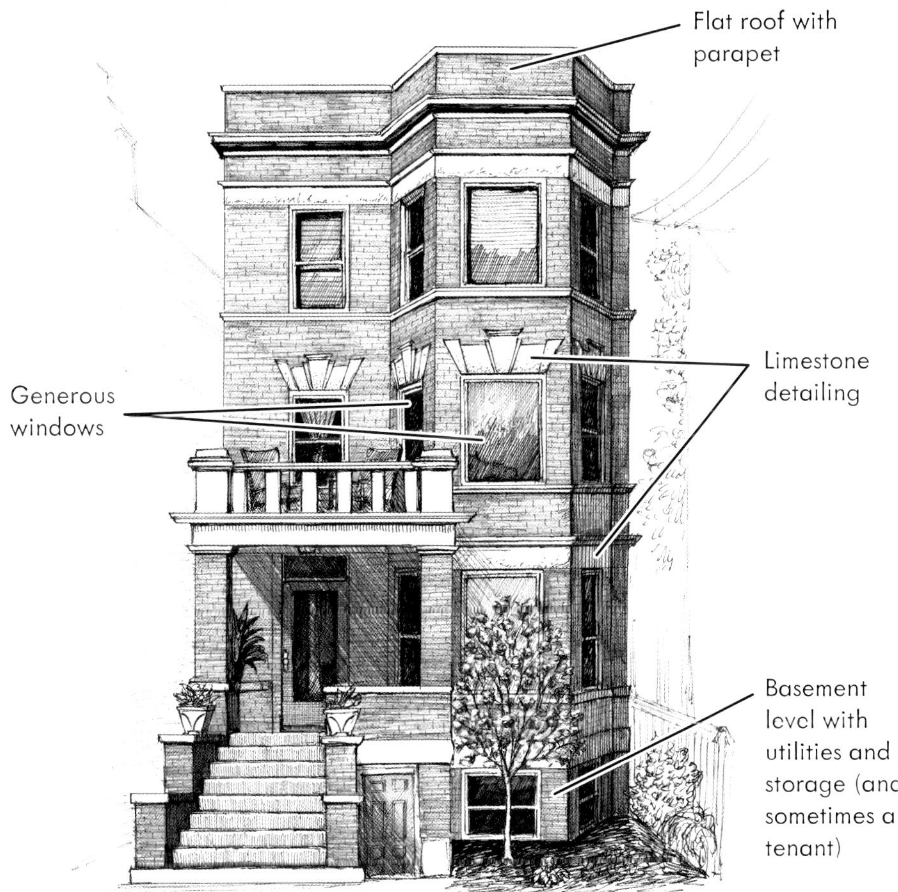

An early-1900s three-flat. Just like a two-flat but taller!

Six-Flats

These are essentially double-wide versions of three-flats with a central entrance and hallway and two mirror-image apartments on each floor. Like their smaller cousins, they're also constructed of brick, with face brick on the street-facing side, and have Bedford limestone detailing. Classical Revival and Craftsman styles are most common, and occasionally they'll feature large front porches. There is also a front-and-back variation of this form with three stacked units facing the street and three units behind those that are accessible through a rear side entrance.

One-Flats

These Napoleonic one-story homes have all of the charm and detailing of their multi-flat siblings but are one-story, single-family homes versus stacked flats. They have the same layouts, brick construction, limestone detailing, and even parapet walls. They also have virtually the same interior plan as Chicago bungalows, minus the attic, and are sometimes referred to as "shoebox bungalows." We recommend oohing and aahing when you see these relatively rare treats in neighborhoods like K-Town in North Lawndale.

A 1914 six-flat, each with generous front porches, where the illustrator lived for ten years.

A heroic 1915 one-flat in Forest Park.

The Back Porch

Fire Codes

By the early 1900s, fire codes had already been evolving for decades, but the 1903 Iroquois Theater fire caused the deaths of six hundred people—twice as many as the Great Chicago Fire—and with that came enough enraged Chicagoans to merit more serious regulations. How were six hundred people trapped in a burning building? One of the many issues that contributed was the exit doors, which swung inward instead of outward, leading to a massive pileup. Because of that tragedy, the city passed an ordinance requiring exit doors to swing outward, and required all Chicago theaters to be equipped with levers for simultaneously opening emergency exits—one lever for exits to fire escapes and another for exits to streets and alleys. The ordinances enacted in Chicago after the Iroquois Theater fire influenced fire safety regulations in other cities that were struggling to prioritize safety over profits, such as New York.

By 1906, the building code also required that every two- or three-flat apartment have two means of egress: either a fire escape, or one staircase located at the front of the building and another at the back. Today, anyone who's lived in or peeked around an old Chicago building has seen a wooden staircase out back. Some have been enclosed, but they're in there.

Why wood and not metal? Even though we were quickly exhausting the forests of the Upper Great Lakes region, Chicago still had relatively cheap lumber. It was a matter of economics. But is it a good idea to build a fire exit out of wood, you might reasonably ask? While it *will* burn, the wood should hold out long enough for the fire department to arrive—there are calculations for this that we just have to trust—and Chicago code specifies what wood must be used to ensure this is the case. Other factors weigh into this calculation, such as the dimensions of porches, which can't be wider than ten feet. A broader porch could be unwieldy and collapse. Porches must also be built behind a fire-rated wall made of brick or another material that will burn more slowly than wood.

View from the rear: a common sight from a Chicago alley.

Myriad Functions

Back staircases built with wood can have a number of other functions. Because of Chicago's open back alleys, we can build roomy platforms, unlike the narrow metal fire escapes of New York. These outdoor spaces became much more than fire escapes—they were used for garbage pickup, and served as a place for milk and ice deliveries in the early decades of the century. Of course, these wide landings were also used to cool off and get fresh air when you weren't feeling well, like a makeshift sanatorium. Imagine living with Uncle Sal as he coughed up a lung in a packed apartment. You'd just kick him out onto the porch, especially during the flu pandemic that found its way to Chicago in the late 1910s. These outdoor spaces were also used for more uplifting activities like meals away from the kitchen heat on a July evening, maybe playing a board game in the 1930s, or folding over the pages of the *Chicago Daily Tribune* and sipping coffee in the early hours. These means of egress were very real and welcomed extensions of Chicagoans' dwellings.

In 2003, a porch collapsed during a party in Lincoln Park, killing thirteen people and injuring dozens more. This triggered tenants and owners all over the city to look more closely at their century-old porches, and others that were recently constructed, with a new set of eyes. Inspections boomed, more porches collapsed, and the codes were updated. Today, Chicagoans still use porches like backyards, perhaps more than ever thanks to a renewed appreciation during the recent Covid-19 pandemic and mandates. Isolation sparked a huge bump in patio furniture, hanging plants, and outdoor rug sales as apartment dwellers clawed their way out of confining living spaces for some fresh air and space. While fires do happen, thanks to burning cigarettes or grills gone wild, these porches are so utterly woven into our culture that we're happy to take our chances on their inherent flammability. ■

Beaux Arts: Still Fabulous

Despite all the stripping down of flourishes and pulling oneself up by the bootstraps during this era, some Beaux Arts buildings continued to be constructed. These extroverts found a way to make do and survive, and even thrive in some cases. For example, the 1913 Cook County Hospital building is flaunting every sexy, "look at me!" attribute of the style with zero shame, and at eight stories tall and spread across two city blocks. To give you some sense of the size and ornamentation of the building, during the early phase of restoring this beautiful beast, which began in 2018 after almost two decades of fighting to save the structure, architectural firm Skidmore, Owings & Merrill had to replace more than 4,500 pieces of terra cotta on the facade.

Some residential buildings also sported the style, though admittedly not many. Unlike the mass production of many single-family homes at this time, most Beaux Arts residential structures still required architects due to their more sophisticated designs, and that took money. You can find twelve Beaux Arts residential structures in the Chicago Park Boulevard System Historic District, with a couple of notables at 4321 South Dr. Martin Luther King Jr. Drive, designed in the 1910s, and a six-flat located at 622–624 South Independence Boulevard, designed in 1900.

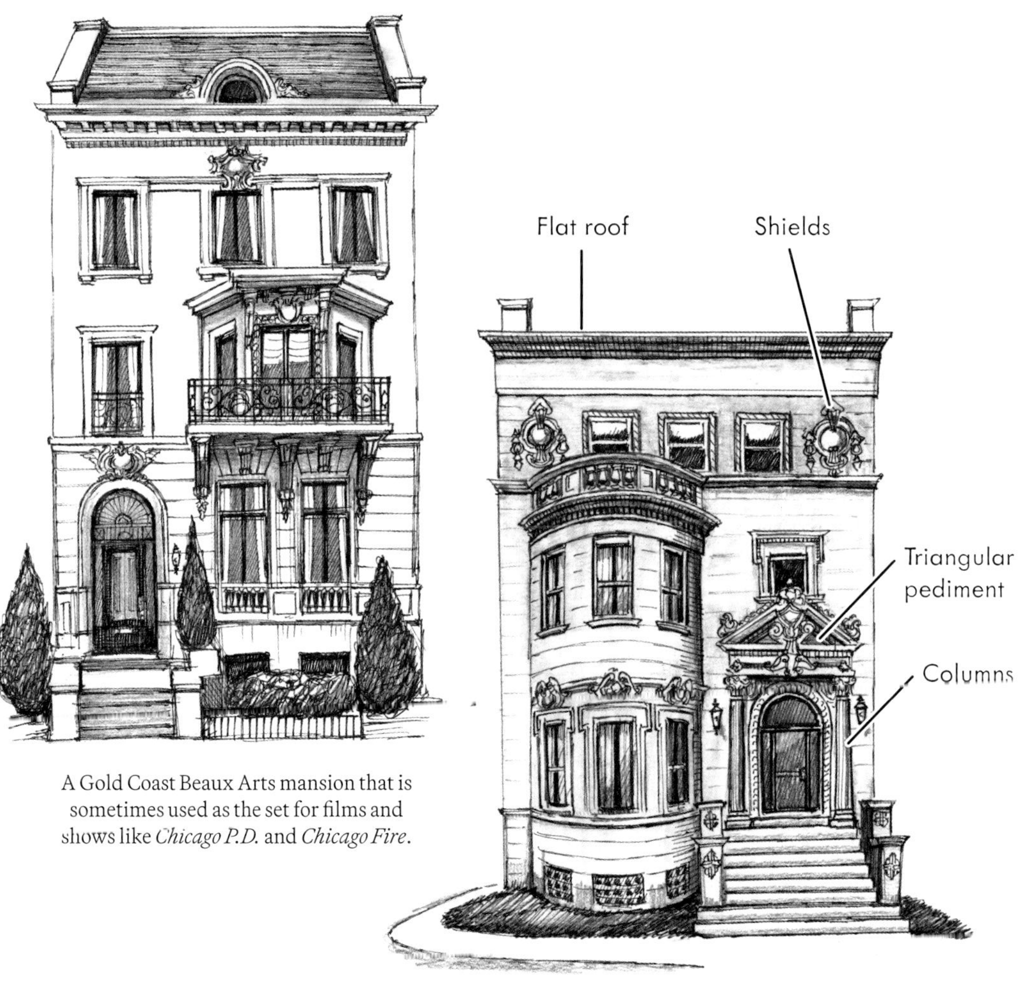

A Gold Coast Beaux Arts mansion that is sometimes used as the set for films and shows like *Chicago P.D.* and *Chicago Fire*.

A Beaux Arts home on South King Drive.

CHAPTER

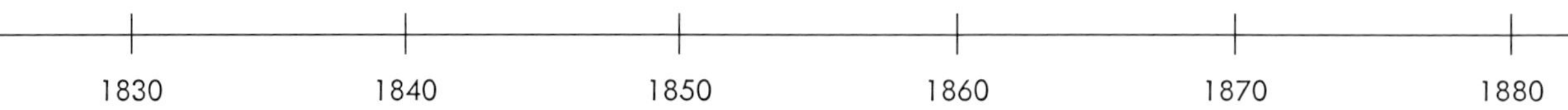

Death, Speed, and a Bit of Whimsy

1917–1929

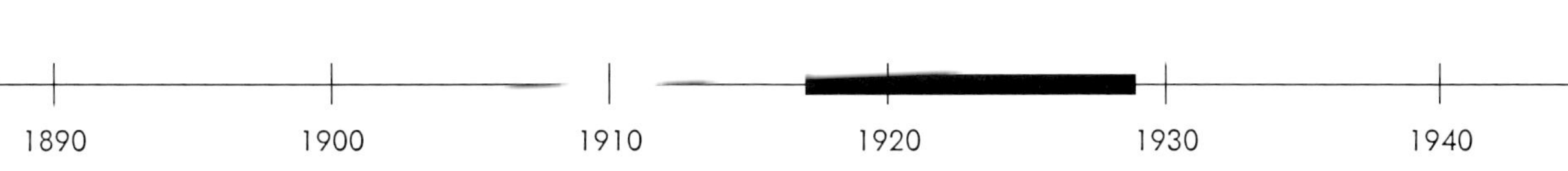

“There’s only one thing for Chicago to do, and that’s to move to a better neighborhood.”
—Herman Fetzer

THE LATE 1910S WERE ROUGH ON CHICAGOANS. Immigration slowed to a crawl, the industries that powered the city came to a halt, and growing racial tensions boiled over into bloody riots. On top of this, organized crime and corrupt officials created such a culture of lawlessness that a group of businessmen had to take it upon themselves to form an independent Chicago Crime Commission. This was not to address business-related thefts, but the massive backlog of murder cases.

And these were just the homegrown challenges.

After three years of watching a war rage overseas, in 1917, the United States entered what was originally called the Great War. Almost five million Americans served in the military during World War I, including thousands from Cook County.[1] One of the effects of this was a deepening hostility towards German immigrants, a group that made up a substantial percentage of Chicago’s population. Neighborhood enclaves in Chicago originally designed to attract Germans were now changing street names from Bismarck, Berlin, Hamburg, Cologne, and Rhine to Ancona, Canton, Custer, Eleanor, and Coyne. By 1918, many Chicagoans, and even the *Chicago Tribune*, began referring to sauerkraut as “liberty cabbage.”[2]

In addition to the mass casualties of war, another 63,000 non-combat-related deaths occurred—due to a global pandemic. The influenza pandemic of 1918, or “Spanish Flu”—which actually originated in Kansas[3]—made its way into the city via the nearby Great Lakes Naval Training Station. In a matter of months, there were 38,000 cases of influenza in Chicago and 13,000 cases of pneumonia.[4] The loss of able-bodied workers found local meatpacking plants, steel mills, and railroads stretched almost to the point of breaking.

Historically a go-to city for new immigrants eager for manual work, Chicago was used to replacing any population losses with ease. But yet another factor complicated matters—the steady flow of folks seeking the American dream had encountered a dam. Actually, three dams. Just before the U.S. entered the war, Congress passed a law limiting immigration to only literate applicants, banned most Asians from entry, and added a hefty immigration tax. As a result, residential, commercial, and industrial growth ground to a halt.

The answer was to find workers elsewhere. The U.S. government decided to waive the literacy provision for Mexican citizens and opened its southern border, populating warehouses, railroads, and farms across the country with new Spanish-speaking residents. While the city's Mexican population grew considerably, they were not the largest group of new Chicagoans. A much larger demographic shift came from the Great Migration, the movement of African Americans from Southern states to the urban North. From 1916 to 1918, Chicago's Black population doubled from 58,000 to almost 110,000.[5]

Work opportunities became available during the war, causing an expansion of the narrow band of Black ghettos on the South Side and two additional areas on the North and West Sides. There was a massive housing shortage, and despite entire Black families cramming into single rooms, there simply were not enough of those, either. Movement into historically white neighborhoods was necessary and inevitable, but tensions rose sharply. Dozens of bombings took place from 1917 to 1919, determined to displace Black residents or scare real estate agents who allowed transitional property. Tensions finally came to a head on a hot July day in 1919 when a Black teenager named Eugene Williams floated across an invisible color line in Lake Michigan. White beachgoers threw rocks at him from the beach, striking him and causing him to drown. This resulted in race riots breaking out across the city, and an eruption of racial violence targeting Black Americans spread across at least twenty-six cities around the country.[6]

Adding to the violence and unrest, German Chicagoans were on a collision course with prohibitionists, who gained support against companies like Pabst, Schlitz, Blatz, and Miller, as well as beer houses, which were often owned by Germans. Alphonse Capone rose to the head of the Chicago crime syndicate and used his connections with public officials and police to win control of bootleg alcohol through the beer wars of 1924–30. Chicago was cementing its reputation as a violent, corrupt, and crime-ridden city.

Still, the gears kept on cranking. The 1920s ushered in massive social and technological advances, widespread electrification of homes, automobiles with a price point for the masses, and new forms of entertainment and media. And, naturally, construction! Home building exploded after the war, wages rose, and homeownership became attainable for the first time to tens of thousands of Chicagoans. The kitchens and bathrooms of Chicago bungalows and other newly constructed homes available to the working class were tricked out with the latest plumbing fixtures. A new middle class, made up of hard-working people who suddenly had expendable income, shed its inclination towards austerity.

The new middle class needed to buy things. "Main Streets" popped up in neighborhoods around the city and these localized commercial areas meant that Chicagoans no longer had to make their way to the Loop for most of their shopping needs. As of 1930, twenty-six principal retail areas had sprung up in neighborhoods, and homes clustered around them, creating the equivalent of town centers. Most of the shops were modest developments occupying twenty- or thirty-foot-wide lots with second-floor residential units. But collectively, they added up to hundreds of miles of frontage, lining both sides of streets in some areas, and dotting lots here and there in other areas.[7]

Chicago bungalows upped their game in the 1920s, especially the late 1920s, with more elaborate detailing and more revival styles incorporated into their form.

Political realities also improved for many in this era. In 1920, Illinois and another thirty-five states ratified the 19th amendment, declaring for the first time that American women, like men, deserve all the rights and responsibilities of citizenship. Despite intense segregation in Chicago, unsegregated "black-and-tan" nightclubs flourished, and Black musicians, visual artists, and writers were able to achieve nationwide fame and notoriety for their work during this period. Some nightclubs on the South Side also provided LGBTQ+ spaces for Black and white patrons. Blues singer Ma Rainey and others put out overtly queer music, and drag shows were common in many Chicago clubs.[8]

Chicago's nightlife was booming and skyscrapers were soaring to unimaginable heights. There seemed no boundary we couldn't break, and break with style. But the higher you climb, the further you fall. And the 1930s landed the City of Big Shoulders flat on its back.

Chicago Bungalows Embrace Cocktail Attire

Chicago bungalows in the late 1910s and early '20s retained their solid, get-'er-done vibes, and dominated the single-family home market. The Bungalow Belt widened at a breakneck pace after the war, with peak building in the mid- to late 1920s, yet remained affordable to the growing middle class through a range of pricing and new funding mechanisms. White-collar professionals were also happy to share the block with railroad workers and clerks.

When the stock market crashed in 1929, building slowed considerably while builders and investors held onto hope. Most building stopped around 1930, though you will find a few Chicago bungalows built as late as 1934–35. Even so, construction ceased almost entirely within a couple of years of the crash. It would be another decade before building began to slowly rebound. Ranches, Cape Cods, Tudor Revivals, and Georgian Revivals would take the place of the beloved Chicago bungalow in the 1940s and '50s, often functioning as infill in the lots that were never developed.

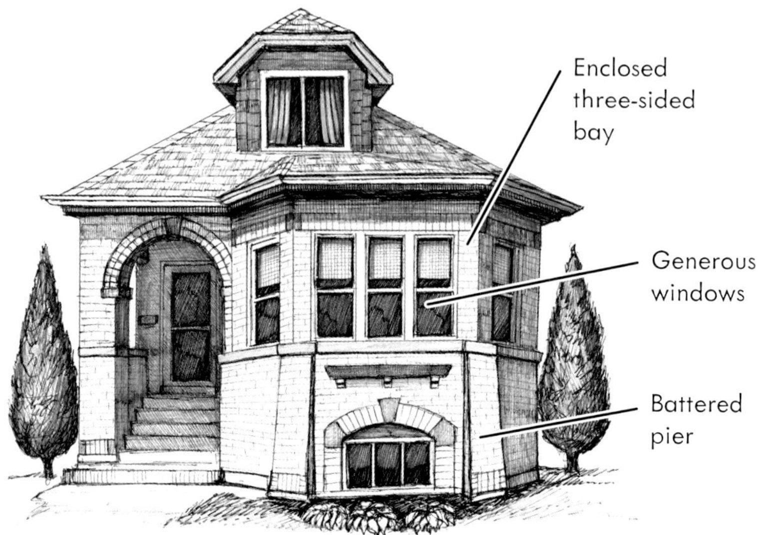

A typical mid- to late 1920s Chicago bungalow.

Front gables were less common than hipped roofs with Chicago bungalows, but there are still plenty to be found. These were usually frame (wood) half stories, and this one is sporting a jerkinhead or "clipped" gable. Bungalow developers would sometimes alternate these gabled roofs with hipped roofs to create more variety on a street.

Sub-Styles

- Tudor Revival
- Gothic Revival
- Mediterranean Revival styles
  - Spanish, Italian, Moorish influences
- Detroit-style bungalow
  - Same characteristics and layout as Chicago bungalow but with a side-gable roofline
- Dutch gambrel two-story (likely a 1940s postwar addition)
- "Bungaloids," or massive bungalows, often on corner lots

Stylistic Changes

As with the humans of the time, Chicago bungalows have a little more fun in the second half of this era. They experiment with form, materials, colors, and even some exotic styling. Some wear earthy clay roof tiles, while others shift from the brown and red brick of the 1910s to a more glamorous yellow brick (with a slightly glossy sheen). The open front porches of many 1910s bungalows are enclosed for added interior space, and art glass filled with geometric patterns may fill front bays and smaller side windows.

Bungalows were always designed to work with nature by incorporating large groupings of windows and emphasizing local plantings and informal topography—an intentional departure from the formal landscaping of the late nineteenth century. Often, a hefty stone planter box sat under the front bay windows on limestone brackets, though most of these have disappeared thanks to freeze-thaw cycles. Unlike during Victorian times, front fencing was rarely installed and neighbors shared collective views and lawns.

More whimsical revival styles are woven into these otherwise simple beauties. Some Mediterranean Revival homes are so ornate that they bring to mind images from the actual Mediterranean—seaside villas, tiled courtyards, cousin Spiros dragging an octopus into the kitchen after a tussle at the beach. Tudor and Mediterranean Revival styles emphatically scoff at the suggestion that these homes are uniform or overly conventional.

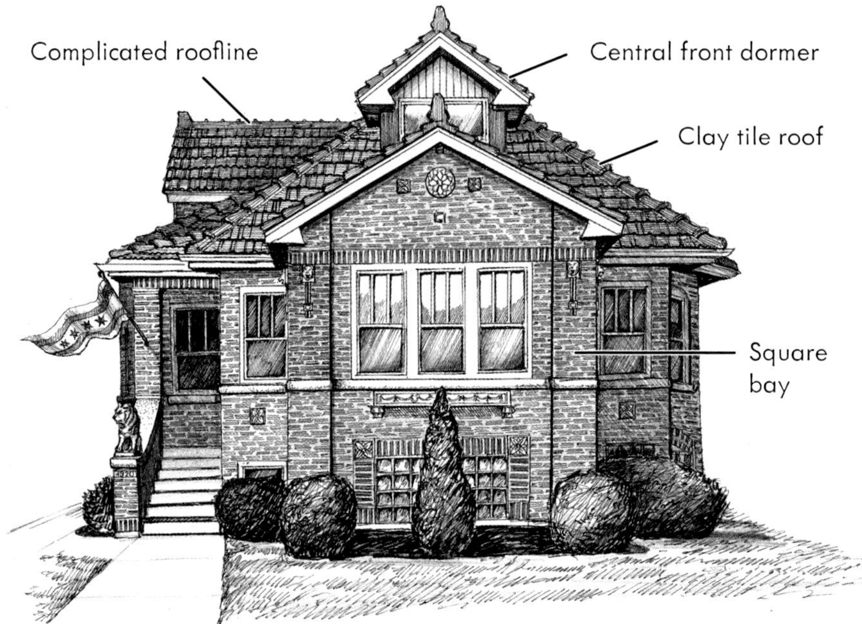

A Chicago bungalow with a clay tile roof and other Mediterranean Revival details.

Angel gilding was a distinctly Chicago phenomenon. In the window pictured here, the small shaded squares in the corners and the center diamond are angel gilded in gold. The other pieces of glass are clear or nature-inspired colors.

Some 1920s bungalows also incorporated double-sided gold mirror elements into their stained-glass windows. The technique used to achieve this effect is called angel gilding, and Chicago is the only city in the U.S. to use this in residential buildings. To make the gilding, gold chloride is dissolved in water, mixed with other chemicals, and poured onto the glass. Pieces are set back-to-back within the frame to reflect light both in and out of the front room, like flapper dresses shaking at a Gatsby-style party.

Evolution of Form

In terms of form, the bungalow bay—the face of the bungalow—evolves during this period. Some bungalows have an enclosed flat front that stretches the entire length of the facade, while others have a projecting square bay, a curved bay, or a three- or five-sided polygonal bay—perhaps the most recognizable and iconic form of this housing type. If the bay spans the entire facade, the "front door" is actually located on the side of the home.

Polygonal bays with either three or five sides became common in the mid- to late 1920s. This modification, which gives a little extra flair, became the iconic bungalow shape. Some of these also have stained glass in their bay windows as well as in smaller windows along the sides of the home and next to the front door.

"Bungaloids" enter the scene as well. These are bungalows on growth hormones—proportional, but with far more square footage than the typical 1,200–1,400 square feet of their older siblings. These mansion-sized bungalows often anchor streets on wide corner lots that allow them to spread out and push the definition of what the Chicago bungalow represents. Bungalows were still homes for the working class striving for upward mobility, but they were also for those who had, as far as they were concerned, already arrived. One of the most endearing things about bungalow blocks is the economic diversity. There might be a doctor in a bungaloid, married with no children, sharing a block with a railroad worker, a clerk, and their six children in a 1,200-square-foot bungalow.

The rooflines of bungaloids were generally more complicated, moving away from the simple hipped or front gable. These much larger homes needed to break up the roofline with cross gables, massive dormers, and other attractively lumpy layouts. Because the style retained many of the original bungalow characteristics, like the low-slung massing of the home, a bungaloid may appear only slightly larger than average. Then, when you go inside, it magically unfolds like *Doctor Who*'s TARDIS.

Example of a corner-lot bungaloid with an expansive lawn and a long, street-facing stretch of brick and windows.

Example of a Dutch gambrel roofline on a Chicago bungalow.

One particularly interesting form change is the brick gambrel roofline. These can be a half story or a full story, and it's difficult to know how many are original because they tend to blend seamlessly with the first story. We do know that many were added to the typical one-and-a-half story Chicago bungalow in the 1940s, well after they were built, as a way to accommodate the large numbers of people who moved into the city for work after the war. These gambrel additions became apartments. Large "shed" dormers that reach all the way to the peak of the roofline were also added at this time for the same reason. Throughout their time as the dominant form of single-family housing in Chicago, bungalows continued to fulfill their original intention of being attractive and affordable to most, regardless of social status, but adaptable to the economic climate and able to grow with population booms.

Brick Flats & Variations: A Little Extra

A 1924 article in *The National Builder* describes a scene in South Chicago as "One day a prairie, the next day a city. . . . One day quiet, no noise but the wind sweeping through the weeds—the next day, a bang of hammers, the sound of saws, and the chug, chug, chug of a concrete mixer—sweet music to a builder's ears."[9] Brick flats were often built concurrently with Chicago bungalows, along the same streets and by the same builders and architects. And there were loads of them. These were sometimes called "two-apartments" in advertisements, and even Al Capone lived in a two-flat in the late 1920s, though some attribute this modest home choice to the fact that there was a convenient tunnel built from the flats to the garage.

A grand 1929 three-flat in Rogers Park with warm yellow brick and beige terra cotta details surrounding its porches and anchoring its columns.

During this period, the formal stone facades of Classical Revival greystones gave way to warmer, Prairie-inspired details and the earthy comforts of brick and wood and clay. These more economical flats dominated the stacked apartment market throughout the city for decades to come, with post–World War II versions especially prevalent along the western edge of the city limits. From their inception and up until today, owner-occupied brick two-flats have been critical to maintaining high-quality affordable housing in Chicago.

A Note on Affordability

While it certainly saved some money to build with face brick instead of limestone cladding, material costs weren't the only reason that high-quality buildings were able to be sold at moderate prices. Careful planning was critical. Selecting the building forms in advance, knowing how the floor plans were to be arranged, and carefully determining the order in which the work was to be done were the first steps. This may seem obvious, but when you're constructing entire streets at one time, such planning and timing are everything. Any changes that happened while the work was underway were expensive, so as much as possible, any alterations needed to be done on paper before the shovel hit the dirt. There was definitely a "Give me six hours to chop down a tree and I will spend the first four sharpening the axe" approach.

For one ambitious development, two hundred bungalows and two-flats were planned at once, with buildings going up in groups of seven. When the foundations were completed for one group, digging began for a second group, and then bricklayers were set to begin the walls on the first group. Pressure was on contractors, who were held to some strict choreography, and if they screwed up the footwork, the superintendent would raise hell. If the timing was off, the contractor would rapidly lose money and that would either obliterate profits or be passed on to homebuyers.

Materials & Appearance in the 1920s

There are many kinds of flats—see the section on flats in the previous chapter for more on these distinctions. All of these forms continued into the late 1920s. Like their bungalow neighbors, brick two- and three-flats continued to function as attainable, attractive, and practical housing. But they did indulge in a little whimsy as they moved into the mid- to late 1920s. In some cases, they also got a little roomier.

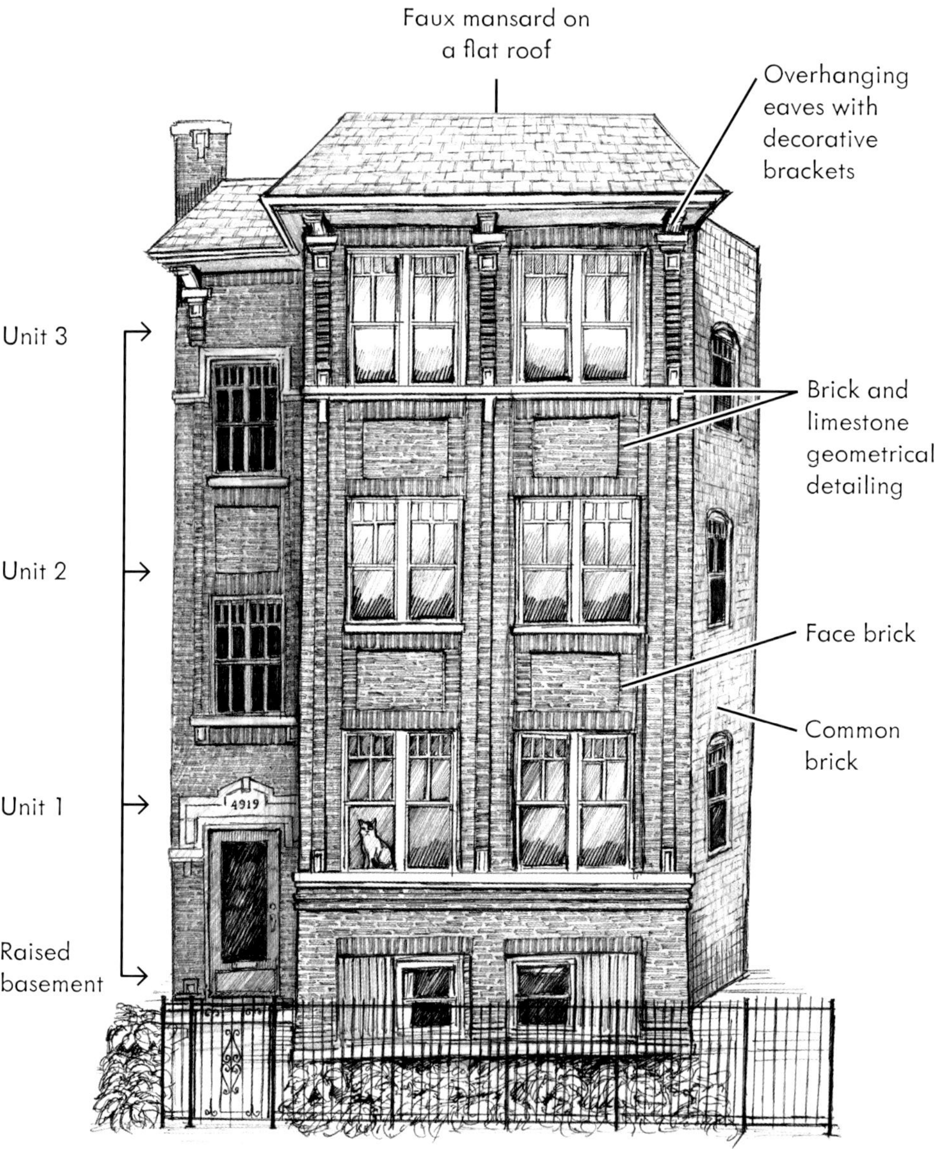

A dark brown brick three-flat in Uptown with a faux mansard roof and Prairie and Craftsman details.

While we always assume twenty-five-foot lot widths in Chicago, the truth is that many are irregular, and by the 1920s, thirty-foot-wide lots were common. By the late 1920s on the Far North Side, there were even some "jumbo" flats that were designed for thirty-three-foot and forty-foot-wide lots.[10] Some conjured up Spanish Revival themes by finding ways to incorporate decorative clay tile onto parapets, or by adding a small clay tile roof above the top bay.[11] Tudor Revival half-timbering—the non-structural wood elements added to stuccoed walls and gables—achieved that Henry XIII feel. Numerous variations like these—sometimes only very minor decorative pieces—could turn a Craftsman building into a revival style with minimum expense.

Brick appearance and patterning in the 1920s also became more elaborate with checkered or diapered (diamond-shaped) patterns, and yellow brick became more common on these building forms as well as on single family homes. The face brick was still decorated with limestone detailing and that detailing became increasingly more complicated and ornate as the stock market boomed. Despite the material upgrades, the same affordable, unevenly colored common brick wrapped around the sides and rear. Back porches were now mandatory at the time of construction, and all that wood behind buildings became colloquially known as the "Chicago Lumberyard."

In terms of interior spaces, the long flats interiors generally kept the same order of rooms with kitchens in the rear, bedrooms and dining rooms in the center, and living rooms in the front—often functioning as a sun porch or half sun porch and half living room hybrid. Economy of space was now also a focus as architects worked to eliminate the wasted square footage of long hallways.

While developers will always rush to build brick two-flats due to their value (two houses stacked on one lot!) and renters and buyers will always appreciate their economy, these easily identifiable, classic Chicago flats with their handsome Craftsman detailing said goodbye alongside their Chicago bungalow cousins in the early 1930s. The two-flats that came back after the war had a decidedly different appearance and didn't dominate throughout the heart of the city in the same numbers. While countless from this era remain standing, many have been recently converted into single-family homes, shifting the affordability quotient and rearranging the interior flow of the space. Still, purchasing a 1920s brick two-flat is the dream of so many Chicagoans and likely will be for the foreseeable future.

Courtyard Apartments Get Gussied Up

Like their smaller, single-lot cousins, the two- and three-flats, these popular neighborhood anchors thrived in the 1920s with material upgrades and decorative motifs to give them a little extra flair. The green space around their set-back exterior walls, and of course in their fountained courtyards and limestone details, continued to set them even farther apart from their tenement ancestors.

While this building type had been around for a while, first appearing in the 1890s, large, multi-unit buildings still had something to prove. The prevailing culture continued to equate morality with single-family homeownership, and multi-unit housing still had a bit of a chip on its shoulder. A 1925 display ad in the *Chicago Tribune* made it clear who was welcome to live in the Greenview Apartments in Rogers Park—a boxed proclamation gobbling up the bottom quarter of the ad begins: "HIGH CLASS RESIDENTS ONLY. Only high-class people, who have furnished complete information about themselves, may buy apartments from us."[12] Not a tenement. Got it.

A late 1920s courtyard building in Lake View with a creamy, white-colored brick and central bays clad almost entirely in limestone.

During this period, courtyard apartment buildings retained their low, three-story height (though sometimes with a raised basement) to stay in scale with the single-family homes and flat buildings around them. That height limit actually helped keep the units affordable as well—three stories or less meant the building didn't have to be fireproofed, and it also meant that folks were still willing to walk up to their apartment and wouldn't complain about a lack of elevators—as they might in taller walk-ups in New York. The developers saved a buck and so did the renters.

In fact, tenants saved more than a buck. That same *Chicago Tribune* advertisement, despite implying that its tenants wore crowns and carried scepters, spent the other three-quarters of the ad talking about how cheap the units were to acquire through a cooperative ownership plan. "The average monthly rental of this class of apartment in Rogers Park is $120 . . . you can live in the Greenview Apartments at a monthly cost of only $61.39."[13]

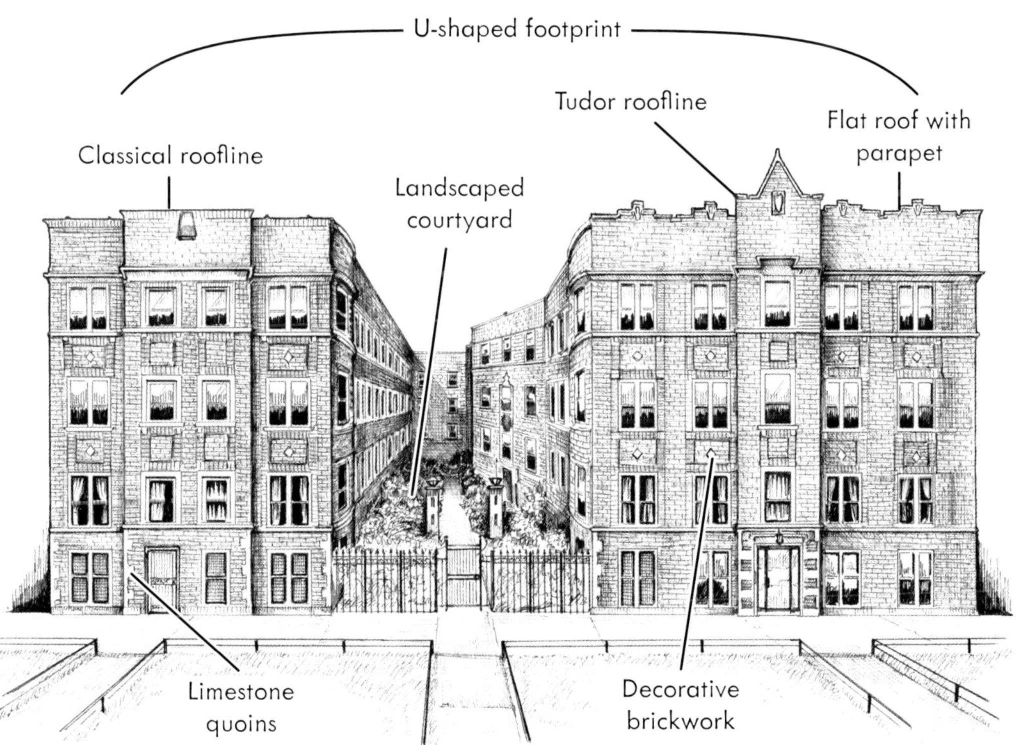

A massive red-brick courtyard building in Rogers Park with a mixture of classical and Tudor Revival details, built 1924.

A Bit of Flash

Like two-flats and bungalows, courtyard apartments were experimenting with Classical, Spanish, and Tudor Revival elements in the 1920s. The street-facing facades were clad in red, brown, creamy white, or yellow brick. Good old Chicago common brick still wrapped around the rear and alley-facing sides of the building. Brick pattern variations brought a bit of extra charm, while playful touches—like urns or cast concrete crests—were perched on parapets or above windows to catch the eye. Variations in brick patterning could add a little extra pizzazz and funky elements like urns or cast concrete crests were plunked onto parapets or above windows.

These typically maintained a U-shaped layout, though some variations included an L-shaped design with a half courtyard, an S-shaped layout with one-and-a-half courtyards—often found on block corners—and a W-shaped form featuring double courtyards.

The "Own Your Own Home" Movement

Home buying became an attainable option for many working-class Chicagoans in the late 1910s through 1920s thanks to the developers who subdivided land, the builders and contractors who constructed the houses, and the financial institutions distributing the loans. This holy trinity removed many of the home-buying barriers for the massive European immigrant population that was building the city's social and physical infrastructure. Thousands left cramped, substandard tenement apartments in industrial neighborhoods for single-family homes in areas that looked and felt like landscaped suburbs.

But of course, it wasn't just benevolence on the part of the developers, builders, and banks. Land values around the edges of the city were relatively cheap as compared to areas closer to the city's core. Developers saw opportunity here, especially as soldiers flooded home after World War I. Because the war had stopped residential construction, there was a massive housing shortage by the time soldiers returned, and workers returning to jobs in urban areas, as well as newly married couples, had few housing options. Meanwhile, the cost of renting an apartment in Chicago had nearly doubled between 1919 to 1924.

All of this led to the "Own Your Home" movement, a social and economic campaign where real estate agencies joined with social and civic groups to promote homeownership, especially for families. The newspapers were promoting this crusade by implying that it was a kind of spiritual and patriotic duty to be a homeowner, but also because it just made more economic sense.

One 1919 write-up in the *Chicago Daily Tribune* titled "Own Your Own Home" explained that "the homeowner is inclined to be contemptuous of apartment dwellers. He says they are apt to be childless, frequently lazy, often fond of mere garishness, and usually of unstable disposition," then ended with, "We doubt whether it is any longer true, except in special cases, that it is cheaper to pay rent than to buy. . . . It cannot be cheaper in the long run if a man has any pride in possession or finds satisfaction in the family life of the home, using the word in its traditional sense."[14]

Another article titled "Own Your Own Home and Kill 'Red' Parasite" made the case that homeownership was the best cure for Bolshevism.[15] Perhaps that pricked up the ears of the federal government, because it joined the crusade in 1922 with the *Better Homes in America* movement. President Calvin Coolidge was the honorary chairman and secretary of commerce, and Herbert Hoover was chairman, working with civic organizations and other governmental agencies for support.

While all of this pro-homeownership propaganda was compelling, it still had to make economic sense for the working families who were being targeted. Access to capital with manageable terms was critical, and that meant monthly mortgage payments needed to be the same as what it would cost to rent. And that's exactly what happened.

Developers and builders helped potential homeowners secure first mortgages of up to 50 percent of the value of the house, and then they worked with the buyer to secure a second mortgage through a broker. Sometimes, they even provided the second mortgage themselves. European immigrants and their children developed building and loan associations as a way to help members purchase real estate. New banks were created in parts of the city where construction was booming. There was financial and social support at every level, at least for white Americans, providing a path to stability and generational wealth. ■

Tudor Revival: More Medieval

During the 1920s, Tudor Revivals really ramped up, and many of the same architects designing bungalows and flats buildings were also designing these handsome abodes. Tudor-style buildings continued to feature a mix of exterior wall materials, including decorative half-timbering, medieval-inspired crests, brick, stone, and stucco. This style can be seen across a variety of forms, from single-family homes to two-flats and courtyard buildings. The steeply pitched roofs that characterize the single-family version of the style have one advantage over the Chicago bungalow: more second-story headroom. While, like bungalows, they had a relatively small footprint with two-bedroom floor plans, those taller roofs allowed for more room upstairs and could easily be expanded with dormers.

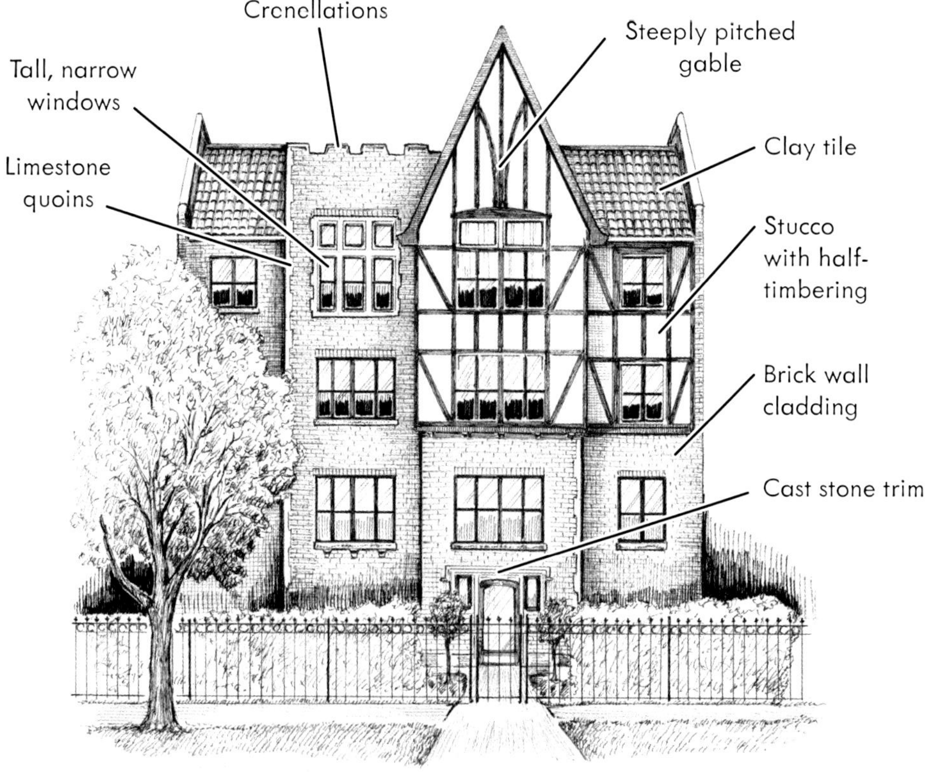

A multi-unit Tudor Revival with red brick, stucco, half-timbering, and green clay tile shingles in Rogers Park.

Some Evolution of Style

As with most styles at the time, Tudors became more whimsical with some "storybook" details and forms showing up in the mid- to late 1920s and into the 1930s. Brick dominated residential architecture at this time, and while stucco and half-timbering still showed up in gables and on second stories, the lion's share of exterior walls were made of brick, sometimes with limestone quoins incorporated at the corners and around doorways. Massive multi-unit courtyard and corner apartment buildings also had Tudor Revival flourishes like crests and false wooden gables emulating peaked roofs—an easy and relatively inexpensive way to turn a large brick box into a romantic medieval estate. Indeed, some of the late 1920s Chicago bungalows wore enough medieval detailing to warrant a British accent.

To further encourage the style, *Chicago Tribune* display ads were lousy with advertisements for Tudor dining room sets with chairs that could be decked out in "beautiful tapestries or blue leather." Field houses like Indian Boundary Park, numerous churches, and schools like Hirsch High School also got that medieval England fever. The fact that we were also experiencing a building boom in the 1920s meant there was no small supply of this influence, especially in neighborhoods like Beverly, Norwood Park, Gladstone Park, West Ridge, Forest Park, and South Shore.

Colonial Revival: Peak Romance

This revival style peaked in the 1920s, along with a growing fascination with the Colonial era. American art and architecture wasn't taken very seriously until we started to claim our unique national identity in the early decades of the 1900s. In 1924, it was a big deal when the Metropolitan Museum of Art opened its American wing, which incorporated twenty-five rooms from Colonial- and Federal-era buildings to display the domestic arts of the seventeenth to early nineteenth centuries. It was the first of its kind.

Up until the 1920s, and in some cases after, many scoffed at the idea of "American art." The young culture seemed juvenile or reductive as compared to the "real deal" European stuff, or the ancient wonders that archaeologists were uncovering in Egypt. But European-descended Americans decided to look at what they'd created since colonizing North America and to claim it in a new way. Three years after the American wing opened, ground broke on Colonial Williamsburg, with the help of various preservation and legacy organizations (such as the Colonial Dames of America and the Daughters of the Confederacy), and its main bankrollers, John D. Rockefeller Jr. and his wife, Abby Aldrich Rockefeller.

There was a renewed push to historicize and modernize America—this time, we were not as focused on the Founding Fathers as we were on art and architecture as a symbol of who we were. What have we built? What could it mean? This reflection, of course, required some heavy romanticization of the past. The simultaneous rise of the automobile and more affordable luxury passenger trains meant that people could visit these architectural holy lands in droves. Tourism was amping up and Colonial Revival was hot.

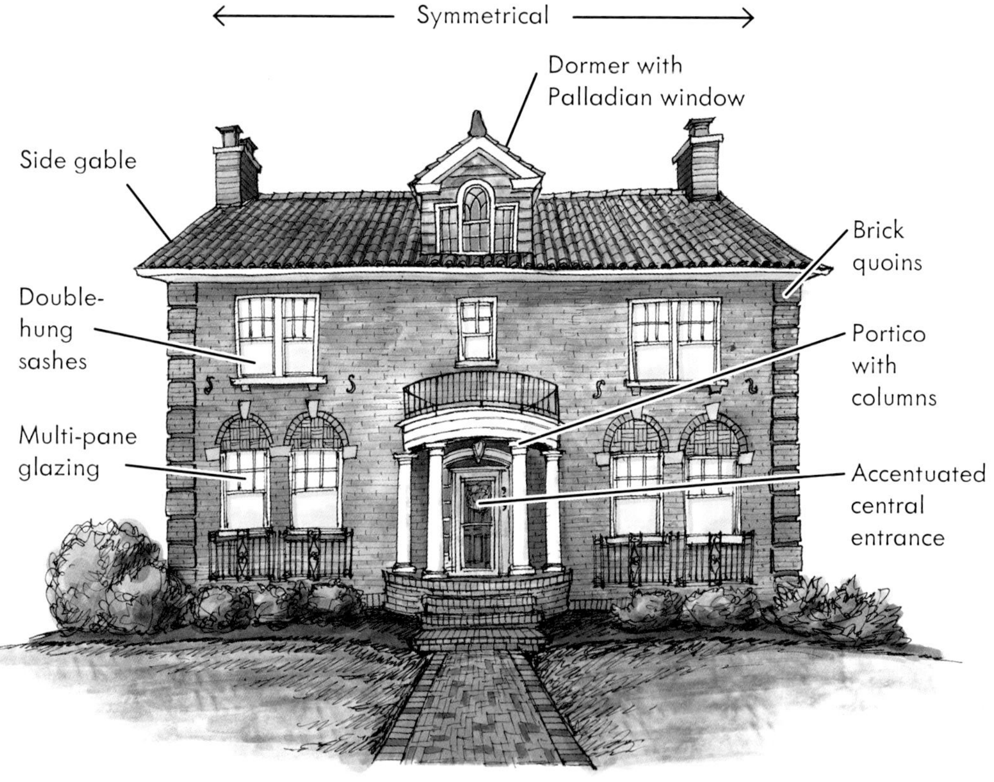

A 1926 Colonial Revival with a symmetrical facade, a central front door with portico, a large dormer, and a green clay tile roof in Oak Park.

Stylistic Changes

In terms of how this revival style changed since becoming popular in the early 1900s, the answer is not much. It kept its pared-down, stately good looks and didn't go the way of the bungalows and two-flats with their increased ornamentation and stained glass. This is because the style was a response to the frilly 1890s stuff and defined itself as a "pure," non-eclectic style. There was less need to add ornament to attract buyers since the popularity of this style only increased with the idea of Americans claiming their own "authentic" past. The selling point was the nostalgia of simpler times, even if they never existed.

Nationwide, from 1910–20, 40 percent of U.S. homes were built in the Colonial Revival style. Yet another, more simplified version of the style sprung up in the 1950s and '60s, bringing an incalculable number of funeral home buildings and modest single-family homes to the Chicago suburbs. A lot of new construction can also be considered a form of Colonial Revival, or at least borrows elements of the style.[16]

Spanish Revival: Bienvenido a Chicago

The Spanish Revival style is based on Spanish Colonial and Mexican buildings that were built in California, Texas, and the American Southwest between the early 1600s and the 1840s. The style regained popularity as a revival style during the 1920s. Various building types with this style can be found all over the city, including Beverly, Edison Park, South Shore, and Rogers Park.

You will often see features like clay tiles and rounded window arches laid over bungalows, flats, and courtyard apartment buildings, and often these "Spanish" details are mixed with other revival styles. While they're frequently combined with other influences, their presence was distinctive enough during this era to warrant a bit of background information. Also, it may be obvious why the southwestern United States would use Spanish Revival styles, due to Spanish settlement that happened in those regions—but Chicago?

How It Got Here

Rest assured, conquistadors did not subjugate the Great Lakes Region in the early decades of the twentieth century. Like so many trends that don't seem to make sense for the region, the style became popularized through a World's Fair. In fact, if you're ever participating in a trivia night and get a question about how a revival style popped up in an unexpected part of the U.S., you can

SPANISH REVIVAL

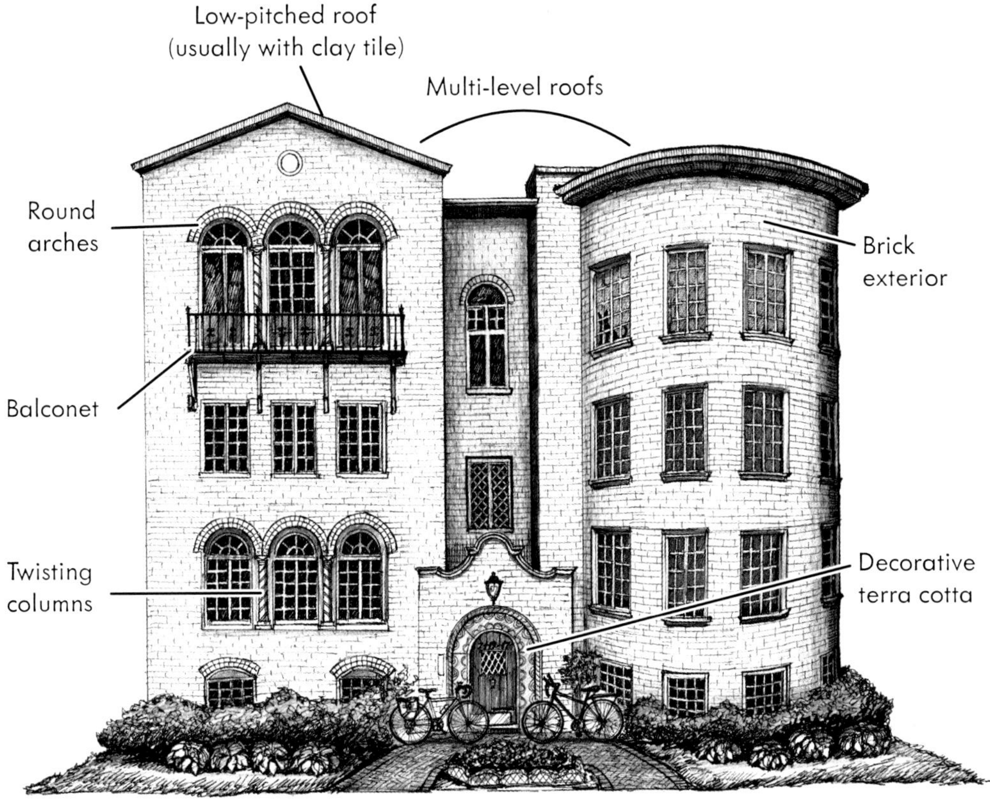

Rogers Park Spanish Revival six-flat with twisting columns, rounded arched windows, and creamy white brick.

COMMON FEATURES

- Brick or stucco walls
- Twisting columns
- Decorative terra cotta shields
- Round arched windows
- Elaborately rounded roof parapets
- Low-pitched clay tile roofs
- Yellow-cream brick wall surfaces
- The occasional nod to a bell tower

pretty safely make a guess now. This particular style crept into Chicago after the 1915 Panama-California Exposition held in San Diego, which showed off elaborate Spanish prototypes, common in the southwestern states.[17] Architects travel.

In addition to the Panama-California Exposition, World War I caused architects longing to study architecture in Europe to study in Spain instead of the usual spots like France and Italy due to their involvement in the war.[18] Hollywood movies also influenced the development of the style. Folks watching films and reading magazines about movie stars were exposed to their glamorous lifestyles and mansions and got some ideas, many even more playful and off-brand as the Revivals they were ogling. This Hollywood effect may also be why a lot of movie theaters reflect the style or something like it, one example being the Music Box Theater, described by *Chicago Tribune* architecture critic Paul Gapp as "an eclectic melange of Italian, Spanish and Pardon-My-Fantasy put together with passion."[19]

American Foursquares: Straightforward to the End

The classic, boxy, two-story home with a half-story attic became even more popular during this era, but like Colonial Revival homes, American Foursquares didn't get fancy in the 1920s. For the most part, they kept it simple, their form always identifiable. Despite their practicality and ample space, they lost popularity in the 1930s and ultimately went the way of their Prairie style predecessor. Somehow, the shape that embodies what a house is supposed to look like went out of fashion.

Changes in Appearance

Foursquares were covered in wood siding, built of brick, or clad in stucco or textured concrete blocks. Most built in Chicago at this time would have been brick construction with Arts and Crafts detailing. A "shirtwaist Foursquare" had contrasting exterior materials on the first and second floors to add a little visual interest and harken to the horizontality of Prairie style. Colonial Revival detailing was also common at this time, which is no great surprise given how popular the style was in this era.

Cost & Materials

Looking to throw down some roots after returning from the war? Look no further! One could order the materials to build a wood frame Foursquare from Aladdin Co. for around $1,100. The frame Sears "Woodland" model might run you around $2,500, and the "Hillrose" $3,500 four years later. Size, details, and amenities could alter the cost of materials considerably, and one could save by going with plaster exterior walls versus wood siding, forgoing storm doors, ditching a mantel, choosing a more economical shingling material, etc. Labor, of course, was not included in these costs.

A 1918 Foursquare in the Ravenswood neighborhood.

Homes for Cars

Garages are weird, ubiquitous additions that forever changed our residential landscape. They're tiny houses for cars that, during this time, looked like they were birthed by their parent house. While they excel as cozy hideouts for stray kittens and locations for Domino tournaments, their main job is to keep inanimate objects safe and dry, providing homes for workbenches, bikes, holiday decorations, and those hand-embroidered linens from your great aunt that you're honor-bound to keep as the unofficial family archivist. So, when and how did these tiny homes for cars—the first of their kind—begin taking up our real estate?

Public Parking Garages

In 1899, only one in 1.5 million Americans owned a car. Within three years that number would jump to one in 6,500, but it would take more than a decade for the middle class to be able to comfortably afford their own automobiles. When the Model T dropped to less than the cost of an upright piano, sales exploded. The massive increase in personal car ownership created a need for a new building type—the parking garage.

Unlike horses, who would get aggressive and bite-y if hitched to a post for too long, an automobile could lounge about on a curb all day. And they often did, without bolting into traffic or requiring an apple. As cars clogged up narrow streets that weren't designed for all that large, sedentary machinery, parking became an issue for the first time in history.

Architects Holabird and Roche, known for high caliber buildings like the Palmer House, designed the first high-rise parking garage in 1917. Parking at the five-story Hotel LaSalle cost you seventy-five cents for ten hours or less.[20] It was likely the oldest example of a commercial parking garage in the United States, but was razed in 2005 thanks to plaster chunks falling off of the ceiling and large SUVs trying to fit into spaces designed for Model Ts. A few years later, in the 1920s, parking entrepreneurs Richard G. Lydy and Ben Kissel bought up some old buildings on Franklin Street, Wells Street, and Printers Row and converted them into garages. Residents loathed these early garages and complained that they were defacing the street. Some things never change.

Mainstreaming the Single-Family Garage

Before the automobile, alleys were lined with chest-high, solid board fences and were used as transportation paths for services like ice and coal delivery, and other activities that would otherwise result in dragging mud through the house. Then the automobile came along, complete with its cloth roofs and delicate machinery, and these expensive and finicky contraptions needed protection. The servicemen found themselves moving their wagons down the same narrow alleys behind homes, but they suddenly felt more like thoroughfares. The alley had a more complicated job now that it was shared, and it required a more robust infrastructure. Most of them were paved after 1910.[21]

Unlike early public parking structures, these detached, private garages could not be carved out of existing buildings. This was an entirely new form of architecture. Naturally, we took to experimenting with a variety of shapes, sizes, and materials early on, resulting in a somewhat disorganized look along alleyways.

Builders decided to lean on the horse stable look since folks were calling automobiles "horseless carriages" at the time. The old barnlike garages you sometimes see were never meant for horses; those who owned horses at the time generally kept them in stables, not on their own property, unless they were wealthy. (For information on carriage houses, see Chapter 5.)

By the 1920s, numerous companies sold garage plans. For Aladdin and Sears, already well known for their kit homes, it was a small leap to jump to kit garages. Newspapers advertised "permanent garages" with single or double options in a variety of sizes, and offered payment plans. Even after Chicagoans got used to the automobile and adapted their garages, many doors continued to be built with a barn look into the 1940s.[22]

While a tiny barn may be charming, it's not terribly functional as a garage. Sliding doors and doors that swung on hinges weren't especially fun to deal with when snow piled up in the winter. The improved design? The overhead door that rolled up and back into the ceiling of the garage, which began to appear in the 1930s.

1920s garage with Spanish Revival and Craftsman details that likely matched its parent house.

The Hard Parts

If you had a car, you really did need a garage. Today, people will chase down a tornado in a Camry, but early automobile features like a cloth top made such endeavors an even worse idea, and these delicate machines could be put out of commission with just a little cold weather. If you wanted to run your car during the winter months, it had to be kept in a heated space. Of course, a heated garage had to be close enough to the house to tap into the domestic furnace, or it had to have its own fireproof boiler room and wall-mounted steam pipes or radiators. Every now and again, you'll still see one with a chimney. As one might imagine, these amenities would add up, so some would use cars in the warmer months and switch to a horse and sleigh to move things around in the winter. Garages also had to be roomy enough to have a work bench and lighting system, and ideally a water system like any typical repair shop, since repairs were needed so often.

Gas was another issue. For early automobile owners, gas was bought by the bucket in repair shops and general stores. The Chicago Public Library Digital Collections have images of early stations, including a 1906 photo that shows an early filling station at Broadway and Devon. The station had no gas pumps or service bays so you had to purchase the gasoline in canisters. Over the next two decades, things evolved considerably, and a 1925 postcard of Super-Service Station No. 2, located at 6919 Stony Island Avenue, shows pumps, shelter, and four gas station attendants in white uniforms.[23] From the 1920s to 1960s, major oil companies adopted distinctive logos, slogans, and new services like oil checks and auto repair. Gas stations reflected the corporate image and were designed by some of Chicago's top architects, including Frank Lloyd Wright, Mies van der Rohe, and Bertrand Goldberg.

Prohibition gave garages another job. Bootlegger Joe Saltis, supposedly on his way to Florida after his release from prison in 1929, was immediately nabbed when prohibition agents found 18 cases of Canadian ale and 125 slot machines in the garage behind his home at 5658 South Albany Avenue.[24]

But more sinister than smuggling spirits was good old carbon monoxide. Car owners regularly tinkering with their finicky vehicles, sometimes shirked the warnings of poisonous gasses released in their private "death chambers."[25] According to the *Chicago Daily Tribune*, the first recorded case of home garage poisoning was in 1911. Dr. John Aloysius Hemsteger was cleaning the carbon out of a muffler in his garage at 1035 East 42nd Street, but things didn't go as planned. He managed to drag himself out of his garage and even go to see a few patients before slumping to the ground and being taken up by that chariot in the sky. Physicians agreed that he died of "direct poisoning of the heart from carbon gas."[26] There were many such cases going forward.

Tens of thousands of original garages still exist, but original garage doors are rapidly disappearing due to deterioration and loss of functionality—or, in some cases, a lack of imagination. There are still examples around the city; this is a great excuse to spend a Sunday morning wandering down alleyways with a thermos and some curiosity. ■

Art Deco: Anti-Classical

Art Deco architecture was popular from the 1920s to around 1940, and got its name from the Paris Exposition of 1925—the *Exposition internationale des arts décoratifs et industriels modernes*. Of course, we well-mannered Midwesterners could have taken the opportunity to thumb our noses at the Parisians, since Art Deco had already wowed at its debutante ball a few years earlier in the land of the hog butchers.

In 1922, in observance of its seventy-fifth birthday, the *Chicago Tribune* held an international competition to design its headquarters—"the most beautiful office building in the world"[27]—to sit at the corner of Michigan Avenue and the Chicago River. The $100,000 prize was awarded to American architects Raymond Hood and John Mead Howells, who created the Gothic-inspired Tribune Tower, drawing on European architectural traditions. But the second prize went to an Art Deco design by Finnish architect Eliel Saarinen. A lot of local architects, no doubt tired of the relentless return to classical precedents, preferred the young Saarinen's exciting design, and shortly thereafter, stylistic elements found their way onto the tables of draftsmen around the city.

Examples, Big & Small

Art Deco loved to borrow non-Western stylistic elements, principally from Egyptian, Asian, and Indigenous sources. While we tend to think of Art Deco architecture in terms of the big buildings you'd find downtown like the Carbide and Carbon Building (230 North Michigan), Chicago Board of Trade (141 West Jackson), Adler Planetarium (1300 South Lake Shore Drive), or the Merchandise Mart (222 West Merchandise Mart Plaza), it did find its way to smaller commercial streets as well as bank buildings, garages, news buildings, and various other businesses. The style also dominates sections of cemeteries like Rosehill in Edgewater, which is brimming with striking Deco monuments, mausoleums, and tombs. Large, older cemeteries often reflect the architectural styles of the times, and some of these Deco tombs will really knock your socks off with their Egyptian themes and dramatic angular shapes.

Single-family homes were also built in this style, but they were rare and didn't make their way to Chicago until the 1930s. There are, however, extant examples of large Art Deco apartment buildings in neighborhoods around the city from the 1920s, usually with retail on the ground floor. Some

ART DECO

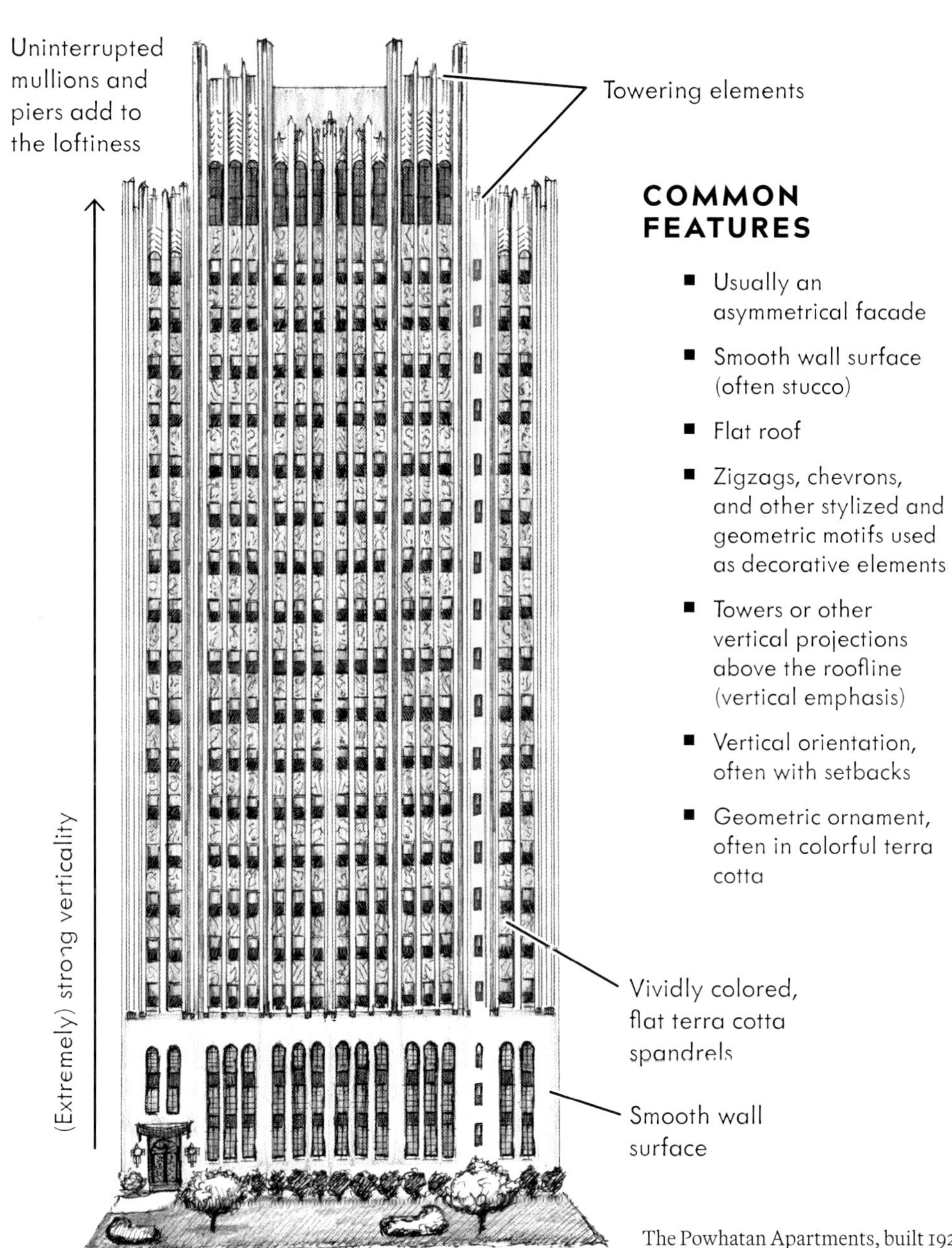

COMMON FEATURES

- Usually an asymmetrical facade
- Smooth wall surface (often stucco)
- Flat roof
- Zigzags, chevrons, and other stylized and geometric motifs used as decorative elements
- Towers or other vertical projections above the roofline (vertical emphasis)
- Vertical orientation, often with setbacks
- Geometric ornament, often in colorful terra cotta

The Powhatan Apartments, built 1927–30.

examples include the striking four-story apartment building at 4025–4027 North Pulaski Road; the stretched, three-story, multi-colored brick apartment building at 2201–2207 West Montrose; and the Egyptian-themed, eight-story Belle Shore Apartments in Edgewater at 1062 West Bryn Mawr Avenue, clad in rich green and cream terra cotta.

Perhaps the residential Art Deco building most influenced by Eliel Saarinen's submission for the Tribune Tower is the twenty-two-story Powhatan Apartments high-rise at 4950 South Chicago Beach Drive, built 1927–30. Architects Charles Morgan and Robert S. DeGoyler added vibrant mosaics to the facade, lobbies, and swimming pool of the Powhatan Apartments, along with terra cotta ornamental panels featuring scenes from Native culture—the building was named for a famous Algonquin Indian chief, although the imagery is vague and eclectic. The east and south entrances have silver metal outlines of two Native men facing one another with light fixtures at either side, decorated with arrows and feathers.

FACING PAGE: There are an astonishing number of brightly colored terra cotta panels spanning the upper 17 stories of the Powhatan. But even more astonishing is that each panel is unique, featuring abstractions of Indigenous imagery.

CHAPTER

Hard Times, New Deals, and a Century of Progress

1930–1941

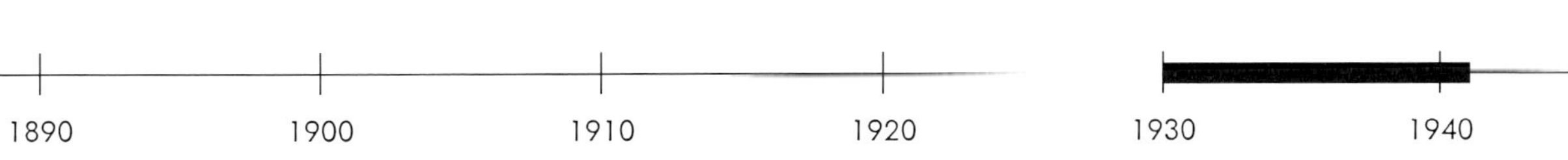

You've lost your job
You've lost your dough
Your jewels and handsome houses
But things could be worse, you know
You haven't lost your trousers

—A Valentine's Day comic laid on the body of "Machine Gun" Jack McGurn, mastermind of the Saint Valentine's Day Massacre, moments after he was shot dead at a Milwaukee Avenue bowling alley; February 15, 1936.[1]

WHILE THE BULLDOZER WOULDN'T BE INVENTED for another decade, you wouldn't know it by looking at the domestic realities of Chicagoans in the 1930s. The Great Depression hit this city hard. Harder than many other cities, in fact, because Chicago's jobs were production jobs and little was being produced. After a period of unprecedented prosperity, it only took a few years to make rubble of lives and replace the urban landscape with soup kitchens, a massive homeless population, and a groundswell of labor strikes. New construction was stopped in its tracks and no major buildings were added to the downtown skyline until after the next World War.

The City of Big Shoulders—a name coined by Carl Sandburg in a 1914 poem that made you want to strut around in overalls and wipe your forehead with a filthy handkerchief—was now a city slouching. Once America's capital of industry, Chicago was now distinguished primarily by its high unemployment rate. A whopping 700,000 Chicagoans were unemployed in 1931—40 percent of the city's population.[2] As a result, in just the first half of 1931 alone, nearly 1,400 families were evicted from their homes.[3]

Political Upheaval

That year, the city had an insolvent city government led by a notoriously corrupt Republican mayor—incidentally, Chicago's last Republican mayor—which resulted in protests and a population that felt abandoned by its leadership. Desperate Chicagoans came together to elect Mayor Anton Cermak. Cermak was an Austro-Hungarian-born Democrat who worked the coal mines as a youth, then the horse stables of Chicago's Pilsen neighborhood after moving to the city as a teenager. He was seen as a man who understood the plight of the struggling Chicagoan, and boy were Chicagoans struggling. But there were few happy endings to be found in these years. Just two years after taking office, during a brief visit from President Franklin Delano Roosevelt, Cermak was shot by a bullet intended for the president-elect, and died shortly after.

In the early 1930s, conditions were even worse for Black and Mexican workers who had swooped in to fill the labor shortages during World War I and had been so vital to Chicago's growth over the past decade. By 1932, 40 to 50 percent of Black workers in Chicago were unemployed, and many Mexican immigrants were forced to return to their home country or face retaliation.[4] In the fall of 1931, the *Chicago Tribune* reported that rental agents were creating armed patrols on the South Side meant to prevent evicted tenants in "colored districts" from reentering their homes after being forced out. A judge shut down these violent groups, declaring their vigilantism illegal.[5]

Because Chicagoans of all backgrounds were affected by the economic conditions, the shared experience created bridges between groups as well. Faced with a surge of evictions throughout the city, a desperate population united, sparking some of the earliest instances of cross-racial organizing in Chicago. One result was the formation of "Unemployed Councils," which were racially integrated at both the membership and leadership levels. The primary purpose of these councils was to push back on evictions for nonpayment of rent. By September 1931, there were forty-five branches of Unemployed Councils in Chicago alone, and around twenty thousand members. The massive resistance, coupled with violence against protestors and enforcement agents, got the attention of the mayor. Before his assassination, Mayor Cermak decreed a temporary moratorium on forced evictions and rent debts in response to the resistance.[6]

In 1933, mayor number three picked up the torch. Despite being unexpectedly thrust into leadership, the third time seemed to be the charm when Edward Kelly came into power. Kelly would become one of Chicago's most powerful mayors, and that is saying a lot if you know a thing or two about Chicago mayors. He strategically shaped the Democratic Party for the next fourteen years by aligning the city with New Deal policies, drawing Black Republican voters into the Democratic party, and using the resources of the organized crime syndicate. That same year, despite monumental challenges, Chicago held its second World's Fair: the 1933–1934 Century of Progress—a beacon of bright colors and futuristic forms against a gray and beaten down city.

Technology Marches On

Regardless of the economic hardships bulldozing the psyche of everyday Chicagoans, technological advancements continued to transform urban life. Fueled in part by the massive mail-order businesses of Sears Roebuck and Montgomery Ward, the Chicago Post Office—the largest mail transfer facility in the world at the time—was completed in 1932. By 1933, two-thirds of American homes had at least one radio,[7] and indoor plumbing, which had once been a luxury for the wealthy, had become so commonplace that the federal government identified housing *without* plumbing as substandard.[8] General Electric refrigerators—a.k.a "sealed-in-steel cold-makers"—were introduced in 1927, and by 1936, were being used by 200,000 Chicagoans.[9]

The promise of air conditioning was also on the horizon. While it would not become commonplace in homes until after the second World War, it was now available in public gathering spaces like movie theaters where folks could escape their stressful realities and cool down after burning their rubbish on a Sunday in August. Places like the Avalon Theater at 79th and Stoney, which boldly advertised "Always Cool-Air Conditioned" in a frosty font, drew crowds for relief from the heat in the warmer months.[10] Food technology advanced as well, with miracles like stable, moist, and inexpensive spiced ham in a can entering the scene in 1937. SPAM was being baked and fried and added to soups, chilis, and "SPAMwiches" in the kitchens of carved up Queen Annes and crowded bungalows in the late, lean years of the Depression.[11]

New Deal Relief Programs

But contrary to what one might think, SPAM was not the pinnacle of the era. There were also some bright spots brought about by President Roosevelt's New Deal relief agencies, such as the Federal Emergency Relief Administration and the Social Security Administration. Programs targeted the elderly, sick, and unemployed. While elegant, older, single-family homes were being subdivided to allow for cheaper rents and mortgage relief, the New Deal provided emergency loans to the middle and working classes in order to again provide a path to homeownership.[12]

While some of these new policies were a blessing for many, they were a curse for others. A newly created Federal Housing Administration provided funds to lending institutions that guaranteed mortgages and encouraged construction on the edges of the city and suburbs, though this also served to discourage investment in the city's crumbling apartment buildings.[13] The new loan policies *also* created and sanctioned systems like redlining, a practice that withholds financial services from areas that have significant numbers of racial and ethnic minorities. This practice would continue on into the 1960s, when the 1968 Fair Housing Act finally deemed it unlawful, but the effects on real estate prices and lack of access to home improvement loans in predominantly Black neighborhoods continues to have devastating effects into the present day.

Beyond housing, the city's flagging infrastructure enjoyed a huge boost of federal funding in the 1930s. This pool was tapped to complete projects like Lake Shore Drive, from Foster Avenue to Jackson Park, construct dozens of new schools, and create some semi-idyllic public housing projects. Roads were resurfaced, sewers were repaired, and the airport was expanded. As intended, the work provided desperately needed jobs for thousands of Chicagoans. And not just construction crews. Unemployed architects, photographers, artists, and historians also benefited. Roosevelt created the Historic American Buildings Survey (HABS), a program that used the skill sets of these professionals to document America's architectural heritage. Many of these sketched and photographed places are the only existing records of long-obliterated buildings and landscapes around Chicago and the rest of the U.S. You can look up detailed documentation of everything from pueblos to skyscrapers on the Library of Congress website.

Chicago Straightens Its Shoulders

Chicagoans were still struggling to return to a sense of normalcy in the late 1930s, but a few rays of hope were beginning to break through the fog. By 1940, Chicago had a solvent, unified, and powerful city government.[14] A new comprehensive land use plan for the city was in the works to stimulate residential construction and shape housing policy. There was also a push for transportation development as cars had changed circulation patterns, and for subways and highways that would flow out from downtown. Then another World War happened, and everything was put on hold.[15] But this hardly hurt the city.

When the U.S. entered the war in 1941, Chicago became a global center of production again, thanks to its location as a transportation hub, its industrial infrastructure, and its willingness to convert everything from hotels to local businesses and civilian backyards into spaces that could contribute to the war effort. Chicagoans fabricated everything from airplane frames and engines to GI rations and torpedoes. In the end, this city was responsible for the manufacture of $24 billion in war-related goods.[16] Chicago found itself, very abruptly, on the other side of a depression. It also found itself making a bomb that would forever change the political and literal landscape of the world.

The National Mortgage Crisis and Public Housing

While reforms in the early part of the twentieth century had improved housing conditions for those living in tenements and other crowded housing situations, these milestones became a moot point for Chicagoans unable to stay in their homes during the Depression. The National Mortgage Crisis of the 1930s was characterized by thousands of unpaid home loans. Once a home was in default, the bank would seize the property and auction it off to pay off the mortgage. Between 1928 and 1933, home prices declined by almost 26 percent and foreclosures were rampant.[17] In 1933, one thousand people per day lost their homes nationwide and 40–50 percent of all home mortgages were in default.[18] Construction came to a halt and there was no money for repairs and maintenance on existing buildings.

Housing had always been seen as an individual's responsibility in America, not a government issue. But social reformers had begun making the case for government intervention as early as the mid-nineteenth century. During the Depression, the federal government finally stepped in and made some bold and creative moves to stem the bleeding, adopting sweeping new policies that allowed for public works programs and regulation of the financial industry. The results included job creation across multiple sectors, nationally funded unemployment relief, long-term and low-interest mortgages and refinancing, and national standards for home appraisal and construction methods.[19]

All of that was great, as long as you were a middle-class individual with some means to buy a single-family home on the outskirts of the city. In 1939, a Chicago Land Use Survey found that about 8 percent of Chicago's inner-city housing stock—about 76,000 units—were in such bad shape that they were unfit places to live.[20] These new mortgage terms, while addressing some of the issues that created the housing bubble and collapse of the financial industry, in no way benefited older buildings and the residents who were struggling most. Instead of offering repair funding and relief to the Chicagoans who needed it most, the Federal Housing Administration effectively served to empty out the city by stimulating homeownership in the suburbs.

Public Housing: Experimentation & Integration

Despite this inequity, Roosevelt knew his programs had to at least address some of the "slums" that were spreading across U.S. cities. The federal government decided to use public tax money to build homes for those who could not afford to pay market rates for housing, and the Wagner-Steagall Housing Act of 1937 became the first social housing legislation in the country. At the time, public housing was not a popular idea in the U.S., even amid the suffering and evictions of the 1930s, and many of the initiatives were hobbled by opposition.

Chicago did have some earlier success with public housing, however, having experimented with it during the previous decade. First, in 1928, the Julius Rosenwald Fund created the Michigan Boulevard Garden Apartments, a complex of 421 units brimming with social amenities. Notably, this complex was on the South Side and intended to serve Chicago's chronically ignored and disproportionately impacted Black population. A year later, in 1929, the Marshall Field Garden Apartment Complex was created—a similar complex on the North Side along the 1500 block of North Sedgwick.[21] These were not basement-level apartments in the way we use the term "garden apartment" today, but were instead notable for their "spacious garden courts" and "rooms full of light and air." Field's buildings created homes for 628 families at an average cost of only fifteen dollars per room, per month. According to a brochure for the development, an apartment of similar size with the same amenities in other parts of the city could fetch as much as twenty-five or thirty dollars per room, per month.[22]

While these complexes were much needed, they certainly were not sufficient to deal with the thousands of homeless families and individuals in the years after the stock market crash. The Chicago Housing Authority (CHA) was created in 1937 to own and operate public housing complexes that resulted from the New Deal policies. This signaled a move away from temporary shelters for the unhoused and toward the creation of lasting housing solutions that addressed the root challenges facing society's most vulnerable.[23] The first three New Deal housing projects in Chicago were the Jane Addams Homes, the Julia C. Lathrop Homes, and the Trumbull Park Homes. These complexes were located in white, working-class neighborhoods and were created to benefit unemployed white workers, again ignoring the conditions of Chicago's Black neighborhoods. But CHA's first director, the politically progressive Elizabeth Wood, served from 1937 to 1954 and made housing integration a top priority. She also believed strongly in access to green space—no concrete jungles—and access to cultural and recreational activities for tenants.[24] She likely pointed to the Rosenwald and Field projects to show what these kinds of environments could look like.

In 2025, Chicago's National Public Housing Museum moved into the only remaining building from the once massive Jane Addams Homes complex. The museum has recreated some of the housing units and brought in programming that brings together artists, historians, scholars, and public housing residents to grow the public's understanding of social housing and ultimately help shape policy.[25] The museum also restored and reinstalled the Art Deco "animal court" sculptures that Edgar Miller designed for the complex in the late 1930s using Works Progress Administration (WPA) funds.[26] ■

Lingering Chicago Bungalows

Chicago bungalows continued to be built into the early 1930s, but these were mostly hangovers from the late '20s boom years. A few trickled in as late as 1934–35, and ranged from modest red brick bungalows to elaborate yellow brick bungalows with polygonal bays and stained glass. Some even showed up wearing towers and peaks with Mediterranean or Tudor Revival details, as if they missed the memo about the economic catastrophe and showed up to a backyard potluck in a ball gown. But, alas, all good things must come to an end. These were the last soldiers of a residential building style that came to define Chicago's landscape during the most prolific building boom the city had ever seen.

Tudor Revival: Fairytale Vibes

As the 1930s progressed, fewer newly constructed Tudor Revivals featured the dark half-timbering, stucco facades, and tall, narrow multi-pane windows of their predecessors. More typically in Chicago neighborhoods, Tudors were smaller homes built with a variety of brick colors and patterns, often accentuated with some limestone accents. You can find concentrations of these in Norwood Park, Forest Park, Beverly, and Gladstone Park.

While increasingly modest in size, the style was giving a little more "fairytale" and "tiny castle" than it had in the past. Rounded doorways surrounded by chunky limestone voussoirs, swooping rooflines, and towers sporting conical roofs began sprouting up like sturdy mushrooms. Contemporized "thatch" roofs created by architect R. Harold Zook brought the Cotswold Cottage look into vogue and added some Alice in Wonderland energy. Despite the drama, their relatively modest footprints, local materials, and uniform setbacks allowed them to blend in seamlessly with existing housing. This style stretches into the 1940s, sometimes indistinguishable from Cape Cods outside of the limestone details surrounding the windows or door. You can find especially delightful examples of 1930s Tudor Revival homes on the Northwest Side in Gladstone Park.

FACING PAGE, BELOW: A nearby suburban "Zook home" showing off a collection of fanciful details. While Zook is perhaps best known for his signature "thatch" roof, not all of his homes were designed to wear them.

An early 1930s Tudor Revival in Peterson Park.

The World's Fair of 1933 and 1934

Amid the longest and steepest economic downturn in the history of the United States, folks needed something to look forward to. "Levity" was a major theme at the Expo, which emphasized speed and flight, and showcased soaring, spacious buildings that gave a sense of freedom and openness. Walking past the unemployed and hopeless, being above it all sounded pretty good.

The 1933 Century of Progress Exposition was not interested in resurrecting the ancient "greats" by dunking a piece of the city into a Neoclassical baptismal font. Interestingly, the fair was dreamt up and designed by an architectural team that included Daniel Jr. and Hubert Burnham, the sons of the venerable Daniel Burnham who had been the force behind those white, Neoclassical buildings forty years earlier. The younger Burnhams and other planners adopted a dynamic and modern aesthetic that translated to Art Deco and Art Moderne.

The Expo was originally scheduled to run from May 27 to November 12, 1933, but was so successful that it reopened from May 26 to October 31, 1934. Over those two years, almost 49 million people visited Chicago.[27] Somehow, during the worst years of a depression, the fair made money. Nearly two dozen corporations developed dazzling displays that convinced Americans that they needed to spend money to modernize pretty much everything, including their homes.

The fair's central theme was "progress," and it was often described as a "utopia, or perfect world, built on democracy and manufacturing." Of course, the reality was that many social inequities in Chicago and beyond remained stagnant—or in some cases were growing worse. Technology offered a kind of neutral and benevolent hope against the social and economic realities of the time, the idea being that in the near future, lives would be made easier for all with increased luxuries and conveniences on the horizon. Transportation would move faster, lights would be brighter, food would last longer via preservatives and refrigerators. The Home Planning Hall and Gas Industry Hall showed off advancements in home heating, plumbing, air conditioning, and building materials. Innovations that we take for granted today—from gas cooking stoves to dishwashers to vacuum cleaners—delighted tired visitors looking for some proof that things would get easier.[28]

As with most world's fairs, in the interest of time and money, the buildings were meant to be temporary structures and were quickly demolished after closing. Only a handful escaped their sentence. One was discovered in Wilmette in the late 2010s and dismantled; another was demolished in the 1990s in Palos Heights. There is a bit of good news, however. When the Fair closed, real estate developer Robert Bartlett came up with the idea of floating some of the model homes across Lake Michigan—fifty miles southeast to Michigan City, Indiana—in hopes to attract more people to his new development. Five homes that were once part of the Homes of Tomorrow Exhibit still stand: the Cypress Log Cabin, the Wieboldt-Rostone House, the Armco-Ferro House, the House of Tomorrow (currently being restored), and the Florida Tropical House. While these homes supposedly had an eye on affordability, they were, of course, largely aspirational for a struggling public.[29] The homes are now part of Indiana Dunes National Park and are open for tours one day each October. ■

The flamingo-pink Florida Tropical House from the Century of Progress Exposition, now in Beverly Shores, Indiana. On clear days, the Chicago skyline is visible across the lake.

Art Deco's Farewell & the Short, Streamlined Life of Moderne

The 1933 Century of Progress Exposition amped up the idea of small, modern homes and brought the Art Deco style down to a human scale after almost a decade of scraping the clouds. Chicago's second World's Fair showed the country examples of "homes of the future," wrapped in modernistic styles and equipped with innovative technologies. There was a focus on affordability when conceiving these homes for the Fair, but perhaps because the Exposition took place during the throes of the Great Depression, or perhaps because some of the technology had yet to be truly accessible, "pure" Art Deco single-family homes just never took off in the city. Or really anywhere, in any great number.

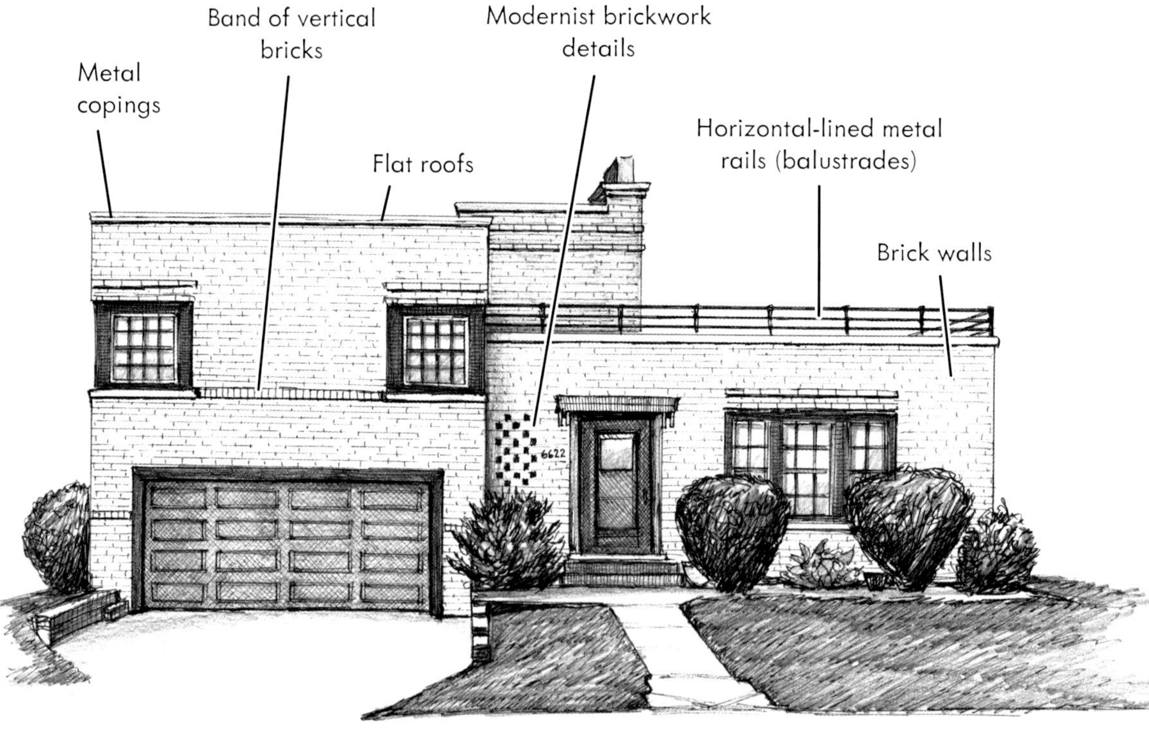

A rare example of a late 1930s single-family Art Deco home in Chicago at 6622 N. Ponchartrain Blvd.

MODERNE

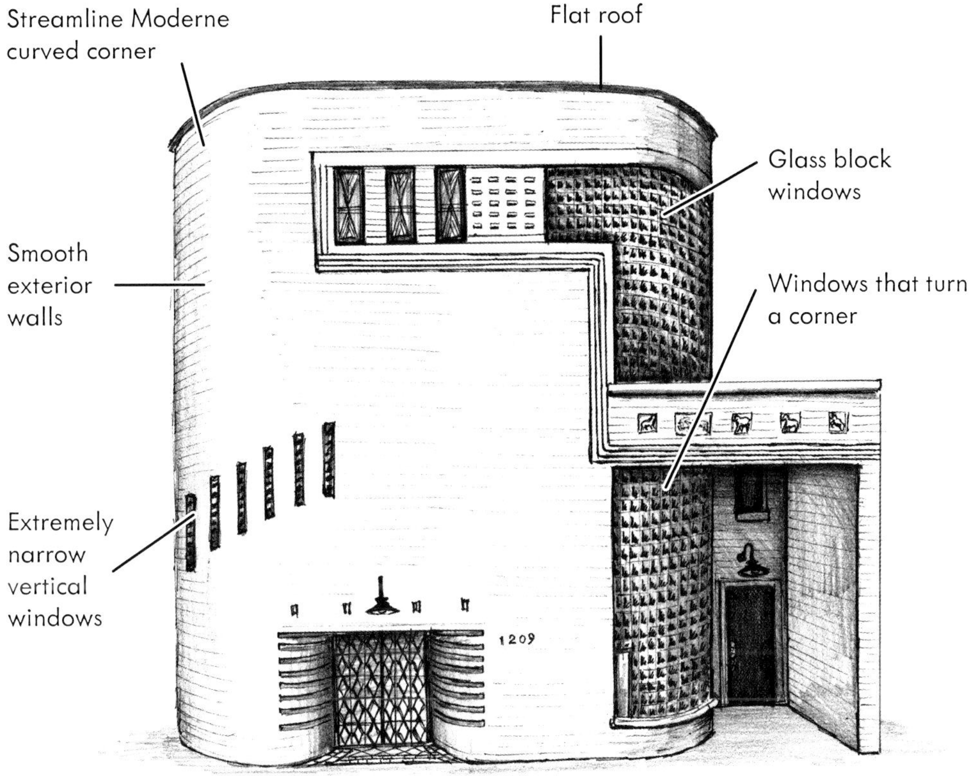

Fischer Studio Houses, made up of twelve units with a common, narrow courtyard at 1209 N. State Pkwy., designed by Andrew Rebori and Edgar Miller in 1936.

COMMON FEATURES

- Horizontal orientation
- Glass block windows
- Flat roofs and ledges with metal ledges (copings)
- Horizontal-lined balustrades
- Smooth stucco wall surfaces and/or unique brickwork
- Rounded edges, corner windows, and glass block walls

Deco's Last Echoes

Examples of Deco commercial buildings can be found around the city, and Deco-inspired WPA buildings from this era anchor neighborhoods as post offices and other public buildings. While there are very few single-family Deco homes, some can be found here and there in neighborhoods like Old Town and Wrightwood. When you spot one, you should wave or honk!

Art Deco continued to endure into the 1940s in commercial and public buildings and was expressed as a pared-down version of its 1920s iterations. Uniformly gray, Bedford limestone is the primary exterior material for almost every larger Art Deco building in the city, sometimes coupled with a swirly, metamorphic, Morton gneiss at the base for some contrast. The entire Adler Planetarium is clad in Morton gneiss.

A rare tan-brick Moderne beauty on West 83rd Street, built c. 1940.

Distinguishing Between Deco & Moderne

During the interwar era, Art Deco split and evolved in a new direction, and as a result, there are some blurred lines between Art Deco and Art Moderne. While Art Moderne was born in this era, it has the same DNA as Art Deco, like a shorter, curvier fraternal twin.

Even with so many similarities, Moderne—sometimes called Streamline Moderne—has a horizontal emphasis, little ornamentation, and curved corners so it often looks like a ship. Deco, on the other hand, is marked by angular, geometric forms and forces you to look upward, often with vertical elements that extend past the roofline. The tricky part is when a building displays both of these characteristics, which is often. When this happens, folks usually just lump both variations together as "Deco."

Some buildings didn't so much evolve as change their clothes. Humans, and especially artists and designers, tend to embrace the latest trends and technologies, and during an economic downturn, that can look mighty funky. To see how late nineteenth century buildings were transformed into Deco-Moderne-Craftsman hybrids, see if you can hop on a tour of Carl Street Studios on West Burton Place in Old Town.

West Burton Place and the Creative Response to the Depression

If you've ever strolled down West Burton Place after a long lunch on Wells, you may have paused about midway down the block to look at a mishmash of tile, stone, and concrete reliefs embedded into both the sidewalk and a low brick wall with an iron gate. The collection of apartments behind that delightfully incongruous wall is Carl Street Studios, and it's the anchor of the West Burton Place District. (West Burton Place was actually known as Carl Street until 1936—in case you wondered who on earth Carl was.) The district is relatively small and lives on a short residential block between Wells Street and LaSalle Drive in Old Town. There are twelve main buildings, the oldest dating from the mid-1870s and early 1880s. So why are you reading about them in this chapter? The facades and interiors were remodeled from the 1920s through early 1940s and turned into artist studios.

Many artists, designers, and craftspeople were involved in these conversions, including some who had national and even international stature. But artist Edgar Miller led the charge on these conversions, alongside his former classmate at the School of the Art Institute, Sol Kogan, and they are most associated with these spaces. Miller once described his work at Carl Street Studios as the process of taking "an obsolete structure and setting out to make it into something new, fascinating, and living." The result of this process is a collection of buildings that were reimagined into a wild, eclectic mix of styles: Art Deco, Art Moderne, and Arts and Crafts (sometimes all three styles at once, and then some).

If you are ever able to hop onto a tour of Carl Street Studios, you'll find courtyards with heavy, carved wood doors, winding paths of brightly colored tile leading to various apartment entrances, plenty of murals, mosaics, and stained glass, and a general sense of delighted bewilderment. The interiors of the apartments are carved up into unusual configurations, and basements were converted into living spaces, which was a new idea at the time of the remodels.

While Carl Street Studios was the first conversion on the block, the second was led by Sol Kogan (Miller was not involved) and involved a two-story, 1880s two-flat at 151 West Burton Place. The former rooming house was converted into artist studios similar to the Carl Street spaces. This exterior remodel was heavily Moderne,

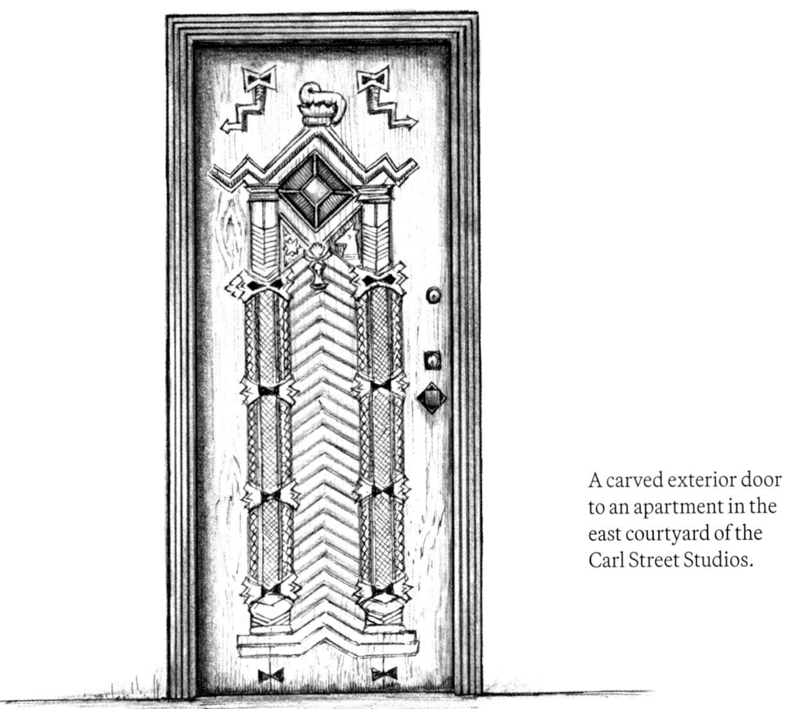

A carved exterior door to an apartment in the east courtyard of the Carl Street Studios.

but with a spin. The front facade has a series of curved, stacked windows that incorporate stained-glass pieces that were salvaged from the Swift and Company exhibit at the Century of Progress World's Fair.

Why did artists converge upon Old Town in the interwar era? Old Town is one of Chicago's oldest residential neighborhoods, and it was pretty run-down by the 1920s. The area was a magnet for intellectuals, members of the LGBTQ+ community, artists, and birds of every feather, and was teeming with rooming houses where single adults could afford to live and work on their creative pursuits. Themes of free love and atheism washed into neighborhood cafés and nightclubs. On the South Side, in the first decades of the twentieth century, Bronzeville had a similar reputation in terms of its acceptance of the queer community and its role as a hub for the arts, music, literature, civil rights, and human expression.

While it may be difficult to imagine today, the U.S. government saw great value in supporting artists in the 1930s, leading to astonishing public art works by artists like Edgar Miller, Ivan Albright, Willem de Kooning, Walker Evans, Dorothea Lange, Jacob Lawrence, Jackson Pollock, and many others. In Chicago, murals and sculptural works sprung up in post offices, schools, public housing developments, and government buildings to provide some relief to struggling artists and some joy to those who got to experience works of art while doing their day-to-day activities. A bright spot in an otherwise dreary time—or in the case of Pollock, a bright splatter. ■

CHAPTER

Common Modifications to Homes: How We Live

1890 1900 1910 1920 1930 1940

As soon as we started creating shelters, we began adapting them, upgrading the materials, and incorporating new technologies. Forms and styles were regularly revived, made up, modified, and built concurrently, creating funky combinations that are difficult to pin down, retroactively, as one revival style or another. Even if you squint, you may not be able to tell which side of the family your house takes after most. Humans just love to tinker. Especially with their homes.

In recent centuries, fashion has dictated a lot of our choices. The post-Columbian Exposition zeitgeist was one of increased austerity due to a depression and a feverish love of stately classicism. Down with the fussy Victorians! Sometimes organic forms were in, sometimes geometric. Sometimes metal, sometimes wood. We get bored and we like to fit in with our neighbors.

There is also a phenomenon in Chicago, and likely everywhere else in the world, where a run of several homes may have the same addition or modification. Maybe the Perma-Stone salesman promises a good price if your neighbors sign up, or there's a deal if everyone on the west side of the block gets a dormer on the right side of their roof, especially if you let the contractors stash their giant ladders overnight. Things are always cheaper in quantity, and a construction crew's time going to and from a neighborhood costs a lot more money than the commute down a single block. All the better if the addition isn't customized to a specific home but can just be added to the flat plane of any old roof or wall. Most importantly, if you wait to decide, you'll miss out on the deal of the century.

According to Virginia McAlester, the author and architectural historian whose *Field Guide to American Houses* sits on an altar in the home of every historic preservationist, there are three primary reasons we monkey with our homes:

- To update the appearance of the house
- To add additional living space to the house
- To minimize exterior maintenance of the house

Porches are added, removed, or changed from spindly to robust or vice versa. Windows, doors, and wall cladding change like our shoes, hats, and coats. Small houses grow into big houses and are sometimes almost completely swallowed by additions and alterations. For these reasons, when someone asks an architect or historian to date a house—after the inescapable joke about how they tried but they ultimately wanted different things—they may say that it's sometimes impossible to know when a building was built simply by looking at the current iteration of it. We learn early that to understand something, you sometimes have to peel back some layers to see what's underneath.

There are incalculable ways we can adapt and reimagine a home, so not all will be covered here. We've included some of the more common modifications that may offer clues as to how your own home has changed and why on earth they covered, replaced, added, or removed that thing.

Dormer & Second-Story Additions

A dormer is an addition that extends from the side of the roof. Because attics are often dark and gloomy (or cozy and mysterious, if you're a romantic), a dormer window brings in some light while also adding a little visual pizzazz to the exterior. Unlike skylights, dormer windows let light and heat into the space without risk of water leakage, and also have operable windows that are easy to access for some fresh air. Most of these dormers are frame elements, meaning they're constructed of wood and are often covered in clapboards, or in asbestos or asphalt shingles that match the rest of the roof. Some dormers feature decorative wooden eaves, and most include small casement or double-hung windows in groups of two or three.

Another addition you may see is called a "pop top," where that half story roof is completely removed and a full second story is added to the home. Sometimes the second story blends with the original first story; other times it intentionally differentiates itself. One particularly sneaky addition is a gambrel roof—a common addition that blends seamlessly with the first floor. These can be a half- or a full-story tall.

Many of these additions, especially the gambrel roofs and larger dormers, were added in the 1940s to accommodate large numbers of people flooding into the city. During WWII, production boomed in many industrial cities, including Chicago, which received over nine *billion* dollars in war supply contracts. The industrial workers followed, and these additions were built to create apartments for those workers.

In Chicago many homes were built with a half story above the primary story, which could be converted into living space as money allowed. Bungalows, Tudor Revivals, and cottages often popped out dormers on either side of their roof for some added head room and living space.

Enclosed Porches

One thing most homeowners covet is a little extra space. Enclosing front and rear porches as money allowed or as babies were born was a relatively inexpensive way to create another room that could be used year-round. The advent of air conditioning also made that outdoor space less critical, since folks were no longer as dependent on their open porches as a way to avoid melting.

You can generally tell when a porch was not originally enclosed by looking for differences between the exterior wall material and the rest of the house. Often a brick single-family home or two-flat with brick piers will have a front porch enclosed with another material like wood, stucco, or vinyl. The windows on these added walls may be smaller or otherwise not match those of the rest of the house.

Back porch enclosures are also common. On two- and three-flats, the height can make the enclosure look like a mobile home turned on its end, but they are certainly functional. The enclosed space allows for extra storage, keeps you safe from the wind and rain when you're running down to the basement with laundry, and will also protect the wood from rain and sun damage, extending its life. It's also a pretty effective way to hide porch violations.

This porch was likely open when built, with the primary entrance located on the porch itself.

Metal Awnings

According to a 2012 *New York Times* article covering the decline of metal awnings,[1] most of these funky and character-giving overhangs became a casualty of gentrification. Frankly, seeing them in neighborhoods usually implies that there are longtime homeowners who are either emotionally and functionally attached to them, or newer homeowners who simply haven't gotten around to tearing them off due to time or expense. In some cases, as with the fabulous midcentury homes along 5100 North Kilbourn, original metal awnings have been retained along almost the entire street face. Go check them out, they are magnificent.

After World War II, awnings were virtually discontinued thanks to the miracle of air conditioning—the thought being that there was no longer a need to keep out the heat from the outside when air conditioning units could now create a cool climate from the inside. Luckily, awning manufacturers pushed back, explaining that you'd need far less conditioned air if you added shade to your home. It turns out air conditioners are also unable to keep the rain off you when you're fumbling with your house keys. In the 1950s, bright, modernist aluminum awnings became a popular alternative to fabric awnings because they were easier to clean and far more durable. These new metal awnings were made with slats called "pans" that could be arranged either horizontally or vertically. To match the homes and to offer some variety for homeowners, different colored slats could be arranged in a variety of ways, with some folks even putting their initials on them.[2]

Perma-Stone/Formstone

Perma-Stone is a cementitious material that is applied to exterior walls in sheets, or formed on-site and shaped, usually over an applied layer of lath. It is also a thing that inspires both rabid hatred and nostalgic delight among anyone who pays attention to houses. Perma-Stone is a locally known name brand for faux stone siding, which came on the scene in the 1940s. This cladding may also be known as formed concrete, simulated stone, or Formstone. First seen when the Rostone Company of Lafayette, Indiana, brought its own early version of the product to the 1933 Century of Progress Exposition in Chicago, the siding was billed as "futuristic" at the time, and accurately so. Almost a century later, there's still a lot of simulated stone around this town.

There are many reasons people might have wanted to live in a home with a stoney appearance. Perhaps they always wanted to visit the castles in England, or they had a frame home and knew that a masonry home meant you had made it in life. Perhaps they were funky by nature, or perhaps they were practical sorts and they didn't want to have to deal with the cost of repairing their exterior stucco walls. This was a popular way to bypass finicky home repairs from its earliest days and was probably a bit cheaper than new stucco.

Perma-Stone and Formstone were created on the job site. The installer would first nail metal or wood lath to the exterior of the home. Chicken wire was often used with Formstone for extra reinforcement, and then the cement was formed and applied. Some products also claimed to not need the lath base and installers applied cement directly to the exterior walls.

Interestingly, while Perma-Stone was sometimes used to cover stucco because it was cheaper to cover the stuff than replace it, stucco may have been used in the same way. An advertisement in a *Home and Gardens* supplement discusses how expensive it is to maintain wood clapboarding, so why not just cover your home in stucco?

If you'd like to watch an in-depth examination of Formstone and its legendary popularization among Baltimore rowhouses, there is a thirty-minute documentary film about this trend directed by Skizz Cyzyk of the punk band Berserk, and featuring interviews with various homeowners, manufacturers, installers, and John Waters.

Removing and Hiding of Fireplaces & Stained Glass

Ever been in a home that has a chimney but not a visible fireplace inside? There are also countless stories of new homeowners discovering walled-over stained-glass windows that would have been on either side of a fireplace mantle in the early 1900s—scroll around on social media if you need proof. This kind of alteration was fashion-driven, and it became somewhat of a trend beginning in the late 1940s, according to numerous *Chicago Tribune* articles showing off these kinds of design ideas as well as testimonials of homeowners who wanted to spruce up the place and make it more modern.

One *Chicago Tribune* story from 1949 highlighted an updated 1926 Chicago bungalow where the owner remodeled his living room to hide the stained-glass windows and mantle with a large bookcase and a shockingly gigantic mirror. Others ripped out the original mantels and covered that "outdated" stained glass on both the interior and exterior of the house.

While stained glass and mantles are again our friends, a more recent alteration in this wheelhouse is the dismantling of the chimney itself. Many chimneys are in disrepair—they are especially vulnerable elements, sticking out like a thumb and taking on weather from all four sides—and need to be taken down for safety reasons. The reality is that so few chimneys are used today as a way to actually vent smoke from a fire that there is little incentive to spend money to retain them aside from aesthetics, and for venting appliances like furnaces, boilers, and water heaters.

Vinyl Siding

Vinyl siding is a plastic exterior siding you'll find on enclosed back porches and frame homes. Made of polyvinyl chloride (PVC) resin, this stuff is most popular in the U.S. and Canada, and was usually installed to update a house's look or protect it from the elements. There was also the promise of it looking forever new and never fading—whether that promise held is another matter. Perhaps unsurprisingly, this was also popularized in the 1950s, a time when everything old was suddenly "the worst." Beginning in the 1970s, the vinyl siding industry improved the production process so it was more durable and easier to maintain, making it even more popular. The newer stuff also fades less quickly in the sun than other exterior cladding products.

While it seems like artificial siding would be easy to remove, and may even protect the original features of a home, that's not necessarily the case. Unlike carpeting that has protected a hardwood floor for half a century or more, there are often casualties created by installing siding. Because exterior siding has to be installed on a flat surface, all kinds of architectural doodads may have been knocked off or cut down to accommodate the installation. Then there are the nails. Sometimes installers directly nailed the siding to the building fabric; other times they nailed the furring strips to the old siding. This means that if you remove the siding, it may look like a woodpecker spent a lot of time hanging out with your wood siding, molding, trim, window, and door frames. Or if you've got a brick building, the nails may have cracked the masonry. It's definitely worth poking around and investigating before spending the money to go all-in on a restoration project.

A frame cottage covered with vinyl siding for ease of maintenance.

Glass Block & Picture Windows

Glass block is an inexpensive replacement material that allows you the freedom to wear your birthday suit while also enjoying some solar gain. Bathrooms in older homes were most likely built with a double-hung wood sash window, but many have been replaced with glass block, likely because these windows often experience rot due to taking on a whole lot of moisture over the years. Many have also replaced their original wood basement windows with glass block for the same reasons, and the added bonus of increased security. It's going to make a lot more noise smashing through layers of glass block and mortar than a single-pane wood window from 1920.

Picture windows were also a popular window replacement choice, especially during the midcentury modernization craze. If you're walking down a street where there is a row of the same style house—a bungalow block is an easy example—slow your pace a wee bit and notice the front windows. Likely, many will have something like three central double-hung windows all lined up. But then, there's that one that had to be different. The three windows are gone and replaced with a single giant, fixed window.

A two-flat with picture windows as well as glass block basement windows (left); a Tudor Revival that also went the picture window route after removing the original double-hung wood sashes (right).

Raised Workers Cottages

This is discussed elsewhere in the book, but it bears mentioning again in case you missed it. Many workers cottages went from one story to two stories, but not by adding a second story on top as we would today. These homes were often raised off the ground while a new first floor was built underneath the original structure.

A frame workers cottage that was raised and plunked on top of two stories of brick.

This was not uncommon in the nineteenth and early twentieth centuries and provided a way to add a rental unit for extra income or expand space for a growing family. All this while saving owners the cost of constructing a new roof! The former front door may have been turned into a second-story window, or in other cases, a front staircase might lead to the original front door. The wonderful thing about this kind of expansion is that cottages retained their original rooflines and details, like decorative brackets, keeping some key parts of their historic appearance intact while doubling their interior space.

Metal Handrails & Porch Rails

Not unlike chimneys, brick cheek walls—the walls on either side of your concrete steps—were especially vulnerable to the elements because they "peninsula" out into space. As a result, the mortar can deteriorate quickly and maintenance can be expensive, especially if they've been deteriorating for a while—which is common, as most of these were built from the 1910s through 1930s. If the walls have started pulling apart, they may need to be completely rebuilt and the limestone caps replaced.

Sounds pricey, right? So, you'll see loads of thin, black metal handrails, and sometimes porch rails, installed to replace those original maintenance-heavy brick walls. In some cases, wood rails were also used, along with wood steps that would have replaced the original concrete stairs. In the case of slightly older buildings like greystones, wood or concrete steps may have replaced original stone steps and the thinner, newer black metal handrails may have replaced original black pipe railings with cast-iron newel posts and fancy wrought iron (these were generally found on Victorian-era greystones).

Black metal hand- and porch-rail replacements are common throughout the city.

Greystones may also have had a wood or stone awning and railings that rotted or deteriorated over time and were removed. Sometimes the awnings are replaced with the original materials, sometimes fiberglass awnings appeared, and sometimes the entryways decided to spend their later years going topless. In general, people fixed what they could based on what they could afford, what was available, and what required the least amount of maintenance.

Street- or Courtyard-Facing Metal Balconies

While the trend may have been to enclose front porches for added interior space in the twentieth century, we seem to be craving more fresh air and sunshine in the twenty-first century. Metal balconies have been added to countless multi-unit buildings in recent decades, creating new hangouts for book readers and large grills. Often a window opening was enlarged to create a door and black metal supports were added without significant disruption to the masonry.

Recessed areas to either side of the bays have had balconies added, likely after 2000.

Animistic Additions

This unique Tudor Revival in Edgewater is actually a two-flat with an additional rear unit. The late 1890s building boasts the addition of a large skeleton, as well as two adorable living canines. These additions do not negatively impact the historic integrity of the building and in fact add value to both the home and landscape.

Skeleton and dogs were added in the early 2020s.

EPILOGUE

Part 1: Be Your Own Architectural Historian

Before barreling into spoilers of what happened next in Chicago's architectural evolution, we thought you might like some action items and tips for your own homegrown research. In addition to clutching this book to your breast every time you leave the house, here are a few ways to keep learning and drill down into your specific interests:

Go outside.

Seriously. Just walk around and look at things. Maybe one day you just look at roofs. How are they different? Do you remember what a hipped roof is versus a gable? What's a side gable? What do you call it when there are two roofs that intersect? Do certain styles seem to have the same kinds of roofs? It's a game. It's a good time. Then, on your next walk, look at bays. Can you name the shapes? Then windows—what do you call that wood window where you can open the bottom pane but usually leave the top pane in place? Which style has the tall, skinny windows? Then, when you feel you're ready, brace yourself to be rocked by variations in brick colors and patterns—maybe go on a Brick of Chicago tour!

Go to the library. And get a library card.

Chicago has the best libraries. In 2014, an international study ranked Chicago Public Libraries number one in the United States and number three in the world. Get a library card if you don't already have one. They are free and also entitle you to use numerous historical databases online, such as the *Chicago Defender* archives beginning in 1910 and the *Chicago Tribune* archives beginning in 1849. You can search these with terms and date ranges and your mind will be blown.

Your neighborhood library may be smaller than some other libraries, but it may also have hyper-local resources that are relevant to your neighborhood. A lot of cultural and housing organizations also schedule free public programming to be held at these libraries.

Regional libraries have special collections and a massive number of resources. Our three regional libraries are Carter G. Woodson Library (south), Conrad Sulzer (north), and the Henry E. Legler Library (west). You'll need to make appointments for access to any of the special collections, but there's plenty to look at before you tap into those.

Our Central Library is the Harold Washington Library downtown. This is the top banana of research facilities. Their architecture resources are currently on the eighth floor and history resources are on the sixth floor. Check out the atrium on the ninth floor, and make an appointment to visit the special collections housed there, where you can rummage through the boxes of your choice. They even give you gloves to wear.

Focus on a specific address for individual home research.

Find a step-by-step home research guide. There are a few versions of these around the city—some are newer and some need updating. For a more recent step-by-step guide on how to research your home, visit the Chicago Bungalow Association (CBA) website at ChicagoBungalow.org and look for their blog post from 2020 titled "House Research 101" (just call or email CBA if you can't locate it). It even comes with a downloadable form to track your progress, which will keep you on track as you inevitably go down some pretty wild rabbit holes. The CBA website also has an accompanying webinar on this topic that takes you through each step.

Find your original building permits. The University of Illinois Chicago (UIC) has an online database called the "Building Permits Digital Collection 1872–1954." These permits are also available on microfilm at the Chicago History Museum, where a human librarian can walk you through how to find your house. If you are able to find your permit (the earlier the building, the more difficult to find, typically), you can learn the name of the architect (if there was one), builder, and owner (often a developer), as well as the date the house was completed, its exterior dimensions, and cost to construct. It's pretty neat.

Do some neighborhood research.

Context matters, as you may have gleaned from the few hundred pages that came before this one. When researching a specific building, it really adds to the narrative if you can learn more about the area surrounding that building.

Search the *Encyclopedia of Chicago*. This can be done online, complete with a search bar, or you can find a hard copy at many of our public libraries. This is an absolute treasure trove of information about neighborhood histories and Chicago history in general.

Visit the Chicago History Museum (CHM) Abakanowicz Research Center. To do this, go to the main desk for check-in on the first floor and they will give you a pass and direct you upstairs to the Research Center. In the Research Center, ask a librarian if there is a "neighborhood file" for the area you are researching. Usually there is. Also ask whether they recommend any other sources to research that neighborhood within the Resource Center. The hours at the Center are short, so look them up before making the trek to the CHM.

Find some online or in-person lectures about architectural history. Many organizations offer seminars and webinars and a lot of them are free. A few local organizations and institutions that offer regular programming are the Chicago Architecture Center, the Chicago Bungalow Association, the Chicago History Museum, and Landmarks Illinois. Check their websites regularly for updates.

There are so many ways to do this research, but this will get you pretty far. Just get out there. Start trying to name the things you see. It's the best kind of nerdy fun that money can't buy.

Part 2: A Portrait of the City, Addendum to a Love Letter

So, to recap . . . our city has seen some stuff. It took a lot of work and a lot of nerve to transform groves of wild ramps and a trading post into one of the most architecturally significant cities in the world. Population booms, pandemics, catastrophic fires, world wars, world's fairs, an abundance of clay, formidable mayors, and brazen innovation shaped our streets and lit our living rooms.

This book takes you through the Second World War. Often, we break architecture into pre- and postwar eras because of the massive societal and technological shifts that manifest in our buildings after such pivotal events. When peace returned in 1945, the U.S. economy expanded and wages rose for the next two decades. Advancements in materials like concrete, steel, and glass, which were heavily developed during the war for military applications, became widely used in architecture, changing some of the literal bedrock of the city. Air conditioning became affordable, leading to all kinds of modifications to homes like lower ceilings and smaller windows. Sanitary conditions improved, and the bathhouses of the Progressive Era were made obsolete thanks to indoor plumbing requirements. Cultural changes were also afoot. The jazz melodies emanating from clubs were drowned out by electric guitars riffing

Population booms, pandemics, catastrophic fires, world wars, world's fairs, an abundance of clay, formidable mayors, and brazen innovation shaped our streets and lit our living rooms.

the blues along Maxwell Street. Postwar housing was stripped of its ornamentation, reflecting more austere social views and limited building materials after the war effort. Racial tensions again grew, as did civil rights activism.

While the postwar years are known as a period of expansion and rapid home building, they are equally significant for their large-scale destruction. The bulldozer, invented to clear land for military bases overseas, was looking for a new job once the war was done. So the U.S. government found one. The war on "blight" wiped out a jaw-dropping number of existing homes in urban areas across the country—especially areas where people of color and ethnic minorities lived—and Chicago saw heavy losses. The addition of highways did similar damage. Between 1950 and 1980, 7.5 million dwelling units were demolished. In the 1960s, one in seventeen dwelling units were destroyed nationwide. As exuberantly as our city was built up in the first three decades of the twentieth century, it seemed to be equally undone.

At the same time, returning servicemen had zero-down-payment loans for new housing, provided they were white servicemen. New Deal redlining policies barred all but 2 percent of Black servicemen from receiving these loans, keeping Black families in a city that was rapidly demolishing housing in the narrow sections available to them. Many white veterans decided to move to new suburban developments, recently made accessible with highways, and the city tax base was increasingly drained. The result was an even more segregated city. The National Trust for Historic Preservation was established in 1949 to tamp down the desire to smash our old neighborhoods to bits, and by the 1960s, citizen activists like Richard Nickel and Jane Jacobs were pushing back against the devastating effects of urban renewal on both the urban landscape and the people who lived there.

Chicago can never sit still.

But Chicago can never sit still, and amid the dust clouds of demolition, buildings continued to rise. In the 1950s and '60s, new housing forms, loosely based on old forms, filled in areas of the city where development had ceased during the Depression. New, low-slung ranch homes that put a new spin on Prairie style principles were built on empty lots next to Chicago bungalows. Bungalows, now in their thirties, were pleased to realize how harmoniously they could coexist with their young, hip neighbors. New subdivisions sprang up along the western boundaries of the city. Tudor Revivals were yet again resuscitated and simplified, and Georgian Revivals tried out the long and narrow

Chicago lot, forcing themselves into two-story box forms that look, admittedly, very little like Georgians. We also saw a resurgence of large public housing projects with the construction of Cabrini-Green, the Robert Taylor Homes, and Henry Horner Homes. There was another wave of ever-efficient brick two-flats, this time wearing bright, textural, horizontal panels between windows. For perhaps the first time ever, we looked to places like Florida for building form inspiration as we tested out breezeway apartment buildings that opened up their hallways to the elements.

Chicago in the 1970s saw rising crime rates—an unsurprising outcome given the often destructive "urban renewal" practices that continued into that decade—and those still living in the city longed for a more suburban lifestyle. We see this longing reflected in a rise of larger homes with attached garages and some split-levels—suburban stuff from the 1950s and '60s. In 1977, fifty-one acres of railroad yards became Dearborn Park, a neighborhood of apartments and townhouses that were hailed as a late urban renewal success story that continued to expand into the '90s. Rowhouses also made a long-awaited comeback, though these later versions we refer to as "townhouses" (locally, it would be sacrilege to use this term for older versions of this building type) because they are decidedly non-urban. The postmodernism of the '80s brought buildings that trended big—the larger, more open, and more exaggerated, the better. Maximizing indoor square footage was king, resulting in larger homes on smaller lots.

The city experienced an economic turnaround towards the end of the twentieth century, and we continued to demolish, split, "McMansion," rebuild, flip, and adapt our homes. Chicago's 54th mayor, Richard M. Daley, went to Germany in the mid 1990s and returned obsessed with energy efficient housing technologies. Countless garages, warehouse buildings, and even City Hall were suddenly topped with rooftop gardens, and real estate agents learned they could bump up the price of units with views of those rooftops. New home products featuring renewable bamboo or countertops with ground-up recycled glass embedded in it became signals of our environmental virtues, and new styles of homes sprung up with solar panels, jaunty angles, and an astonishing amount of orange interior paint.

In many cases, these new homes began filling the spaces where workers cottages had recently stood, picking off the smaller homes to build lots out to their "highest and best use." Reusing old building materials, if not old homes, became cool again. Bike lanes and farmers markets sprung up as prolifically as the saloons of the 1890s. And as all of these changes happened, various housing organizations emerged to protect the city's existing housing stock.

Events like the Covid-19 pandemic of the early 2020s and the increasing effects of climate change continue to transform the way we live. Thanks to new flu varieties and the dangers of swirling germs, open floor plans are not as enticing as they used to be. Homes are moving away from natural gas and towards electric heat pumps and appliances. Office buildings have emptied out as people make home offices of extra bedrooms, basements, and closets. For folks with some extra money, second homes in rural areas have become commonplace, shifting demographics and real estate prices in once-cheap farm towns. Architects are getting ahead of future challenges by designing houses that float or resist the burning embers of wildfires.

We've seen this level of change before. Chicago was built on change. We're still culturally the same old city, and our homes are still extensions of who we are, individually and collectively. Architecture is politics. Architecture is whimsy. Architecture is people.

We hope this book has made you even more curious about your city. We hope that during a lunchtime walk, you take too long trying to categorize a transitional style and are subsequently late for a meeting. We hope you try to woo someone with a passionate description of the Iroquois Theater fire and the rise of Bedford limestone (explain the trick about determining limestone versus concrete for extra points—you're welcome). We hope a suspicious homeowner confronts you for getting too close to their house and you take the opportunity to explain how insanely unique their brick patterning is. We hope you are endlessly stimulated by your neighborhood and find immense joy with this new infrastructure of stories. Let us know how we did. And don't forget to look up.

Architecture is *politics*. Architecture is *whimsy*. Architecture is *people*.

THANK YOUS

All work is collective work. Period. This book has had many eyes and hands on it and we are so grateful for the labor and wisdom of peer reviewers, advice-givers, and confidence boosters. We could not have done this without your brains and care. Some of you, with indomitable strength, also managed to endure a never-ending onslaught of monologues about topics like decorative festoons and the history of garages while we gorged ourselves in a bacchanalia of research. We see you.

Endless thanks to: The Agate Publishing team, Sabrina Atria, Julia Bachrach, Lauren Bakos, Gigi Barbara, Martha Bayne, Matt Bergstrom, Kim Bookless, Bethany Brown, Frank Bruni, Kathleen Bruni (thanks for forcing a love of history, Mom), Philip Bruni, Anne Cadigan, Seth Captain, Jenny Carney, Lucie-Ann Chen, The Chicago Bungalow Association staff (extra big hug to each of you), The Chicago Workers Cottage Initiative staff, Morgan Clark, Matt Cole, Franklin Cosey-Gay, Steve Costello, Stacey Crowley, Shannon Downey, Romella Ferguson, Jean Follett (x3), Rachel Freundt, Marjorie Fritz-Birch, Eleanor Gorski, Mary Ellen Guest, Cathy Halley, Mike Jackson, Amelia James, Tonika Johnson, David Kadavy, Mariah Karson, Ellen Kaulig, Jordan Kost, Maria Krysan, The Lakeside Inn staff, Jeanne Lambin, Kelly Little, Maria Lopez, Sarah Marsom, Michael Massart, Paula Mauro, Bonnie McDonald, Vince Michael, Wendy McClure, Kate McNamee, Sara Minard, Kevin Mott, Mr. Nancy, Dominic Pacyga, Frankye Payne, Jim Peters, Andy Pierce, Charlie Pipal, Kat Powers, Will Quam, Lara Ramsey, Sarah Ratcliffe, Bob Remer, Amanda Roelle, Donovan Rypkema, Julia Scalzo, The School of the Art Institute Department of Historic Preservation, Arijit Sen, Larry Shure, Christin Sogge, Patti Swanson, Tamara Talansky, Kate Tannian, Shelby Tannian, Terry Tatum, David Thompson, Mark Thompson, Angie Walden, Emily Wallrath Schmidt, Vincent, Rachel Webster, Collene Wells, Krista Weir, Brad White, Matt Wolf, Cass Cleghorn, Meegan Czop, Amy Keller, Katie Lauffenburger, Jeremiah Posedel, and so many others.

Finally, we would also like to acknowledge this city's institutions of history and architecture, its local pubs, quiet-ish cafés, and public libraries for the rent-free writing tables and bottomless research materials. Special shout-out to the heavenly Sulzer Library, where we definitely added some patina to the seats. These public institutions, civic organizations, and small, local businesses are critical infrastructure for our beloved neighborhoods, and we owe them a great deal.

GLOSSARY

American Foursquare A popular residential architectural style that emerged in the late nineteenth and early twentieth centuries. The style sounds like its name and is known for its interior layout (generally divided into four rooms), as well as its simple, boxy shape, efficient use of space, and practical, unornamented design. This style was a popular choice for the middle class because it was roomy yet relatively affordable.

Arts and Crafts movement A design and architectural movement that originated in the late nineteenth century, emphasizing traditional craftsmanship, simplicity, and natural materials. It emerged as a reaction against industrialization and mass production, advocating for the beauty of handmade objects and a harmonious relationship between form and function. *Arts and Crafts* and *Craftsman* are sometimes used interchangeably when describing a style.

Art Deco This style emerged in the 1920s and 1930s, characterized by bold geometric patterns, verticality, smooth walls, and the use of non-Western motifs (especially Indigenous and Egyptian themes locally). Deco blends modernist forms with decorative elements like vibrant terra cotta panels, and patterns like zigzags, chevrons, and fluted designs are often seen in the facades and interior details of Deco buildings.

Art Moderne Sometimes called "Streamline Moderne," this style is a subset, or cousin, of Art Deco. Moderne emerged in the 1930s and is often associated with smooth, efficient design with minimal ornamentation, and curved corners that sometimes make the building resemble a ship. The style emphasizes horizontality and sleek lines, frequently using materials like glass and chrome. There is a lot of overlap with Art Deco and the two styles are often used interchangeably. If you're not sure if it's Deco or Moderne—if there's a curve, it's Moderne.

balloon frame A type of wood-frame construction that uses long, continuous studs that run from the foundation to the roof, allowing for faster construction.

balustrade A row of small columns topped by a rail, often used on staircases, balconies, and porches.

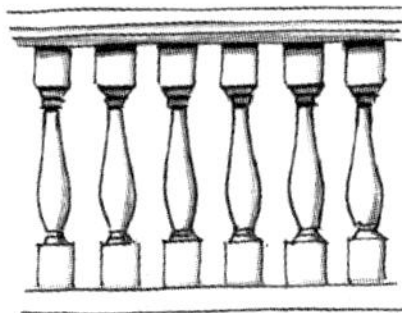

Balustrade.

bargeboard Decorative trim on the edge of a gable roof, often carved or ornamented.

battered piers Tapered vertical supports often found in Craftsman style architecture. This was a popular feature especially on Chicago bungalows and some brick two-flats.

bay A division of a facade, typically defined by architectural elements like columns, pilasters, or windows. It serves as a way to organize the space rhythmically. For example, a three-bay Colonial Revival house has three evenly spaced window sections on its facade.

Beaux Arts A grand and highly decorative style that was influenced by the classical traditions of the École des Beaux-Arts in Paris and popularized by the Columbian Exposition. Grand local examples include the Art Institute of Chicago and the old Cook County Hospital. While there are some exceptions, many residential expressions of Beaux Arts in Chicago are pared-down versions of the style, and it can be difficult to distinguish it from the omnipresent Classical Revival facades of greystones, rowhouses, and flats.

Bedford limestone Bedford limestone is a high-quality, dense, and durable stone quarried from Bedford, Indiana. It's a ubiquitous building material in Chicago's homes, often used for window sills, wall and parapet caps, and various decorative elements. It's also the famous gray stone that clads our beloved Chicago greystones.

belvedere A belvedere, or *bel vedere*, meaning "beautiful view" in Italian, is an architectural feature meant to be used to take in a panoramic view—as opposed to a cupola, which is for light, ventilation, and decoration.

Belvedere.

board and batten siding Type of exterior cladding common in Carpenter Gothic homes that combines wide vertical boards and narrow strips, called battens, to cover the seams between the boards.

bousillage A mixture of mud, clay, and Spanish moss or straw used in traditional French Creole construction.

bracket A decorative support piece used under eaves, shelves, or overhangs.

brick course A brick course is a single horizontal layer of bricks in a masonry structure. Courses are laid in succession to form walls or other brickwork. Different types of brick courses create various bonding patterns, affecting the strength and appearance of the wall.

bungalow First built of wood, and sometimes clad in stucco, bungalows in Chicago began popping up in the first two decades of the twentieth century. By the mid-1910s, brick became the preferred building material for this home type, and the iconic Chicago-style bungalow was born. Both frame and brick bungalows are one-and-one-half stories tall with a low-pitched roof and overhanging eaves, reflecting a simple, functional design with a strong connection to the surrounding landscape. They were built as an alternative to tenement housing for the working class and middle class, and quickly became a form of affordable housing for tens of thousands of Chicagoans.

capital (on a column) The topmost part of a column, serving as a transition between the column shaft and the structure it supports. Capitals are often decorative and structural, helping to distribute weight while making the column look impressive and fancy. The most common capital styles are Doric (simple shapes), Ionic (looks like a scroll), and Corinthian (highly ornate), though there are some other varieties, such as Tuscan.

Chicago window This style of window came out of the Chicago School, which was a school of architects active in the late nineteenth and early twentieth centuries. These windows are found primarily in early skyscrapers, and consist of a large, fixed, central-pane window with two narrower, double-hung sash windows on either side. This allowed for lots of light but also ventilation via the side sashes.

chinking The material used to seal gaps between logs in log cabin construction. Traditionally made of clay or lime, modern versions use synthetic compounds.

clapboard siding Overlapping horizontal wooden boards used as exterior cladding.

Classical Revival Classical Revival, sometimes called Neoclassical architecture (there are distinctions, but the terms are often swapped), draws inspiration from the architecture of ancient Greece and Rome. This style can be smacked onto any building form, and is characterized by details like triangular pediments, balustrades, columns, cornices, and decorative shields.

coach house Often two stories, these structures are located behind the main house and were originally designed to store horse-drawn carriages (coaches), and related equipment. Larger, fancier coach houses might have also had a milk cow and/or living spaces for a groom or coachman. Over time, many of these houses were converted into living spaces and rented out.

Colonial Revival Colonial Revival architecture is a style that emerged in the late nineteenth and early twentieth centuries, drawing inspiration from early American colonial buildings. This style is notoriously conservative with key features like symmetrical facades, brick exteriors, gable roofs, and decorative elements like columns and dormer windows.

common brick Brick made from locally sourced clay, often rougher and less uniform than face brick. This brick wraps around the non-street-facing side and rear walls of most masonry buildings in Chicago.

coping The protective cap or covering placed on the top of a wall, parapet, or another exposed structure to keep water out and protect the top of an exposed wall.

cornice The projecting upper edge of a building, typically decorative and used to cap walls.

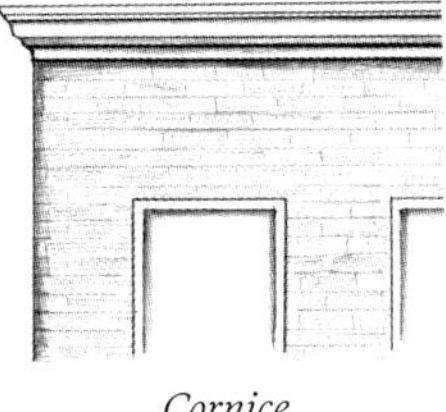

Cornice.

courtyard apartments A type of multi-unit residential building that is arranged around an open-air courtyard. The most common courtyard building configuration is a U-shape, though there are other variations in form. The courtyard design was a result of much-needed tenement reform, and promotes air circulation, natural light, and a sense of dignity for multi-unit building dwellers at a time when single-family homeownership was equated with morality. These were first seen in the late nineteenth century in Chicago and boomed during the 1920s.

Craftsman style An architectural style popular in the early twentieth century emphasizing handcrafted materials and simple, functional design. In Chicago, common exterior features are low-pitched roofs, overhanging eaves, brick and limestone geometric designs, brick cladding, limestone sills and caps, and wide front porches.

crenellations These are the distinctive, repeated gaps or notches along the top of a wall or parapet, harkening to castles or defensive structures. While this architectural feature is pretty common in Chicago, it still allows us to feel like we have sturdy, fortified homes, and assures us that we are the king of our castle. A crenellated parapet can also be called a battlement, but locally, we usually just describe the wall as being crenellated.

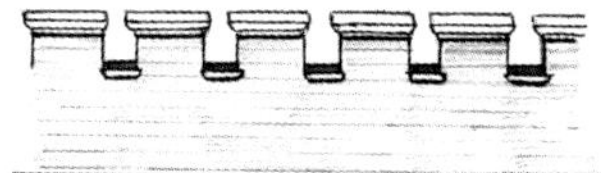

Crenellations.

cresting Decorative ornamentation along the ridge of a roof, often made of iron or terra cotta.

Cresting.

cross gable A roof design that features two or more gable ends intersecting.

Cross gable.

crown The uppermost part of a structure, element, or ornament. Its specific meaning can vary depending on the context, but generally, it denotes a feature that caps or finishes an architectural element.

cupola A small dome-like structure on top of a building, often for ventilation, light, and/or decoration.

dentil molding A series of small rectangular blocks resembling teeth, used as decorative trim on cornices.

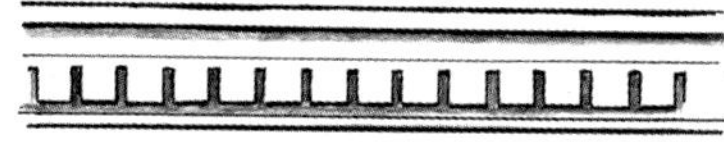

Dentils.

dimensional lumber Standardized lumber cut to specific sizes, commonly used in construction.

dog-trot cabin A log cabin type with an open breezeway through the center, connecting two enclosed living areas.

dormer A window that projects vertically from a sloping roof, often used to create, illuminate, and ventilate additional living space.

double-hung window A type of window that features two vertically sliding sashes—one on the top and one on the bottom. Both sashes can be moved up and down independently, allowing for ventilation at the top, bottom, or both. Traditionally, double-hung windows use a system of weights and pulleys to keep the sashes in place, though modern versions often use springs or friction mechanisms.

eaves The overhanging edges of a roof, which protect the walls from rain and summer sun. Squirrels also vacation here.

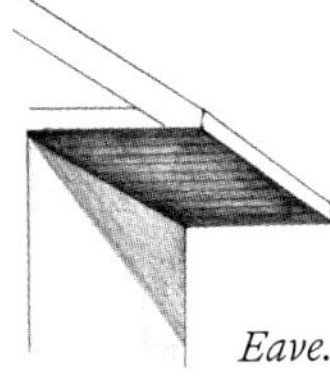

Eave.

egg and dart A classic decorative molding pattern featuring alternating egg-shaped and dart-like elements, thought to represent the interplay between birth and death.

Egg and dart molding.

elevation Elevation refers to a two-dimensional representation (a drawing) of a building's exterior that shows the details of a structure from a specific viewpoint. While it is a term used to describe architectural drawings, it is sometimes used interchangeably with "facade" in general architectural descriptions.

equilateral gable A gable that forms an equilateral triangle—meaning all three sides are equal in length and all angles are 60 degrees.

fanlight A semicircular or fan-shaped window often found above doors.

facade The exterior "face" or surface of a building, particularly the front or most prominent side unless otherwise noted. Sometimes the principal elevation/side of a building, usually facing a street or other public way, is called the "primary facade." Conversely, the back elevation of a building would be called a "rear facade" and the side elevations would be described directionally, as in the "western facade," etc.

face brick Bricks that are specifically manufactured and used for the exposed or visible surface of a wall or structure, like in the construction of street-facing exterior walls and chimneys, where appearance is important. These bricks are made to be aesthetically pleasing and also to help differentiate buildings from their neighbors, and they tend to be more expensive than common brick, which is why they are often not used on all elevations.

fenestration The arrangement and design of windows and doors on a building's facade.

festoon A decorative motif resembling a garland of flowers, ribbons, or foliage.

finials Ornamental tops or spires commonly used on roofs, towers, or gables. Chateauesque and Gothic Revival buildings are lousy with them.

Finial.

flanking Elements positioned on either side of a central feature, such as columns flanking a doorway.

flats In Chicago, "building flats" typically refer to multi-unit residential buildings, often two-flats, three-flats, or larger walk-up apartments. Within a building, each unit (flat) is typically laid out in the same way.

frame construction A building method in which the structural framework of a building is made of wood.

fretwork Ornamental design consisting of interlaced patterns, often carved into wood or stone.

front gable A gable facing the front of the building, usually the street. If you see one side of the roof while looking at the main entrance of a home, it's a side gable, but if you see the "triangle" formed by the roof planes, it's a front gable.

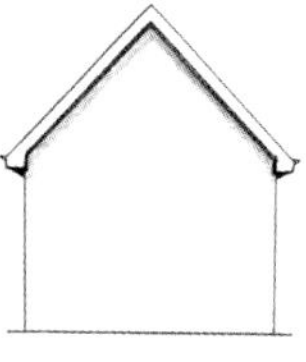

Front gable.

gable roof When we draw a roof, this is what we draw—two sloping sides that meet at a ridge. If a roof has a peak and forms an upside-down "V," it's a gable roof.

gambrel gable A roof design with two slopes of varying pitches on each side, typically found on barns but also in homes with Dutch Colonial inspiration.

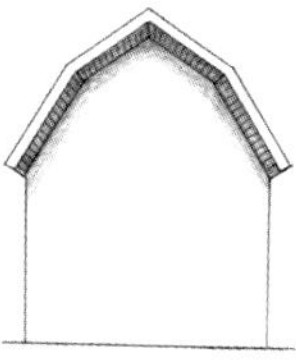

Gambrel roof.

garlands Decorative motifs resembling hanging foliage, often carved or painted.

glazing Glass is also referred to as "glazing," as in, "there is so much glazing on the south side of this house, we could cook our bacon without a stove during peak sun."

greystone A type of residential building popular in Chicago, particularly in the late nineteenth and early twentieth centuries. These buildings are named for their distinctive gray limestone facades, sourced from quarries in Indiana. Greystones are typically two- or three-story structures, but can also be large single-family homes, rowhouses, or multi-unit flats.

Greek Revival A style inspired by classical Greek architecture, characterized by columns, pediments, symmetrical facades, the use of marble (or materials made to look like marble) and an emphasis on simplicity and proportion.

Gunter's chain A measuring device used for surveying land, consisting of 100 links, totaling 66 feet in length.

half-timbering A traditional building technique where exposed wood framing is infilled with plaster, brick, or wattle and daub. In Chicago, you will most often see plaster infill (sometimes brick), and the wood "framing" is purely cosmetic. You'll find this detailing on Tudor Revivals.

Decorative half-timbering.

hipped roof A roof style where all sides slope down to the walls, often with a gentle pitch. This roof form is extremely common, especially with Chicago bungalows and American Foursquares.

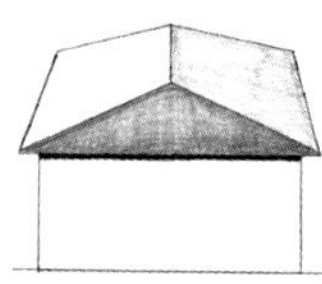

Hipped roof.

hood mold A hood mold is an architectural feature, often made of stone, that runs above an arch, doorway, or window. Its primary function is to keep rainwater away from openings, though it is sometimes just a handsome, decorative element.

Italianate style An architectural style inspired by Tuscan villas and characterized by wide eaves with decorative brackets and cornices. The windows are often tall and narrow with arched tops and crowns.

Joliet limestone A buttery yellow limestone quarried in Joliet, Illinois. It was cheap to acquire, easily accessible by water, and widely used in Chicago in the nineteenth century before it was replaced with the more durable Bedford limestone. While incorporated into many of Chicago's early homes, its most recognizable use may be the fully clad Chicago Water Tower.

keystone The central, wedge-shaped stone at the apex of an arch, which locks the other stones into place.

lights (windows) The individual panes of glass within a window sash. For example, a sash with six lights on the top pane and one light on the bottom pane (an open pane with no dividers) is called a six-over-one window.

lintel A horizontal structural element spanning an opening, such as a door or window, often both decorative and supportive.

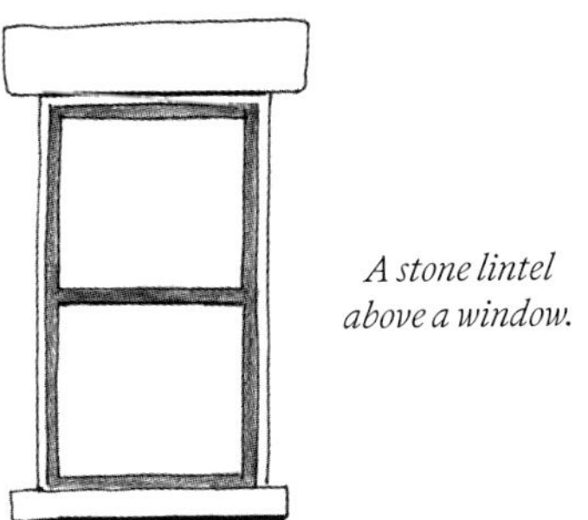

A stone lintel above a window.

mansard roof A roof with two slopes on each side, the lower slope being much steeper than the upper.

Mediterranean Revival A style that emerged in the United States during the early twentieth century, primarily in the 1910s through the 1930s. Inspired by the architecture of the Mediterranean region—including Spanish, Italian, and Moorish influences—this style has a lot of low-slung red tile roofs, arches, columns, courtyards, and balconies.

moldings Trim or detailing used to enhance a structure's aesthetic appeal, often found along walls, ceilings, and doors. Rumor has it that this was also a trick used to cover up the imperfect seams between walls and ceilings and floors, especially after buildings settled.

mortise and tenon A traditional wood-joining technique in timber-frame construction in which a projecting tenon fits snugly into a mortise, or hole, for a strong joint.

multi-light window A window with multiple panes of glass, separated by muntins or mullions.

mullions and muntins Mullions are the thicker vertical or horizontal supports between adjacent windows, while muntins are the narrow dividers within a single sash that separate panes (lights) of glass.

Nicolson paving An early method of street paving using wooden blocks soaked in tar to create a durable surface.

ornamental parapet gable A decorative gable with a parapet wall extending above the roofline, often found in Gothic or Tudor Revival styles, and always found with Chateauesque styles in Chicago, topped by a finial.

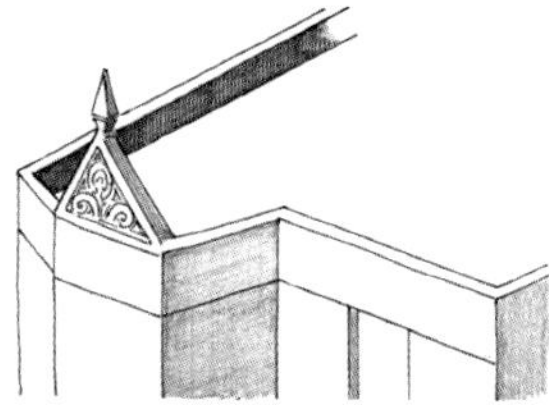

Parapet gable.

Palladian window A three-part window with a large arched central section flanked by two smaller, rectangular sections.

A Palladian window.

parapet wall A low wall or barrier that extends above the edge of a roof.

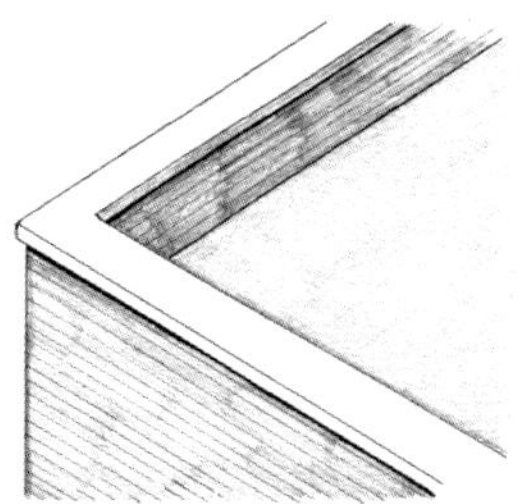

Bird's eye view of a parapet wall.

pediment The triangular upper part of a building's front, typically above a portico or gable, and sometimes decorated with sculpture or relief. Pediments were the crowning feature of Greek temples and are one of the most common details found on Classical Revival buildings.

piers In terms of residential architecture, these refer to vertical support posts or column-like structures that help hold up porches, entryways, or roof extensions. They can also be purely decorative features.

pilasters Flat, decorative columns projecting slightly from a wall, often with a base and capital.

plank roads Roads constructed with wooden planks laid across the route, an early solution to muddy paths.

platted lot A plot of land subdivided from a larger tract and officially recorded on a plat map.

portico A covered entryway or porch supported by columns, often leading to the primary entrance of a building. It can be a simple structure or a grand, elaborate feature, and is commonly found on Greek Revival, Classical Revival, and Colonial Revival homes.

Prairie style A uniquely American architectural style that emerged in the 1890s, pioneered by Frank Lloyd Wright and the Prairie School architects. Its low-slung orientation was developed as a response to the flat, open landscapes of the Midwest and the style is characterized by horizontal lines, open floor plans, and integration with nature.

pressed brick Popular during the late nineteenth and early twentieth centuries, this brick was formed under high pressure to create a smooth, uniform surface. This process created dense bricks with sharp edges and a refined appearance, which were often used for decorative or facade work.

Queen Anne style The quintessential Victorian home, defined by asymmetrical facades, decorative gables, towers and turrets, wraparound porches, and a mix of eye-catching textures and colors.

quoins Cornerstones of a building, often larger or differently dressed than the surrounding stone or brick used for visual emphasis. They can be used for structural support or just decoratively.

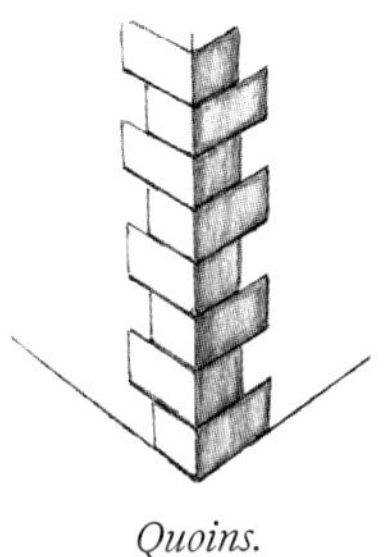

Quoins.

ribbon window A continuous row of windows, often horizontal, separated by narrow mullions.

Richardsonian Romanesque style A popular style of Romanesque Revival named for H.H. Richardson, characterized by heavy stone construction, rounded arches, deep-set windows, and a sense of massiveness.

Romanesque Revival style A style that emerged in the late nineteenth century, inspired by medieval Romanesque architecture, which was characterized by heavy masonry, round arches, and a fortress-like appearance.

rowhouse Narrow but deep home that shares walls and a uniform facade with its neighbors, typically with a continuous roofline and cohesive look.

rusticated stone Masonry with rough-textured surfaces and emphasized joints, creating a bold, decorative appearance.

sash A sash is a full pane of glass. Many windows have two sashes, with upper and lower panes.

Second Empire style Defined by mansard roofs with dormer windows, often highly ornamental cresting and window hoods, inspired by the fashionable Parisian buildings of the time.

Shingle style A style characterized by the use of continuous wood shingles covering walls and roofs, irregular shapes, and minimal ornamentation.

shotgun house A narrow, rectangular house style that's only one room wide and has rooms arranged in a straight line—one behind the other—with no hallways.

sidelights Vertical windows placed on either side of a door, often decorative and used to admit light.

side gable A gable roof where the gable ends face the sides of the structure.

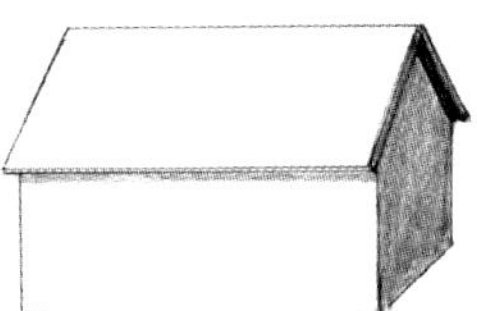

Side gable.

spandrel A panel between the top of a window on one floor and the bottom of a window on the floor above in a multi-story building. Over time, these shifted from highly ornamental to functional and expressive designs and are used to define rhythm, texture, and identity in buildings.

steeply pitched roof A roof with a sharp incline, often found in Gothic and Tudor architecture.

Stick style Characterized by exposed wooden framing on exteriors, steep roofs, and overhanging eaves, emphasizing vertical and diagonal patterns reminiscent of medieval timber construction.

sunken homes Homes in Chicago on which the first floor or part of the structure appears to sit below the current street level due to past street raisings.

swag A decorative motif resembling a draped fabric or garland.

symmetry Balanced proportions in architecture, where elements on either side of a central axis mirror each other. Horizontal symmetry is when the top and bottom halves are mirrored. Vertical symmetry is when the left and right halves are mirrored.

tenement housing Working-class housing, generally characterized by low rents, overcrowding, and poor sanitary conditions. While cities like New York generally had massive, multi-unit tenement buildings and areas of concentrated poverty, Chicago's poverty was scattered across the city in a mix of multi-unit buildings and single-family homes that were carved up into smaller units. Under the leadership of activists like Jane Addams, major tenement reforms were undertaken at the beginning of the twentieth century.

terra cotta "Baked earth" in Italian, this is a fired clay material used for decorative, structural, and fireproofing purposes.

tower A large, self-supporting structure that can be placed at the corner or center of a building or even stand alone. Towers always reach the ground, in contrast to a turret, which is not self-supporting.

transom window A transom window is a small window positioned above a door or another window, often separated by a horizontal beam called a transom. Some of these windows open up for added ventilation and are called awning windows (if they swing open at the bottom) or hopper windows (if they swing down from the top).

triangular pediment A triangular feature, often seen in classical and neoclassical architecture, above porticos, entrances, windows, or niches.

Tudor Revival style Tudor Revival homes in the U.S. spanned the 1890s through the 1930s and are named after the Tudor Dynasty (1485–1603), a period of time in England when that country was shifting from church-inspired Gothic architecture to medieval and Renaissance-inspired architecture. Steeply pitched roofs, decorative half-timbering, tall narrow windows, and brick and stone exteriors are defining features.

turret A small, tower-like structure projecting from a building. It is often cylindrical or polygonal and does not reach the ground.

vernacular architecture A kind of architecture that's based on local needs, materials, traditions, and climate.

vertical timbers Timber framing where vertical posts provide structural support, often visible in half-timbered buildings.

Victorian era The period of history during the reign of Queen Victoria, from 1837 to 1901, marked by profound social, cultural, political, and technological changes that shaped not only Britain and the U.S. but much of the world.

voussoirs The wedge-shaped stones or bricks that form an arch. The central voussoir at the highest point of the arch is called the keystone, which helps distribute weight and stabilize the structure.

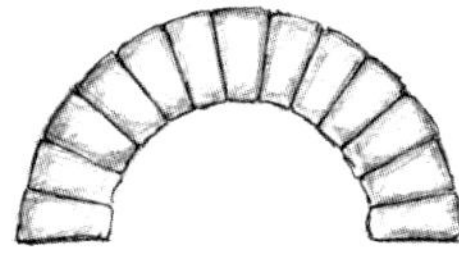

Voussoirs.

window crown Decorative trim placed above a window, often adding a touch of elegance to the exterior facade.

window hood / hood mold This feature is often made of stone and runs above an arch, doorway, or window. Its primary function is to keep rainwater away from openings, though it is sometimes just a handsome, decorative element.

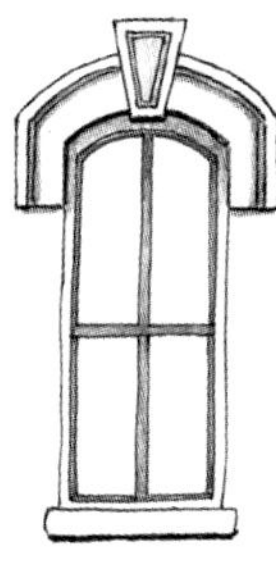

Window hood.

workers cottage A modest house originally built for the working class, typically with a simple rectangular plan and a gable roof.

wood clapboard Horizontal wooden boards used for exterior cladding, overlapping to protect against the elements.

BIBLIOGRAPHY

CHAPTER 1

Andreas, A.T. *History of Chicago, Volume 1*. Chicago: A.T. Andreas, 1884.

Chicago Architecture Center. "Clarke-Ford House." Accessed April 2023. https://www.architecture.org/learn/resources/buildings-of-chicago/building/clarke-ford-house/.

City of Chicago, Department of Transportation. "Street and Site Plan Design Standards." October 2, 2020. https://www.chicago.gov/dam/city/depts/cdot/StreetandSitePlanDesignStandards407.pdf.

Conference on Research in Income and Wealth. *Trends in the American Economy in the Nineteenth Century*. Princeton: Princeton University Press, 1960.

Cronon, William. *Nature's Metropolis: Chicago and the Great West*. New York: W. W. Norton & Company, 1991.

Encyclopedia of Chicago. "Origins of the Grid." In *Encyclopedia of Chicago*, edited by Janice L. Reiff, Ann Durkin Keating, and James R. Grossman. Chicago Historical Society, 2005. http://www.encyclopedia.chicagohistory.org/pages/410050.html.

Greenberg, Joel. *A Natural History of Chicago*. Chicago: University of Chicago Press, 2020.

Grimm, Eric. "Ecosystem." In *Encyclopedia of Chicago*, edited by Janice L. Reiff, Ann Durkin Keating, and James R. Grossman. Chicago Historical Society, 2005. http://www.encyclopedia.chicagohistory.org/pages/410.html.

Hoyt, Homer. *One Hundred Years of Land Values in Chicago: The Relationship of the Growth of Chicago to the Rise in Its Land Values, 1830-1933*. Chicago: University of Chicago Press, 1933.

Karamanski, Theodore J. "Lumber." In *Encyclopedia of Chicago*, edited by Janice L. Reiff, Ann Durkin Keating, and James R. Grossman. Chicago Historical Society, 2005. http://www.encyclopedia.chicagohistory.org/pages/767.html.

Kubal, Joseph D., Ruth D. Nelson, and Maria R. Traska. "That Other Marquette Monument." Illinois Route 66 Association. Accessed May 2023. https://www.il66assoc.org/2017/08/that-other-marquette-monument/.

Lebergott, Stanley. "Wage Trends, 1800-1900." In *Handbook of Labor Economics*, vol. 1, edited by Orley Ashenfelter and Richard Layard, 9–29. Amsterdam: Elsevier Science Publishers, 1986. http://www.nber.org/chapters/c2486.

Low, John N. "*Pokégnek Bodéwadmik*: The Pokagon Band of Potawatomi Indians. Keeper's of the Fire: A History and Introduction to the Community through Text & Images." Presentation, Department of Comparative Studies, Ohio State University—Newark.

Marquette, Jacques. "Journal of the First Voyage to the Illinois." In *The Jesuit Relations and Allied Documents: Travels and Explorations of the Jesuit Missionaries in New France, 1610-1791*, vol. 59, 3–110. Cleveland: Burrows Brothers Company, 1900.

Mattson, Richard Leonard. "The Gable Front and Upright-and-Wing: An Historical Geography of Two Common American House Types." PhD diss., University of Illinois at Urbana-Champaign, 1988.

McAlester, Virginia Savage. *A Field Guide to American Houses*. New York: Alfred A. Knopf, 2020.

Meehan, Thomas A. "Jean Baptiste Point du Sable, the First Chicagoan." *Journal of the Illinois State Historical Society* 56, no. 3 (Autumn 1963): 439–453.

Milwaukee Public Museum. "Fur Trade." Accessed April 2023. https://www.mpm.edu/wirp/ICW-121.html.

Milwaukee Public Museum. "Potawatomi Culture." Accessed April 2023. https://www.mpm.edu/content/wirp/ICW-56.

Nabokov, Peter, and Robert Easton. *Native American Architecture*. New York: Oxford University Press, 1989.

Peterson, Fred W. *Homes in the Heartland: Balloon Frame Farmhouses of the Upper Midwest*. St. Paul: Minnesota Historical Society Press, 1991.

Quaife, Milo M. *Checagou: From Indian Wigwam to Modern City, 1673-1835*. Chicago: The Caxton Club, 1933.

Randall, Frank Alfred. *History of Building Construction in Chicago*. Urbana: University of Illinois Press, 1999.

Randolph Society. "James Thompson." Accessed May 2023. https://randolphsociety.org/james-thompson/.

Schock, Robert E., and Eric J. Risberg. "120 Years of Caisson Foundations in Chicago." Paper presented at the Seventh International Conference on Case Histories in Geotechnical Engineering, Roselle, IL, May 2, 2013.

Sells, Benjamin. *A History of the Chicago Portage: The Crossroads That Made Chicago and Helped Make America*. DeKalb: Northern Illinois University Press, 2019.

Shiloh Museum of Ozark History. "Log Cabins." Accessed May 2023. https://shilohmuseum.org/log-cabins/.

Tallmadge, Thomas. *Architecture in Old Chicago*. Chicago: University of Chicago Press, 1941.

Walter, William. "Selling Location: Illinois Town Advertisements." *Journal of the Illinois State Historical Society* 95, no. 2 (2002): 109–135.

CHAPTER 2

Abbott, Edith. *The Tenements of Chicago, 1908–1935*. University of Chicago Press, 1936.

BBC History. "The Irish Famine." Accessed February 2024. http://www.bbc.co.uk/history/irishfamine.

Brunet, François, and Jessica Talley. "Exhibiting the West at the Paris Exposition of 1867: Towards a New American Aesthetic Identity?" *Transatlantica* 2 (2017).

Cain, Louis P. *Sanitation Strategy for a Lakefront Metropolis: The Case of Chicago*. Northern Illinois University Press, 1978.

Carey, Heidi Pawlowski. "Prairie Avenue." In *Encyclopedia of Chicago*, edited by Janice L. Reiff, Ann Durkin Keating, and James R. Grossman. Chicago Historical Society, 2005. http://www.encyclopedia.chicagohistory.org/pages/1003.html.

Chicago Historical Society and Northwestern University. "A Bird's Eye View of Pre-Fire Chicago." Accessed February 2024. https://greatchicagofire.org/birds-eye-view-of-pre-fire-chicago/.

Chicago Park District. "History of Chicago's Parks." https://www.chicagoparkdistrict.com/about-us/history-chicagos-parks.

Chicago Press and Tribune. "Proof Graphic and Photographic." *Chicago Press and Tribune*, August 6, 1859. ProQuest Historical Newspapers: *Chicago Tribune*.

Colbert, Elias, and Everett Chamberlin. *Chicago and the Great Conflagration*. Cincinnati: C. F. Vent & Co., 1871.

Cronon, William. *Nature's Metropolis: Chicago and the Great West*. W. W. Norton & Company, 1991.

Duis, Perry. *Challenging Chicago: Coping with Everyday Life, 1837–1920*. Urbana: University of Illinois Press, 1998.

Encyclopedia of Chicago. "Development of Railroad Lines from Chicago." In *Encyclopedia of Chicago*, edited by Janice L. Reiff, Ann Durkin Keating, and James R. Grossman. Chicago Historical Society, 2005. http://www.encyclopedia.chicagohistory.org/pages/1461.html.

Encyclopedia of Chicago. "Houses and Water: Connecting Houses to Water Networks." In *Encyclopedia of Chicago*, edited by Janice L. Reiff, Ann Durkin Keating, and James R. Grossman. Chicago Historical Society, 2005. http://www.encyclopedia.chicagohistory.org/pages/300101.html.

Flynn, Katherine. "128 Years of Justice: Jane Addams and Chicago's Hull House." National Trust for Historic Preservation. September 27, 2017. https://savingplaces.org/stories/128-years-of-justice-jane-addams-and-chicagos-hull-house.

Gruber, John, Chris Guss, Michael Blaszak, and Brian Solomon. *Chicago: America's Railroad Capital: The Illustrated History, 1836 to Today*. Voyageur Press, 2014.

Jentz, John B., and Richard Schneirov. *Chicago in the Age of Capital: Class, Politics, and Democracy During the Civil War and Reconstruction*. University of Illinois Press, 2012.

Lewinnek, Elaine. *The Working Man's Reward: Chicago's Early Suburbs and the Roots of American Sprawl*. Oxford: Oxford University Press, 2014.

Library of Congress. "German Immigrants in America." Updated April 17, 2024. https://www.loc.gov/rr/european/imde/germchro.html.

Mayer, Harold M., and Richard C. Wade. *Chicago: Growth of a Metropolis*. Chicago: University of Chicago Press, 1973.

Norwood Park Historical Society. "History of Norwood Park." Accessed March 2024. https://norwoodparkhistoricalsociety.org/about-chicagos-norwood-park-neighborhood/.

Nugent, Walter. "Epidemics." In *Encyclopedia of Chicago*, edited by Janice L. Reiff, Ann Durkin Keating, and James R. Grossman. Chicago Historical Society, 2005. http://www.encyclopedia.chicagohistory.org/pages/432.html.

Parton, James. "Chicago." *Atlantic Monthly*, March 1867.

Randall, Frank A. *The History of the Development of Building Construction in Chicago*. Revised and expanded by John D. Randall. University of Illinois Press, 1999.

Schuyler, David. *Apostle of Taste: Andrew Jackson Downing, 1815–1852*. The Johns Hopkins University Press, 1996.

Spula, Ian. "Historic Hopkinson House and 2.8 Acres List for $525K." Curbed Chicago, November 21, 2013. https://chicago.curbed.com/2013/11/21/10171984/historic-hopkinson-house-and-28-acres-lists-for-525k.

The Great Chicago Fire. "Bellinger Home." Accessed March 2024. https://greatchicagofire.org/landmarks/bellinger-home/.

The Great Chicago Fire. "The O'Leary Legend." Accessed March 2024. https://greatchicagofire.org/oleary-legend-library/official-report/.

CHAPTER 3

Cain, Louis P. "Annexation." In *Encyclopedia of Chicago*, edited by Janice L. Reiff, Ann Durkin Keating, and James R. Grossman. Chicago Historical Society, 2005. http://www.encyclopedia.chicagohistory.org/pages/53.html.

Chicago Daily Tribune. "French Flats in New York." December 18, 1880.

Chicago Daily Tribune. "French Flats: A Genuine Apartment House." December 19, 1875, 6.

City of Chicago. "Arlington-Deming District Landmark Designation Report." City of Chicago Department of Planning and Development. Approved October 4, 2006. https://www.chicago.gov/content/dam/city/depts/zlup/Historic_Preservation/Publications/Arlington_Deming_District.pdf.

Follett, Jean A. "The Hotel Pelham: A New Building Type for America." *American Art Journal* 15, no. 4 (Autumn 1983): 58–73.

Lamb, John. "Joliet Limestone: The Rise and Fall of a Nineteenth Century Building Material and Its Architectural Impact on the Joliet, Illinois Area." *Will County Historical Society Quarterly Publication*. Lockport, IL: Will County Historical Society, Winter 1997. Accessed March 24, 2025. https://www.lewisu.edu/imcanal/JohnLamb/section_46.pdf.

Larson, Gerald. "How Did the 1871 Fire Change Chicago?" *The Architecture Professor* (blog), The Chicago School of Architecture. May 16, 2020. https://thearchitectureprofessor.com/2020/05/16/chap-3-how-did-the-1871-fire-change-chicago/.

Lee, Carol E. "Obama Returns to Chicago." *Politico*. July 23, 2009. https://www.politico.com/story/2009/07/obama-returns-to-chicago-025368.

Lewinnek, Elaine. *The Working Man's Reward: Chicago's Early Suburbs and the Roots of American Sprawl*. New York: Oxford University Press, 2014.

Mayer, Harold M., and Richard C. Wade. *Chicago: Growth of a Metropolis*. Chicago: University of Chicago Press, 1973.

Powers, Robert. "An Old Preservation Victory: Hotel St. Benedict Flats." *A Chicago Sojourn* (blog), December 9, 2014. https://achicagosojourn.wordpress.com/2014/12/09/an-old-preservation-victory-hotel-st-benedict-flats/.

Preservation Chicago. "THREATENED: Demolition Looming: Historic Three-Flat at 2240 N. Burling after Demolition Delay Expires." *Preservation Chicago*, January 12, 2023. https://www.preservationchicago.org/threatened-demolition-looming-historic-three-flat-at-2240-n-burling-after-demolition-delay-expires/.

Reiff, Daniel D. *Houses from Books: Treatises, Pattern Books, and Catalogs in American Architecture, 1738–1950: A History and Guide*. University Park, PA: Pennsylvania State University Press, 2000.

The Great Chicago Fire. "Kate the Barn Is Afire." Chicago Historical Society. https://greatchicagofire.org/oleary-legend-library/%E2%80%9Ckate-barn-afire%E2%80%9D/.

The Great Chicago Fire. "The O'Leary Legend." Chicago Historical Society. https://greatchicagofire.org/oleary-legend/.

University of Illinois School of Architecture. "History of the School of Architecture." Accessed March 2024. https://arch.illinois.edu/about/history-of-the-school-of-architecture/.

Vernon, J.R. "Unemployment Rates in Postbellum America." *Journal of Macroeconomics* 16, no. 4 (Autumn 1994): 701–714. https://delong.typepad.com/1-s2.0-0164070494900086-main.pdf.

WTTW. "Red Bridge." Chicago Time Machine. https://interactive.wttw.com/timemachine/red-bridge.

WTTW. "Shelter Cottages." Chicago Time Machine. https://interactive.wttw.com/timemachine/shelter-cottages#:~:text=More%20than%205%2C200%20of%20the,on%20to%20more%20permanent%20housing.

CHAPTER 4

Adams, Sean Patrick. *Home Fires: How Americans Kept Warm in the 19th Century*. The Johns Hopkins University Press, 2014.

Bruegmann, Robert. *The Architects and the City: Holabird & Roche of Chicago, 1880–1910*. Chicago: University of Chicago Press, 1997.

Chicago Daily Tribune. "Chicago's Sky-Scrapers: Interesting Facts About Three Tall Buildings." January 13, 1889.

Chicago Daily Tribune. "Saratoga: The Past and Present of the Season at the Spa." August 26, 1877.

Chicago Public Library. "Coal Continued: Technology That Changed Chicago." Chicago Public Library Blogs, February 3, 2014. https://www.chipublib.org/blogs/post/technology-that-changed-chicago-coal-continued/.

Chicagology. "Driehaus Museum Tour." Accessed March 2024. https://chicagology.com/goldenage/goldenage171/.

City of Chicago. "Arlington-Deming District Landmark Designation Report." City of Chicago Department of Planning and Development. Approved October 4, 2006. https://www.chicago.gov/dam/city/depts/zlup/Historic_Preservation/Publications/Arlington_Deming_District.pdf.

City of Chicago. "Preliminary Summary of Information: Martin Schnitzius Cottage." Commission on Chicago Landmarks, submitted June 2012. https://www.chicago.gov/dam/city/depts/zlup/Historic_Preservation/Publications/Schnitzius_Cottage_Prelim_Sum.pdf.

Clark, Emily. "Samuel Eberly Gross's Subdivisions." In *Encyclopedia of Chicago*, edited by Janice L. Reiff, Ann Durkin Keating, and James R. Grossman. Chicago Historical Society, 2005. http://www.encyclopedia.chicagohistory.org/pages/2449.html.

F. B. W. "Chicago Architecture: A Critical Essay." *Chicago Daily Tribune*, October 28, 1883.

Illinois Secretary of State. "Communication from the Coroner to the Mayor Concerning Unsafe Elevators." *From the Ashes, 1872-1900: A Selection of Documents from the Illinois State Archives*. https://www.ilsos.gov/departments/archives/teaching_packages/from_the_ashes/doc11.html.

Inland Architect and Builder 1, no. 5 (June 1883). Chicago: Inland Pub. Co.

Keating, Ann Durkin. *Building Chicago: Suburban Developers and the Creation of a Divided Metropolis*. Urbana: University of Illinois Press, 2002.

Knox, Douglas. "Boardinghouses." In *Encyclopedia of Chicago*, edited by Janice L. Reiff, Ann Durkin Keating, and James R. Grossman. Chicago Historical Society, 2005. http://www.encyclopedia.chicagohistory.org/pages/152.html.

Larson, Gerald. "How Did the 1871 Fire Change Chicago?" *The Architecture Professor* (blog), The Chicago School of Architecture, May 16, 2020. https://thearchitectureprofessor.com/2020/05/16/chap-3-how-did-the-1871-fire-change-chicago/.

Larson, Gerald. "The Influence of H. H. Richardson." *The Architecture Professor* (blog), The Chicago School of Architecture, October 4, 2020. https://thearchitectureprofessor.com/2020/10/04/7-16-the-influence-of-h-h-richardson-v-1-0/.

Larson, Gerald. "The Two Variables of the Chicago School: Ornament and Architectural Expression." *The Architecture Professor* (blog), The Chicago School of Architecture, April 21, 2020. https://thearchitectureprofessor.com/2020/04/21/4-the-two-variables-of-the-chicago-school-ornament-and-architectural-expression/.

Morse, Patricia L. Acting Archivist, Hyde Park Historical Society. archives@hydeparkhistory.org.

National Park Service. "A Brief Overview of the Pullman Story." Updated January 2025. https://www.nps.gov/pull/learn/historyculture/a-brief-overview-of-the-pullman-story.htm.

New York Times. "Pullman's Body Sealed Up; Put in Tar Paper in a Steel Casket and Incased in Concrete." October 25, 1897. https://timesmachine.nytimes.com/timesmachine/1897/10/25/102098611.html?pageNumber=7.

Nichols, Ralph, and Harold Doerr. "The History, Construction, and Design of Caisson Foundations in Chicago." Bachelor's thesis, University of Illinois, 1913.

Platt, Harold L. "Gas and Electricity." In *Encyclopedia of Chicago*, edited by Janice L. Reiff, Ann Durkin Keating, and James R. Grossman. Chicago Historical Society, 2005. http://www.encyclopedia.chicagohistory.org/pages/504.html.

Platt, Harold L. *The Electric City: Energy and the Growth of the Chicago Area, 1880-1930*. University of Chicago Press, 1991.

Preservation Chicago. "Terra Cotta Buildings Throughout Chicago – 2023 Most Endangered." *Preservation Chicago*. March 8, 2023. https://www.preservationchicago.org/terra-cotta-buildings-throughout-chicago-most-endangered-2023.

Reardon, Patrick T. "It all starts downtown." *Chicago Tribune*, July 26, 2004. https://web.archive.org/web/20180626054732/http://articles.chicagotribune.com/2004-07-26/features/0407260184_1_south-loop-cable-cars-chicago-transit-authority.

Reiff, Daniel D. *Houses from Books: Treatises, Pattern Books, and Catalogs in American Architecture, 1738–1950: A History and Guide*. University Park, PA: Pennsylvania State University Press, 2000.

Roth, Leland M. *American Architecture: A History*. Boulder, CO: Westview Press, 2001.

The Skyscraper Museum. "Foundations: Construction History in New York and Chicago." March 22, 2022. https://skyscraper.org/programs/foundations/.

Tunick, Susan. *Terra-Cotta Skyline: New York's Architectural Ornament*. First edition. New York: Princeton Architectural Press, 1997.

Turnbull, Craig. *An American Urban Residential Landscape, 1890-1920: Chicago in the Progressive Era*. Cambria Press, 2009.

Twombly, Robert C. *Louis Sullivan: His Life and Work*. New York: Viking, 1986.

Weiner, Lynn Y. "Work Culture." In *Encyclopedia of Chicago*, edited by Janice L. Reiff, Ann Durkin Keating, and James R. Grossman. Chicago Historical Society, 2005. http://www.encyclopedia.chicagohistory.org/pages/1382.html.

Wright, Gwendolyn. *Moralism and the Model Home: Domestic Architecture and Cultural Conflict in Chicago, 1873-1913*. Chicago: University of Chicago Press, 1980.

CHAPTER 5

Azu, Lauryn. "Home of the Week: Wicker Park 6-Bedroom Home with 2-Story Coach House: $4M." *Chicago Tribune*, May 19, 2024. https://www.proquest.com/newspapers/home-week/docview/3056344307/se-2.

Bachrach, Julia. "Home on the Park." *Julia Bachrach Consulting* (blog). June 3, 2019. https://www.jbachrach.com/blog/2019/6/3/home-on-the-park.

Bachrach, Julia. "Ode to the American Foursquare." *Julia Bachrach Consulting* (blog). January 27, 2022. https://www.jbachrach.com/blog/2022/1/27/ode-to-the-american-foursquare.

Bigott, Joseph C. "Housing Types." In *Encyclopedia of Chicago*, edited by Janice L. Reiff, Ann Durkin Keating, and James R. Grossman. Chicago Historical Society, 2005. http://www.encyclopedia.chicagohistory.org/pages/609.html.

Bluestone, Daniel. "Framing Landscape While Building Density." *Journal of the Society of Architectural Historians* 76, no. 4 (December 2017): 506–531. https://www.jstor.org/stable/pdf/26419054.pdf.

Brooks, H. Allen. "Architecture: The Prairie School." In *Encyclopedia of Chicago*, edited by Janice L. Reiff, Ann Durkin Keating, and James R. Grossman. Chicago Historical Society, 2005. http://www.encyclopedia.chicagohistory.org/pages/63.html.

Brooks, H. Allen. *Frank Lloyd Wright and the Prairie School*. New York: George Braziller, Inc., 1984.

Bruni, Carla. "The Garalow: Grandmama of Tiny Homes and ADUs." Chicago Bungalow Association. July 13, 2021. https://www.chicagobungalow.org/post/the-garalow.

Build Your Own Chicago. "Chicago Greystone." *Chicago Vernacular Architecture* (blog). Accessed March 2024. https://www.buildyourownchicago.com/BYOKC/Greystone.html.

Burke, Daniel. "The Lavish Homes of American Archbishops." CNN. August 2014. https://www.cnn.com/interactive/2014/08/us/american-archbishops-lavish-homes/index.html#:~:text=George%2C%20whose%20private%20quarters%20occupy,house%20near%20the%20main%20residence.

Chicago Architecture Center. "What's With That Odd Closet? What Chicago's Architectural Clues Reveal About How We Lived." Accessed April 2025. https://www.architecture.org/news/happening-caf/whats-with-that-odd-closet-what-chicagos-architectural-clues-reveal-about-how-we-lived/.

Chicago Architecture Center. "World's Columbian Exposition of 1893." Accessed April 2024. https://www.architecture.org/learn/resources/architecture-dictionary/entry/world-s-columbian-exposition-of-1893/.

Chicago Daily Tribune. "Among Architects and Builders: Contracts Let and Work Began on the Dexter Office Building." February 14, 1892. https://www.proquest.com/historical-newspapers/among-architects-builders/docview/174595333/se-2.

Chicago Daily Tribune. "Street and Alley Report: Mileage and Cost of Cleaning and Paving—Sidewalks—Garbage Collection and Disposal. Sewer Work of the Year." December 31, 1899. https://www.proquest.com/historical-newspapers/street-alley-report/docview/172949384/se-2.

Chicago Greystone & Vintage Home Program. Interview with Matt Cole, former Program Manager, in discussion with the author. November 9, 2024.

Chicago History Museum. "Chicago Ancient Building Permits." Microfilm. https://libguides.chicagohistory.org/buildings/buildingpermits.

Chicago Workers Cottage Initiative. "A History of the Chicago Workers Cottage." Accessed April 2025. https://www.workerscottage.org/history.html.

Chicago Workers Cottage Initiative. "Field Guide for Identifying Chicago Worker Cottages." Accessed April 2025. https://www.workerscottage.org/WCIdentification.pdf.

Chmelik, Samantha. "Frederick Rueckheim." In *Immigrant Entrepreneurship: German-American Business Biographies, 1720 to the Present*, vol. 4, edited by Jeffrey Fear. German Historical Institute. Last modified October 10, 2013.

City of Bedford, Indiana. "Bedford Limestone Walking Tour." August 2021. https://limestonecountry.com/wp-content/uploads/2021/08/Bedford-Limestone-Walking-Tour.pdf.

City of Chicago. "Chateauesque." Chicago Landmarks, City of Chicago. Accessed April 2025. https://webapps1.chicago.gov/landmarksweb/web/styledetails.htm?styId=200.

City of Chicago. "Cook County Hospital Administration Building Landmark Designation Report." City of Chicago Department of Planning and Development. Adopted November 1, 2018. https://www.chicago.gov/content/dam/city/depts/zlup/Historic_Preservation/Publications/Cook_County_Hospital_Administration_Bldg.pdf.

City of Chicago. "Design Guidelines." Historic Chicago Greystone Initiative. 2009. https://issuu.com/nhsgreystoneandvintage/docs/greystone_design_guidelines_final_2.

City of Chicago. "K-Town Historic District Registration Form." National Register of Historic Places Registration Form. Submitted July 21, 2010. https://web.archive.org/web/20180626083003/http://gis.hpa.state.il.us/pdfs/223505.pdf.

City of Chicago. "Prairie School." Chicago Landmarks, City of Chicago. Accessed April 2025. https://webapps1.chicago.gov/landmarksweb/web/styledetails.htm?styId=201.

City of Chicago. "Preliminary Summary of Information: Martin Schnitzius Cottage." Commission on Chicago Landmarks, submitted June 2012. https://www.chicago.gov/dam/city/depts/zlup/Historic_Preservation/Publications/Schnitzius_Cottage_Prelim_Sum.pdf.

City of Chicago. "The Chicago Park Boulevard System Historic District Registration Form." National Register of Historic Places Registration Form. Accessed April 2025. https://www.chicago.gov/dam/city/depts/zlup/Historic_Preservation/Publications/ParkBlvdsHD_NR_nom_FINAL_DRAFT_pt1.pdf.

City of Chicago. "Tudor Revival." Chicago Landmarks, City of Chicago. Accessed April 2025. https://webapps1.chicago.gov/landmarksweb/web/styledetails.htm?styId=215.

City of Chicago. "West Burton Place District Landmark Designation Report." Adopted April 7, 2016. https://www.chicago.gov/content/dam/city/depts/zlup/Historic_Preservation/Publications/West_Burton_Place_District.pdf.

Cressey, Paul Frederick. "Population Succession in Chicago: 1898-1930." *American Journal of Sociology* 44, no. 1 (July 1938): 59–69.

Duis, Perry R. *Challenging Chicago: Coping with Everyday Life, 1837-1920*. Urbana: University of Illinois Press, 2006.

Frank Lloyd Wright Trust. "The Prairie Style." Accessed April 2025. https://flwright.org/explore/prairie-style.

Geological Society of London. "Limestones." *The Rock Cycle*. Accessed April 2025. https://www.geolsoc.org.uk/ks3/gsl/education/resources/rockcycle/page3524.html.

Hanchett, Thomas Walter. "The Four Square House in the United States." Master's thesis, University of Chicago, April 1986. https://www.historysouth.org/wp-content/uploads/2015/06/FourSquareThesis.pdf.

Hirsch, Susan E., and Robert I. Goler. *A City Comes of Age: Chicago in the 1890s*. Chicago: Chicago Historical Society, 1991.

Historic Chicago Greystone Initiative. *A Users Guide to Renovating Your Home*. Published by the City Design Center in the College of Architecture and the Arts at the University of Illinois at Chicago, 2007.

Hogan, David. "Education and the Making of the Chicago Working Class, 1880-1930." *History of Education Quarterly* 18, no. 3 (Autumn 1978): 227–270. https://www.jstor.org/stable/368088.

Hoyt, Homer. *One Hundred Years of Land Values in Chicago: The Relationship of the Growth of Chicago to the Rise in Its Land Values, 1830-1933*. Chicago: University of Chicago Press, 1933.

Hubka, Thomas C., and Judith T. Kenny. "Examining the American Dream: Housing Standards and the Emergence of a National Housing Culture, 1900-1930." *Perspectives in Vernacular Architecture* 13, no. 1 (2006): 49–69.

Irving, Bruce. "Colonial Revival Architecture." *This Old House*. Accessed April 2025. https://www.thisoldhouse.com/21015409/colonial-revival-architecture.

John, Richard R. "Telephony." In *Encyclopedia of Chicago*, edited by Janice L. Reiff, Ann Durkin Keating, and James R. Grossman. Chicago Historical Society, 2005. http://www.encyclopedia.chicagohistory.org/pages/1236.html.

Karamanski, Theodore J. "Lumber." In *Encyclopedia of Chicago*, edited by Janice L. Reiff, Ann Durkin Keating, and James R. Grossman. Chicago Historical Society, 2005. http://www.encyclopedia.chicagohistory.org/pages/767.html.

Khyl, Carson P. "How Daniel Burnham and the 1893 Columbian Exposition Influence Innovation at Burnham Nationwide." *Burnham Nationwide* (blog). https://www.burnhamnationwide.com/final-review-blog/how-daniel-burnham-and-the-1893-columbian-exposition-influence-innovation-at-burnham-nationwide.

Lambert, William A. *Lambert's Suburban Architecture*. New York: Wm. A. Lambert, 1894. https://archive.org/details/WmALambertLambertssuburbanarchitecture0001.

Mayer, Harold M., and Richard C. Wade. *Chicago: Growth of a Metropolis*. Chicago: University of Chicago Press, 1969.

McAlester, Virginia Savage. *A Field Guide to American Houses*. New York: Alfred A. Knopf, 2020.

Monet, Dolores. "The History of Baltimore Rowhouses." *Wander Wisdom*. February 18, 2024. https://wanderwisdom.com/travel-destinations/Row-HouseTheHistoryofBaltimoreRowhouses.

Morris, John. "Five of a Kind: The Chicago Greystone." Tiny City Press. https://tinycitypress.bigcartel.com/product/five-of-a-kind-the-chicago-greystone.

Moss Design. "Chicago Building Types: Coach House." November 6, 2018. https://moss-design.com/chicago-building-types-coach-house/.

Moss Design. "Chicago Building Types: The Greystone." February 19, 2015. https://moss-design.com/greystone/.

Moss Design. "Chicago Building Types: Worker Cottage." February 2, 2016. https://moss-design.com/worker-cottage/.

Nugent, Walter. "Demography: Chicago as a Modern World City." In *Encyclopedia of Chicago*, edited by Janice L. Reiff, Ann Durkin Keating, and James R. Grossman. Chicago Historical Society, 2005. http://www.encyclopedia.chicagohistory.org/pages/962.html.

Pennsylvania Historical & Museum Commission. "Beaux Arts Style 1885–1930." *Pennsylvania Architectural Field Guide*. Updated August 26, 2015. https://www.phmc.state.pa.us/Portal/Communities/Architecture/Styles/beaux-arts.html.

Retrospective Vaughan. "Foursquare." *Retrospective Vaughan* (blog). Accessed April 2025. https://www.retrospectivevaughan.ca/foursquare.

Rose, Julie K. "The World's Columbian Exposition: Idea, Experience, Aftermath." Master's thesis, University of Virginia, 1993. https://libraetd.lib.virginia.edu/public_view/v979v310m.

Skogan, Wesley G. *Chicago Since 1840: A Time-Series Data Handbook*. The Institute of Government and Public Affairs. University of Illinois Urbana, 1976.

The University of Chicago Library. "Chicago in the 1890s." The University of Chicago Library's Map Collection. https://www.lib.uchicago.edu/collex/collections/chicago-1890s/.

University of Illinois at Chicago. "Historic Chicago Greystone Initiative: Planning Phase Report." City Design Center. December 2005. https://issuu.com/mit-dusp/docs/cdc_greystone_planning_report_2005.

University of Illinois Library. "World's Columbian Exposition of 1893: Planning and Vision." Accessed April 2025. https://omeka-s.library.illinois.edu/s/idhh/page/worlds-columbian-exposition-planning-and-vision.

Urban Studies Center. "The World's Columbian Exposition of 1893: The Innovations." Accessed April 2025. https://urbanstudieschi.weebly.com/the-innovations.html.

Wagner, Kate. "Looking Around: American Foursquares." *McMansion Hell* (blog). October 29, 2017. https://mcmansionhell.com/post/166916762911/looking-around-american-foursquares.

Wheeler Kearns Architects. "Coach Homes." Accessed April 2025. https://www.chicagocityscape.com/uploads/964.pdf.

Williams, David B. "Greystones: Chicago's Answer to Brownstones." *Stories in Stone* (blog). May 4, 2010. https://stories-in-stone.blogspot.com/2010/05/greystones-chicagos-answer-to.html.

Wilson, Mark R. "Quarrying, Stone Cutting, and Brick Making." In *Encyclopedia of Chicago*, edited by Janice L. Reiff, Ann Durkin Keating, and James R. Grossman. Chicago Historical Society, 2005. http://www.encyclopedia.chicagohistory.org/pages/1031.html.

Wolski, Tamara. "The World's Columbian Exposition's Lasting Effect on Chicago." Paper for Master's program in Historical Administration, Eastern Illinois University, 2009. https://www.eiu.edu/historia/2010Wolski.pdf.

World's Columbian Exposition, Chicago, IL. "New Jersey building." 1893. https://www.loc.gov/item/2020771322/.

WTTW. "Ask Geoffrey: A Brief History of Chicago's Coach Houses." Ask Geoffrey. August 6, 2020. https://news.wttw.com/2020/08/06/ask-geoffrey-chicago-s-coach-houses.

WTTW. "History of Chicago's Bike Industry." Biking the Boulevards with Geoffrey Baer. https://interactive.wttw.com/a/biking-the-boulevards-history-bike-industry.

Yang, Robert. "Shadow of the White Cloud: Architecture Criticism at the 1893 World's Fair." *Radiator Design Blog*. February 7, 2012. https://www.blog.radiator.debacle.us/2012/02/shadow-of-white-cloud-architecture.html.

CHAPTER 6

Abid, Ayesha. "Sears Is Fading, But Memories Of Its Mail-Order Homes Endure." WBEZ Chicago, October 20, 2018. https://www.npr.org/2018/10/20/657770791/sears-is-fading-but-memories-of-its-mail-order-homes-endure.

Addams, Jane. "The Housing Problem in Chicago." *Annals of the American Academy for Political and Social Science* 20 (July 1902): 99–107. Accessed May 13, 2023. https://digital.janeaddams.ramapo.edu/items/show/1162.

American Carpenter and Builder 7, no. 6 (September 1, 1909): 694.

Andre, Kathryn. "The Evolution of Skyscrapers: The Chicago School of Architecture, 1870-1920." Master's thesis, University of Vermont, 2006.

Bauer, William. "Early Colonial Revival Architecture." Old House Online. Accessed May 13, 2023. https://www.oldhouseonline.com/house-tours/early-colonial-revival-architecture/.

Big Shoulders Realty. "Dutch Colonial Architecture." Accessed May 17, 2023. http://www.bigshouldersrealty.com/resources/architectural-styles/dutch-colonial/.

Bluestone, Daniel. "Framing Landscape While Building Density: Chicago Courtyard Apartments, 1891-1929." *Journal of the Society of Architectural Historians* 76, no. 4, (2017): 506–531.

Breckinridge, Sophonisba P., and Edith Abbott. "Chicago Housing Conditions, IV: The West Side Revisited." *American Journal of Sociology*, XVII, no. 1 (July 1911): 13.

Brick and Clay Record. "A Converted Carpenter Who Now Builds with Burned Clay." February 15, 1916.

Burnham, Daniel H., and Edward H. Bennett. *Plan of Chicago*. Prepared under the Direction of the Commercial Club During the Years MCMVI, MCMVII, and MCMVIII. Chicago: The Commercial Club, 1909.

Chicago Architecture Center. "Prairie Style." Architecture Dictionary. Accessed May 14, 2023. https://www.architecture.org/learn/resources/architecture-dictionary/entry/prairie-style/.

Chicago Architecture Center. "Two- and Three-Flats." Accessed May 13, 2023. https://www.architecture.org/learn/resources/buildings-of-chicago/building/two-and-three-flats/.

Chicago Bungalow Association. *The Chicago Bungalow*. Edited by Dominic A. Pacyga and Charles Shanabruch. Chicago: Arcadia Publishing, 2001.

Chicago Daily Tribune. "Display Ad 9 — no Title." *Chicago Daily Tribune* (1923-1963), January 26, 1939. https://www.proquest.com/historical-newspapers/display-ad-9-no-title/docview/182009173/se-2.

Chicago Daily Tribune. "Plan of Two-Room Model Tenement." March 20, 1900, 7.

Chicago Daily Tribune. "The Bungalow Craze." April 26, 1908.

Chicago Metropolis 2020. "The Plan of Chicago: A Regional Legacy." The Burnham Plan Centennial Committee. May 2008. https://burnhamplan100.lib.uchicago.edu/files/content/documents/Plan_of_Chicago_booklet.pdf.

Chicago Workers Cottage Initiative. Accessed March 10, 2023. https://workerscottage.org/.

City Homes Association. *Tenement Conditions in Chicago*. Chicago: City Homes Association, 1901.

City of Chicago. "Avalon Park." Chicago Park District. www.chicagoparkdistrict.com/parks-facilities/avalon-park.

City of Chicago. "Cook County Hospital Administration Building Landmark Designation Report." City of Chicago Department of Planning and Development. Adopted November 1, 2018. https://www.chicago.gov/content/dam/city/depts/zlup/Historic_Preservation/Publications/Cook_County_Hospital_Administration_Bldg.pdf.

City of Chicago. "Prairie School." Chicago Landmarks, City of Chicago. Accessed April 2025. https://webapps1.chicago.gov/landmarksweb/web/styledetails.htm?styId=201.

City of Chicago. "Preliminary Summary of Information: Martin Schnitzius Cottage." Commission on Chicago Landmarks, submitted June 2012. https://www.chicago.gov/dam/city/depts/zlup/Historic_Preservation/Publications/Schnitzius_Cottage_Prelim_Sum.pdf.

City of Chicago. "The Chicago Park Boulevard System Historic District Registration Form." National Register of Historic Places Registration Form. Accessed April 2025. https://www.chicago.gov/dam/city/depts/zlup/Historic_Preservation/Publications/ParkBlvdsHD_NR_nom_FINAL_DRAFT_pt1.pdf.

Columbian Guide Company. "Official Guide to the World's Columbian Exposition." Compiled by John J. Flinn. October 26, 1893. Accessed June 16, 2023. https://www.google.com/books/edition/Official_Guide_to_the_World_s_Columbian/6BEaAAAAYAAJ.

Connors, Maura, Jonathan Katz, Lee Kuhn, Hannah Loftus, and Jennifer Brandel. "Chicago's Flammable Fire Escapes." WBEZ Chicago. October 25, 2013. https://www.wbez.org/stories/chicagos-flammable-fire-escapes/b53874e6-1c66-42c6-b705-8fd9f2c482c0.

Curbed Chicago. "Getting to Know Chicago's Smallest Neighborhood: The Villa." February 24, 2015. https://chicago.curbed.com/2015/2/24/9988278/getting-to-know-chicagos-smallest-neighborhood-the-villa.

Editors, Charles River. *Chicago in the 20th Century: The History and Legacy of the Windy City's Modernization*. CreateSpace Independent Publishing Platform, 2018.

Grossman, James. "The Great Migration." In *Encyclopedia of Chicago*, edited by Janice L. Reiff, Ann Durkin Keating, and James R. Grossman. Chicago Historical Society, 2005. Accessed May 10, 2023. http://www.encyclopedia.chicagohistory.org/pages/545.html.

Hanchett, Thomas W. "The Four Square House Type in the United States." *Perspectives in Vernacular Architecture* 1 (1982): 51–53. https://www.jstor.org/stable/3514266.

Hirsch, Arnold R. "The Labor Force of Chicago: Historical Trends and Future Prospects." In *Chicago: A Historical Guide to the Neighborhoods*, edited by Ann Durkin Keating, 335–57. Chicago: University of Chicago Press, 1986.

Hoyt, Homer. *One Hundred Years of Land Values in Chicago: The Relationship of the Growth of Chicago to the Rise in Its Land Values, 1830-1933*. Chicago: University of Chicago Press, 1933.

Hubka, Thomas C., and Judith T. Kenny. "Examining the American Dream: Housing Standards and the Emergence of a National Housing Culture, 1900-1930." *Perspectives in Vernacular Architecture* 13, no. 1 (2006): 49–69.

Hunter, Rebecca. "Kit House History." Accessed June 18, 2023. http://www.kithouse.org/.

Hunter, Robert. *Tenement Conditions in Chicago*. Chicago: City Homes Association, 1901. Accessed May 13, 2023. https://babel.hathitrust.org/cgi/pt?id=hvd.32044025682253&view=1up&seq=160.

Illinois Historic Preservation Agency. "Chicago Bungalows." Multiple Property Documentation Form, National Register of Historic Places.

Illinois Secretary of State. "Rushing to Open the Canal, 1900." Illinois State Archives. Accessed May 13, 2023. https://www.ilsos.gov/departments/archives/online_exhibits/100_documents/1900-photo-reverse-chicago-river.html.

Institute for Housing Studies at DePaul University. "Characteristics of the 2 to 4 Stock in Chicago Neighborhoods." May 13, 2021. https://www.housingstudies.org/releases/characteristics-2-4-stock-chicago-neighborhoods/.

Journal of the Illinois State Historical Society. "Politics and Potable Water: The Chicago Water Tower." *Journal of the Illinois State Historical Society* 108, no. 3 (2015): 353–76.

Lancaster, Clay. "The American Bungalow." *The Art Bulletin* 40, no. 3 (1958): 239. https://doi.org/10.2307/3047780.

Landmarks Illinois. "Old Cook County Hospital Rehabilitated." Accessed April 2025. https://www.landmarks.org/old-cook-county-hospital-rehabilitated/.

McAlester, Virginia Savage. *A Field Guide to American Houses*. New York: Alfred A. Knopf, 1984.

McCarthy, Michael P. "Chicago Businessmen and the Burnham Plan." *Journal of the Illinois State Historical Society* (1908-1984) 63, no. 3 (Autumn 1970): 228–56. University of Illinois Press on behalf of the Illinois State Historical Society.

Moberg, David. "Work." In *Encyclopedia of Chicago*, edited by Janice L. Reiff, Ann Durkin Keating, and James R. Grossman. Chicago Historical Society, 2005. http://www.encyclopedia.chicagohistory.org/pages/1381.html.

National Public Radio. "Contract Buying Robbed Black Families in Chicago of Billions." NPR.org. May 30, 2019. https://www.npr.org/local/309/2019/05/30/728122642/contract-buying-robbed-black-families-in-chicago-of-billions.

New York Times. "Multiple Levers for Exits." January 3, 1904.

Perry, Marilyn Elizabeth. "Villa District." In *Encyclopedia of Chicago*, edited by Janice L. Reiff, Ann Durkin Keating, and James R. Grossman. Chicago Historical Society, 2005. Accessed May 14, 2023. http://www.encyclopedia.chicagohistory.org/pages/1306.html.

Plotkin, Wendy. "City Homes Association." In *Encyclopedia of Chicago*, edited by Janice L. Reiff, Ann Durkin Keating, and James R. Grossman. Chicago Historical Society, 2005. Accessed May 13, 2023. http://www.encyclopedia.chicagohistory.org/pages/289.html.

Rent Confident. "The Rise and Fall of Chicago's Courtyard Apartment Buildings." *Rent Confident* (blog). November 1, 2019. Accessed May 13, 2023. https://blog.rentconfident.com/2727/the-rise-and-fall-of-chicagos-courtyard-apartment-buildings/.

Sears Archives. "Sears Modern Homes." Accessed June 18, 2023. http://www.searsarchives.com/homes/.

Sears, Roebuck & Co. *Sears Modern Homes Fall 1914 - Spring 1915*. Chicago: Sears, Roebuck & Co., 1914–1915.

Sidler, Scott. "The History of Sears Kit Homes." *The Craftsman Blog*. Accessed June 18, 2023. https://thecraftsmanblog.com/the-history-of-sears-kit-homes/.

Sinclair, Upton. *The Jungle*. Doubleday, Page & Company, 1906.

Smith, Henry T., and Lloyd Lewis. *Chicago: The History of Its Reputation*. New York: Harcourt, 1929.

Sonne, Wolfgang. "Dwelling in the Metropolis: Urbanity as a Paradigm in Modern Housing 1890–1940." *Positions*, no. 1 (2010): 122–45. http://www.jstor.org/stable/25835104.

Spivack, Dolores. "Amending the Building Code of the City of New York: Exploring Forces That Influenced Change." PhD diss., New Jersey School of Architecture, New Jersey Institute of Technology, 2016.

The Pennsylvania Historical & Museum Commission. "Georgian Architecture." Accessed May 14, 2023. http://www.phmc.state.pa.us/portal/communities/architecture/styles/georgian.html.

Twombly, Robert. "Foreword: New Forms, Old Functions: Social Aspects of Prairie School Design." *Art Institute of Chicago Museum Studies* 21, no. 2 (1995): 85–182.

United States Census Bureau. "Historical Census Statistics on Population Totals by Race, 1790 to 1990, and by Hispanic Origin, 1970 to 1990, for Large Cities and Other Urban Places in the United States." February 2005.

United States Work Projects Administration (Ill.). "Residential Chicago." In *Report of the Chicago Land Use Survey, 1942*. Chicago: Chicago Plan Commission. Accessed May 10, 2023. https://www.google.com/books/edition/Report_of_the_Chicago_Land_Use_Survey/xJYkxAEACAAJ.

University of Chicago. *Local Community Fact Book: Chicago Metropolitan Area*. Chicago: University of Chicago, 1963.

Workers Cottage. "A Field Guide for Identifying Chicago Workers Cottages." Accessed May 10, 2023. https://www.workerscottage.org/WCIdentification.pdf.

Yang, Mimi. "The Prairie Style: Rethinking the American Identity." *South Atlantic Review* 81, no. 1 (2016): 81–93. https://www.jstor.org/stable/soutatlarevi.81.1.81.

CHAPTER 7

Aladdin Homes Company. *The Aladdin Homes "Built in a Day" Catalog*. Aladdin Company, 1918. https://archive.org/details/aladdinhomesbuil00alad/page/50/mode/2up.

Chicago Bungalow Association. *The Chicago Bungalow*. Edited by Dominic A. Pacyga and Charles Shanabruch. Chicago: Arcadia Publishing, 2001.

Chicago Daily Tribune. "Blotting German Names from City Map: Plan to Rename Streets for U.S. Heroes Up Today." *Chicago Daily Tribune* (1872-1922), January 3, 1919. https://chipublib.idm.oclc.org/login?url=https://www.proquest.com/historical-newspapers/blotting-german-names-city-map/docview/174459973/se-2.

Chicago Public Library. "Working Horses: Technology That Changed Chicago." Chicago Public Library Blogs. November 25, 2013. https://www.chipublib.org/blogs/post/technology-that-changed-chicago-working-horses/.

Chicago Tribune. "Chicago Garages." August 22, 2021. https://www.chicagotribune.com/news/ct-xpm-2005-11-10-0511090385-story.html.

Chicago Tribune. "Hailed for Its Innovation, but Razed as Out-of-Date." August 22, 2021. https://www.chicagotribune.com/news/ct-xpm-2005-04-01-0504010258-story.html.

City of Chicago. "Spanish Revival." Chicago Landmarks, City of Chicago. Accessed April 2025. https://webapps1.chicago.gov/landmarksweb/web/styledetails.htm?styId=211.

City of Chicago. "The Chicago Park Boulevard System Historic District Registration Form." National Register of Historic Places Registration Form. Accessed April 2025. https://www.chicago.gov/dam/city/depts/zlup/Historic_Preservation/Publications/ParkBlvdsHD_NR_nom_FINAL_DRAFT_pt1.pdf.

Cooper, M. L. "Heating the Private Garage." *House Beautiful* 33 (January 1913): 61–66.

Goat, Leslie G. "Housing the Horseless Carriage: America's Early Private Garages." *Perspectives in Vernacular Architecture* 3 (1989): 62–72.

Hautzinger, Daniel. "How World War I Transformed Chicago." WTTW. April 10, 2017. https://interactive.wttw.com/playlist/2017/04/07/how-world-war-i-transformed-chicago.

High Speed [pseud.]. "Order Is First Law of Success in Home Garage." *Chicago Daily Tribune* (1872-1922), October 21, 1917.

Keating, Ann Durkin. "Water and Urban Life." In *Encyclopedia of Chicago*, edited by Janice L. Reiff, Ann Durkin Keating, and James R. Grossman. Chicago Historical Society, 2005. http://www.encyclopedia.chicagohistory.org/pages/300020.html.

Library of Congress. "American Expeditionary Forces." Accessed April 2025. https://www.loc.gov/collections/stars-and-stripes/articles-and-essays/a-world-at-war/american-expeditionary-forces/.

Library of Congress. "American War and Military Operations Casualties: Lists and Statistics." Congressional Research Service. Updated July 29, 2020. https://crsreports.congress.gov/product/pdf/RL/RL32492.

Literary Digest. "Gasoline and Oats." *Literary Digest* 44 (February 1912): 28.

Mabwa, Nasutsa M. "Parking." In *Encyclopedia of Chicago*, edited by Janice L. Reiff, Ann Durkin Keating, and James R. Grossman. Chicago Historical Society, 2005. Accessed April 22, 2025. http://www.encyclopedia.chicago-history.org/pages/959.html.

McAlester, Virginia Savage. *A Field Guide to American Houses*. New York: Alfred A. Knopf, 2020.

Mina, B. Elizabeth. "English Style: Tudors, Georgians, Victorians." Accessed April 2025. https://gladstonepark.net/architecture/english/.

National Park Service. "Colonial Williamsburg." National Historic Landmarks Program. Archived from the original on October 6, 2012. https://web.archive.org/web/20121006162209/http:/tps.cr.nps.gov/nhl/detail.cfm?ResourceId=704&ResourceType=District.

Sears Modern Homes. "Sears Pre-Cut Kit Garages: A Dandy Place for Your Automobile." October 17, 2011. https://searshomes.org/index.php/2011/10/17/sears-pre-cut-kit-garages-a-dandy-place-for-your-automobile/.

Sears, Roebuck & Co. *Sears Modern Homes Catalog*. Chicago: Sears, Roebuck & Co., 1923.

Turner, Walter R. "Travel by Railroads, Cars, and Planes in the 1920s." *Tar Heel Junior Historian* 43, no. 2 (2004). https://www.ncpedia.org/transportation/overview-1920s.

CHAPTER 8

Architectural Observer. "Queen Anne Window Sash." January 14, 2019. https://architecturalobserver.com/queen-anne-window-sash/.

Biles, Roger. "New Deal." In *Encyclopedia of Chicago*, edited by Janice L. Reiff, Ann Durkin Keating, and James R. Grossman. Chicago Historical Society, 2005. http://www.encyclopedia.chicagohistory.org/pages/883.html.

Chicago Architecture Center. "Carl Street Studios." Open House Chicago. Archived 2019. https://app.openhousechicago.org/archive/sites/recoYQDVqtPj1deQS.

Chicago Daily Tribune. "Display Ad 8 — no Title." *Chicago Daily Tribune*, July 22, 1935. https://www.proquest.com/historical-newspapers/display-ad-8-no-title/docview/181650585/se-2.

Chicago Daily Tribune. "Display Ad 9 — no Title." *Chicago Daily Tribune*, January 26, 1939. https://www.proquest.com/historical-newspapers/display-ad-9-no-title/docview/182009173/se-2.

Chicago Daily Tribune. "Display Ad 11 — no Title." *Chicago Daily Tribune*, May 10, 1936. https://www.proquest.com/historical-newspapers/display-ad-11-no-title/docview/181774559/se-2.

Chicago Daily Tribune. "Rental Agents Form Special Eviction Police: Mayor Told Plan Is Not Legal." *Chicago Daily Tribune*, September 25, 1931. https://www.proquest.com/historical-newspapers/rental-agents-form-special-eviction-police/docview/181298499/se-2.

Chicago History Museum. "Chicago Ancient Building Permits." Microfilm. https://libguides.chicagohistory.org/buildings/buildingpermits.

Chicago Navy Memorial. "Local Businesses Step Up." *Views from the Pier* (blog). November 16, 2019. https://chicagonavymemorial.org/insights-from-the-pier-blog/local-chicagoland-businesses-step-up-world-war-2.

Chicagology. "Marshall Field Garden Apartment Homes." Accessed April 2025. https://chicagology.com/skyscrapers/skyscrapers030/.

City of Chicago. "West Burton Place District Landmark Designation Report." Adopted April 7, 2016. https://www.chicago.gov/content/dam/city/depts/zlup/Historic_Preservation/Publications/West_Burton_Place_District.pdf.

Cordell, William H., and Kathryn Coe Cordell. "Unions Among the Unemployed." *The North American Review* 240, no. 3 (December 1935): 502. https://www.jstor.org/stable/25114676.

Deutsch, Tracey. "Great Depression." In *Encyclopedia of Chicago*, edited by Janice L. Reiff, Ann Durkin Keating, and James R. Grossman. Chicago Historical Society, 2005. http://www.encyclopedia.chicagohistory.org/pages/542.html.

Edgar Miller Legacy. "Animal Court." National Public Housing Museum. Accessed April 2025. https://www.edgarmiller.org/animal-court.

Encyclopedia.com. "Housing, 1929-1941." Accessed April 2025. https://www.encyclopedia.com/education/news-and-education-magazines/housing-1929-1941.

Federal Reserve. "Redlining." Federal Reserve History. June 2, 2023. https://www.federalreservehistory.org/essays/redlining#:~:text=The%20FHA%20began%20redlining%20at,20%2Dyear%20loans%20they%20were.

Fishback, Price, Jonathan Rose, Kenneth A. Snowden, and Thomas Storrs. "New Evidence on Redlining by Federal Housing Programs in the 1930s." *Journal of Urban Economics* 141 (May 2024). https://www.sciencedirect.com/science/article/abs/pii/S0094119022000390.

Franklin D. Roosevelt Presidential Library and Museum. "FDR and Housing Legislation: 75th Anniversary of the Wagner-Steagall Housing Act of 1937." Accessed April 2025. https://www.fdrlibrary.org/housing.

Gleisten, Samantha. *Chicago's 1933-34 World's Fair: A Century of Progress in Vintage Postcards*. Arcadia Publishing, 2002.

Greer, James L. "Historic Home Mortgage Redlining in Chicago." *Journal of the Illinois State Historical Society* 107, no. 2 (2014): 204–33. https://doi.org/10.5406/jillistathistsoc.107.2.0204.

Hunt, D. Bradford. "Redlining." In *Encyclopedia of Chicago*, edited by Janice L. Reiff, Ann Durkin Keating, and James R. Grossman. Chicago Historical Society, 2005. Accessed April 20, 2025. http://www.encyclopedia.chicagohistory.org/pages/1050.html.

Kahn, Mitch. "Paradise Lost." Shelter Force. November 1, 2004. https://shelterforce.org/2004/11/01/paradise-lost/.

Keating, Ann Durkin. "Water and Urban Life." In *Encyclopedia of Chicago*, edited by Janice L. Reiff, Ann Durkin Keating, and James R. Grossman. Chicago Historical Society, 2005. http://www.encyclopedia.chicagohistory.org/pages/300020.html.

Kruse, Jeff. "Home Is Where the Art Deco Is: Modernist Design Around the Corner." Chicago Art Deco Society Newsletter. April 28th, 2020. https://mailchi.mp/e4478d00fa0a/cads-4810527.

Leslie, Thomas. "Glass and Light: The Influence of Interior Illumination on the Chicago School." *Journal of Architectural Education (1984-)* 58, no. 1 (September 2004): 13–24. https://www.jstor.org/stable/40480520.

Logan, John R., and Brian J. Stults. "Metropolitan Segregation: No Breakthrough in Sight." Diversity and Disparities Project, Brown University, August 12, 2021. https://s4.ad.brown.edu/Projects/Diversity/Data/Report/report08122021.pdf.

Mayer, Harold M., and Richard C. Wade. *Chicago: Growth of a Metropolis*. Chicago: University of Chicago Press, 1969.

National Public Housing Museum. https://www.nphm.org/.

Northwestern University Institute for Policy Research. "IPR at 40." September 2018. https://www.ipr.northwestern.edu/documents/year-in-review/iprat40.pdf.

Rodkin, Dennis. "Architecture Sleuths Solve Mystery of That World's Fair House." *Crain's Chicago Business*, December 19, 2017. https://www.chicagobusiness.com/article/20171219/CRED0701/171219874/historic-steel-house-in-wilmette-is-original-world-s-fair-model.

Sweeney, Ginia. "Harnessing American Creativity: The WPA and Chicago." Art Institute of Chicago, The Collection in Context. December 1, 2020. https://www.artic.edu/articles/890/harnessing-american-creativity-the-wpa-and-chicago.

Swiatosz, Susan. "A Technical History of Late Nineteenth Century Windows in the United States." *Bulletin of the Association for Preservation Technology* 17, no. 1 (1985): 31–37. https://www.jstor.org/stable/1494065.

Yoon, Al. "Home Price Drops Exceed Great Depression: Zillow." Reuters, January 11, 2011. https://www.reuters.com/article/us-usa-housing-prices-idUSTRE70961E20110111/.

CHAPTER 9

Chicago Workers Cottage Initiative. "Two Rhine Street Cottages." Accessed April 2025. https://workerscottage.org/hist-2728Belden.html.

Friedman, Daniel. "Perma-Stone Exterior Siding." Inspectapedia. Accessed April 2025. https://inspectapedia.com/exterior/Perma-Stone.php.

Harris, Elizabeth A. "On City Stoops, a Familiar Shelter Is Losing Its Appeal." *New York Times*, June 25, 2012. https://www.nytimes.com/2012/06/26/nyregion/once-a-staple-awnings-are-losing-their-appeal.html.

McAlester, Virginia Savage. *A Field Guide to American Houses*. New York: Alfred A. Knopf, 2013.

Myers, John H., revised by Gary L. Hume. "Aluminum and Vinyl Siding on Historic Buildings." National Park Service Preservation Brief 8. Accessed April 2025. https://www.okhistory.org/shpo/docs/08Preserve-Brief-Aluminium-Vinyl.pdf.

Randl, Chad. "The Use of Awnings on Historic Buildings: Repair, Replacement, and New Design." National Park Service Preservation Brief 44. April 2005. https://www.nps.gov/orgs/1739/upload/preservation-brief-44-awnings.pdf.

Schmidt, Emily Wallrath. "Where Did All the Fireplaces Go?" Chicago Bungalow Association. December 17, 2019. https://www.chicagobungalow.org/post/2019/12/16/where-did-all-the-fireplaces-go.

Ultralocal Geography. "Stucco Bungalows on Arthur, 1915." February 15, 2018. http://ultralocal.blogspot.com/2018/02/stucco-bungalows-on-arthur-1915.html.

Wikipedia. "Vinyl Siding." Updated June 26, 2024. https://en.wikipedia.org/wiki/Vinyl_siding.

Williams, Paul K. "History of Formstone & Permastone: Love It or Hate It?" *House History Man* (blog). February 17, 2012. https://househistoryman.blogspot.com/2012/02/history-of-formstone-permastone-love-it.html.

ENDNOTES

CHAPTER 1

1 Juliette Magill Kinzie, *Wau-Bun: The Early Day in the Northwest* (J. B. Lippincott & Co., 1873).

CHAPTER 2

1 John B. Jentz and Richard Schneirov, *Chicago in the Age of Capital: Class, Politics, and Democracy During the Civil War and Reconstruction* (University of Illinois Press, 2012).

2 "The Irish Famine," BBC History, accessed February 2024, http://www.bbc.co.uk/history/irishfamine.

3 "A Bird's Eye View of Pre-Fire Chicago," Chicago Historical Society and Northwestern University, accessed February 2024, https://greatchicagofire.org/birds-eye-view-of-pre-fire-chicago/.

4 Elias Colbert and Everett Chamberlin, *Chicago and the Great Conflagration* (Cincinnati: C. F. Vent & Co., 1871).

5 "Proof Graphic and Photographic," *Chicago Press and Tribune*, August 6, 1859, ProQuest Historical Newspapers: *Chicago Tribune*.

6 Edith Abbott, *The Tenements of Chicago, 1908–1935* (University of Chicago Press, 1936).

7 James Parton, "Chicago," *Atlantic Monthly*, March 1867.

8 "Houses and Water: Connecting Houses to Water Networks," *Encyclopedia of Chicago*, accessed March 2024, http://www.encyclopedia.chicagohistory.org/pages/300101.html.

9 François Brunet and Jessica Talley, "Exhibiting the West at the Paris Exposition of 1867: Towards a New American Aesthetic Identity?," *Transatlantica* 2 (2017).

10 Perry Duis, *Challenging Chicago: Coping with Everyday Life, 1837–1920* (Urbana: University of Illinois Press, 1998), 89.

11 "Epidemics," *Encyclopedia of Chicago*, accessed March 2024, http://www.encyclopedia.chicagohistory.org/pages/432.html.

12 Katherine Flynn, "128 Years of Justice: Jane Addams and Chicago's Hull House," Saving Places, May 3, 2022, https://savingplaces.org/distinctive-destinations/jane-addams-hull-house-museum.

13 Ian Spula, "Historic Hopkinson House and 2.8 Acres List for $525K," Curbed Chicago, November 21, 2013, https://chicago.curbed.com/2013/11/21/10171984/historic-hopkinson-house-and-28-acres-lists-for-525k.

CHAPTER 3

1 "Kate the Barn Is Afire," The Great Chicago Fire, https://greatchicagofire.org/oleary-legend-library/%E2%80%9Ckate-barn-afire%E2%80%9D/.

2 "Shelter Cottages," Chicago Time Machine, WTTW, https://interactive.wttw.com/timemachine/shelter-cottages#:~:text=More%20than%205%2C200%20of%20the,on%20to%20more%20permanent%20housing.

3 J.R. Vernon, "Unemployment Rates in Postbellum America," https://delong.typepad.com/1-s2.0-0164070494900086-main.pdf.

4 "Red Bridge," Chicago Time Machine, WTTW, https://interactive.wttw.com/timemachine/red-bridge.

5 "Obama Returns to Chicago," *Politico*, https://www.politico.com/story/2009/07/obama-returns-to-chicago-025368.

6 Elaine Lewinneck, *The Working Man's Reward: Chicago's Early Suburbs and the Roots of American Sprawl* (Oxford University Press, 2014).

7 Gerald Larson, "How Did the 1871 Fire Change Chicago?" The Chicago School of Architecture, *The Architecture Professor*, May 16, 2020, https://thearchitectureprofessor.com/2020/05/16/chap-3-how-did-the-1871-fire-change-chicago/.

8 Daniel D. Reiff, *Houses from Books: Treatises, Pattern Books, and Catalogs in American Architecture, 1738–1950: A History and Guide* (University Park, PA: Pennsylvania State University Press, 2000).

9 John Lamb, "Joliet Limestone: The Rise and Fall of a Nineteenth Century Building Material and Its Architectural Impact on the Joliet, Illinois Area," Will County Historical Society, Quarterly Publication, (Lockport, IL: Will County Historical Society, Winter 1997), accessed March 24, 2025, https://www.lewisu.edu/imcanal/JohnLamb/section_46.pdf, 270.

10 "History of the School of Architecture," University of Illinois, accessed March 24, 2025, https://arch.illinois.edu/about/history-of-the-school-of-architecture/#:~:text=Nathan%20Clifford%20Ricker%2C%20the%20first,the%20University%20of%20Illinois%20Archives.

11 Jean A. Follett, "The Hotel Pelham: A New Building Type for America," *American Art Journal* 15, no. 4 (1983): 58–73.

12 "French Flats: A Genuine Apartment House," *Chicago Daily Tribune* (1872-1922), December 19, 1875, 6.

13 "French Flats in New York," *Chicago Daily Tribune*, December 18, 1880.

14 Robert Powers, "An Old Preservation Victory: Hotel St. Benedict Flats," *A Chicago Sojourn* (blog), December 9, 2014, https://achicagosojourn.wordpress.com/2014/12/09/an-old-preservation-victory-hotel-st-benedict-flats/.

CHAPTER 4

1 Harold L. Platt, *The Electric City: Energy and the Growth of the Chicago Area, 1880-1930*, (University of Chicago Press: 1991).

2 F B W, "Chicago Architecture: A Critical Essay Concerning its Most Notable...," *Chicago Daily Tribune* (1872-1922), October 28, 1883. Accessed via ProQuest Historical Newspapers: *Chicago Tribune*, 18.

3 Homer Hoyt, *One Hundred Years of Land Values in Chicago: The Relationship of the Growth of Chicago to the Rise in Its Land Values, 1830-1933*, (University of Chicago Press, 1933), 195.

4 Hoyt, *One Hundred Years of Land Values,* 190.

5 Gerald Larson, "The Two Variables of the Chicago School: Ornament and Architectural Expression," *The Architecture Professor*, April 21, 2020, https://thearchitectureprofessor.com/2020/04/21/4-the-two-variables-of-the-chicago-school-ornament-and-architectural-expression/.

6 Robert C. Twombly, *Louis Sullivan: His Life and Work* (New York: Viking, 1986).

7 Though two cable cars made a transit "loop," the word is still a few years off. It actually came into usage for the loop of the elevated tracks some years later. See Patrick T. Reardon, "It all starts downtown," *Chicago Tribune,* July 26, 2004, https://web.archive.org/web/20180626054732/http://articles.chicagotribune.com/2004-07-26/features/0407260184_1_south-loop-cable-cars-chicago-transit-authority.

8 "Chicago's Sky-Scrapers: Interesting Facts About Three Tall Buildings," *Chicago Daily Tribune* (1872-1922), January 13, 1889, ProQuest Historical Newspapers: *Chicago Tribune*, 2.

9 "Foundations: Construction History in New York and Chicago," Skyscraper Museum, March 22, 2022, https://skyscraper.org/programs/foundations/.

10 "Communication from the Coroner to the Mayor Concerning Unsafe Elevators," *From the Ashes, 1872-1900: A Selection of Documents from the Illinois State Archives*, https://www.ilsos.gov/departments/archives/teaching_packages/from_the_ashes/doc11.html#:~:text=In%20Chicago%20the%20first%20steam,warehouse%20on%20West%20Lake%20Street.

11 "How Did the 1871 Fire Change Chicago?" *The Architecture Professor*, May 16, 2020, https://thearchitectureprofessor.com/2020/05/16/chap-3-how-did-the-1871-fire-change-chicago/.

12 *Inland Architect*, no. 1, 5 (1883).

13 Robert Bruegmann, *The Architects and the City: Holabird & Roche of Chicago, 1880–1910* (Chicago: University of Chicago Press, 1997).

14 Susan Tunick, *Terra-Cotta Skyline: New York's Architectural Ornament*, 1st ed. (New York: Princeton Architectural Press, 1997).

15 Craig Turnbull, *An American Urban Residential Landscape, 1890-1920: Chicago in the Progressive Era*, (Cambria Press, 2009), 54.

16 "Samuel Eberly Gross's Subdivisions," *Encyclopedia of Chicago*, http://www.encyclopedia.chicagohistory.org/pages/2449.html.

17 Turnbull, *An American Urban Residential Landscape,* 67.

18 Ibid., 65.

19 "Boardinghouses," *Encyclopedia of Chicago*, http://www.encyclopedia.chicagohistory.org/pages/152.html.

20 "Pullman's Body Sealed Up; Put in Tar Paper in a Steel Casket and Incased in Concrete," *New York Times*, October 25, 1897, https://timesmachine.nytimes.com/timesmachine/1897/10/25/102098611.html?pageNumber=7.

21 Ann Durkin Keating, *Building Chicago: Suburban Developers and the Creation of a Divided Metropolis* (Urbana: University of Illinois Press, 2002).

22 Reiff, *Houses from Books,* 133.

23 "Gas and Electricity," *Encyclopedia of Chicago*, http://www.encyclopedia.chicagohistory.org/pages/504.html.

24 Harold L. Platt, *The Electric City: Energy and the Growth of the Chicago Area,* 39.

25 Sean Patrick Adams, *Home Fires: How Americans Kept Warm in the 19th Century* (Johns Hopkins University Press: 2014), 126–7.

26 "Technology That Changed Chicago: Coal Continued," Chicago Public Library, https://www.chipublib.org/blogs/post/technology-that-changed-chicago-coal-continued/.

27 "Saratoga: The Past and Present of the Season at the Spa," *Chicago Daily Tribune* (1872-1922), August 26, 1877; ProQuest Historical Newspapers: *Chicago Tribune,* 16.

28 Gwendolyn Wright, *Moralism and the Model Home: Domestic Architecture and Cultural Conflict in Chicago, 1873-1913*, 93.

CHAPTER 5

1 "World's Columbian Exposition of 1893," PBS, https://www.pbs.org/wgbh/americanexperience/features/chicago-worlds-columbian-exposition-1893/.

2 "Demography," *Encyclopedia of Chicago*, http://www.encyclopedia.chicagohistory.org/pages/962.html.

3 "Business Panics as They Pass: 'Good Times' Should Come Soon in Course of Nature—Duration of Past Panics—Concise and Interesting Review," *Chicago Daily Tribune* (1872-1922), July 27, 1897, https://www.proquest.com/historical-newspapers/business-panics-as-they-pass/docview/175412192/se-2.

4 See Hoyt, in *One Hundred Years of Land Values*: "The demand for vacant property is at the lowest ebb in the history of the city" (p. 180). "In 1896 real estate was in such a dull and disorganized condition that land values were difficult if not impossible to determine in many cases" (p. 181). The decline in the volume of building activity is discussed on p. 179.

5 Hoyt, *One Hundred Years of Land Values,* 181.

6 Harold M. Mayer and Richard C. Wade, *Chicago: Growth of a Metropolis* (University of Chicago Press, 1969), 200, 206.

7 Susan E. Hirsch and Robert I. Goler, *A City Comes of Age: Chicago in the 1890s* (Chicago Historical Society, 1991), 125.

8 Duis, *Challenging Chicago*, 27.

9 Duis, *Challenging Chicago*, 17.

10 "Street and Alley Report: Mileage and Cost of Cleaning and Paving—Sidewalks—Garbage Collection and Disposal. Sewer Work of the Year," *Chicago Daily Tribune*, December 31, 1899, https://www.proquest.com/historical-newspapers/street-alley-report/docview/172949384/se-2.

11 "History of Chicago's Bike Industry," WTTW, https://interactive.wttw.com/a/biking-the-boulevards-history-bike-industry.

12 "Street and Alley Report," *Chicago Daily Tribune*, https://www.proquest.com/historical-newspapers/street-alley-report/docview/172949384/se-2.

13 The University of Chicago Library, "Chicago in the 1890s," The University of Chicago Library's Map Collection, https://www.lib.uchicago.edu/collex/collections/chicago-1890s/.

14 "The World's Columbian Exposition of 1893: The Innovations," Urban Studies Center, https://urbanstudieschi.weebly.com/the-innovations.html.

15 Julie K. Rose, "The World's Columbian Exposition: Idea, Experience, Aftermath" (Master's thesis, University of Virginia, 1993), https://libraetd.lib.virginia.edu/public_view/v979v310m.

16 "New Jersey building," World's Columbian Exposition, Chicago, IL, 1893, https://www.loc.gov/item/2020771322/.

17 "Early Colonial Revival Architecture," *This Old House*, https://www.thisoldhouse.com/21015409/colonial-revival-architecture.

18 "Five of a Kind: The Chicago Greystone," Tiny City Press, https://tinycitypress.bigcartel.com/product/five-of-a-kind-the-chicago-greystone.

19 "Bedford Limestone Walking Tour," Limestone Country, https://limestonecountry.com/wp-content/uploads/2021/08/Bedford-Limestone-Walking-Tour.pdf.

20 "What's with That Odd Closet? What Chicago's Architectural Clues Reveal About How We Lived," Chicago Architecture Center, https://www.architecture.org/news/happening-caf/whats-with-that-odd-closet-what-chicagos-architectural-clues-reveal-about-how-we-lived/.

21 "William Winslow House," Frank Lloyd Wright Trust, https://flwright.org/explore/william-winslow-house.

22 "N Is for Narrow Gauge Brick, a Lancaster Building Material That Recalls Ancient Rome," LancasterOnline, March 8, 2024, https://lancasteronline.com/features/yesteryear/architecture/n-is-for-narrow-gauge-brick-a-lancaster-building-material-that-recalls-ancient-rome-architecture/article_ec361eb2-dc9e-11ee-af27-cf22acca2c73.html.

23 J.B. Achrach, "Ode to the American Foursquare," February 1, 2022, https://www.jbachrach.com/blog/2022/1/27/ode-to-the-american-foursquare.

24 Carla Bruni, "The Garalow: Grandmama of Tiny Homes and ADUs," Chicago Bungalow Association, July 13, 2021, https://www.chicagobungalow.org/post/the-garalow.

25 Daniel Burke, "The Lavish Homes of American Archbishops," CNN, https://www.cnn.com/interactive/2014/08/us/american-archbishops-lavish-homes/index.html#:~:text=George%2C%20whose%20private%20quarters%20occupy,house%20near%20the%20main%20residence.

CHAPTER 6

1 Hoyt, *One Hundred Years of Land Values,* 214–215.

2 Leslie Mann, "An All-American Standout the Foursquare, a Century-Old Design, Attracts New Buyers," *Chicago Tribune*, August 18, 2001, https://www.proquest.com/newspapers/all-american-standout-foursquare-century-old/docview/419373973/se-2.

CHAPTER 7

1 "Chicago and the Great War," Chicago History Museum, https://www.chicagohistory.org/exhibition/chicago-and-the-great-war/.

2 "Sauerkraut to Be 'Liberty Cabbage,'" *The Chicago Defender*, May 4, 1918, https://chipublib.idm.oclc.org/login?url=https://www.proquest.com/historical-newspapers/sauerkraut-be-liberty-cabbage/docview/493372796/se-2.

3 John M. Barry, "The Site of Origin of the 1918 Influenza Pandemic and Its Public Health Implications," *Journal of Translational Medicine* 2, no. 3 (January 20, 2004), https://www.ncbi.nlm.nih.gov/pmc/articles/PMC340389/.

4 "Influenza Encyclopedia: Chicago, Illinois," University of Michigan Center for the History of Medicine, https://www.influenzaarchive.org/cities/city-chicago.html#.

5 Daniel Hautzinger, "How World War I Transformed Chicago," WTTW, https://interactive.wttw.com/playlist/2017/04/07/how-world-war-i-transformed-chicago.

6 Mayer and Wade, *Chicago: Growth of a Metropolis*, 283–284.

7 Mayer and Wade, *Chicago: Growth of a Metropolis*, 344.

8 Jacob Arnold, "Chicago's 1920s Nightlife Incubated World-Changing Musical and Social Experiments," *Chicago Reader*, https://chicagoreader.com/music/chicagos-1920s-nightlife-incubated-world-changing-musical-and-social-experiments/.

9 "Careful Planning Shows Itself Here," *The National Builder* (1896-1924) 67, no. 2 (February 1, 1924): American Periodicals, 64.

10 R. Gnat, "Chicago Flat Type Planning: Sustainability and the 1902 Tenement House Ordinance," 1st Residential Building Design & Construction Conference, February 20–21, 2013, www.phrc.psu.edu/assets/docs/Publications/2013RBDCCPapers/Gnat-2013-RBDCC.pdf.

11 "8011 South Princeton Avenue, Chicago, IL 60620," Compass Real Estate, https://www.compass.com/listing/8011-south-princeton-avenue-chicago-il-60620/1364118973316943289/.

12 "Display Ad 11 — no Title." *Chicago Daily Tribune* (1923-1963), March 3, 1925, https://www.proquest.com/historical-newspapers/display-ad-11-no-title/docview/180634893/se-2.

13 Ibid.

14 "Own Your Own Home," *Chicago Daily Tribune* (1872-1922), May 18, 1919, https://www.proquest.com/historical-newspapers/own-your-home/docview/174443837/se-2.

15 "Own Your Own Home and Kill 'Red' Parasite: Best Cure for Bolshevism, George M. Reynolds Tells Bankers," *Chicago Daily Tribune* (1872-1922), October 2, 1919, https://www.proquest.com/historical-newspapers/own-your-home-kill-red-parasite/docview/174551717/se-2.

16 Virginia Savage McAlester, *A Field Guide to American Houses: The Definitive Guide to Identifying and Understanding America's Domestic Architecture*, Revised ed. (New York: Knopf), 3, 68, 414.

17 National Register of Historic Places Registration Form, The Chicago Park Boulevard System Historic District, https://www.chicago.gov/dam/city/depts/zlup/Historic_Preservation/Publications/ParkBlvdsHD_NR_nom_FINAL_DRAFT_pt1.pdf. Also, Virginia Savage McAlester, *A Field Guide to American Houses*, 533–534.

18 McAlester, *A Field Guide to American Houses,* 533–534.

19 "Music Box Theatre History," Music Box Theatre, https://musicboxtheatre.com/about/music-box-theatre-history, and "Arts and Books," *Chicago Tribune,* July 21, 1983.

20 "Hotel LaSalle Public Garage," *Chicago Reader*, https://chicagoreader.com/news-politics/hotel-lasalle-public-garage/.

21 Hoyt, *One Hundred Years of Land Values,* 199.

22 "Display Ad 42 — no title," *Chicago Daily Tribune* (1923-1963), February 16, 1941, https://www.proquest.com/historical-newspapers/display-ad-42-no-title/docview/176491939/se-2.

23 "Gas Stations: Photos from the Archives," Chicago Public Library, https://www.chipublib.org/blogs/post/gas-station-photos-from-the-archives/.

24 *Chicago Daily Tribune* (1923-1963), February 21, 1929, 1, https://www.proquest.com/hnpchicagotribune/pubidlinkhandler/sng/pubtitle/Chicago+Daily+Tribune+$281923-1963$29/$N/$N/46851/PagePdf/181007306/fulltextPDF/63FA8B9679ED42C5PQ/4?accountid=26320.

25 J. L. Jenkins, "Motordom: Uncle Sam Warns Against Deadly Automobile Gas Closed Garage Is Death Chamber, Report Declares," *Chicago Daily Tribune* (1923-1963), November 16, 1924, 1.

26 "Automobile Gas Fatal to Doctor: Dies in Kenwood Day After He Tried to Clean Carbon Out of Muffler in Garage," *Chicago Daily Tribune* (1872-1922), January 6, 1911, 7.

27 "Chicago Tribune Tower Competition Entry Section," Art Institute of Chicago, 1922, https://www.artic.edu/artworks/189755/chicago-tribune-tower-competition-entry-section.

CHAPTER 8

1 Richard C. Lindberg, *Quotable Chicago* (Wild Onion Books, Loyola Press Chicago, 1996), 119.

2 Mauritz Hallgren, *Seeds of Revolt: A Study of American Life and the Temper of the American People During the Depression* (New York: Alfred A. Knopf, 1933).

3 Mayer and Wade, *Chicago: Growth of a Metropolis*, 360.

4 "Great Depression," *Encyclopedia of Chicago*, http://www.encyclopedia.chicagohistory.org/pages/542.html.

5 "Rental Agents Form Special Eviction Police: Mayor Told Plan Is Not Legal," *Chicago Daily Tribune* (1923-1963), September 25, 1931, https://www.proquest.com/historical-newspapers/rental-agents-form-special-eviction-police/docview/181298499/se-2.

6 William H. Cordell and Kathryn Coe Cordell, "Unions Among the Unemployed," *The North American Review* 240, no. 3 (December 1935): 502, https://www.jstor.org/stable/25114676.

7 Samantha Gleisten, *Chicago's 1933-34 World's Fair: A Century of Progress in Vintage Postcards* (Arcadia Publishing: 2002), 50.

8 "Water and Urban Life," *Encyclopedia of Chicago*, http://www.encyclopedia.chicagohistory.org/pages/300020.html.

9 "Display Ad 11 — no Title," *Chicago Daily Tribune* (1923-1963), May 10, 1936, https://www.proquest.com/historical-newspapers/display-ad-11-no-title/docview/181774559/se-2.

10 "Display Ad 8 — no Title," *Chicago Daily Tribune* (1923-1963), July 22, 1935, https://www.proquest.com/historical-newspapers/display-ad-8-no-title/docview/181650585/se-2.

11 "Display Ad 9 — no Title," *Chicago Daily Tribune* (1923-1963), January 26, 1939, https://www.proquest.com/historical-newspapers/display-ad-9-no-title/docview/182009173/se-2.

12 "New Deal," *Encyclopedia of Chicago*, http://www.encyclopedia.chicagohistory.org/pages/883.html.

13 Mayer and Wade, *Chicago: Growth of a Metropolis*, 364.

14 "Great Depression," *Encyclopedia of Chicago*, http://www.encyclopedia.chicagohistory.org/pages/542.html.

15 Mayer and Wade, *Chicago: Growth of a Metropolis*, 368.

16 "Local Businesses Step Up," Chicago Navy Memorial, November 16, 2019, https://chicagonavymemorial.org/insights-from-the-pier-blog/local-chicagoland-businesses-step-up-world-war-2.

17 "Home Price Drops Exceed Great Depression: Zillow," Reuters, January 11, 2011, https://www.reuters.com/article/us-usa-housing-prices-idUSTRE7096IE20110111/.

18 "Housing, 1929-1941," Encyclopedia.com, https://www.encyclopedia.com/education/news-and-education-magazines/housing-1929-1941.

19 James L. Greer, "Historic Home Mortgage Redlining in Chicago," *Journal of the Illinois State Historical Society (1998-)* 107, no. 2 (2014): 204–33, https://doi.org/10.5406/jillistathistsoc.107.2.0204. Greer cited: William E. Leuchtenburg, *Franklin D. Roosevelt and the New Deal* (New York: Harper and Row, 1963), 46–62; Nathaniel S. Keith, *Politics and the Housing Crisis Since 1930* (New York: Universe Books, 1973), 22–27; Susan Estabrook Kennedy, *The Banking Crisis of 1933* (Lexington: University Press of Kentucky, 1973), 216–22; Kenneth Finegold and Theda Skocpol, *State and Party in America's New Deal* (Madison: University of Wisconsin Press, 1995), 8–9.

20 Mayer and Wade, *Chicago: Growth of a Metropolis*, 366.

21 Mayer and Wade, *Chicago: Growth of a Metropolis*, 364.

22 "Marshall Field Garden Apartment Homes," Chicagology, https://chicagology.com/skyscrapers/skyscrapers030/.

23 "Housing, 1929-1941," Encyclopedia.com, https://www.encyclopedia.com/education/news-and-education-magazines/housing-1929-1941.

24 Mitch Kahn, "Paradise Lost," Shelter Force, November 1, 2004, https://shelterforce.org/2004/11/01/paradise-lost/.

25 National Public Housing Museum, https://www.nphm.org/.

26 "Animal Court," Edgar Miller Legacy, https://www.edgarmiller.org/animal-court.

27 "The Fair Grounds," https://www.rgusrail.com/ilcwf.html.

28 Gleisten, *A Century of Progress in Vintage Postcards*, 75.

29 Lindsay Fullerton, "The Afterlives of the 1933 Century of Progress Homes," *Belt Magazine*, August 30, 2019, https://beltmag.com/1933-century-progress-homes/.

CHAPTER 9

1 Elizabeth A. Harris, "On City Stoops, a Familiar Shelter Is Losing Its Appeal," *New York Times*, June 25, 2012, https://www.nytimes.com/2012/06/26/nyregion/once-a-staple-awnings-are-losing-their-appeal.html.

2 Chad Randl, "The Use of Awnings on Historic Buildings: Repair, Replacement, and New Design," National Park Service Preservation Brief 44, https://www.nps.gov/orgs/1739/upload/preservation-brief-44-awnings.pdf.

INDEX

C

D

E

F

ABOUT THE AUTHORS

Carla Bruni has spent close to twenty years preserving, studying, and writing about historic architecture across dozens of U.S. cities. She teaches graduate students at the School of the Art Institute of Chicago, where she holds a Master of Science degree in Historic Preservation. Carla has been a recurring guest discussing architecture and environmental issues on WGN and WLS Radio, and her work has been featured on StoryCorps Chicago, *Newcity*, *NBC Nightly News*, PRX, NPR, the *Chicago Reader*, *Chicago* magazine, the *Chicago Tribune*, *The Washington Post*, and various other national and international publications.

Carla also works to support the Chicago Bungalow Association, overseeing energy efficiency work, creating history and home maintenance resources, and leading the charge to list thousands of vintage homes in the National Register of Historic Places. Her professional work and involvement in community repair and revitalization has taken her to every corner of Chicago, her native city, where she currently resides with Mr. Nancy, her above-average cat.

Phil Thompson is the co-founder and illustrator behind Wonder City Studio (wondercitystudio.com), a company dedicated to creating artwork of the places worth preserving, with a special love for Chicago. For ten years, Phil has captured over a thousand homes and buildings with his pen-and-ink illustrations and sold prints of his artwork celebrating history and architecture to customers all over the world. His work has been featured in dozens of media outlets, including the *Chicago Tribune*, *Chicagoist*, *Curbed*, *Business Insider*, and *Chicago* magazine. Clients have included University of Chicago, Northwestern University, and the Chicago Architecture Center, among others. He and his wife, Katie, who creates ceramics of Chicago architecture, love to walk city streets admiring architecture with their dog, Vincent.

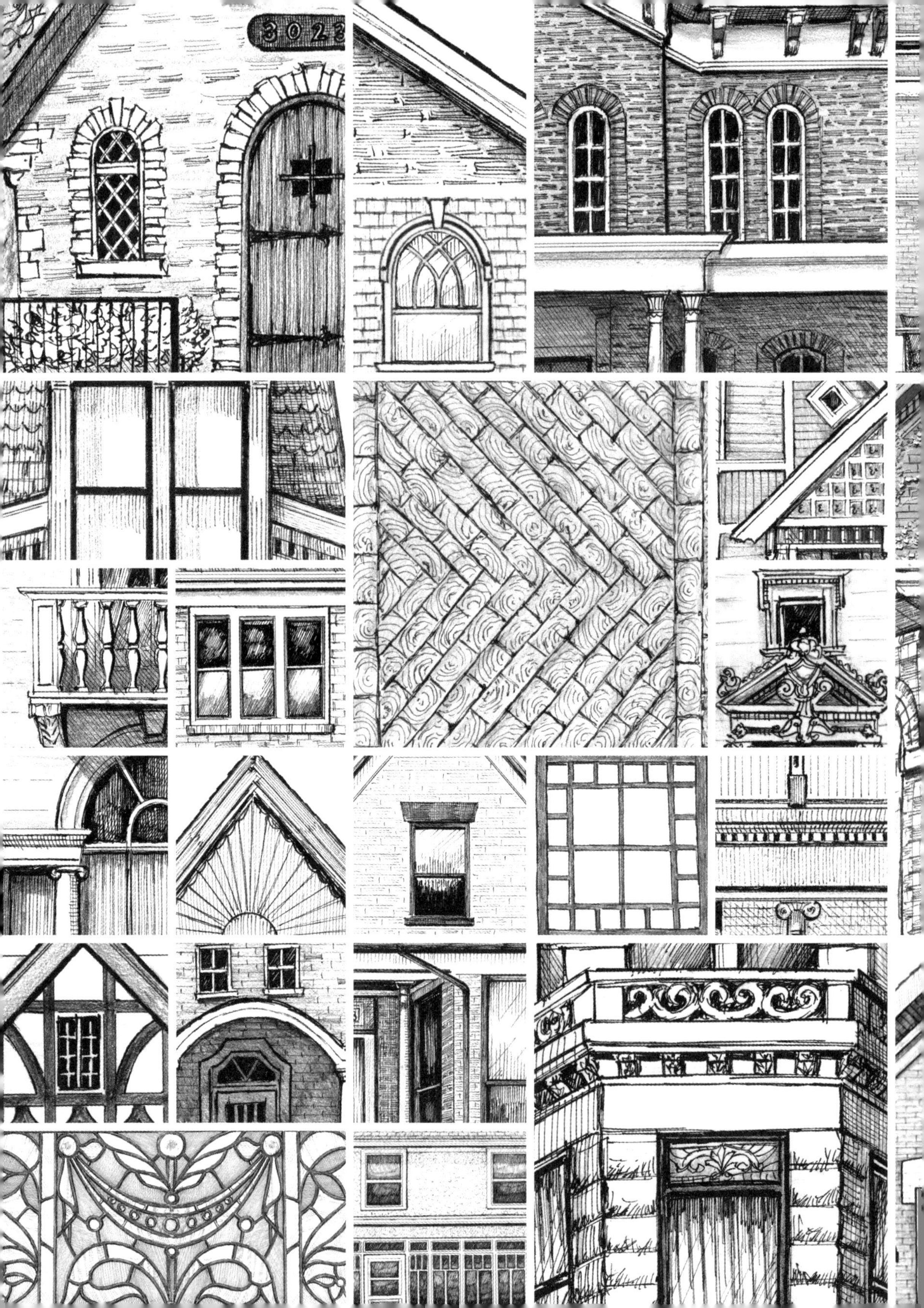
3023